AF738542

THE EUROPEAN UNION AND TURKEY: AN ANCHOR/CREDIBILITY DILEMMA

To Sema, Deniz and Süha

The European Union and Turkey: An Anchor/Credibility Dilemma

MEHMET UGUR
University of Greenwich

Routledge
Taylor & Francis Group
LONDON AND NEW YORK

First published 1999 by Ashgate Publishing

Reissued 2018 by Routledge
2 Park Square, Milton Park, Abingdon, Oxon, OX14 4RN
52 Vanderbilt Avenue, New York, NY 10017

Routledge is an imprint of the Taylor & Francis Group, an informa business

Copyright © Mehmet Ugur 1999

All rights reserved. No part of this book may be reprinted or reproduced or utilised in any form or by any electronic, mechanical, or other means, now known or hereafter invented, including photocopying and recording, or in any information storage or retrieval system, without permission in writing from the publishers.

Notice:
Product or corporate names may be trademarks or registered trademarks, and are used only for identification and explanation without intent to infringe.

Publisher's Note
The publisher has gone to great lengths to ensure the quality of this reprint but points out that some imperfections in the original copies may be apparent.

Disclaimer
The publisher has made every effort to trace copyright holders and welcomes correspondence from those they have been unable to contact.

A Library of Congress record exists under LC control number: 99072362

ISBN 13: 978-1-138-35874-4 (hbk)
ISBN 13: 978-0-429-43417-4 (ebk)

Contents

List of Figures and Tables

Preface

This book is the result of my work on the European Union's external policy-making and its relations with Turkey. In that work, I used state-society interaction within the member states as an analytical framework for identifying the variables likely to impinge on: (i) the dynamics of European integration; (ii) the nature of EU policy-making procedures; and (iii) the EU's capacity to take decisions which go beyond the lowest common denominator. I conceptualised these variables as 'societal assertiveness' and 'issue transparency/divisibility'. While the former depicts the extent to which societal groups try to influence policy decisions by shifting loyalties to other jurisdictions and/or lobbying, the latter captures the extent to which implications of policy decisions are quantifiable and affect different societal groups differently. Work on these issues led to the completion of a Ph.D. thesis, which examined EU-Turkey relations with a view to test the hypothesis that different combinations of societal assertiveness and transparency/divisibility at the national level generate different degrees of integration and different mixtures of supranational and intergovernmental procedures at the EU level.

Meanwhile, my reading of the evidence on EU-Turkey relations prompted me to think about a new question: why did EU-Turkey relations tend to be characterised by recurrent crises which, ironically, emerged after significant steps forward in upgrading the contractual arrangements between the two parties? The first crisis emerged in 1960, when a military coup followed the signing of the Association Agreement and indicated the vulnerability of Turkey's democratic institutions. The second crisis occurred in 1970, when Turkey 'realised' that the trade liberalisation envisaged in the Additional Protocol signed in 1970 was incompatible with the requirements of the import-substitution policy which had been in place since 1963. Then, throughout the 1970s, a number of crises recurred around issues including the extent of unilateral preferential treatment to be granted to Turkish agricultural products, the flexibility with which Turkey should implement the AP, and the gradual introduction of the free movement of workers. In 1980, Turkey tried to break the deadlock in her relations with the EU by accelerating the preparations for a membership application. This policy change proved a premature step and was followed by the military coup of 12

September 1980.

Following the interregnum caused by the military coup, Turkey placed a membership application in 1987. The membership bid was followed not only by a panic in the EU but also by Turkey's failure to embark on a credible process of convergence towards European standards, leading to the rejection of the membership application in 1989. Finally, the customs union agreement of December 1995 was followed by the decision of the Luxembourg Summit of December 1997 not to include Turkey in the list of candidates for membership. Turkey's response was to freeze relations with the EU, including the implementation of the customs union agreement. Although the Cardiff Summit of June 1998 signalled a change in the EU's position and Turkey was eventually classified as a candidate in November 1998, uncertainty continued to prevail as Turkish policy-makers continued to reflect their inability to tackle three major issues: persistent violations of human rights, including the treatment of the Kurdish population; the civilian government's control over the military; and the resolution of the Cyprus problem as well as other issues in Greco-Turkish relations.

Given these regularities, the question above led to a secondary question: can recurrent crises in EU-Turkey relations be explained within a single analytical framework allowing for a simultaneous analysis of both EU and Turkish policy decisions? The search for an answer suggested that state-society interaction can be a useful framework for two reasons. First, it can be used to identify, at a given time, the level of the societal assertiveness and issue transparency/divisibility not only in the EU but also in Turkey. Second, it allows for incorporating the effect of past EU and Turkish policy decisions on societal expectations which, in turn, influence societal assertiveness and issue transparency/divisibility. In fact, the second reason suggests that there is scope for taking a step forward from my earlier work on EU policy-making and EU-Turkey relations by incorporating expectation formation into the analysis.

Taking these properties into account, this book argues that recurrent crises in EU-Turkey relations are endogenous outcomes of an anchor/credibility dilemma, which reflects two tendencies working at cross purposes. On the one hand, state-society interaction in EU member states limits the EU's capacity to undertake commitments and/or impose sanctions with a view to anchor Turkey's convergence towards European standards. On the other hand, the type of state-society interaction in Turkey induces Turkish policy-makers to engage in frequent deviations from the policy reform required for convergence. The combination of both tendencies leads to a typical prisoners' dilemma where the EU's failure to act as an effective anchor increases the probability of policy reversals in Turkey which, in turn, induces the EU to be even more reluctant about anchoring Turkey's convergence towards European standards. What I add to this standard strategic interaction analysis is that the anchor/credibility dilemma in EU-Turkey relations is exacerbated by the impact of the sub-optimal policy decisions on societal expectations in the EU and Turkey. In other words, the level of societal assertiveness and issue transparency/divisibility which may initiate the anchor/credibility dilemma are not constant. They may also be influenced by past policy decisions, which may or may not be conducive to ameliorating the anchor/credibility dilemma.

Because of this endogenous dynamic, the anchor/credibility dilemma continued to haunt EU-Turkey relations since the early 1970s despite repeated declarations confirming both parties' commitment to the original goals of integration and convergence. For example, both sides interpreted the Association Agreement as a step that confirmed Turkey's European vocation and her importance for the 'free world'. Similarly, the membership application of 1987 was presented not only as the ultimate proof of Turkey's commitment to European values, but also as a step that would eliminate any ambiguity about that commitment by anchoring the destiny of Turkish people to that of Western Europe. Finally, the establishment of a customs union was described as a development that would anchor Turkey firmly in Europe and contribute to her economic modernisation. Underlying these declarations was the assumption that Turkey's link with Europe was not only a natural result of the country's modernisation but also a necessary condition that would reduce the probability of deviations from that trajectory in the face of internal as well as regional challenges. This assumption was held so strongly that it survived the collapse of the Soviet bloc and was upgraded to portray Turkey as a secular and democratic 'role model' not only for her neighbours but also for the newly independent countries of the Central Asia.

In addition, the anchor/credibility dilemma continued to generate sub-optimal outcomes despite significant developments in the international as well as domestic environment within which EU and Turkish policy decisions were made. Therefore, the persistence of sub-optimal outcomes could not be explained by changes in the exogenously-given environmental factors. The persistence was rather due to the failure of both parties to learn from past mistakes and address the core problem in EU-Turkey relations - i.e., the introduction of transparent and enforceable rules for distributing the costs and benefits associated with Turkey's convergence towards EU standards and her eventual integration. On the contrary, both the EU and Turkey preferred to maintain a high level of discretion and ambiguity in existing contracts so that deviations from contractual obligations were either not penalised or penalised by discretionary actions which were not necessarily designed to discourage deviations. Discretion and lack of transparency exacerbated the anchor/credibility dilemma for two reasons. On the one hand, either EU member states or Turkish governments were enabled to equate a certain policy issue with a non-negotiable national interest. On the other hand, societal groups in the EU or Turkey were induced to be more vocal in their demands for special treatment.

This analytical perspective is introduced in chapter 1 and applied to the EU and Turkish policy-making processes in chapters 2 and 3. What emerges from these chapters is an analytical framework which suggests that the EU's anchoring capacity would be limited and the probability of policy reversals in Turkey would be high. Put in other words, the analysis in chapters 1-3 suggests that the crisis-ridden continuity in EU-Turkey relations can be analysed as an anchor/credibility dilemma determined endogenously as a result of the interaction between the state (the policy-maker as a proxy) and societal groups. Although the endogenous character of this dilemma implies that it is perpetuated over a long period, the analysis in these chapters will also suggest that the dilemma can be resolved if two conditions are met: learning from past mistakes; and willingness to reduce the scope for discretion in the interpretation as well as implementation of the contractual provisions that govern EU-Turkey relations.

Following the general evidence provided in chapters 1-3, detailed evidence on the anchor/credibility dilemma in EU-Turkey relations is presented in chapters 4-7. For example, chapters 4 and 5 demonstrate that the EU was capable of undertaking commitments with respect to transparent/divisible policy issues such as trade and improvement in the rights of Turkish workers - mainly with a view to increase the attractiveness of the association link and induce Turkey to remain committed to convergence towards European standards. However, parts of chapter 5 and chapters 6-7 will demonstrate that the EU's anchoring capacity remained highly limited or lacking in non-transparent/non-divisible policy areas such as free movement of workers, foreign policy and human rights. Against this anchor failure, chapters 4-7 will also show that the ability of either the Turkish state or societal groups to blur the transparency/divisibility of the policy issues was the major factor which led to frequent deviations from Turkey's declared commitment to policy reform and convergence towards EU standards. The analysis in these chapters will also highlight the way in which these mutual failures were exacerbated and perpetuated over a long period because of both parties' reluctance to learn from past mistakes and agree on transparent rules that would reduce the scope for discretionary action.

Although the chapters in this book are organised as modular units, they form an integrated whole in terms of narrative and unity of analysis. This combination is designed to enable the reader to enjoy the flexibility offered by edited books as well as the analytical unity that characterises monographs. Because of this arrangement, the book can be read either as a full text on EU-Turkey relations or as a collections of analytical/empirical chapters analysing specific issues in the EU and Turkish policy-making processes. The referencing style had to be in the form a Harvard system incorporated into footnotes rather than the text itself. This style is adopted with a view to accommodate the type of sources quoted (especially official documents and periodicals with full dates) and to ensure that the reading is not interrupted by detailed footnotes. Another presentational point to be indicated here relates to the use of 'European Union' or 'EU' consistently despite the fact that the entity referred to has evolved from the 'European Economic Community' through 'European Communities' to 'European Union' over the period covered in the book. This choice reflects the change brought about by the Treaty on European Union and aims to make the text less complicated. An exception is made where the source quoted or the issuing institution bears a different title.

This book is intended to offer a different perspective on EU policy-making and EU-Turkey relations. The perspective offered here is inspired by a genuinely felt need to foster a better understanding of the issues involved rather than engaging in product differentiation. As such, it is hoped that the book will be appealing for readers interested in EU-Turkey relations, students of European integration, researchers and policy-makers. It is also hoped that the questions to be raised by the readers will only contribute to the solution of the anchor/credibility dilemma depicted in this book - as new questions inevitably increase the transparency/divisibility of the issues in EU-Turkey relations and make the solution more feasible.

Mehmet Ugur
London, November 1998

Acknowledgements

A large number of colleagues, friends and unanimous reviewers have contributed to this book not only by making constructive comments on my previous work but also by encouraging me to maintain my interest in EU-Turkey relations. I would like to express my gratitude to all of them. I owe special thanks to Professors Paul Taylor and Christopher Hill of the LSE, and Professor John Redmond of the University of Birmingham for their help and constructive criticism in relation to my Ph.D. dissertation on which this book is based. Special thanks also to Professor Mike Kelly as the head of School of Social Sciences at the University of Greenwich, without whose support the completion of this book may well have been an elusive task. I would also like to thank my colleagues in Economics, Psychology and Sociology subject groups who, during the course of writing, provided support, encouragement and accommodated my absence from meetings. I owe a special debt to Jenny Boyle of the Warburg Institute and Jonathan Sugden of the Amnesty International for their valuable comments on the manuscript, which helped me clarify my ideas and correct a large number of stylistic/linguistic errors. I would also like to thank the publishers, Ashgate, for their patience and understanding over the delay in delivering this book.

I must indicate that the completion of this book would have been impossible without the unwavering support and diligent help of my research assistant, Dr. Murad Shaheen, with whom I have also developed a close friendship. Murad worked long hours, shared my joy and anguish, and engaged in long discussions on a number of theoretical and empirical issues covered in the book. A special thank you to him for all his contributions and for keeping me up-to-date with developments in the Middle East - the part of the world with which I have a linguistic and ethnic affinity.

Last but not least, my overriding debt is to my loved ones - Sema, Deniz and Süha - who have been a continuous source of support and inspiration throughout the process of researching and writing. Not only did they cope outstandingly well with my 'absenteeism' but also did their best to bring me back to 'sanity' when, as they put it, I allowed myself to be 'carried away'. The sad fact about research and writing is that the pleasure of the activity is not as easily transferable as the accompanying negative externalities. Therefore, I would like to dedicate this book to Sema, Deniz and Süha with a heart-felt gratitude.

This book draws on some of my work published elsewhere. Chapter 2 incorporates a substantial part of the article entitled 'State-Society Interaction and European Integration: A Political Economy Approach to the Dynamics and Policy-Making of the European Union' published in volume 23 of the *Review of International Studies*. Chapter 5 draws on an article entitled 'Freedom of Movement vs. Exclusion: A Reinterpretation of the "Insider" - "Outsider" Divide in the European Union', published in volume 29, no. 4 of the *International Migration Review*. I would like to thank the copyright holders, the British International Studies Association and the Centre for Migration Studies of New York Inc., respectively, for their permission to use this material.

Despite the devoted efforts of those listed and detailed comments from many others, I am aware that a book covering EU-Turkey relations since the early 1970s and trying to suggest a novel interpretation may not be free of errors, omissions and/or inconsistencies. I assume sole responsibility for any such deficiencies.

List of Abbreviations

AA	EU-Turkey Association Agreement
AC	EU-Turkey Association Council
ACP	African, Caribbean and Pacific countries linked to the EU with preferential trading and cooperation agreements
AI	Amnesty International
AP	EU-Turkey Additional Protocol
ATC	Agreement on Textiles and Clothing
CAP	Common Agricultural Policy
CCP	Common Commercial Policy
CEECs	Central and Eastern European Countries
CET	Common External Tariff
CFSP	Common Foreign and Security Policy
CHD	Conference on Human Dimension
COREPER	Committee of Permanent Representatives
CSCE	Conference on Security and Cooperation in Europe
CU	Customs union
EAGF	European Agricultural Guarantee and Guidance Fund
EC	European Community
ECHR	European Commission of Human Rights
ECJ	European Court of Justice
ECU	European Currency Unit
EEC	European Economic Community
EIB	European Investment Bank
EP	European Parliament
EPC	European Political Cooperation
ERDF	European Regional Development Fund
ESC	Economic and Social Committee
EU	European Union
FDI	Foreign direct investment
GNA	Grand National Assembly
GSP	Generalised System of Preferences
HDIM	Human Dimension Implementation Meeting
İKV	*İktisadi Kalkınma Vakfı* (Economic Development Foundation)

JPC	EU-Turkey Joint Parliamentary Committee
LPP	Law on Political Parties
MEP	Member of the European Parliament
MFA	Multifibre Arrangement
NAM	Non-Aligned Movement
NATO	North Atlantic Treaty Organisation
OECD	Organisation for Economic Cooperation and Development
OSCE	Organisation for Security and Cooperation in Europe
PKK	Kurdistan Workers' Party
PoCo	Political Committee
RPP	Republican People's Party
SEA	Single European Act
SEEs	State-owned Economic Enterprises
SPO	State Planning Organisation
T&C	Textiles and clothing
TEU	Treaty on European Union
TL	Turkish Lira
TRNC	Turkish Republic of Northern Cyprus
TUSİAD	*Türk Sanayicileri ve İs Adamları Derneği* (Turkish Industrialists and Businessmen's Association)
UNIFCYP	UN Peacekeeping Force for Cyprus
UNHCR	United Nations High Commission for Refugees

1 The Anchor/Credibility Dilemma in EU-Turkey Relations: Introduction

Turkey's formal application will herewith eliminate any ambiguity by anchoring once and for all the destiny of the Turkish people with that of Western Europe
Prime Minister, Turgut Özal, 14 April 1987

The EU wants a stable, prosperous, democratic Turkey that is anchored in Europe and is part of the European security architecture
Council president, Alain Lamassoure, 6 April 1995

1.1 EU-Turkey Relations: Current Interpretations

Since the 1830s, reform movements of the Turkish political elite have been marked by a close link between modernisation and westernisation. The political elite of that period, observing the forces unleashed by European revolutions, concluded that pre-modern Ottoman institutions would not survive the onslaught of Western modernity.[1] A similar tendency characterised the reform movements of the early republican era - despite the anti-imperialist rhetoric used during the War of Independence. As a result, Turkey adopted Western standards ranging from the republican constitution through the civil code to the introduction of Latin script. It was against this background that Turkey greeted the end of World War II by introducing a multi-party regime in 1946 and a market-oriented development plan in 1947. These reforms were closely related to the aim of securing a place in the post-war international system in which Europe and the United States (US) were the closest allies.[2]

---

1 Ahmad (1993), p. 3.
2 See Zürcher (1993); Shaw (1976); Lewis (1988); and Mardin (1983).

After 1945, however, 'westernisation' meant not only the adoption of an externally-given model for reform; but also a way of ensuring the irreversibility of the modernisation process itself. In other words, relations with the West and membership of the post-1945 Western institutions became not only a reflection of the Turkish political elite's choices, but also an *anchor* that would reduce the probability of deviations from the modernisation trajectory. This upgrading of the 'westernisation' objective from a preference into an anchor was due to two factors. First, a Turkey outside the post-war Western defence and economic architecture would have remained isolated and, therefore, deprived of the opportunity to secure Western economic and military assistance. Second, the Turkish policy-makers of the time came to realise that the lack of popular support for the state-led modernisation strategy was a major weakness that would be exacerbated by the introduction of a multi-party regime. Although this reform was an essential condition for securing a place in the emerging Western institutions, it also carried the risk of undoing the past reforms should new parties play the populist game of cultivating grass-root hostility to state-led reforms of the past. The solution to this dilemma was sought in anchoring the modernisation project through participation in Western institutions that would tie the hands of populist parties.

That was the context in which Turkey signalled her willingness to integrate with the market-based capitalist economy by adopting a liberal development plan in 1947, which was in stark contrast with the *étatist* (state-led economic development) policy of the 1930s.[3] Two years later, in 1949, Turkey joined the Council of Europe in an attempt to demonstrate its commitment to European values. This went hand in hand with intensive lobbying to ensure that Turkey was included in the North Atlantic Treaty Organisation (NATO) and the Organisation for European Economic Cooperation (OEEC).[4] European policy-makers accommodated Turkey in these European structures reluctantly - mainly because of US pressure.[5]

Turkey's application in 1959 for association with the European Economic Community (EEC) constituted yet another step inspired by similar considerations. Existing evidence clearly suggests that both Turkey and the

---

[3] The rationale for the 1947 Plan and its drafting history can be found in Tekeli and İlkin (1974). The 1947 Plan was prepared in 1946-47 to replace the 1945 Plan which had been inspired by the *étatist* development strategy of the 1930s.

[4] On Turkey's attempts to secure a place in the OEEC, see Tekeli and İlkin (1988). On Turkey's foreign policy orientation in this period; see Ankara University, Faculty of Political Sciences (1968). On Turkey's push for NATO membership, see Ataöv (1970).

[5] On the role of the United States in securing Turkey's NATO membership, see McGhee (1990), pp. 72-113.

European Union (EU) did indeed perceive of the EEC-Turkey association as an arrangement that would contribute to Turkey's modernisation. Speaking on behalf of the Commission, Walter Hallstein stated that the Agreement 'constitutes, on the part of the Community, a recognition of Turkey's political importance for the free world.' Therefore, it '... goes beyond purely economic matters and takes its place in a wider political context.' For Turkey, 'the political aspects' of the Agreement were '... at least as important as its purely economic aspect', because it constituted '... a formal recognition and final consecration of Turkey's European vocation.'[6] Similar statements were made repeatedly later on - especially following significant crises in the region or developments in EU-Turkey association. For example, the membership application of 1987 was presented not only as the ultimate proof of Turkey's commitment to European values, but also as a step that would eliminate any ambiguity about that commitment by anchoring the destiny of Turkish people to that of Western Europe.[7] Similarly, the Association Council decision of 6 March 1995 on the establishment of a customs union was also described as a development that would anchor Turkey firmly in Europe and contribute to her economic modernisation.[8]

A common approach of commentators on EU-Turkey relations is to take these policy announcements as given and try to ascertain the extent to which either party has acted in line with the declared political will. Those who examine the process from a Turkish point of view tend to highlight the failures of the EU to fulfil its obligations under the Association Agreement (AA) and the Additional Protocol (AP). Looked at from this perspective, the list of broken promises includes: quantitative restrictions on textiles and clothing products; insufficient concessions for agricultural products; withholding the right to free movement; the negative response to membership application; and so on.[9] Those writing from a European perspective can produce a no less comprehensive list of Turkish failures: Turkey's suspension of tariff dismantling and her failure to adopt the EU's common external tariff (CET) *vis-à-vis* third countries; introduction of new surcharges on imports from the EU; lack of protection for intellectual and

---

6 Bulletin of the EC, no. 9-10/63 (September), p. 22.

7 This is from the statement by the Prime Minister, Turgut Özal, on Turkey's membership application of 14 April 1987. For similar statements concerning the political significance of the EU-Turkey relations, see Özal (1986), pp. 131-35. See also, Bozer (1987), pp. 9-14; and Özal (1991).

8 From the statement made by Turkey's foreign minister following the Association Council decision. See Agence Europe, 8 March 1997, p. 4.

9 See for example, Kılınç (1990). See also, Tacar (1989); and Birsel (1983).

industrial property; weak democratic institutions and violation of human rights; and Turkey's continued occupation of Northern Cyprus, etc.[10]

Such accounts may be informative in that they draw our attention to salient issues in EU-Turkey relations. They are, however, less illuminating for those concerned with the underlying dynamics that induce both parties to deviate from declared commitments. This shortcoming is only partly addressed by other studies pursuing a more detached and critical approach. Despite their attempt to take into account the internal and external factors affecting EU-Turkey relations, these contributions tend to lack an explicit analytical framework that captures the EU's policy-making process and the implications of Turkey's political economy for closer links with Europe. For example, Eralp suggests that recent problems in EU-Turkey relations are related to the deepening of European integration and the dynamics of the post-Cold War era. These developments have eroded Turkey's strategic importance for the West and induced the Turkish policy-makers to look beyond Europe for exploiting the new opportunities presented by the collapse of the Soviet bloc.[11] The problem with this approach, however, is twofold. First, it cannot explain why EU-Turkey relations had been problematic before late 1980s. Second, Eralp's explanation is inconsistent: it acknowledges the need to examine the impact of intra-EU dynamics on EU's approach to Turkey, but turns a blind eye to internal factors that might influence Turkey's approach to Europe. As a result, two interrelated questions remain unaddressed. First, has the EU's approach to Turkey changed as European integration deepened or has it always been characterised by a tendency to minimise the cost of anchoring the policy reform in Turkey? Second, is the current decline in Turkey's commitment to closer links with Europe related to post-Cold War developments or is it due to factors internal to Turkey which have generated frequent policy reversals?

Similar comments can be made about Redmond's argument that the widening-deepening debate in the EU has limited the scope for further enlargement.[12] No doubt, this was a major factor cited by the Commission and the member states when Turkey's membership application was rejected in 1989. EU institutions with a supranational dimension, such as the

---

[10] As far as Turkish failures in the economic areas are concerned, the most extensive study is that of the Commission. See Commission of the EU (1989a). See also, Cendrowicz (1992); and Schwed (1989). Although written from a different perspective, the book by Birand can also be included in this category because of its emphasis on the lack of a coherent Turkish strategy towards the EC. See Birand (1986).

[11] Eralp (1993, 1998).

[12] For a general discussion on enlargement, see Redmond (1993), pp. 1-16. For issues in EU-Turkey relations, see Redmond (1993), pp. 17-61.

Commission and the European Parliament, were clearly in favour of consolidating the Single Market as well as their competence. Therefore, they were interested in institutional reform rather than enlargement. This pro-deepening tendency was supported by Germany, France, and the Benelux countries, who suspected that the United Kingdom's pro-enlargement argument was designed to detract attention from institutional reform. Nevertheless, Redmond cannot explain why the EU responded positively to accession demands of not only Central and Eastern European countries but also Cyprus and Malta despite the fact that the debate about widening and deepening is still not resolved. Secondly, Redmond's study concludes that the major problem in EU-Turkey relations was mutual misunderstanding and the two sides' apparent pursuit of different agendas, but it offers no explanation as to why these asymmetric tendencies may have persisted.

Other studies try to come to terms with these asymmetries by focusing on the cultural or economic incompatibility between Turkey and the European Union. Keyder, for example, offers a cultural account of the EU-Turkey relations and argues that the problematic evolution of the association has been due to the inconsistency between the cultural ambivalence the modernising Turkish political elite and the hegemony of the capitalistic cultural values in the EU system.[13] Similarly, Huntington also suggests that Turkey is a typical 'torn country' in the sense that the Turkish elite's claim that Turkey is a Western country is shared neither by the Turkish population nor by the Western elite. No doubt, the issue of cultural differences is important and has begun to be raised more frequently by both sides - especially in the second half of the 1990s and with respect to religion. Nevertheless, it is impossible to establish the impact of cultural incompatibility on EU-Turkey relations as long as one cannot prove that cultural differences determine the differences over policy issues ranging from human rights through economic reform to the settlement of the Cyprus problem. In addition, cultural explanations are prone to overlook the possibility that both the EU and Turkey may raise cultural differences in an attempt to blur the transparency of the issues in EU-Turkey relations and justify their failures which may be due to other reasons.

Tekeli and İlkin, on the other hand, identify a different source of incompatibility. They argue that the Turkish policy of import substitution was incompatible with European integration. While import substitution required state intervention into the economy and protection of domestic industries, the aim of European integration was to transcend the nation state

---

13 Keyder (1992).

on the basis of an essentially liberal economic policy.[14] Indeed, this source of incompatibility has been a significant factor in EU-Turkey relations and goes a long way in explaining some of the problems mentioned above. The protectionist bias inherent in import-substitution prevented Turkey throughout the 1970s from complying with the provisions of the Additional Protocol, which required tariff dismantling and structural reform. Nevertheless, Tekeli and İlkin cannot explain why problems in EU-Turkey relations have persisted despite the fact that Turkey's import-substitution policy was replaced, in 1980, with an export-oriented development strategy based on trade and foreign exchange liberalisation. Ironically, the tension between the EU and Turkey increased as the latter embarked on an accelerated process of tariff dismantling since the mid-1980s onwards. In addition, Tekeli and İlkin's conceptualisation of European integration is too simplistic to capture the complex linkages between supranationalism and intergovernmentalism in the EU. They tend to exaggerate the scope for policy integration and, therefore, the EU's ability to act as an external anchor for policy reform in Turkey.

1.2 An Alternative Approach: State-Society Interaction and Endogenous Policy Outcomes

The brief review above suggests that two major issues have been either ignored or addressed inadequately in the existing literature on EU-Turkey relations: the internal determinants of both parties' policy choices, and the impact of past and current policy choices on the range of future policy options. Because of this shortcoming, the existing work tends either to exaggerate the impact of the structural factors on EU and Turkish policy decisions or to provide mainly short-term explanations which overlook the continuity in EU-Turkey relations. To address these shortcomings, we shall use an alternative analytical framework which would: (i) capture the internal determinants of policy choices made by the EU and Turkey; and (ii) explain why EU and Turkish policy decisions concerning Turkey's integration and her convergence towards EU standards might remain sub-optimal over a long period even if the cost/incentive structure faced by policy-makers changes over time. Briefly stated, the proposed analytical framework would suggest that EU and Turkish policy decisions are determined by state-society interaction, which generates different levels of commitment to integration and convergence depending on the levels of societal assertiveness and transparency/divisibility of the policy issues.

---

[14] Tekeli and İlkin (1993a), pp. 11-34; Tekeli and İlkin (1993b), pp. 18-21, 124-39.

Societal assertiveness reflects the extent to which societal groups try to secure favourable policy decisions either by capturing the policy-making process or by shifting their loyalties to other jurisdictions. Issue transparency/divisibility, on the other hand, reflects the extent to which the implications of a policy decision are quantifiable and affect different societal groups differently. Finally, state-society interaction is defined as a dynamic process reflecting the way in which the state (or the policy-maker as a proxy) interacts with societal forces and supplies a special type of public good called public policy. Like ordinary public goods, public policy is characterised by non-excludability - i.e., once it is available it can be 'consumed' by all constituents. Therefore, it induces the constituents to free ride - i.e., to benefit from the available policy without contributing towards the cost of supplying and implementing it. Nevertheless, public policy differs from ordinary public goods in a significant way. In the case of ordinary public goods, free riding takes the form of avoiding payment towards the cost of providing the good in question. In the case of public policy, however, the free riding problem emerges not only in the previous form but also in the form of lobbying activities aiming to influence the policy stance of another in one's favour.

This difference implies that the standard theory of public goods is inadequate for public policy analysis because it examines only the way in which 'consumption' of the policy should be regulated to ensure that beneficiaries contribute towards the cost of providing the good in question. In other words, it only provides the principles upon which taxation should be based. What is also necessary is to analyse how and whether the free riding problem can be resolved before a public policy decision is made. State-society interaction is a useful analytical tool that enables us to explore this aspect of the public policy-making because it captures two relevant variables: the extent of societal assertiveness and the transparency/divisibility of policy issues. While the former reflects the level of demand for favourable public policy decisions, the latter depicts the extent to which either societal groups (the demand side) or the state itself (the supply side) can justify a sub-optimal policy decision by equating the issue at hand with an overarching national interest that the state must defend. Given this specification and assuming a certain level of societal assertiveness, the extent to which the free riding problem can be resolved in public policy-making becomes a function of issue transparency/divisibility. The higher the level of issue transparency/divisibility the less able is the state or societal groups to equate policy issues with an overarching national interest. Therefore, under a given level of societal assertiveness, higher levels of issue transparency/divisibility would be associated with a more efficient supply of public policy.

Once this is established, the task is to ascertain the extent to which societal assertiveness and issue transparency/divisibility may be exogenous and/or endogenous variables. We would argue that these variables are both exogenous (i.e., shaped by structural, institutional or cultural parameters of the country's political economy) and endogenous (i.e., dependent on past decisions of the policy-makers themselves). To illustrate this point, we shall refer to three modes of governance suggested by Etzioni: control-reliant, mixed-scanning, and consensual.[15] In control-reliant or consensual polities, the state is either too strong or too weak *vis-à-vis* societal forces. Therefore, either the state itself or societal forces may act as 'veto groups' who equate the policy issue(s) at hand with a non-divisible national interest and justify the supply of sub-optimal policies. In mixed-scanning polities, however, neither the state nor societal groups are strong enough to dictate an unchallenged definition of the national interest. Under this condition, it is in the interest of the state to capitalise on issue transparency/divisibility as a means of resolving the free riding problem involved in the supply of public policy.

Etzioni's typology suggests that societal assertiveness and issue transparency/divisibility - as independent variables affecting the efficiency of the public policy supplied - would depend on the mode of governance within which the state interacts with society. Although this is a useful construct which depicts the scope for the supply of efficient policy decisions, a backward reiteration would also show that a given mode of governance would depend not only on structural parameters but also on past policy choices - which might have consolidated or weakened the mode of governance in which they have been made in the first instance. Therefore, societal assertiveness and issue transparency/divisibility would also be dependent on both structural parameters of the country's political economy as well as past policy decisions, which could drive a wedge between the current levels of societal assertiveness and issue transparency/divisibility and those which would have been implied by structural parameters only. Simply stated, societal assertiveness and issue transparency/divisibility are both exogenously-given and policy-dependent qualities and, therefore, the efficiency with which public policy is supplied is an endogenous outcome that would depend on both structural factors as well as past policy decisions.

In that sense, future policy options available to the policy-maker are determined by a constraint/incentive structure reflecting not only structural exigencies such as existing institutions, level of economic development, cultural variables, etc., but also the past decisions of the policy-makers themselves. Similarly, the extent to which societal groups are able to capture the public policy process will also depend on the structural parameters of the country's political economy as well as the past policy decisions. In this context, a policy

15 See Etzioni (1967, 1968).

decision made in the current period is not necessarily optimal or inevitable even if it is shaped by constraints and incentives implied by the structural parameters of the country's political economy. That is because there is always scope for improving on the current decision if the structural parameters themselves have been affected adversely by sub-optimal policy decisions made in the past and/or the policy-maker is prepared to act rationally and base his/her current and future policy decisions on all relevant information, including that concerning his/her past mistakes.

This analysis is in the tradition of explaining inter-state relations by referring to domestic determinants of state behaviour. The literature in this tradition is extensive and has provided useful insights into cooperation and conflict relations between states. One early example is Immanuel Kant's argument that the mode of governance determines the state's attitude towards war and peace. According to Kant, a republican mode of governance is the only polity compatible with perpetual peace - a hypothesis that has been tested extensively after World War II.[16] Another example is Rosenau's 'domestic-international linkages' thesis, which posits a correlation between domestic structure and international state behaviour. According to Rosenau, international politics is determined by a large number of domestic variables ranging from the mode of governance to socio-economic and political development indicators.[17]

Although this literature is rightly critical of the realist approach to international relations which treats the state as a closed entity, its analysis remains weak on two counts. First, it implies parametric tests based on stable coefficients that can be assigned to independent domestic variables. In other words, they examine the correlation between the attributes of the domestic regime as independent variables and international policy outcomes as the dependent variables by assuming away the impact of the policy decision in the current period on the value of the test parameters in the next period. Second, it offers no coherent rule for deciding on the number of relevant variables that must be taken into account. This number can vary from a single variable as is the case in Kant to multiple variables as is the case in Rosenau. The consequence is that parametric tests yield either unreliable or over-determined results - depending on the number of variables taken into account and the quality of the data available.[18]

16 See Reiss (1970); and Williams et al. (1993), pp. 112-21.

17 Rosenau (1969).

18 See Rosenau (1969). The drawback emanating from the multiplicity of variables was elegantly avoided by the international regimes theory, which focused on interdependence as an alternative. See Keohane and Nye (1977); Keohane (1984).

Other contributions can be seen in the writings of Andrews and Cox. According to Andrews, one should focus on a 'domestic paradigm' rather than an undivided national interest. Then foreign policy can be said to grow out of the need to reproduce and deepen that domestic paradigm. Similarly, Cox conceptualises the state as an institution that mediates between the level of production and world order which, in turn, is determined by the forms of state that compose it. The forms of state, on the other hand, are determined by the configuration of social forces which, again, is shaped by what goes on in the sphere of production. The problem with these analyses is reductionism. The quest to base the analysis on a structural basis leads both Andrews and Cox to deny the policy-maker of a meaningful capacity to act as a proper agent and, thereby, reduce his/her actions to those required by either the domestic paradigm or the production process.[19]

Putnam's contribution avoids this type of reductionism by pursuing a strategy of treating the domestic and international levels on an equal footing. At the national level, domestic groups exert pressure on the government to enhance their interest, while the latter seeks power by constructing coalitions among the former. At the international level, governments seek to maximise their ability to satisfy domestic demands, while minimising the adverse consequences of international developments. Given this setting, external policy decisions will reflect the overlap between the sets of domestically and internationally feasible options - which Putnam defines as a 'win set'.[20] This perspective has inspired Moravcsik's liberal intergovernmentalist approach to national preference formation and inter-state bargaining in the EU.[21] Similarly, Ikenberry has argued that the interplay between international, societal and state-centred variables can be best explained through an institutional approach which focuses on both state and society.[22] Although the 'two-level game' and institutionalist approaches can avoid reductionism, they take us back to square one: they do not analyse the policy-making process endogenously. They take the preferences of the policy-maker as given and introduce the implications of the state-society interaction into their analysis in an *ad hoc* manner and retrospectively to justify the observed policy outcomes.

Therefore, we believe that there is a case for developing an analytical framework in which state-society interaction is the source of endogenous

19 See Andrews (1984), pp. 321-27; and Cox (1990), pp. 41, 49.

20 See Putnam (1988). Putnam's two-level game metaphor was later on used in the context of international reputation and domestic popularity objectives of the governments. See Guerrieri and Padoan (1989).

21 See Moravcsik (1993).

22 Ikenberry (1988).

policy outcomes. The theory of endogenous macroeconomic policy-making has gone a long way in addressing this problem. For example, Kydland and Prescott's seminal work demonstrates that optimal policy choices may be time-inconsistent or time-consistent policies may be sub-optimal if the policy-maker is granted discretion.[23] Optimal policy choices may be time-inconsistent because the announced policy, if credible, induces the private agents to revise their expectations accordingly. For example, a credible announcement of anti-inflationary policy induces the wage setters to settle on lower wages. That is because the wage setters would know that high wages coupled with a low level of inflation (the government declared objective) would lead to a high level of unemployment. Once this is the case, and provided that the optimal policy choice has been made under constraints imposed by some market imperfections, the policy-maker will have an incentive to deviate from the declared policy because it is now possible to relax the stance of the monetary policy and engineer a surprise boom by taking the advantage of low wage settlements. Once, however, the policy-maker reneges on the announced policy commitment, his/her credibility is lost and any attempt at stimulating the economy will lead only to inflation.

As indicated by various contributors to this debate, Kydland and Prescott's analysis may be qualified in various ways. First, the conflict between optimal and time-consistent policy choices may be resolved if the policy-maker has a non-finite time horizon, i.e., if the strategic game between the policy-maker and the private agents is repeated indefinitely. Then it is in the interest of the policy-maker to develop a reputation by refraining from policy reversals.[24] This proposal, however, is weakened by its assumption of an infinite time horizon. In representative democracies, the time horizon of the policy-maker is generally limited to the electoral cycle. Aware of this, the private agents will expect the policy-maker to renege on the policy commitment at least in the penultimate year before elections. Then the game will unravel into a single-shot game and the conflict between optimal and time-consistent policy choices will prevail.[25]

---

[23] Kydland and Prescott (1977). It must be noted here that Kydland and Prescott's analysis is rooted within the wider debate on policy effectiveness. In this debate, the policy-maker is unable to influence the future path of the economy if private sector expectations are rational and if the markets are flexible. On this, see Lucas (1972); and Sargent and Wallace (1976). The novelty of the credibility literature is that it is compatible with a weak version of rational expectations and market rigidity.

[24] On this, see Backus and Driffill (1985); Tabellini (1986); and Barro (1986).

[25] For a recent and accessible text on game theory, see Hargreaves Heap and Varoufakis (1995). Our analysis here draws on some game theory concepts, but we utilise game theory as a metaphor rather than as a comprehensive analytical framework.

A more significant criticism of the credibility problem posed by Kydland and Prescott relates to multiple-equilibria that may obtain when the policy-maker is concerned about reputation. As Rogoff has pointed out, credibility models do not specify any rule about how the policy-maker and the private agents may co-ordinate and settle on one of the possible equilibrium solutions to the strategic game. It is obvious that the political economy variables are important here. The solution to the co-ordination problem will be comparatively easy when the political economy of the country reflects some traits of corporatism, where the cost of co-ordination is low because of the small number of large interest group organisations bargaining with the government on behalf of their members. The co-ordination problem may not be resolved, however, if the policy-maker is faced with a large number of atomistic interest group organisations.[26] These political economy factors can be extended to include the specification of government and private sector objectives/behaviour. For example, is the policy-maker concerned about societal welfare, his/her own specific interests or a combination of both? Also, what happens if the announced policy has different effects on different sections of the society, i.e., if the median voter assumption is too simplistic? Last but not least, what happens if the preferences of and information held by the non-elected civil servants formulating policies are different from those of the government eager to capitalise on those policies to increase its chance of re-election?

Finally, Kydland and Prescott are concerned about the consequences of the credibility problem rather than the factors that generate it. Although the model assumes that the lack of credible commitments are due to existing distortions, there is no specification about whether such distortions are given exogenously (i.e., reflect a structural aspect of the relevant markets) or resulting from the type of interaction between the policy-maker and the private agents. It is obvious that these distortions will be variant to the announced policy if they are determined by the interaction between the policy-maker and the private sector. In this case, the requirement for an internal binding rule becomes less stringent as the policy-maker may anchor the policy to an external regime. Anchoring might be more effective and/or convenient compared to an internal rule that may be both susceptible to discretionary interpretation and/or require sufficient political support. Not only that, the external anchor can always be used as a means of circumventing particular societal demands for special treatment. One

26 On these issues, see Rogoff (1987); and Persson (1988), p. 523.

example of anchoring an announced policy is the fixing of exchange rates as a substitute for an internal monetary policy rule aimed at low inflation.[27]

Despite these shortcomings, the 'credibility analysis' can still provide a useful framework for the study of EU-Turkey relations where policy reversals in Turkey and EU failures to reduce their incidence have been the norm. The question to be examined here, however, is radically different. Instead of focusing only on how non-credible policies lead to inferior results, we also take a step back and ask the twin questions of: (i) why Turkey's announced policy has been non-credible, and (ii) to what extent an external anchor may or may not reduce the credibility problem faced by Turkish policy-makers. This is especially necessary because the relationship between the policy-maker announcing a policy commitment and the external anchor is an interactive rather than a one-way process. Under these circumstances, the solution to the credibility problem faced by Turkey depends not only on the existence of the *acquis communautaire* (the cumulative EU legislation) as a set of rules and procedures that Turkish policy reform could be anchored to, but also on the way in which the costs and benefits of Turkey's convergence towards EU standards are distributed between the two parties.

Therefore, the argument that free trade or customs union agreements with the EU may enable third countries to anchor their policy reform to the EU regime is too simplistic.[28] The over-optimistic expectation underlying this argument can be detected easily when one takes into account the fact that a third country's (in our case, Turkey's) convergence towards EU standards is nothing but a special case of international policy co-ordination. What is involved here is a policy co-ordination that is perceived to be beneficial for both parties in the long run but the short-term costs of which are distributed unevenly. In other words, Turkey stands to bear the short-term costs of convergence towards EU standards even though the long-term benefits may accrue to both parties. Under this condition, policy co-ordination is highly likely to remain limited unless a transparent contract can be drawn to 'tie Turkey's hands' with a view to increase the cost of policy reversals and commit the EU to share the short-term costs of convergence in order to increase the incentives for Turkey to remain committed to policy reform. The evidence examined in chapters 4-7 indicates that neither the

---

27 On the theoretical case for the use of exchange rate as an external anchor, see Melitz (1988). On the French experience, see Sachs and Wyplosz (1986). On the Italian experience, see Giavazzi and Pagano (1988); and Collins (1988).

28 This argument is developed in the context of the EU-Mediterranean agreements with Morocco, Tunisia and Egypt. See, Francois (1997); and Hoekman and Djankov (1997)

Association Agreement nor the customs union between the EU and Turkey have been compatible with this requirement.

1.3 The Anchor/Credibility Dilemma in EU-Turkey Relations

As will be demonstrated in chapter 2, the EU's anchoring capacity is a function of state-society interaction, which determines the extent of integration, the choice of policy-making procedures, and the ability of the EU to undertake commitments and/or impose sanctions. The type of state-society interaction in EU member states is similar to what Etzioni calls 'mixed-scanning'.[29] In 'mixed-scanning' polities, the policy-making process is characterised by a mixture of planning and consensus building. This combination enables the policy-makers to avoid the policy reversals encountered in control-reliant polities where the lack of a consensus forces governments to scale down their original plans and/or seek more consensus than necessary in order to implement the policy decisions arising out of those plans. Mixed-scanning is also more efficient than the consensual mode of governance, where the lack of planning induces societal groups to penetrate the public policy-making process and force the government to pursue a muddling-through strategy.

Therefore, the ability of the member states and the EU itself to undertake credible policy commitments is higher than what is likely to be the case in mainly control-reliant or consensual polities. The proviso here, however, is that the commitments must relate to transparent/divisible policy issues so that their consequences can be quantified and the adversely affected member states or societal groups can be compensated through issue linkage and package deals. In other words, EU policy-makers can undertake commitments in favour of associated countries only if the consequences of such actions are compatible with either inter-country or inter-group traded-offs within the EU. Similarly, EU policy-makers would be prepared to impose sanctions and penalise the associated country's deviations from the convergence towards EU standards only if the risks associated with those sanctions are manageable or they are functional for avoiding higher risks associated with alternative policy options. Therefore, the EU's capacity to undertake credible policy commitments may be impressive compared to control-reliant or consensual polities, but this is mainly due to the fact that the EU can undertake such commitments only when the cost involved is either low or divisible between the member states.

One implication of this analysis is that the EU's ability to act as an effective anchor for policy reform in Turkey (i.e., its ability to provide

29 See Etzioni (1967, 1968).

incentives and impose sanctions that would reduce the probability of policy reversals in Turkey) will be limited to transparent/divisible policy issues such as trade where inter-country or inter-group package deals are feasible. In non-transparent/non-divisible policy areas such as foreign policy or free movement of Turkish workers, the EU will lack an effective anchoring capacity as either the member states themselves or some societal groups can equate the policy issue with an overarching national interest that cannot be negotiated as part of an intra-EU package deal. In chapters 4-7, we shall demonstrate that the EU's anchoring capacity was indeed characterised by these tendencies. The EU tended to grant only gradual and partial concessions in the area of trade policy, where the costs are quantifiable and could be traded off through intra-EU package deals. In addition, these concessions were either not significant enough to counter-balance the incentives for policy reversals in Turkey or they were given with a view to secure a delay in Turkish membership, which was considered to entail higher risks. The EU's failure to act as an anchor was even more obvious in non-transparent/non-divisible policy areas such as of human rights or the Cyprus problem, where the EU refrained from imposing sanctions that would increase the costs of Turkey's deviation from European standards.

Another implication of the analysis above is that the EU and the member states can enhance or blur the transparency/divisibility of policy issues in EU-Turkey relations. That is because of the compatibility of the mixed-scanning mode of governance with policy innovation, which provides scope for discretion that can be deployed either way. In other words, the transparency/divisibility of the policy issues in EU-Turkey relations is not only an exogenously-given but also a policy-dependent variable. To the extent that the scope for policy innovation is utilised for re-enforcing the transparency/divisibility of policy issues (i.e., for increasing the efficiency of supplying public policy), the range of policy issues where the EU can undertake commitments and risks expands and the association link becomes a more attractive anchor for Turkey. Otherwise, the EU's ability to undertake commitments and risks declines and the probability of Turkey's deviations from EU standards increases. The evidence examined in chapters 4-7 indicates that both tendencies were observable in EU's policy towards Turkey. While EU policy-makers tended to inject a certain level of transparency/divisibility into trade policy issues by designing partial and conditional concessions, they also tended to blur the transparency/divisibility of other issues such as human rights by subsuming them under non-transparent defence, security and economic interests.

Similarly, the credibility problem faced by Turkish policy-makers is also a function of state-society interaction. Governance in Turkey fluctuates between what Etzioni describes as control-reliant and consensual modes.[30] As a result of the control-reliant strategy, the Turkish state has become a major economic actor and the sole arbiter defining the national interest. As indicators of heavy state involvement in the economy, one can point to the fact that the state sector, over the 1960-90 period, accounted for over 50% of fixed capital formation, about 40% of employment in firms employing 10 employees or more, 50-60% of total value added in the manufacturing sector, and 40-60% of imports. Despite the liberalisation program introduced in 1980, the share of public sector investment in the gross domestic product remained higher than the corresponding share of the private sector.[31] On the other hand, the imposition of a state-defined national interest upon the society can be inferred not only from the top-to-bottom approach to modernisation, but also from the oppression of political dissent challenging the legitimacy of the control-reliant mode of governance. This tendency was epitomised in 1982, when the Turkish state bucked the trend of democratisation in developing countries and introduced a constitution designed to defend the state against the individual.[32] Consequently, Turkey deviated not only from the essentially liberal economic policy but also from the principle of representative democracy that underpinned the process of European integration.

Control-reliance also paved the way for societal penetration of the state, especially by organised interests. On the one hand, it generated a tendency among societal forces to expect the state to supply not only 'public goods' such as a stable macroeconomic environment but also 'private goods' such as employment in state-owned industries and low-priced industrial inputs. On the other hand, it enabled the private sector to argue that its losses arising out of private contracts were actually due to the uncertainty caused by the state's interventionist policies. The combination of these dynamics meant that the legitimacy of the Turkish polity became dependent not on the state's ability to strike a balance between interest aggregation and the regulation of externalities arising out of societal behaviour, but on the extent to which it could accommodate private sector demands for special treatment.

Policy decisions taken in the context of control-reliance and societal penetration had an exacerbating effect on the credibility problem faced by Turkish policy-makers. On the one hand, the Turkish government's receptiveness to societal demands induced the organised producer groups to expect that the state would bail them out either by delaying the convergence

---

30 See Etzioni (1967, 1968).

31 See TOBB (1990), pp. 24-25, 49-50, 104. Also, see Uçtum (1992), pp. 146-48.

32 On the state-centred Turkish constitution, see Heper (1988, 1991).

towards EU trade, industrial and competition policies or by insisting on special arrangements during negotiations on the terms of Turkey's accession. The impact of this expectation formation can be seen in chapter 3, where we demonstrate that Turkish industrialists remained highly reluctant to undertake the structural adjustment measures that would enable them to compete in an integrated European market. The lack of enthusiasm for structural adjustment at company level reflected not only the fact Turkish industrialists did not take the government's commitment to integrate with the EU seriously, but it also made the government's credible commitment to integration less likely. Therefore, it was not surprising to observe that successive Turkish governments avoided tariff dismantling and alignment, introduced non-tariff barriers to trade with the EU, and granted high levels of subsidies on investment as well as export at a time when the EU was moving away from protectionism. On the other hand, heavy state control also affected the expectations of the societal forces favouring democratic reforms. State oppression of the reform and minority movements marginalised the mass support for democratisation and encouraged the emergence of extremism, both of which enabled and induced the Turkish state to deviate from its commitment to converge towards EU standards requiring representative democracy and respect for human rights.

Under these conditions, an external anchor - no matter how attractive and effective it is - may not lend sufficient credibility to policy reform in Turkey. Therefore, one must exercise due caution in apportioning responsibility for the problematic evolution of the association between Turkey - as the party committing itself to a European orientation - and the EU - as the external anchor expected to make this policy commitment less reversible. Turkey's announced policy might remain non-credible even if the EU were capable of acting as an external anchor *par excellence*. Given the distortions that make policy commitment in Turkey time-inconsistent and the possibility of reducing the cost of convergence towards EU standards by extracting new concessions from the EU, there will always be incentives for Turkish policy-makers to deviate from the announced policy and secure short-term gains. This fact, however, should not detract attention from the EU's failure to emerge as an effective anchor in the first place. Although the factors that determine the non-credibility of Turkey's declared European orientation are internal to Turkey's political economy, it must be acknowledged that the EU's failure to act as an anchor has exacerbated the credibility problem with which the Turkish policy-makers are faced.

1.4 Issues in EU-Turkey Relations and Organisation of the Book

As a result of the anchor/credibility dilemma specified above, Turkey has remained outside the EU after three successive enlargements - the Mediterranean enlargements of 1981 and 1986, the Scandinavian and Austrian accessions of 1995, and the eastern enlargement currently being negotiated. Turkish policy-makers tended to ignore the fact that Turkey's non-credible commitment to policy reform have contributed to this outcome. On the contrary, they preferred to interpret Turkey's exclusion as evidence of the EU's preference to keep Turkey - a Muslim country - out of the European club. The mirror-image of this interpretation was the EU's tendency to ignore the consequences of its own failure to emerge as an effective anchor by arguing that Turkey's exclusion was essentially a self-imposed outcome determined by her failure to converge towards EU standards. The aim of the following chapters is to demonstrate that both interpretations are essentially incorrect and create a chicken-and-egg problem that has more to do with the preference of both parties to maintain discretion than structural exigencies.

For this purpose, we begin in chapter 2 to examine the EU's anchoring capacity in the context of state-society interaction. We argue that the dynamics of European integration and the EU's anchoring capacity are endogenous outcomes of the state-society interaction that induces the member states to approximate their policies in an attempt to equalise the returns on constituent loyalties and, thereby, reduce the scope for loyalty shifts. In that sense, the dynamic of European integration is primordial to the intergovernmental bargaining on the formal codification of the convergent policy choices and the delineation of the EU institutions' competence. This observation questions the relevance of intergovernmentalist approaches to European integration. It also serves as a basis for determining the supranational aspects of the integration process that would be conducive to a high level of EU anchoring capacity. The scope of the integration process (and anchoring capacity), however, will be limited to a range of transparent/divisible policy areas where the costs and benefits of codified policy convergence can be traded off through package deals. This observation, on the other hand, distances the approach adopted here from functionalist/neo-functionalist approaches to European integration and enables us to specify the limits to the EU's capacity as an external anchor for policy reform in an associated country. Two conclusions follow from the analysis in chapter 2: (i) the EU can emerge as an external anchor for Turkish policy reform mainly in transparent/divisible policy areas; and (ii) the EU system requires the convergence of associated countries towards EU standards as a precondition for minimising the membership risks.

Then, chapter 3 examines state-society interaction in Turkey with a view to establishing the extent to which Turkish policy-makers can commit themselves to a credible European orientation and the policy reform associated with it. We shall demonstrate that the political economy of Turkey is such that it reduces the scope for credible policy commitments. This is due to a historically strong state and its heavy involvement in the economy both as regulator and producer. Under these conditions, either the state itself or the organised interest groups have been able to blur the transparency/divisibility of policy issues by equating them with an overarching national interest that cannot be made subject to compromises and package deals. Invoking the national interest, the Turkish state has been resistant to grass-root demands for democratisation (as can be seen in its record of human rights violations and mediocre democratisation) but responsive to organised interest group demands for externalising private risks (as can be seen in non-transparent means of protection and subsidisation). Under these conditions, policy reversals tended to be the norm and thereby undermined the credibility of the announced European orientation. The EU's failure to anchor Turkey's policy reform has undoubtedly exacerbated this credibility problem, but the source of non-credible and time-inconsistent commitments to policy reform has been internal to Turkey. Therefore, the Turkish argument that the EU has failed to fulfil its obligations towards Turkey can be only partly correct as it ignores two significant consequences of Turkey's failure to converge towards EU standards. First, the Turkish government's deviations from convergence towards European standards has induced the Turkish interest groups to revise their expectations accordingly and enabled them to force further policy reversals by refraining from company-level structural adjustment. Second, Turkey's policy reversals have provided the EU with the pretext to avoid its own obligations on the grounds that the flexibility enjoyed by Turkey was a major concession in its own right.

Chapter 4 provides a detailed account of the EU-Turkey trade in sensitive products, i.e., textiles and clothing and agricultural products. This chapter demonstrates that Turkey's undertakings in the Association Agreement (AA) and the Additional Protocol (AP) concerning trade liberalisation have been non-credible. Not only has Turkey failed to converge towards the EU trading regime, but it has also insisted on unilateral EU concessions as a means of reducing the cost of its European orientation. The EU, on the other hand, has been able to commit itself to unilateral concessions but only partially and gradually. The gradual and partial nature of the concessions has been due to the need for intra-EU package deals that would distribute the cost of concessions among the member states.

Nevertheless, and in contrast to the established wisdom about EU protectionism, chapter 4 demonstrates that the EU has been able to extend a favourable yet *ad hoc* regime to Turkish exports in these sectors as a side payment that would enhance the attractiveness of the EU as an anchor.

Chapter 5 examines the issue of free movement between the EU and Turkey and demonstrates that the EU's anchoring capacity in this area has been more limited compared to trade in sensitive products. This has been due to the way in which the transparency/divisibility of third-country immigration has been blurred by the creation of an 'insider - outsider' divide between EU nationals and non-EU nationals. As intra-EU freedom of movement was introduced in a way that would increase the transparency/divisibility of intra-EU migratory flows, the definition of the European 'nationality domain' against third countries exacerbated the non-transparency/non-divisibility of third-country immigration - leading to an exclusionist EU policy stance and intergovernmental policy-making. Therefore, it is not surprising to observe that the EU has failed to extend the right to free movement to Turkish workers despite explicit provisions to that effect in both the AA and the AP. In addition, chapter 5 demonstrates that the EU has been capable of acting as an external anchor by granting concessions in transparent/divisible secondary policy areas such as second priority to Turkish migrants residing in the member states, allowing for limited mobility after a certain period of legal employment, incorporating the migrant workers' families into the labour market, and granting the Turkish migrants the right to social security benefits.

While chapters 4 and 5 examine the anchor/credibility dilemma by focusing on the EU's anchoring capacity in terms of concessions it can grant to reduce the cost of Turkey's convergence towards EU standards, chapters 6 and 7 focus on the extent to which it can impose sanctions to increase the cost of Turkey's deviations from these standards. The Cyprus issue, examined in chapter 6, provides significant evidence not only on the extent to which Turkey was prepared to sacrifice the credibility of her European orientation but also on the limits to the EU's capacity to emerge as an anchor. The EU has proved capable of developing a Cyprus policy only after the European orientation of both Turkey and Cyprus gathered new momentum in the late 1980s and early 1990s. This may be attributed to the need to minimise risks before the accession of either country rather than to a breakthrough in the EU's foreign policy competence. Chapter 6 also demonstrates that the EU's involvement in and its policy on the Cyprus issue may be influenced by the membership of Greece, but this influence has been limited. Therefore, the Turkish argument that Greece has deployed its membership weapon to ensure Turkey's exclusion must be questioned. In fact, Turkey's continued military presence in Cyprus and her objections to a federal solution were factors that not only enabled Greece to rally the support of the member states in scoring diplomatic points against Turkey, but also reflected the non-credibility of Turkey's European orientation.

Chapter 7 examines the extent to which the EU can act as an external anchor for democratisation in Turkey. Due to legitimation concerns and institutional competition, the EU has developed a human rights dimension to its policy towards its partners - especially associated countries. Although this dimension is still in the making, it reflects the extent to which the supranational institutions of the EU, especially the European Parliament, can instigate policy innovation. Because of the ability of the member state to subordinate human rights policy to non-transparent/non-divisible policy issues, however, chapter 7 also demonstrates that the EU has been able to act as an anchor for Turkey only when the latter's European orientation gathered momentum. This can be seen in the contrast between the EU's stance before and after Turkey's membership application in 1987. Inevitably, the EU's inconsistency has not only compromised its ability to emerge as an effective anchor for democratisation in Turkey but also enabled the Turkish governments to blur the transparency/divisibility of the human rights issues by arguing that EU criticism of human rights violations has been essentially a pretext to keep Turkey out.

Finally, in chapter 8, we shall derive a number of general conclusions in the light of the preceding analysis and offer a perspective on how the anchor/credibility dilemma in EU-Turkey relations may be resolved. One conclusion is that the problematic evolution of the EU-Turkey association has been due to the nature of state-society interaction that (i) limits the capacity of the EU to act as an effective anchor for policy reform in an associated country; and (ii) reduces the ability of Turkish policy-makers to undertake a credible commitment to policy reform. As a second conclusion, we shall argue that both Turkey and the EU, instead of addressing the causes of their respective failures, have chosen the easy option of blaming each other in order to justify their respective positions. The third conclusion can be stated as follows: the gradual upgrading of EU-Turkey relations from a loosely specified association into a customs union has actually increased the tension between Turkey and the EU as both sides have failed to upgrade the contract between them in a way that would resolve the policy co-ordination problem on the basis of transparent incentives and sanctions designed to anchor Turkey's policy reform. Given these conclusions, we shall argue that the solution to the anchor credibility dilemma in EU-Turkey relations would depend on whether or not both parties would recognise the fact that Turkey's convergence towards EU standards is a special case of policy co-ordination.

Therefore, the way forward is to revise the existing contracts with a view to reduce the extent of discretion that has enabled Turkey and the EU to avoid their obligations in terms of convergence and integration. Any other option is highly likely to lead to inefficient outcomes even if the declared of objective of both sides - i.e., Turkish membership - is achieved in the distant future.

1.5 A Methodological Note

From a methodological point of view, the approach adopted in this book excludes the use of an exogenously-given objective function as a basis for analysing the relations between the EU and Turkey. In addition, policy issues faced by both EU and Turkish policy-makers are treated not as discrete issues ranging from low to high politics as Hoffmann suggests, but as elements of a single policy portfolio containing different issues with different levels of transparency/divisibility.[33] Therefore, the methodology in this book differs from that of the conventional international relations theories where states (even though sensitive to societal interests) interact with each other on the basis of an assumed national interest. The difference is due to the fact that national interest is an elusive concept that makes it impossible to determine *a priori* when and why it may or may not be invoked by the state to defend a certain position on a specific policy issue in its interaction with other states. Therefore, national interest is rarely defined in international relations or international political economy literature and it is generally introduced into the analysis retrospectively and in an *ad hoc* manner. We have tried here to overcome this shortcoming by deriving the policy outcomes and the policy stance not from interaction between states as entities with exogenously-given objective functions but as endogenous results determined by the level of societal assertiveness and issue transparency/divisibility under which the state interacts with society.

Another aspect of the methodology adopted here is that the impact of systemic changes or external factors on the EU's or Turkey's policy orientation is mediated through state-society interaction that delineates the options available to policy-makers. In this perspective, an external factor such as the collapse of the Soviet bloc may affect the anchoring capacity of the EU and/or the credibility of Turkey's European orientation only to the extent it affects the level of societal assertiveness and the ability of the state to blur the transparency/divisibility of the issues in EU-Turkey relations. Unless this intermediate process is conceptualised and its consequences for

---

[33] On the distinction between high and low politics, see Hoffmann (1966). For an opposite view, see Baldwin (1985).

the available policy options are verified in the light of empirical evidence, establishing a direct and causal relationship between external factors and the policy choices will remain a convenient yet misleading exercise. In fact, this tendency has been the major weakness of Waltz, who argues that systemic changes condition the actions of the states, the internal qualities of which must be assumed away. [34] No doubt, the abstraction from the qualities of the states facilitates the construction of a simplified system of inter-state interaction. Nevertheless, the gain in terms of analytical convenience is more than neutralised by the loss in terms of explanatory power.[35] That is why state-centric accounts ignore the fact that (i) the anchor/credibility dilemma has characterised the EU-Turkey relations both before and after external developments such as the collapse of the Soviet bloc, and (ii) the dilemma has been due to the EU's tendency to assume only a limited anchoring function in the face of Turkey's non-credible policy commitments.

Finally, the analysis in this book is inspired by the game-theoretic and public choice literature, which is best equipped to deal with endogenous policy outcomes.[36] Yet, the methodology we use differs from this literature in two ways. First, we do not subscribe to the assumption that the cost/incentive structure faced by the policy-maker is externally given. This is also a product of the policy-maker's own actions taken on the basis of past and current information.[37] In that sense, the anchor/credibility dilemma in EU-Turkey relations is a product of state-society interaction that determines the definition of the 'national' or 'European' interest which, in turn, delineates the options available for policy-makers in both Turkey and the EU. Second, we agree with the game-theoretic and public choice argument that strategic interaction may lead to sub-optimal results, commonly referred to as prisoners' dilemma outcomes. However, we depart from this literature by rejecting the idea that the sub-optimal results are inevitable given the rationality of the actors. What we propose here is to take a step back and open the concept of rationality by asking two questions: (i) to what extent state-society interaction is limiting the policy options for both Turkey and the EU so that their interaction leads to sub-optimal outcomes; and (ii) to what extent Turkey and the EU are inclined to learn from past experience in order to improve the scope for policy innovation.

---

[34] See Waltz (1979). For a critique, see Ashley (1984); and Cox (1981).

[35] On the limits of neo-realism in the analysis of European integration, see Ugur (1996a), pp. 26-27.

[36] For a review of this literature, see Hargreaves Heap and Varoufakis (1997); Mueller (1997); and Weintraub (1992).

[37] On this, see Giddens (1979).

These questions raise the possibility that the anchor/credibility dilemma in EU-Turkey relations may not be a result of the rational action by each party given the action of the other. It may rather be a result of both parties' tendency to overlook the need for *epistemic rationality* (which requires the recognition that beliefs should be revised continuously on the basis of available information) and satisfice only with *practical rationality* (which takes these beliefs as given).[38] The difference between epistemic and practical rationality is significant in that beliefs can be self-fulfilling without being correct. To the extent that this is the case, the anchor/credibility dilemma in EU-Turkey relations may be due to both parties' failure to learn from past and current information and enhance the consistency of their beliefs with the actual properties of the environment in which they interact. Therefore, the anchor/credibility dilemma in EU relations may not be an inevitable outcome provided that the perceived cost/incentive structure is reinterpreted on the basis of past and current information with a view to enhance the scope for new policy choices.

---

[38] For this distinction and the attempt to develop a game-theoretic theory of learning, see Bicchieri (1993).

2 State-Society Interaction, European Integration and the EU's Anchoring Capacity

Introduction

Research output on European integration was once likened to a blind man's description of an elephant - disjointed and impressionistic.[1] The initial debate between state-centric and society-centric models revolved around the issue of whether the EU was an intergovernmental or supranational organisation. Until 1965, the process of European integration was fairly unproblematic and the society-centric view seemed to be winning the argument. The neo-functionalist view, developed in seminal works of Ernst B. Haas, depicted European integration as a process driven by transnational actors who instigate a norm-generating process that continually weakens the state and increases the competence of EU institutions - especially the Commission. When France, under General de Gaulle, withdrew from the main committees of the EU in 1965 mainly because of the disagreement on the relationship between state sovereignty and European integration, the state-centric view entered a period of ascendancy. According to this view, the EU is essentially an intergovernmental arrangement albeit the member states that created it had gone through a process of transformation after World War II.

Not surprisingly, the polarisation of the debate eventually led to the emergence of intermediate positions which argued that European integration is an arrangement characterised by a combination of intergovernmental and supranational elements. Nevertheless, the intermediate approaches are still state-centric as their starting point is the state and its needs to come to terms with interdependence. Although they provide a better description of the integration process, their theorctical premise remains weak as the member states' willingness to delegate autonomy to European institutions remains unexplained. In other words, why should European political elite choose to

[1] For the original analogy, see Puchala (1972). For a recent use of the analogy, see Haaland-Matlary (1994), p. 1.

create supranational and not purely intergovernmental institutions in order to manage the spill-over effects of interdependence? Surely, there must be some factors at play that induce the elite to go beyond intergovernmentalism. It may be argued that interdependence between European states is too complicated to be managed through intergovernmental arrangements. This argument, however, begs the question as to why the EU system contains both supranational and intergovernmental procedures applicable to different policy issues. For example, the EU's competence in intra-EU and extra-EU trade policy is exclusive, but the procedure has remained essentially intergovernmental in the area of third country immigration or foreign policy. This discrepancy cannot be explained by the level of interdependence as the spill-over effects in the latter are no less significant than those of the former.

Therefore, recent work has begun to pay more attention to societal processes and the way in which public policy is made. In other words, the society-centric approach seems to be enjoying a revival. For example, the policy communities/networks approach examines the process of EU policy-making in the light of a proxy to state-society interaction, i.e., interaction between the public and private actors in policy networks.[2] What is involved here is a new context for public policy-making. In this context, the driving force behind European integration is the exchange of resources between private and public agents rather than the pressure from transnational interest group organisations. Although this might seem an improvement on the neo-functionalist perspective where transnational organisations are posed against the state, it actually suffers from the same weakness: the state concept is blurred even if not neglected. In addition, the perspective remains limited to sectoral snapshots of the policy-making process. The institutional approach, on the other hand, provides new insights into the way in which institutions, defined as formal rules and procedures, may delineate the options available to the policy-maker. Applied to EU policy-making, this approach can explain EU policy outcomes by relating them to the characteristics of the institutional structure within which the policy is made.[3] Its explanatory power, however, is again limited for two reasons. The exogenous approach that takes institutions as given derives the policy outcomes from the constraint/incentive structure imposed by institutions rather than as endogenous outcomes emerging from state-society interaction. The endogenous approach to institutions, on the other hand, can derive the policy

2 Reviews of the policy communities/networks literature can be found in Petersen (1995); and Richardson (1996).

3 For reviews of the institutionalist approach, see Pollack (1996); Keman (1997); and Kerremans (1996).

outcomes endogenously from the interaction between EU institutions and the member states but it cannot take account of state-society interaction.

The aim in this chapter is to propose a different perspective suggesting that European integration and EU policy output are endogenous outcomes of state-society interaction, which induces member states to approximate policies and codify the policy convergence at the EU level. The proposed perspective is built on three interrelated arguments. First, there is no need to ignore either the state or the societal forces in order to explain the dynamics of European integration and the making of EU policies. Second, the need for policy convergence is both internal to European states and primordial to the establishment of supranational institutions. Finally, the incidence of intergovernmental or supranational policy-making procedures is a function of societal assertiveness and issue transparency/divisibility rather than the extent of interdependence between EU member states. As we demonstrate below, this perspective enables us not only to address the shortcomings of the existing literature but also to derive some conclusions concerning the EU's anchoring capacity.

To work out the proposed perspective, this chapter is organised in four sections. Section 2.1 provides a critical assessment of the existing literature with a view to demonstrate that the state-centric *vs.* society-centric dichotomy is still the main characteristic of the debate on European integration. We shall argue that the society-centric view ignores the state and tends to be reductionist as it derives the policy decisions to form European institutions from societal preferences or constraints. The state-centric view, on the other hand, tends to be voluntaristic as it accords the state a fictive objective function detached from the state's interaction with societal forces.

Section 2.2 builds on this review and develops a political economy approach explaining the integration process as an endogenous outcome of state-society interaction. This section will demonstrate that the level of integration and the competence of the EU as a supranational entity are determined endogenously by the level of societal assertiveness and the extent of transparency/divisibility associated with policy issues. While societal assertiveness is defined as a synthetic index of centrifugal societal tendencies and societal capture that constrain the ability of the state to supply and legitimise territorially-binding policies, issue transparency/divisibility is defined as the extent to which (i) the consequences of policy decisions for societal groups can be quantified and (ii) these consequences are distributed unequally over different societal groups with different interests.

Finally, sections 2.3 and 2.4 will examine the implications of this analytical framework for the capacity of the EU to emerge as an external anchor that could lend credibility to policy reform in Turkey. Section 2.3

will summarise the implication of the preceding analysis for the EU's anchoring capacity in general. It will be demonstrated that the EU's anchoring capacity is an endogenously-determined quality that is positively-correlated with the level of integration and EU competence, but constrained by the EU's need to focus on transparent/divisible policy issues. Section 2.4 probes the relevance of this finding by examining the legal-institutional provisions that regulate not only the EU's external policy-making process in general, but also its association with Turkey. This section will demonstrate that the EU can act as an external anchor only to the extent that the issues in EU-Turkey relations are transparent/divisible and the anchor role does not imply either blanket commitments or significant redistribution in favour of Turkey. Therefore, the EU's capacity to emerge as an external anchor will be limited for two reasons. First, the EU is capable of undertaking only partial commitments and risks in favour of Turkey, as common positions are possible only on the basis of package deals through which the consequences of commitments can be distributed among the member states. Second, the EU may impose sanctions only to the extent that these can be implemented through instruments involving transparent/divisible policy issues. As a result, neither the incentive to remain anchored to nor the cost of deviations from European standards can be increased to make policy reversals in Turkey less likely.

2.1 Theories of European Integration and EU Policy-making: An Assessment

The functionalist/neo-functionalist analysis of European integration is characterised by a society-centric bias where the state is either neglected as an actor (the separability thesis of functionalism) or presented as a decomposable pseudo entity (neo-functionalism).[4] Once the state is either ignored or mystified in this manner, then it is fairly easy to construct a theory (or ideology as Milward would suggest)[5] that compels the student of integration to pursue a research strategy of languishing in siege around the state rather than tackling it directly. Having freed itself of the vagaries of power politics, this society-centric approach concentrates on individual or

---

[4] The neglect of the state by functionalists is a result of their subscription to a 'realist' state image that leads them to see the state as an obstacle to cross-border cooperation of non-state actors. See Mitrany (1966, 1975). Neo-functionalism, on the other hand, perceives of the state as an aberration which conceals the pluralist nature of politics. See Haas (1968, 1969, 1964a).

[5] Milward (1992, 1993).

group interests which recognise the possibility of maximising welfare through international organisations. To the extent that this possibility is recognised, societal groups will shift loyalty away from the state system (functionalism) or strengthen the international organisation as the integrative lessons learned in one context are generalised and a process of 'spill-over' sets in (neo-functionalism). Although loyalty shifts and 'spill-over' are not automatic, they are facilitated either by the separability of technical issues from controversial power-political issues (functionalism); or by a norm-generating learning process which favours the '[international] organisation and diminish the powers of the states' (neo-functionalism).[6]

According to this society-centric perspective, EU policy-making is essentially driven by the Commission, but it also involves interactions between EU institutions and transnational interest groups as well as national governments.[7] What is problematic in this approach is the reliance on a pluralist understanding of politics in which the state is either a broker in societal conflict resolution or the agent of a winning coalition of societal forces. As a result, member states are portrayed as soft entities whose powers are encroached upon by supranational institutions and domestic interest groups.[8] In the neo-functionalist research, the member states are accorded with a more visible status, but when examined carefully can be seen that the 'variable-sum' nature of the bargaining among member states tends to generate policy outcomes that expand the mandate of the supranational institutions at the expense of the states themselves - without explaining why and how such unintended outcomes may emerge.[9]

This reductionist bias has led to various theoretical and empirical problems. First, the society-centric approach is faced with what Olson has described as the 'collective action problem', i.e., a situation where actor rationality leads to failure in organising interest groups because of the potential members' tendency to free-ride.[10] Even if this tendency can be

---

6 Haas (1964a), p.48.

7 See Webb (1987), p. 18.

8 Despite the shortcomings of his pluralist approach, Haas' observation that 'interest group politics' is a necessary condition for regional integration remains to be significant. See Haas (1964), pp. 447-57. That is because in polities where interest groups are dominated by the state legitimation would be based on clientelism and a nationalist/populist ideology. In this polity, the transparency/divisibility of policy issues is reduced and so is the capacity of the state to engage in integrative frameworks with binding rules agreed on the basis of trade-offs.

9 Lindberg and Scheingold (1970).

10 The tendency to free-ride becomes more pronounced as the size of the group with a common interest increases. As group size increases the rationally-behaving individual will expect his/her free-riding to have minimal or no effect either on the establishment of the

checked by the introduction of 'selective incentives' designed to make membership attractive, there is the danger that the state, when necessary, would manipulate the group leadership given its awareness of the fact that the organisation is not based on pure altruism.[11] Second, there is the possibility that the state - under certain conditions leading to a deterioration in constituent loyalty - may be induced to intensify its involvement in welfare-related technical issues in order to recover and/or consolidate its legitimacy. In other words, it could well prove possible that the 'technical' issues in which the society-centric approach invests so heavily assume a new status making the distinction between technical and power politics issues meaningless. Finally, empirical support for hypotheses either on the Commission-driven policy-making or the ever declining member state autonomy has been rather weak. As a result, expectations that the Commission's authority will gradually be enhanced at the expense of the member states '... have given way to more sober examinations' of how governments try to maintain their hold on the levers of power.[12]

The major factor that gives rise to these shortcomings of the functionalist/neo-functionalist analysis is its reliance on a crudely pluralistic/technocratic understanding of post-1945 politics in Western Europe.[13] The technocratic nature of politics and the 'spill-over' dynamic is seen by Haas as necessary for a strategy of 'quietly' but 'deviously' subverting the *ancient regime* through technical pressure. This may be an ingenious way of trying to reduce the friction likely to be encountered in the process of integration, but it has -like Hirschman's concept of forward/backward linkages in economic development - a major disadvantage: the whole edifice is highly likely to disintegrate when the process of technocratic change it purports to explain - a grey process lacking an effective ideology - fails to secure the necessary social/political support in the face of difficulties.[14]

---

interest group organisation or on its success in providing the collective good. See Olson (1965), pp. 31-42. For examples of work on group theory, see Hansen (1985); and Wallerstein (1989).

11 In other words, the state would recognise that the leadership of the interest group organisation is inclined to advance not only the collective welfare of the group, but also their own interests. On this, see Dunleavy and O'Leary (1987), pp. 163-64.

12 Webb (1987), p. 14.

13 For example, Haas observes that economic planning and reliance on technocracy have become the most significant features of national governance in the post-war period. The elevation of these norms to the European level would then require merely an adaptation of the national forms. See Haas (1964b), pp. 65-71.

14 See Hirschman (1981), pp. 276-77.

Given these shortcomings, it is not surprising to observe a state-centric reaction that considers the functionalist/neo-functionalist approach as a pre-theory which may be useful in explaining the process of integration only if it is restricted to the account of the 'spill-over' that follows major intergovernmental bargains.[15] Therefore, various students of European integration began to focus on how the state succeeded in maintaining its authority and in shaping the pace of the integration process.[16] Although these criticisms were not new, they generated a more lively debate compared to earlier critiques by Hoffmann and Waltz. Writing after de Gaulle's veto in 1965, Hoffmann had already made a case for a state-centric approach based on a transformed yet obstinate state image. Also, in an attempt to redefine the realist approach on a structural basis, neo-realism had introduced the bi-polarity of the post-1945 system as a variable that explains the change in European politics and the establishment of the EU.[17]

The weakness of the state-centric analysis is due to its attempt to construct an 'analytically manageable' international system by assuming away the domestic determinants of inter-state relations. Although primordial to the system, the state is over-simplified as an essentially closed entity in order to reduce the number of variables implied by state-society interaction.[18] Once the state is conceptualised in this manner, it is only too easy to construct, analytically, an international system characterised by mechanical interaction between closed entities. Such explanations, however, contradict the empirical evidence on the multiplicity of actors involved in EU policy-making and overlook the fact that the definition of national interests is a subjective exercise that differs not only from one member state to the other but also from one policy issue to the other. For example, how can one

---

15 See Keohane and Hoffmann (1991); and Moravcsik (1993). It must be indicated that Haas himself has also acknowledged obsolescence of neo-functionalism. See Haas (1974). For earlier attempts at coping with the problems posed for the theory, see Lindberg (1966); and Schmitter (1970).

16 For an assessment of the intergovernmentalist drive in the 1970s, see Taylor (1982). For an explanation provided from an international regime perspective, see Keohane and Hoffmann (1990). For other state-centric explanations, see Kahler (1987); and Guerrieri and Padoan (1989). For a historical account based on state-centrism, see Milward (1992); and Milward and Sorensen (1993).

17 See Hoffmann (1966); and Waltz (1979, pp. 71).

18 For example, Morgenthau (1960, pp. 507-512) mentions three state functions performed in the domestic realm, but none of these functions are incorporated into his account of international politics. Waltz (1979, p. 99) is even more unequivocal. He abstracts from '... any particular qualities of states and from all their concrete connections' in order to attain a 'positional picture ... in terms of the placement of the units rather than in terms of their qualities.'

explain the elevation of the textiles industry's interests to the level of national interest in some member states (France and the United Kingdom between 1977 and 1986) and not in others with higher dependence on the sector as a source of export earnings and employment (Greece or Portugal in the 1990s)? Or, how can we explain the difference between a policy issue on which decisions could be taken by majority (trade policy) from another policy issue subject to unanimous procedures (third-country immigration)? It is obvious that concepts such as high-low politics are only of limited value and require a substantial degree of theorisation about how to determine the 'pigeonhole' into which a certain policy issue should be placed.[19]

Against this background, the international regimes theory seemed to possess good explanatory power and to be capable of accounting not only for member state influence on the spasmodic evolution of the integration process (an issue that the society-centric approach is not equipped to deal with), but also for the expanding policy scope and authority of the EU (an outcome that cannot be anticipated by a state-centric analysis). Although it shared the state-centric perspective of the realist/neo-realist tradition,[20] the international regimes theory appeared to be capable of explaining European integration on the basis of interdependence as a constraint implying inter-state cooperation. Thus, European states have been depicted as units of an oligopolistic market which induces the constituent units to cooperate so that they could avoid sub-optimal outcomes that would follow from non-cooperative behaviour.[21]

Although this approach is suitable for examining the demand for international regimes, it fails to specify the supply of such regimes as the latter depends not only on the cost-benefit analysis that Keohane has elegantly developed, but on a number of other factors - including the transparency/divisibility of the policy issues to be regulated within a certain regime and the stability of players' objective functions.[22] Also, the

---

19 Here we share the view suggested by Milward and Sorensen (1993, p. 20) that the high-low politics dichotomy shares common ground with the neo-functionalist premise that posits an antagonism between integration and the nation-state - a premise that '... on the basis of the present state of historical research, appears to be false.'

20 In his attempt to propose a modified research agenda, Keohane (1986) subscribes to the state-centric assumption of the Realist/Neo-realist approach - albeit with some acknowledgement of the roles also played by non-governmental or transgovernmental organisations.

21 On this, see Keohane and Nye (1977) and Keohane (1984). Despite his earlier interest in domestic determinants of international politics, Hoffmann (1982) has also moved towards international regimes theory. For a specific reference to oligopolistic behaviour in the context of European integration, see Guerrieri and Padoan (1989).

22 On the demand for international regimes, see Keohane (1988), pp. 104-16.

international regimes perspective assumes that the state is a rational agent with interests and objectives, but its explanation of how these variables are defined and re-defined remains wanting - largely due to its treatment of the domestic determinants of interest formation as exogenous variables.[23]

As Moravcsik has observed, the international regimes theory is still inspired by traditional 'conceptions of national interests and power' despite Keohane's assertion that '... the concept of international regime is consistent both with the importance of differential power and with a sophisticated view of self-interest.'[24] Consequently, the explanation of international regime formation on the basis of a cost-benefit analysis tends to be either *ad hoc* or tautological. The concept of 'self-interest' is invoked to explain why inter-state cooperation is feasible and desirable, but the lack of theorisation about that very concept begs the questions as to how, when and why self-interest changes over time and calls for different types of international regimes characterised by different levels of authority delegation. In an attempt to address this question, Moravcsik develops a liberal intergovernmentalist approach where preference formation of the member states - i.e., the demand for integration - is the key issue. This is a welcome step, but a careful examination would reveal that the demand for integration is still defined as a function of interaction between member states rather than their legitimation concerns implied by state-society interaction.[25] All that Moravcsik does is to impose constituent preferences as a constraint upon the preference formation of the member states engaged in a continual process of negotiations. Therefore, the demand for integration emerges as a result of the cost-benefit analysis conducted by the member states subject to the constraint of constituent preferences. This is hardly an improvement on the international regimes theory that he attempts to refine.

Recently, because of its emphasis on the interaction between private and public actors of the policy process, the policy communities/networks approach has received positive reviews.[26] This approach is based on the concept of a 'power dependency relationship', which involves resource exchange between public and private agents. In the policy process, the

---

23 It is necessary to indicate that Keohane himself is aware of this problem. He states that international regimes '... could change as a result not only of shifts in the allegedly objective interests of states, ..., but of changes in how people think about their interests...' Nevertheless, he refrains from elaborating on this issue and acknowledges that his analysis remains focused on arguments about power and institutions rather than interest formation. See Keohane (1984), p. 132.

24 See Moravcsik (1991), p. 21, note 5.

25 See Moravcsik (1993), pp. 481, 482-495, and 496-507.

26 See Petersen (1995); Richardson (1996).

public agent receives information and technical expertise while the private actors have the opportunity to influence the policy outcomes.[27] The drawback of this approach is that it does not tackle the consequences of the asymmetry that underpins the distribution of resources between the public and private actors. Therefore, it ignores the implications of the contrast between the territorial and sectoral competences of the public and private actors. This omission deprives the approach of a state theory and limits its value to its descriptive quality that can provide new insights into sectoral policy issues where EU competence is already established.[28] What is also necessary, however, is to explain why EU competence exists in these areas and tends to be less feasible in others.

In addition, the policy networks model can describe the societal actors' role in the making of EU policy only at later stages that follow the initial drive for policy integration. This is in fact acknowledged implicitly or explicitly in sectoral case studies which demonstrate that public-private interaction within policy communities/networks becomes a significant factor only after the Commission begins to work on a policy proposal - either at its own initiative or following instructions from the Council. If state-society interaction is to be limited to the interaction between public and private actors of the policy community/network, then two results follow: either state-society interaction is ignored as a factor that may cause the initial drive towards integration or it is introduced into the analysis only after an intergovernmental bargain is struck in favour of integration. This, however, is hardly an advance either on liberal intergovernmentalism that treats societal preferences merely as a constraint on the member states' preference formation, or neo-functionalism which is already accepted as useful in describing the dynamics of integration after a bargain between member states has been struck.

The application of an institutional perspective to EU policy-making has also attracted positive reviews.[29] Institutions, defined as formal rules and compliance procedures, structure the relationship between actors in various units of the polity and the economy.[30] No doubt, institutions may intervene

---

[27] For analysis of national policy networks, see Rhodes (1990); Rhodes and Marsh (1992). For application of the model to EU policy-making, see Peterson (1992); and Schneider (1994).

[28] On the lack of a state theory in the policy communities/networks approach, see Kassim (1994), p. 17. On sectoral applications, see Grant et al. (1988); Peterson (1992); Schneider et al. (1994); and Anderson (1991).

[29] See Pollack (1996); Keman (1997); and Kerremans (1996).

[30] Hall (1986), p. 19. The exogenous approach to institutions is associated with the work of Hall (1986); Katzenstein (1985); Putnam (1993); and Castles et al. (1987).

between the preferences of society and the state or between member state preferences and EU policy output. Nevertheless, the historical version of institutionalism is constrained by three shortcomings. First, the institutional context is taken as an exogenously-given source of inertia that generates an almost perpetual pattern of policy actions or outcomes.[31] Therefore, the feedback from state-society interaction into the institutional set-up is ignored. Second, institutionalism can explain the way in which EU policy output may 'lock-in' the member states from below because of the societal expectations it generates,[32] but it cannot explain how a given policy convergence codified at the EU level may enable the member states to transcend such societal constraints as a result of the policy convergence itself. Finally, there is the question as to whether institutions can be taken as exogenously-given 'rules *for* use', or they should be considered as 'rules *in* use' determined endogenously by the interaction between the actors involved.

In fact, the last weakness is already recognised by rational choice institutionalism which perceives of institutions as 'rules in use' rather than 'rules for use'. This perspective rightly assumes that institutions are determined by interactions between the actors involved in the policy-making process of the EU. Therefore, it provides useful insights into how EU institutions may induce the member states to agree to policy decisions that might normally not be adopted. Viewed from a principal-agent perspective, this may be due to 'shirking' or 'bureaucratic drift' that enables the agent (i.e., the EU institutions) to secure policy outcomes that the principal (i.e., the member states) could not prevent because of imperfect information or limited sanctioning capacity.[33] The weakness of this perspective, however, is its focus on the interaction between the member states and the EU at the expense of state-society interaction. In that sense, endogenous institutionalism can be seen as a mirror-image of the exogenous approach: it addresses the latter's shortcomings, but fails where the latter is strong.

2.2 Integration and EU Competence as Endogenous Outcomes

It is clear from the preceding review that the emphasis on state or society at the expense of state-society interaction raises various theoretical and

---

[31] On the resilience of the institutional context, see Hall (1986), pp. 233-34, 266.

[32] Pierson (1996) explains the 'lock-in' effect successfully in the area of EU and national social policy.

[33] See Scharpf (1988); Moe (1990); Tesebelis (1990, 1994); North (1990); Garett (1992); and Pollack (1996).

empirical problems in the study of European integration. Although the policy networks and institutionalist approaches have succeeded in addressing some of these problems, they either lack a theoretical basis for state-society interaction (as is the case with policy networks and endogenous institutionalism) or they ignore the endogenous nature of the policy outcomes resulting from the state-society interaction (as is the case with exogenous institutionalism). That is why, we argue that an analysis which has state-society interaction at its centre not only avoids this shortcomings but also provides new insights into the policy-making of the EU and its capacity to act as an anchor for policy reform in third countries. The first step in the direction of developing such an approach is to provide a working definition of the state and society that allows for the conceptualisation of the state-society interaction in a non-reductionist manner.

We define both the state and societal groups/organisations as self-interested actors trying to maximise their respective objective functions and interacting with each other on the basis of territorial and sectoral competences. While the state acts on the basis of territorially-defined competence and supplies territorially-binding policies, societal groups/organisations act on the basis of a sectoral competence and take sector-specific decisions.[34] This definition is characterised by three features. First, the state is not co-extensive with the nation as Northedge would suggest. For Northedge, the state is '... a means of organising people for the purpose of their participation in the international system.'[35] Such a definition is problematic because it is based on the political elite's discourse that has developed over many centuries as a means of legitimation and support mobilisation. Second, the state cannot be understood without reference to its territorial competence and the unequal appropriation of political control techniques that this competence allows for. The public policy-maker is identifiable only within this institutionalised structure and therefore she/he is differentiated from societal decision makers within business or professional organisations. Third, this definition is not based on any *a priori* assumption about state-society interaction. All it suggests is that state-society interaction is to be expected as each side tries to realise its objective function on the basis of different but interconnected domains of competence.[36]

34 This definition is based on the work of Nettle (1968), Mann (1986), and Nordlinger (1981) who demonstrate that the difference between territorial and functional competence has differentiated the state from interest groups even if the former has been created by the latter who eventually become less able to control it.

35 See Northedge (1976), p. 15. For a critique, see Halliday (1989), p. 43.

36 Basing the definition of the state on assumptions concerning state-society interaction is paving the way for reductionism. On this, see Mouzelis (1990). For examples of

Thus defined, the state supplies territorially-enforceable policies, which may be constrained by societal assertiveness revealed in the form of what Hirschman defines as 'exit' or 'voice' tendencies.[37] Given the level of societal assertiveness and depending on the nature of the policy issue over which the state-society interaction unfolds, the state tries to legitimate its policy in two ways. When the policy issue is non-transparent/non-divisible, the state would tend to differentiate its policy from that of other states in order to increase the relative returns on the societal groups' loyalty to its territorial domain. The drawback to this strategy is competitive bidding between states that reduces the returns on policy differentiation but increases societal pressure for higher loyalty pay-off differentials. When the policy issue is transparent/divisible, however, the state may engage in policy approximation as a means of reducing the incentives for loyalty shifts and/or reducing the scope for societal capture. The most developed form of such policy approximation is regional integration based on policy convergence and supported by binding rules as well as supranational institutions. The drawback here is the sharing of territorial competence with other states and agreeing to binding rules that make future policy differentiation less feasible.

This line of reasoning has certain parallelisms with Hirschman and Hotelling who have demonstrated that policy approximation may enable the state (or the firm) to supply policies which may be functional for loyalty maintenance but not in compliance with revealed constituent (or client) preferences that have originally instigated the search for new policies.[38] Societal assertiveness may well induce the state (the firm) to approximate its policies to those of other states (firms), but the implications of reduced choice for constituents (clients) or the reduced incentive for loyalty shifts are not necessarily compatible with the motive underlying societal assertiveness - namely the aim to secure improvement in state (or firm) services. It must be indicated that similar unintended outcomes are faced by the state (firm) too: the state (firm) may stabilise constituent (client) loyalty, but it has to accept the implications of reduced scope for policy differentiation and autonomy because of the commitment to policy approximation.

However, the analysis presented here differs from these early contributions in three ways. First it qualifies Hotelling's assumption about the lack of market segmentation. Hotelling, to some extent legitimately,

---

instrumentalist and structuralist reductionism, see respectively, Miliband (1984); and Poulantzas (1975). For the debate between the two, see Miliband (1983).

37 See Hirschman (1970) for a detailed explanation of how the exit-voice-loyalty metaphor can be used as an analytical framework.

38 See Hirschman (1970, 1981); and Hotelling (1929).

assumes that firms operate in a linear and integrated market where customers can shift their custom from one firm to the other. Unlike firms, however, states are able to limit constituent loyalty shifts by resorting to territorial segmentation through: (i) well-known restrictive measures such as border controls, restrictions on emigration, tariffs, quantitative restrictions on trade, capital controls, etc.; and (ii) effective use of symbolic values such as nationality, traditions and ideologies. Although such segmentation is varied between states and never complete in an international system, it increases the cost for constituents of both 'entry' (i.e. direction of loyalty to another state) and 'exit' (i.e. shifting loyalty away from one's state). Therefore, the pressure on states to equalise the returns on loyalty is not as high as the pressure on firms to equalise prices, quality or wages. Under this condition, not only the coverage of the convergence process, but also the type of international institutions that might be created for its regulation requires further explanation.

Second, we need to be aware of the variations in the state's response to societal assertiveness. As Etzioni has pointed out, some states tend to invest less heavily than others in control-reliant strategies and the same state may be pursuing a differentiated mix of control-reliant and consensual strategies in different policy areas.[39] As a result, the extent of policy convergence or divergence as means of loyalty maintenance is likely to differ from one state to the other or from one policy issue to the other. Last but not least, the analysis here goes beyond Hotelling's and Hirschman's contributions by identifying the factors that would enable us not only to account for these empirical regularities but also to explain the extent to which the EU can emerge as an external anchor for policy reform in an associated country. These factors are the extent of societal assertiveness and the transparency/divisibility of policy issues that capture the most relevant aspects of the state-society interaction.

As indicated in the introduction to this chapter, societal assertiveness is a synthetic index of centrifugal societal tendencies and societal capture constraining the capacity of the state to supply territorially-binding policies. It can be measured by aggregating radical dissent, frequent industrial actions, capital flight, emigration, tax avoidance, intensity of lobbying, strength of interest group organisations, etc. It may emerge as a result of dissatisfaction with domestic policies or incentives/constraints implied by the existence of an international system. In that sense, external factors such as ideological/military threats or interdependence can be captured in this analysis through their impacts on societal assertiveness. For example, the

39 See Etzioni (1968), pp. 282-305; and Etzioni (1967).

emergence of a global capital market can be analysed in terms of its effect on investor behaviour. Similarly, the impact of the Cold War or its demise can be internalised by focusing on how these developments affect constituent loyalty and the perceptions of the states about changes in that loyalty.

On the other hand, the level of transparency/divisibility of policy issues captures the extent to which the consequences of policy decisions can be quantified and are distributed unevenly across societal groups. This can be measured as a composite index combining externally-given and endogenously-determined properties of the policy issue. Although externally-given properties allow for the use of econometric and statistical techniques for measuring and apportioning the consequences of the policy decisions, the endogenous properties are more problematic and depend on the extent to which either the state or societal groups are able to equate the interests affected by the policy decision with an undivided national interest. Therefore, it has to be evaluated qualitatively in the light of state-society interaction underlying the overall policy-making process. If the state is committed to delivering a contracted outcome (such as a high level of economic growth) through intervention and demand management, either the state or societal groups can equate sectoral demands with an overall national interest relatively easily and, therefore, issue transparency/divisibility will be reduced. When, however, the state is engaged in a rule-based regulation aimed at delivering the contracted outcome by reducing the rigidities of the markets, both the state and societal groups are less able to equate a given policy issue with an overarching national interest and, consequently, issue transparency/divisibility will be reinforced.

Bearing in mind these clarifications and the analysis above, we depict in Figure 2.1 four endogenous outcomes of the state-society interaction in EU member states.[40] The underlying assumption here is that both issue transparency/divisibility and societal assertiveness in Europe fluctuate between high and low levels. The relevance of this assumption can be established by referring to three types of theoretical/empirical evidence. First, European states are fairly similar to Etzioni's 'mixed-scanning' polities where governance is based on an institutionalised mixture of control-

40 For further elaboration, see Ugur (1996a), pp. 39-53; and Ugur (1997), pp. 481-93.

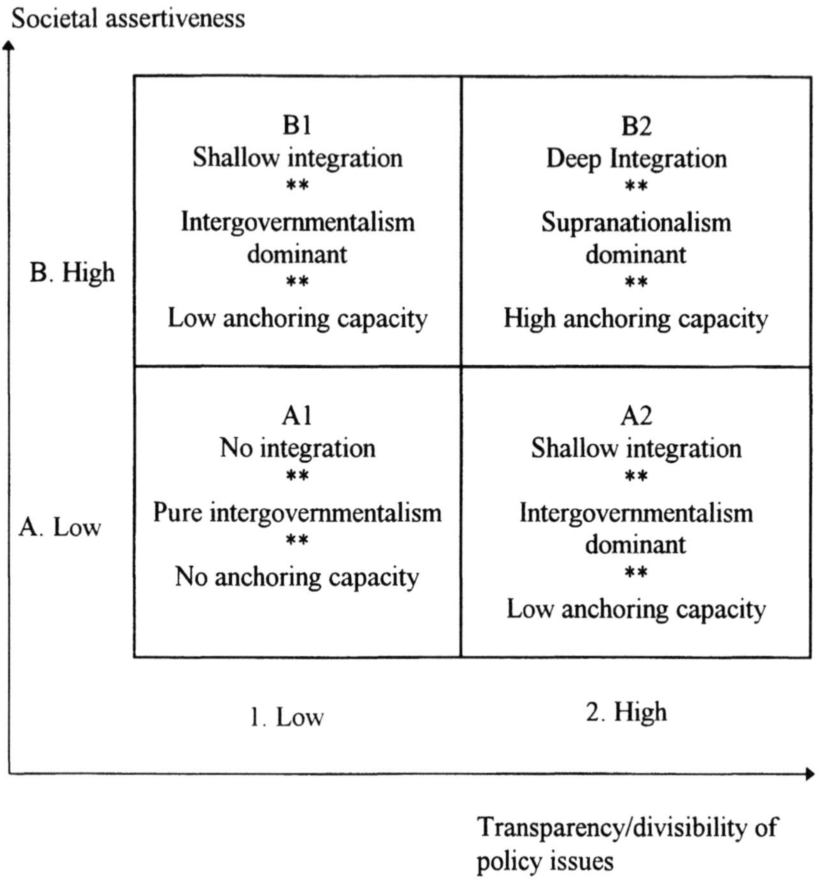

Figure 2.1 Integration, policy-making procedures and anchoring capacity in the European Union: A typology

reliance and consensus building. The relative proportions of these techniques determines the extent of issue transparency/divisibility. Second, societal assertiveness in Europe has followed an upward but variable trend in the post-1945 period with respect to claims made on the state and the methods by which assertiveness has been revealed. This assertiveness has begun as individualistic mobilisation in the 1950s and 1960s, continued as corporatist pressure in the 1970s and has recently taken the form of 'new social movements' tending to question the relevance of the established channels of 'voice'.[41] Although societal assertiveness in Europe has increased over time, the increase has not been uniform across policy issues. Variations in the level of societal assertiveness can be captured from the distribution of interest group organisations or lobby groups with respect to policy issues. Third, and in contrast to what we observe in Turkey, the ability of the European state to blur issue transparency/divisibility has declined over time as the state has moved from interventionism to supply-side regulatory policies. The implied increase in issue transparency/divisibility, however, has not been uniform, as different issues have required different mixes of control-reliance and consensus-building.

Cell A1 in Figure 2.1 corresponds to a situation where state-society interaction in EU member states unfolds under low societal assertiveness and issue transparency/divisibility. Whilst low levels of societal assertiveness reduce the incentives for member states to approximate policies as a means of loyalty maintenance, low levels of transparency/divisibility reduce the scope for package deals as a basis for designing regional institutions and binding rules. Under these conditions, integration is not feasible and any policy co-ordination aimed at dealing with the spill-over effects of interdependence between the member states will be based on intergovernmental procedures. Therefore, the EU's competence will be limited to the provision of services which might facilitate bargaining between the member states.

Cells B1 and A2 depict the outcomes of state-society interaction when societal assertiveness and issue transparency/divisibility are asymmetrical. High levels of *only* societal assertiveness or issue transparency/divisibility may generate some momentum towards policy approximation among EU member states, but this will remain limited because policy integration is either not attractive as a means of loyalty maintenance when the level of societal assertiveness is low (cell A2); or unfeasible when a low level of issue transparency/divisibility enables either the member state or societal groups to equate sectoral interests with an undivided national interest (cell B1). Put differently, state-society interaction under these conditions limits either the incentive or the scope for package deals as a basis for policy integration and institution building. Therefore, intergovernmetalism will be the dominant mode of decision-making to allow for policy reversals or

[41] On individualistic mobilisation in Western Europe, see Pizzorno (1964). On the rise of corporatism in Europe, see Schmitter (1981). Also, see Streeck and Schmitter (1991) on the fall of corporatism in Europe following the breakdown of the Keynesian consensus. On the 'new social movements' and the challenge to established patterns of political representation, see Maier (1995); Richardson (1995); and Offe (1985).

selective integration that may be necessary when either the member states or societal groups equate a salient policy issue with the national interest that cannot be negotiated on the basis of package deals.

Finally, cell B2 depicts the outcomes of state-society interaction when EU member states are faced with high levels of both societal assertiveness and issue transparency/divisibility. Here, policy approximation as a means of loyalty maintenance for EU member states is both desirable and feasible as it can be deployed against high societal assertiveness and may be consolidated on the basis of package deals made feasible by high levels of issue transparency/divisibility. As a result, policy-making procedures in the EU will be closer to supranationalism and EU competence will be significant. The caveat here, however, is that EU competence requires and is conditional on the construction of package deals and trade-offs through which the loss to some member states and/or societal groups/organisations resulting from the integration of a certain issue can be compensated by gains from the integration of other policy issues. This finding is compatible with both statistical modelling and qualitative studies on EU policy-making which suggest that the EU's policy output is positively correlated with the feasibility of package deals or side-payments.[42] Not only that, it also suggests that it is necessary and possible to examine the feasibility of package deals within a wider framework of state-society interaction that may or may not be conducive to integration - depending on the level of transparency/divisibility and societal assertiveness under which it unfolds.

2.3 Integration and the EU's Anchoring Capacity: Theoretical Results

The analysis above suggests that an analytical framework based on state-society interaction and endogenous policy outcomes is comprehensive enough to incorporate the findings of both society-centric and state-centric theories of European integration. It predicts that the EU's policy-making process is characterised by a combination of supranational and intergovernmental procedures that the earlier debate on European integration urged us to consider as mutually exclusive. In addition, it incorporates the findings of both policy networks and institutional approaches that examine EU policies in the light of a truncated framework of public-private

[42] For a statistical modelling approach to voting power and trade policy stance, see Kirman and Widgren (1995). On the significance of side-payments and trade-offs in the conclusion of the Single European Act, see Marks (1992); and Moravcsik (1991).

interaction or interaction between EU institutions and the member states. In that sense, it may contribute to the debate on how the partial and fragmented nature of the work on European integration - i.e., the 'blind man and elephant' syndrome - can be overcome.

Second, it suggests that the level of integration and EU competence are endogenous outcomes of state-society interaction at the national level. Therefore, the dynamic generating the integration process is rooted within the political economy of the member states and primordial to either inter-state or state-EU interaction where the method of policy convergence and integration is negotiated. This does not mean that inter-state or state-EU interaction are irrelevant. All we suggest here is that these types of interaction unfold on the basis of endogenous policy choices that the member states have to make in the light of the societal assertiveness and issue transparency/divisibility they are faced with. Therefore, attempts to explain the integration process and the EU's competence by reference to inter-state or state-EU relations are very likely to remain either incomplete or *ad hoc* as they miss the domestic-level factors that induce the member states to engage in policy approximation or differentiation. The proposed analytical framework bridges the gap between the domestic and international levels by focusing on societal assertiveness and issue transparency/divisibility as variables capturing the nature of the state-society interaction.

Third, the level of integration and EU competence reflects the extent to which state-society interaction induces the member states to opt for policy integration or differentiation. This choice and the resulting level of integration are endogenous outcomes rather than exogenously-given options over which the member states could bargain with one eye gazing the options that can be sold domestically and the other trying to spot the options that are feasible given strategic reactions from other member states. This perspective also suggests that the integration process does not have a stable equilibrium as either the member state or societal groups are likely to continue to improve on current outcomes by revising their expectations in the light of new information as well as constraints and incentives. Such revisions in expectations will affect the level of societal assertiveness and issue transparency/divisibility, and generate a discrete process of integration characterised by deepening at some times and consolidation of intergovernmentalism at others. Unless this aspect of the integration process is recognised, the blind men-elephant syndrome would continue to recur in the form of discovering a federalising trend at times of deepening integration and resurgence of state sovereignty at periods of intergovernmentalism.

Another implication of this analysis, which is more relevant for the purposes of this book, concerns the capacity of the EU to emerge as an external anchor for policy reform in third countries. As can be seen from Figure 2.1, the EU's anchoring capacity is also an endogenous and fluctuating outcome that depends on societal assertiveness and issue transparency/divisibility. With respect to policy issues corresponding to cell A1, the EU cannot emerge as an external anchor because policy outcomes under these conditions tend to be determined by the lowest common denominator. Here, the role of supranational institutions as policy initiators is severely limited. Therefore, they cannot get the member states to undertake significant commitments that would make the anchoring function of the EU attractive for a third country. Not only that, the ability of the EU to impose sanctions is also very limited and therefore the cost for third countries to engage in policy reversals is very low.[43]

In cells A2 and B1 the EU's anchoring capacity is higher than in cell A1, but lower than in cell B2. That is because intergovernmentalism in cells A2 and B1 may be dominant, but it is not the only procedure for policy-making. Therefore, the role of supranational institutions is not limited only to service provision but also involves some degree of policy initiation. This may be the case when issue disaggregation is required for increasing transparency/divisibility as a basis for package deals, or when issue-linkage is implied by past integration or integration in other policy areas. As a result, the EU may undertake some limited commitments towards third countries and make the anchor link attractive. As will be demonstrated later, the EU has been able to undertake such selective commitments towards Turkey in areas of employment and social security for Turkish workers, financial aid, and human rights.

The anchoring capacity of the EU is highest when policy issues fall within cell B2. High levels of societal assertiveness and issue transparency/divisibility are conducive to and compatible with policy integration and EU competence. Here, policy integration and authority delegation to the EU are accepted by member states in return for the dampening effect that the resulting policy integration has on societal assertiveness. Therefore, the EU can undertake commitments towards third countries and try to increase the attractiveness of its anchoring function. Policy issues in EU-Turkey association that fall within cell B2 are essentially trade-related. Again, the evidence to be presented in chapter 4 demonstrates that the EU has been able to undertake unilateral concessions towards Turkey in this policy area. The drawback to this anchoring

43 On the capability-expectations gap in EU foreign policy, see Hill (1993). On the implications of the non-transparent procedures in the common foreign and security policy, see Kiso (1997).

capacity, however, is that EU commitments have to be gradual, sectoral, and conditional. Otherwise, the construction of package deals and issue linkage become difficult if not impossible, and the scope for decisions transcending the lowest common denominator diminishes. Given this limitation, the EU's anchoring capacity may not lead to the undertaking of substantial commitments that would increase the attractiveness of the association link as perceived by Turkish policy-makers. To the extent that this is the case, the limitation to the EU's anchoring capacity would clash with Turkey's tendency to interpret the association link as a means of externalising the cost of policy reform.

2.4 Integration and the EU's Anchoring Capacity: Evidence form Legal and Institutional Arrangements

The analysis above has been concerned with the development of an analytical framework delineating the endogenous levels of integration, EU competence and anchoring capacity. In this section, we will provide some evidence on the extent to which these analytically-derived results are compatible with the legal and institutional framework through which EU external policy is made and implemented. For this purpose, we begin with Table 2.1 which summarises the legal bases of EU competence in the area of external relations and the type of decision-making procedures that apply. A quick examination of Table 2.1 reveals that the decision-making procedures move towards unanimity and the role of the Commission diminishes as the scope of EU competence moves towards non-transparent/non- divisible issues such as association agreements and foreign and security policy. This is in line with the predictions of the proposed analytical framework, but we need to examine the correlation in more details in order to have a better understanding of the EU's anchoring capacity.

From a strictly legalistic point of view, the authority delegated to the EU under Articles 110, 113 and 228 is exclusive -i.e., the member states forego the ability to adopt national policies on these issues. The exclusive nature of the EU's competence under these articles was confirmed in the Court of Justice (ECJ) Opinion of 1975 which, *inter alia*, stated that the common commercial policy should be seen in the light of the operation of a common market which implies that a concurrent power to the member states could compromise the effective defence of the common EU interest. One later, in its *Donckerwolke* judgement, the ECJ consolidated the 'exclusiveness' argument by ruling that national commercial policy measures were permissible only on the basis of a specific authorisation by the EU.[44] Although such a legalistic interpretation may be justified, a close examination of the institutional powers, the decision-making procedures, and secondary legislation reveals that EU competence in this area is more complicated and therefore requires attention to fine details. This is even more the case when one looks at association agreements under Article 238, where EU competence co-exists with concurrent powers to the member states.

Table 2.1 EU competence in the area of external relations: Treaty sources and decision-making procedures

Article	Scope	Procedure
110 (EEC)	Defines the aims of the Common Commercial Policy (CCP). Commits member states to contribute to the harmonious development and liberalisation of international trade.	No procedure is defined as this is a general provision.
113 (EEC)	Provides for a CCP. The Commission has the right to make proposals concerning conclusion, renewal or amendment of trade agreements between the EU and third parties. The Council, on the basis of a mandate, authorises the Commission to negotiate on behalf of the European Community.	Commission proposal may be accepted or modified by qualified majority. Results of negotiations are approved by the Council, in principle, by qualified majority.
115 (EEC)	Provides for safeguard measures to be introduced by the member states. In that sense, it is an anti-dote to the CCP as it allows for the fragmentation of the European Community market along national customs Jurisdictions.	The Council decides by qualified majority when the restriction is introduced by the Commission, and by unanimity when the measure is introduced by a member state.

[44] See Bourgeois (1987), pp. 7-8.

228 (EEC)	Provides for conclusions of preferential trade and cooperation agreements with third countries. The Commission negotiates on behalf of the European Community and on the basis of mandate from the Council.	Results of the Commission negotiations are approved by the Council by qualified majority unless the agreement covers a field for which unanimity is required. The assent procedure applies after the TEU.
237 (EEC)	Provides for accession of European states to the European Community. Application is addressed to the Council	The council approves by unanimity after receiving the Commission's opinion and after the TEU - subject to assent by EP
238 (EEC)	Provides for the conclusion of association agreements with European and non-European countries.	Decisions on the basis of procedures provided in Article 228 above or Article B below. Commission can propose policies.
K1-K3 (TEU)	Member states shall regard the issue of third country immigration as matter of common interest. The Council may draw up conventions to be adopted by member states.	Decision on the basis of two-thirds majority, but it is up to member states to decide on adoption. The Commission my propose policies.
B (TEU)	Sets aims for the EU to assert its identity on the international scene through implementation of a common foreign and security policy (CFSP).	Commission participates in Council meetings, but with no right of policy initiation. Mainly intergovernmental procedures.
C (TEU)	Sets the EU the task of ensuring consistency of its external activities, including external relations, security, and economic and development policies.	Same procedure as Article B.
J1-J15 (TEU)	Sets the EU and its member states the task of defining and implementing CFSP.	Same procedure as Article B.

The exclusive powers of the EU must be qualified even in the commercial policy area where the issue is the least controversial. For example, Article 115 provides for the introduction of national measures with the aim of either protecting domestic markets or maintaining special arrangements with some countries - especially the so-called state-trading countries of the former socialist bloc. Such measures were introduced frequently and on an *ad hoc* basis until 1982-83. In 1982, following the proliferation of protectionist measures, the Council adopted Regulation 288/82 with the aim of bringing some order to a process that had almost gone out of control.[45] Although the aim of this regulation was to provide common rules concerning quantitative restrictions, these 'common' rules proved to be an afterthought that legitimated a *de facto* segmentation of the EU market until the elimination of national restrictions in 1993.[46] It must be noted that this segmentation has been justified by the ECJ on the grounds that the establishment of exclusive EU competence in these areas would require agreement among member states as a prerequisite.[47]

Second, EU competence is based on an elaborate interaction between the supranational and national dynamics of the policy process. Any agreement or EU decision concerning trade relations with a third country is proposed by the Commission. In that sense, the EU system excludes the danger of under-legislation or lowest common denominator outcomes that are likely to obtain when policy initiation is the prerogative of the member states. In addition, the Council decides on the Commission's proposal under articles 113 and 228 by qualified majority - with the implication that the ability of member states to veto a Commission proposal is restricted unless they can construct an alliance with a 'winning minority'. These supranational dynamics are conducive to a significant anchoring capacity as the commitments and/or sanctions implied in the Commission proposals could be significant enough for third countries. The other side of the coin, however, is the intergovernmental constraints that are generally overlooked by legal analysis.

At the policy initiation stage, Commission proposals are negotiated within the Committee of Permanent Representatives (COREPER) and the Article 113 Committee, both of which are composed of national representatives. Although these Committees do not give the Commission

---

[45] Regulation 288/82 covers the so-called sensitive sectors such as textiles and cars. See *Official Journal of the EC*, no. L35. 9.2.1982, pp. 1-44.

[46] For Council Regulation no. 3030/93 on elimination of national quotas, see *Official Journal of the EC*, no. L 275, 1993, pp. 1-9.

[47] European Court of Justice (1984). See also Eeckhout (1994), pp. 153-54; and van Dartel (1987).

direct instructions, the latter is not likely to ignore their views if it wants to secure a 'winning majority' in the Council.[48] This means that prior convergence among member states is a necessary condition for the Commission's ability to initiate policies that are likely to be approved by the Council. In addition, an intergovernmental dynamic is also visible during negotiations with third countries and after the Commission's mandate has been approved by the Council. During these negotiations, not only must the Commission maintain consultation with the committees mentioned above, it must also comply with 'negotiating directives' that the Council may issue unilaterally and without Commission proposal. Although these negotiating directives cannot modify the original mandate (because a modified mandate would require a Commission proposal), they can exert pressure on the Commission to carry out the mandate in line with national preferences to the extent the original mandate is left vague deliberately. Finally, the negotiating mandate of the Commission is not necessarily approved by qualified majority if the agreement to be negotiated with third countries is likely to contain issues that are subject to a unanimous vote in the Council. Because it is impossible to be exactly sure about the content of the final agreement until the negotiations are completed, the practice of approving the Commission's mandate is generally based on a consensus within the Council, which is an implicit unanimity rule.[49]

In the light of these qualifications, we can argue that the seemingly exclusive competence of the EU in the area of commercial policy is actually based on a lengthy process of inter-state and state-Commission bargaining that must be exhausted before EU competence is granted and the stance of the resulting policy is determined. This combination of supranational and intergovernmental dynamics is even more pronounced under Article 238 providing for association agreements. With respect to these so-called 'mixed agreements', member states are granted explicit concurrent powers which imply that common EU positions must be secured on the basis of unanimity for issues that do not fall within the area of common commercial policy.[50]

In the specific case of the EU-Turkey association, this procedure was formalised by an internal agreement concluded between the 'representatives of the member states' rather than the Council'.[51] According to Article 1 of this agreement, the joint position is worked out in accordance with the

---

48 See Macleod et al. (1998), pp. 88; and Nugent (1994), p. 388.

49 Macleod et al. (1998), pp. 89-90.

50 On 'mixed agreements', see Neuwahl (1991); Schermes (1983), pp. 23-28; and Macleod et al. (1998), pp. 142-64.

51 See *Journal Officiel des Communautés Européennes*, no. 217, 29.12.1964, p. 3703.

provisions mentioned above when the matter is within the sphere of Common Commercial Policy. This means that the Community position would be determined mainly by qualified majority within the Council and on the basis of a Commission proposal. In other cases, however, the joint position is determined by the Council or the 'representatives of the member states' meeting in the Council on the basis of unanimity. With respect to such matters, the role of the Commission is limited to consultation only. Two points must be clarified here. First, some issues in EU-Turkey relations are negotiated within the EU through an essentially intergovernmental procedure where the Council is only a convenient forum for the member states to come together. Second, the unanimity principle applicable with respect to such issues implies a significant limit to the capacity of the EU as an entity to undertake risks and commitments or impose sanctions *vis-à-vis* Turkey.

The reconciliation between intergovernmentalism and supranationalism can also be seen in areas of safeguard measures, financial aid, and free movement of workers. With respect to safeguard measures, Council Regulation 1842/71 provides that a member state may introduce quantitative restrictions on Turkish exports either unilaterally or following an authorisation by the Commission.[52] If the first option is exercised, the member state is obliged to notify the Commission only *ex post*. If, on the other hand, the member state seeks authorisation, the Commission must decide within five working days. In either case, any member state can refer the Commission's decision to the Council, which decides by qualified majority. Intra-EU decision-making procedures for financial aid to Turkey were also established by an internal agreement signed in 1964.[53] According to this agreement, financial cooperation between the EC and Turkey was almost entirely a bilateral arrangement. In other words, the role of the Commission or the European Investment Bank (EIB) was limited to monitoring the disposal of the financial aid decided by unanimity. Finally, decisions concerning free movement as well as social security and employment rights of the Turkish workers residing in the EU were also subject to unanimity.

As we move further towards non-transparent/non-divisible policy issues, the oscillation between supranationalism and intergovernmentalism gives way to dominance by the latter. The *ad hoc* nature of the intergovernmentalism in these policy areas (human rights, third-country immigration, and common foreign and security policy) was finally overcome through rules provided in the Treaty on European Union (TEU). These rules

52 See *Official Journal of the EC*, no. L192, 26.8.1971, pp. 14-15.

53 See *Journal Officiel des Communautés Européennes*, no. 217, 29.12.1964, p. 3709.

lock the member states within a co-ordination machinery in which the Commission is represented. However, either Council decisions are taken by unanimity or the Commission's right to initiate policies is restricted. For example, the Commission can initiate policies in the areas of third-country immigration and human rights, but the decision-making is subject to a two-third majority in the former and unanimity in the latter. Also, in the area of common foreign and security policy, the Commission has only the right to participate in Council meetings the decisions of which are subject to unanimity. The obvious implication of these arrangements is that proposals for common policies will be under-supplied and any policy decision will tend to reflect the lowest common denominator. Therefore, the TEU did not bring any significant change to the making of EU policy *vis-à-vis* Turkey in non-transparent/non-divisible areas such as free movement, human rights or the Cyprus problem. In these areas, not only has the Commission had to live with ongoing intergovernmentalism, but it has also failed to devise package deals that would facilitate the undertaking of EU concessions/risk or the imposition of sanctions *vis-à-vis* Turkey.

What does this evidence suggest so far as EU's anchoring capacity is concerned? The analysis in section 2.3 above implies that the EU's ability to undertake commitments and risks or to impose sanctions is positively correlated with the extent of supranationalism and EU competence. Therefore, we would expect the EU's anchoring capacity to be high in policy areas where supranational procedures are dominant. These are generally trade-related - as can be seen from articles 113, 228 and 238 of the Treaty of Rome and specific rules governing trade relations with Turkey. As we move towards less transparent/divisible policy issues such as human rights, foreign policy and immigration covered by Articles 130u, B, C, J and K or TEU, intergovernmentalism tends to be dominant and, therefore, the EU's anchoring capacity is liable to decline. This tendency is also reflected in provisions concerning the free movement in EU-Turkey relations and is compatible with the evidence on the Cyprus issue and human rights to be examined in chapters 6 and 7 below. Moreover, the evidence above suggests that even the EU's anchoring capacity in transparent/divisible policy issues is partial and conditional. For example, the EU can undertake significant commitments in trade-related matters, but these commitments are neither automatic nor free of escape clauses that would enable the member states to take unilateral action when necessary. Although package deals may reduce the incidence of such national withdrawals from EU commitments, the mere existence of such a possibility may reduce the attractiveness of the EU as an anchor for Turkey because of the implicit uncertainty. In addition, the conditional and partial nature of the commitments increases as the transparency/divisibility of the issues in EU-Turkey relations decreases. This is not only an additional source of uncertainty, but also carries the risk of weakening the anchor function dramatically as the non-transparent/non-divisible nature of the policy issues is likely to induce Turkish policy-makers to equate these issues with a non-negotiable national interest.

Conclusions

Two sets of conclusions can be derived from the preceding analysis. The first set concerns the dynamics of integration and EU policy-making. With respect to these issues, we can conclude that a case has been presented for examining the integration process and the making of EU policies as endogenous outcomes determined by state-society interaction. We have demonstrated that European integration is essentially a method of codifying the convergent policy choices made by the member states as a result of state-society interaction at the national level. The extent of convergence and the procedures through which the convergence is codified depend on the extent of societal assertiveness *vis-à-vis* the state and the level of transparency/divisibility associated with policy issues. Therefore, as a means of coping with societal assertiveness, the need for policy convergence is primordial to inter-state or state-EU bargaining on the design of European institutions that would codify the convergent policy choices and/or facilitate the co-ordination of these choices. State-centric approaches are inadequate to examine this process as they capture only the tip of the iceberg, i.e., only the inter-state or state-EU interaction that has been prompted by the primordial need for policy convergence. Society-centric approaches are also inadequate because they misrepresent the bottom of the iceberg by equating the member states' convergent policy choices with the preferences of societal forces. These choices, however, are not only endogenous outcomes determined by state-society interaction, they are also codified and integrated by active participation of the member states.

The analytical framework proposed here also brings some order to the confusion about two aspects of EU policy-making: the co-existence of supranational and intergovernmental procedures; and the technocratic nature of the policy process. The relative incidence of supranational and intergovernmental procedures is determined by the extent of societal assertiveness and the level of issue transparency divisibility. While supranational procedures are an increasing function of societal assertiveness and issue transparency/divisibility, intergovernmental procedures are a decreasing function of these variables. That is why the EU system is characterised by different levels of supranationalism and intergovernmentalism, depending on the level of the societal assertiveness and issue transparency/divisibility as two essential features of the state-society interaction. The technical nature of the policy-making process is also explained by state-society interaction. Policy convergence among member states, as indicated above, is primordial to policy integration and it reflects an attempt to dampen societal assertiveness. Although this reflects an autonomous choice given the state-society interaction within each member state, convergence is never complete due to differences in the mixed-scanning properties of the member states' political systems. Therefore, when these policies are integrated in the form of adopting a common policy (such as a common commercial policy) or harmonisation (such as mutual recognition of standards) with a view to avoid policy reversals, gains and losses due to integration must be traded off both between societal groups and the member states. Technocratic issue dissection and linkage is the result of the need for package deals that would facilitate these trade-offs.

Our second set of conclusions concerns the anchoring capacity of the EU. The co-existence of intergovernmental and supranational procedures enhances the capacity of the EU to act as an external anchor in comparison to purely intergovernmental organisations, but makes it a less viable anchor compared to fully-fledged states endowed with similar economic and political resources. That is because supranationalism enhances the capacity of the EU institutions to secure agreement between member states on the extent of commitments and risks to be undertaken or sanctions to be imposed *vis-à-vis* third countries; whereas intergovernmentalism reduces this capacity. In addition, the technocratic nature of the EU policy-making process is conducive to the delineation of certain commitments and/or sanctions that would increase the EU's attractiveness as an anchor. However, the length of the intra-EU bargaining required by the need to construct package deals and the partial nature of the resulting commitments and/or sanctions would reduce the attractiveness of the anchor link because of the uncertainty implied. These aspects of the EU's anchoring capacity are clearly evident in the general provisions concerning external relations and the specific provisions regulating the EU's relations with Turkey. These provisions contain escape clauses that enable the member states to limit their contributions to the concessions to be granted, or to the cost of the sanctions to be imposed.

Finally, the incidence of supranationalism and the level of anchoring capacity tend to be limited as issue transparency/divisibility declines. This decline may be checked under two circumstances. First, to the extent that the issue area can be disaggregated into smaller areas, it may be possible to define some secondary issues where the implications of the anchoring function can be controlled - for example, differentiation between new immigration and integration of the existing immigrants. Second, EU commitment or sanction concerning a relatively non-transparent/non-divisible policy issue may be functional for legitimating the technocratic nature of EU policy-making. To the extent that this is the case and the risk associated with the commitment or sanction can be controlled, the EU may assume an anchoring role. One example of such policy issues is human rights - where the dominance of intergovernmentalism has not prevented the EU from raising the profile of this issue in its relations with Turkey as well Central and Eastern European countries. Nevertheless, in non-transparent/non-divisible policy areas, the EU's anchoring capacity will remain severely limited if not absent because of two consequences of the dominant intergovernmentalism: (i) the lack of Commission competence for policy initiation will reduce the scope for package deals; and (ii) the tendency towards the lowest common denominator will favour the *status quo* rather than policy innovation.

3 State-Society Interaction and Non-credible Policy Commitments in Turkey

Introduction

Having identified the limitations to the EU's anchoring capacity, we now turn to the issue of policy credibility in Turkey. As indicated in chapter 1, Turkish policy makers have perceived of the link with the EU not only as a particular manifestation of the commitment to modernisation, but also as an anchor that would ensure the irrevocability of the policy reform. We call this choice as European orientation involving convergence towards EU standards. One obvious implication of Turkey's European orientation is that it generates short-term costs associated with institution building, economic policy reform, democratisation and the reduced scope for alternative policy choices. These costs are both economic and political in nature and can be substantial depending on the extent of divergence between Turkey and the EU. Another implication of the European orientation is that it may lead to Turkey's integration within the EU and thereby secure long-term benefits that include stable institutions, increased economic efficiency, enhanced status in the international system, and access to EU agricultural and structural funds. The question that arises here is whether this European orientation can be a credible policy commitment given the cost/incentive structure with which Turkish policy makers are faced with.

We argue that Turkey's European orientation cannot be a credible policy commitment because of the way in which the Turkish state interacts with societal groups in the process of policy-making. State-society interaction in Turkey unfolds in the context of a polity that reflects the characteristics of what Etzioni describes as control-reliant and consensual modes of governance. According to Etzioni, policy performance in these two types of governance is low because of heavy investment in 'control technology' in the former and 'muddling through' in the latter.[1] Applying

[1] See Etzioni (1967, 1968).

this perspective to state-society interaction in Turkish policy-making, we can see that the Turkish state is simultaneously too strong and weak *vis-à-vis* societal groups. Its strength is due to its heavy involvement in the economy and its top-to-bottom approach to policy reform. Its weakness - i.e. its responsiveness to societal demands - is a mirror-image of its strength and is implied by the way in which the state rule is legitimated. The legitimacy of the political regime in Turkey is dependent on the capacity of the state as a major producer, employer and investor to satisfy sectoral claims and counter-claims rather than the efficiency and equity implications of the state's regulatory function.

It is not difficult to see why the oscillation between 'control-reliance' and 'muddling through' is a recipe for failure so far as policy credibility is concerned. If credibility is defined as very low probability of policy reversals, it can be seen neither 'control reliance' nor 'muddling through' is compatible with credible policy commitments. An announced policy choice (e.g., European orientation) is highly likely to be non-credible because Turkish policy makers will be induced to deviate from it either because of changes in state preferences or as a result of societal pressure. In what follows, we examine the constraint/incentive structure that has induced Turkish policy makers to deviate from the announced policy of European orientation. Section 3.1 focuses on the implications for credible policy commitments of the role of the state in Turkey's economic development. This section will highlight the heavy involvement of the Turkish state in the economy and elaborate on the implications of this involvement for: (i) the responsiveness of the state to societal demands, and (ii) the credibility of Turkey's European orientation in terms of economic convergence. Section 3.2 will concentrate on the political domain and demonstrate how the control-reliant mode of governance has enabled the state to determine the way in which the 'national interest' is defined. The aim here is to highlight the implications of this mode of governance for state-society interaction and the credibility of Turkey's European orientation in terms of political convergence. Finally, section 3.3 will examine the extent to which the establishment of the customs union in 1996 can ameliorate the anchor/credibility dilemma in EU-Turkey relations.

3.1 *Étatism* and its Implications for Credible Policy Commitments

The Turkish state has been involved in the economy heavily since 1930. It has played an active role not only in the traditional sense of undertaking large infrastructure projects and regulating the economic environment, but also in terms of being a major producer and employer in the tradable goods sector. As a result, the state has led the private sector by establishing a technological base, training a pool of labour, and providing low-priced consumer goods that have kept the wage level low. This experience has been described as *Devletçilik* (*étatism*) in the literature.[2] As a result, by 1960, the public sector accounted for 53.2% of total output and 56.2% of the total value added in the light industrial sectors. These shares increase to 55.0% and 66.2%, respectively, in the heavy industrial sectors. Also, the public sector accounted for 46.1% of the total investment between 1955 and 1960 - when the government's announced policy was to encourage the private sector to play a more prominent role.[3]

Étatism has continued to shape Turkey's economic development in the last three decades too. Despite the foreign exchange shortages of the 1970s and the liberalisation reforms of the 1980s, the state's share in total fixed capital formation remained high: 44.5% between 1972 and 1979, and 62.5% between 1980 and 1988. After 1988, the share of public sector in total fixed capital formation declined gradually and reached the level of 45% in 1992.[4] These figures reflect not only the rationale for *étatism* as a development strategy, but also its implications in terms of the dependency culture it has created. Due to lack of private sector willingness to invest, the Turkish state has undertaken about half of the total investment over the last three decades. The aim has always been twofold: bridging the investment gap resulting from low levels of private sector investment; and encouraging the latter by signalling the areas of future growth and creating opportunities for private investors as a result of forward and backward linkages.

Given the strategic interaction between the state and the private sector, this strategy led to various unintended outcomes. First of all, *étatism* turned out to be an inefficient policy design. Inefficiency has been due to politically-motivated pricing and employment decisions in the State-owned Economic Enterprises (SEEs), and the private sector's rent-seeking behaviour that the extensive public sector has encouraged.[5] Also, heavy state involvement in the economy generated a dependency culture whereby the private sector expected the state to take on high risks and pave the way for lower-risk investment opportunities to be exploited by private investors. This

---

2 On the role of the state in Turkey's economic development until the 1970s, see Hershlag (1968); Land (1970); Tezel (1986); and Boratav (1982). It is true that the state has begun to pull out of the manufacturing sector since 1980, but this process has proved problematic as will be demonstrated below.

3 Ugur (1988), pp. 85 and 90.

4 Central Bank of Turkey (1982, 1985, 1987, 1989, and 1993)

5 See, for example, Krueger (1974).

dependency culture was so much deep-rooted that it proved difficult to overcome even after the introduction of the export-oriented liberalisation programme in 1980. Although private sector investment increased significantly in magnitude terms after 1980, its share in total investment declined from 55.5% between 1972 and 79 to 37.5% between 1980 and 1988. Finally, the state had to compete with the private sector for investment funds raised from the domestic and foreign markets. This competition was very tense and led to frequent complaints about the crowding-out effects of *étatism* - a strategy purporting to encourage private investment. In addition, *étatism* has placed the public finances under heavy strains and led to macroeconomic instability which increased the risks for private investors.

These consequences have been examined extensively in the academic literature and international organisation reports analysing Turkey's economic performance.[6] It is not our intention to elaborate further on the findings of these studies. Instead, we propose to examine the implications of *étatism* for credible commitments to convergence towards EU standards as a prerequisite for closer integration with the EU. When viewed from this perspective, it is clear that *étatism* has reduced the scope for credible commitments to such convergence. This adverse effect is caused by the way in which the parameters of the Turkish political economy have affected the state-society interaction in Turkey. The effect is twofold: (i) societal assertiveness in Turkey tends to be high as the role of the state in the economy makes it a centre of attraction for private sector claims and counter-claims concerning distribution of economic values; and (ii) both the state and organised interest groups are motivated (and in fact enabled) to blur the transparency/divisibility of policy issues.

It is only natural that societal groups, in their attempts to realise their objectives, try to influence the territorially-binding policy decisions of the state in their favour. After all, this is a rational choice and compatible with evidence concerning the lobbying activities of interest groups across countries. It would be unrealistic to expect a different tendency in Turkey so far as state-society interaction is concerned. We call this tendency externalisation, i.e., a pattern of risk-minimising behaviour reflecting a desire to externalise the risks associated with private decisions and activities but without necessarily accepting the lower returns associated with lower risks. The nearest concept in the political economy is rent-seeking, but this is less comprehensive. In other words, rent-seeking is only a subset of

---

[6] See, for example, OECD (1987, 1988, and 1995); Rodrik (1990); Uçtum (1992); Nas (1992); TUSİAD (1995); and Öniș and Riedel (1996).

externalisation as it refers mainly to influencing the distributional decisions of the public policy maker in one's favour.

What distinguishes the Turkish political economy from the average norm in the EU is that the returns on and scope for externalisation activities are much higher in Turkey. The returns on externalisation are high because the rents that can be derived from favourable policy decisions of a state heavily involved in the economy are substantial. The scope for externalisation is also high because societal demands can be legitimated relatively easily by referring to the uncertainty and risks caused by the discretion that the government draws upon in regulating the economy. Given this incentive/scope structure, societal groups in Turkey tend to be highly assertive with respect to economic policy issues. The implication of this state of affairs is the generation of a ratcheting effect whereby externalisation demands require further state discretion which, in turn, encourages further demands for externalisation.

Under these conditions, even societal groups in favour of closer integration with the EU are likely to try to externalise the short-term costs of the convergence towards EU standards on to others who may or may not be in favour of integration. This may not be a major problem should the policy maker be capable of resisting sectoral or corporate demands for externalisation. The Turkish policy maker, however, is unable to resist such demands not only because of the non-transparent links between societal groups and the state fostered by *étatism*, but also because of the adverse consequences of the discretionary practice built into the policy process. As the Turkish state intervenes in the economy frequently and in an unpredictable manner, contracts between societal actors become less binding because the parties involved can easily associate their private losses arising out of the contract with unpredictable government decisions. As a result, policy makers are more likely to internalise these losses as the discretionary policy they implement enables the societal groups to present their private losses as social losses which the state must internalise.[7]

The unpredictability of the discretionary government policy is due to two factors. First, as the involvement of the state in the economy increases, the public policy maker has to supply policies addressing the needs of the public sector. To the extent that this is the case, the distinction between territorial competence of the state and functional competence of societal groups will be blurred. In other words, the government begins to supply not only territorially-binding policies legitimated through the usual channels of interest representation and aggregation, but also functional/sectoral policies

7 For a similar approach to the stabilisation problem in Turkey, see Saraçoğlu (1995).

concerned with its economic activities and legitimated on the basis of economic rents that these activities create for societal groups - for example low-priced inputs and consumer goods, employment opportunities, etc. Therefore, public policy in Turkey is subject not only to usual societal constraints visible in pluralist societies, but also to additional constraints imposed by the need to sustain its productive activities - which range from food processing through textiles to the production of heavy machinery.

To appreciate the extent of the Turkish state's involvement in the economy, we begin with an overview of the state-owned enterprises involved in productive activities. As of 1985, there were 42 State-owned Economic Enterprises (SEEs) controlling 99 corporate entities with a total work force of some 682,000. In addition, the SEEs were minority shareholders in 429 private companies with a share of no less than 15%.[8] The politically-driven pricing and employment decisions that characterise these institutions have meant that their operating profits have never been adequate for financing the required investment. Therefore, the SEEs have always borrowed from both the domestic and foreign markets, as Table 3.1 demonstrates.

One implication of this borrowing is the competition between the SEEs and private enterprises for investment funds. Given that the capital market is underdeveloped in Turkey, the SEEs have borrowed mainly from the Central Bank, the domestic commercial banks and foreign creditors. The switch between creditors from one year to the other has exacerbated the uncertainty with which the private sector is faced. This is especially the case when the switch is towards the Central Bank or domestic banks. While borrowing from the Central Bank creates inflationary pressure, drawing on private bank credits exerts upward pressure on the interest rates. Another factor that exacerbates this uncertainty is the government's consolidation o has consolidated the SEE debts by converting them into Treasury debts and thereby maintaining the SEEs' ability to borrow fresh funds from the banking system. Consequently, the SEEs net borrowing requirement has increased from 2.64% of the gross national product (GNP) in 1989 to 4.03% in 1993.[9]

Under these circumstances, public policy decisions are bound to be affected not only by the requirements of the economy in general but also by the particular needs of the SEEs. In other words, public policy tends to spill from the territorial to the functional domain, hence providing scope and incentives for societal groups to secure externalisation of private risks. It must also be indicated that the uncertainty implied by extensive SEE

---

8 Under-secretary for Treasury and Foreign Trade (1986), pp. 15-24.

9 Central Bank of Turkey (1993), p. 121.

borrowing is not fully reflected in Table 3.1. When annual projections of the SEEs are compared with year-end results, significant discrepancies can be observed. For example, the projected borrowing requirement for 1987 was TL 1,010 billion, whereas the year-end result turned out to be TL 1,821 billion - reflecting an underestimation of 80%. Although private enterprises may also be liable to incorrect estimations, it is not difficult to see the latter exploiting the failures of the public sector as a significant cause of underperformance and increasing their lobbying for externalisation.

Table 3.1 Net borrowing requirements of the SEEs and financing

Year	Net borrowing requirement	Central Bank credits	Other domestic borrowing	Foreign borrowing
1983	161	-5	28	238
1984	170	-56	49	177
1985	497	80	18	399
1986	910	6	56	848
1987	1821	576	144	1101
1988	2059	308	52	1699
1989	2057	0	2474	964
1990	7426	0	5225	2537
1991	6949	3829	5606	1570
1992	4454	-714	-276	1519
1993	10370	10825	1076	-1955

*: In billions of Turkish Lira. Borrowing requirements and credits do not tally after 1989 because of the changes in cash balances which are not presented here. (-) indicates surplus or debt repayment.

Source: Central Bank of Turkey (1982, 1985, 1987, 1989, and 1993).

The second source of uncertainty that encourages and facilitates externalisation relates to the method with which the Turkish government exercises its discretion in economic policy-making. The Turkish government relies heavily on the use of decrees as substitutes or complements to laws enacted by the parliament. These decrees are drafted by civil servants (who are under-paid comparable to private-sector employees with similar qualifications) and issued subject to *ex post* parliamentary approval. Therefore, not only is the principle of accountability violated, but also members of parliament (MPs) become agents of organised interests as their role is reduced to lobbying civil servants on behalf of their clients. Available evidence clearly suggests that Turkish MPs tend to lobby civil servants on behalf of particular interests through non-transparent channels rather than arguing their case in public (see section 3.2 below). The resulting dependence of MPs on civil servants reduces not only the capacity of the legislative organ to control the executive, but also the predictability of the policy outcomes - thereby increasing the incentive and scope for externalisation demands by societal groups.

The implications of this type of state-society interaction for the credibility of Turkey's commitment to a European orientation are not difficult to detect. The short-term costs of convergence envisaged in the AA and the AP are likely to induce societal groups to demand deviations from the association contract. Societal groups, in line with the externalisation culture, will tend to demand delays in the gradual liberalisation of trade with the EU, special sectoral treatment even if gradual liberalisation is introduced, maintenance of the tax incentives and subsidies granted to exporters, and macroeconomic divergence from the EU to the extent that the latter is engaged in tight fiscal or monetary policies.

Table 3.2 provides some evidence confirming this analysis. The private sector in Turkey has been in favour of EU membership as long as this has remained a long-term target and the short-term costs of convergence are avoided. This is confirmed by the results of a 1988 survey covering 331 firms. Depending on firm size, about 84-97% of the respondents were in favour of Turkey's membership if the time horizon is not specified. However, when the time horizon is specified as 10 years, the level of support drops by half to 32-49% of the respondents. That the fall in the level of support is related to the tendency to avoid the convergence costs can be seen in the next row of the table, where the participants are asked about the adjustment measures they are implementing. The proportion of those taking full or partial measures (29-40%) is even lower than those in favour of membership within 10 years. In addition, large firms (employing 500 people or more) are only marginally more willing to support EU membership or undertake adjustment measures compared to small or medium-size firms. In other words, the tendency to think of EU membership as a distant goal and the reluctance to adjust are general trends that characterise the behaviour of not only the small or medium-size firms which are more likely to be geared towards the domestic market, but also the large firms for which access to external markets should be more significant.

Table 3.2 Percentage of firms responding positively to questions related to EU membership (1988)

Questions asked	Small firms (25-99 employees)	Medium-size firms 100-499 (100 employees)	Large firms (over 500 employees)
Do you want Turkey to accede to the EU?	84.4	95.3	97.3
Do you want accession by 1995?	32.0	42.2	48.7
Are you taking full or partial measures for adjustment?	28.6	37.0	40.7

Source: Kazgan (1989), p. 21.

These results are not surprising and confirm the trends that had been detected earlier. A survey conducted in 1978 by TUSİAD (*Türk Sanayicileri ve İş Adamları Derneği*, Turkish Industrialists and Businessmen's Association) revealed that 64% of the respondents were in favour of EU membership. However, responses to more specific questions demonstrated clearly that this was a qualified support. For example 63% of the respondents thought that newly developing industries would not stand European competition, 64% wanted membership to happen at least 10 years later, 78% thought that Turkey should protect its developing industry more, and 55% wanted the state to provide investment credits to the private sector.[10] This evidence reflects two tendencies.

One is the lack of a committed private sector support for integration with the EU. It is true that some organisations representing the big business such as TUSİAD, İKV (*İktisadi Kalkınma Vakfı*, Economic Development Foundation) and Chambers of Industry in Istanbul, etc. have been in favour of closer links with the EU as an anchor for regime stability. This pro-European stance, however, has been compromised by the private sector's tendency to toe the official policy line when the Turkish government deviates from the convergence towards EU standards on the grounds that this is required by Turkey's national interest. That is why the private sector has

10 TUSİAD (1978).

challenged the government's EU policy only once - in 1978-79 - when the left-of-centre government, faced with the heaviest crisis of the import-substitution strategy, threatened the EU with a new foreign policy orientation. In addition, the private sector has consistently relied on the government's receptiveness to externalisation demands and rent-seeking. Therefore, instead of undertaking the necessary adjustment measures that could have tied the hand of the government, it induced the government to engage frequent deviations from convergence towards EU standards on the grounds that the Turkish industry should be accorded a special treatment. That was why only 28-40% of the respondents to the 1988 survey were in the process of undertaking the necessary adjustment measures despite the fact the membership issue began to be discussed widely since 1985.

The other, and more negative, tendency reflected the private sector's cynicism towards the government's announced policy of integration with the EU. Both survey results clearly indicate that the private sector did not interpret this as a credible policy commitment. Therefore, it discounted the probability of EU membership and concentrated its demands on protection and subsidisation. These demands are reflected in the survey results mentioned above and were reiterated in a 1988 İKV report which asked the government to take into account the special needs of the Turkish industry and carry out the negotiations with the EU accordingly.[11] Given this private sector attitude to integration and adjustment, it was not surprising to observe that the Turkish government avoided tariff dismantling until mid-1980s and introduced non-tariff barriers thereafter, despite the fact the membership application was made in 1987. (See below and chapter 4.)

It must be indicated that this dynamic is only one side of the credibility problem faced by Turkish policy makers. The other side of the coin concerns the interests of the state itself in non-credible policy commitments. Faced with externalisation demands that can be justified relatively easily, the Turkish government has to discover ways of internalising private risks. This involves resources as inter-group competition for externalisation becomes the norm. In other words, the public policy maker cannot shift the private risks of some groups on to the others as the latter are also likely to be engaged in lobbying for externalisation. Possible solutions to the resource problem involves either increased taxation or using fictive resources. The existing evidence suggests that Turkish policy makers have had to resort to the second option. Two indicators can be cited in support of this argument.

---

[11] İKV (1988), p. 122. The İKV (İktisadi Kalkınma Vakfı) is a lobby group established by Turkish chambers of commerce and industry to monitor developments in EU-Turkey relations and express the public sector's views.

First, the Turkish government's taxing decisions have had a dampening effect on the growth of tax receipts relative to gross domestic product (GDP) growth. As can be seen from Table 3.3, the *buoyancy coefficient* for tax receipts, which incorporates the impact of taxing decisions, have been consistently lower than the built-in *elasticity coefficient* which is purged of taxing decision impacts.

Table 3.3 Buoyancy and built-in elasticity coefficients of tax receipts in Turkey: 1975-93

	Indirect tax receipts	Direct tax receipts	Total tax receipts
1975-93	1.43 (1.05)	1.4 (1.02)	1.43 (1.02)
1975-82	1.32 (0.91)	1.56 (1.15)	1.41 (1.03)
1983-93	1.64 (1.25)	1.37 (1.02)	1.55 (1.12)

Note: Buoyancy coefficients are shown in brackets.

Source: Ersel and Kumcu (1995), p. 191.

These figures suggest that the Turkish government's tax receipts would have been higher had no taxing decisions been taken during the period 1975-93. The same can be said of the two sub-periods corresponding to import-substitution (1975-82) and export-oriented industrialisation policy (1983-93). This is not surprising because the receptiveness of the sectoral demands has actually increased in the 1980s and 1990s for two reasons: (i) macroeconomic instability increased as a result of increasing public sector deficit and lax monetary policies; and (ii) the export-oriented strategy was based on large scale subsidisation of exports and investment. Therefore, the taxing capacity of the government during the 1980s and 1990s was even lower than the preceding period - as can be seen from the wider gap between the built-in elasticity and buoyancy coefficients for the period 1983-93.

The inevitable consequence of the weak taxing capacity was the resort to fictive resources in the form of central bank credits - as can be seen from

Table 3.4. A simple calculation shows that, over 1981-93 period, 61.7% of the general government deficit (excluding the SEE deficits examined above) has been financed by short-term borrowing. Of this, 56.5% has been in the form of central bank credits. In other words, the Turkish government has tried to compensate for its weak taxing capacity by printing money and imposing an inflation tax on the society at large. Inflation rates during the 1990s fluctuated between 60% and 85%, reaching a peak level of 106% in 1994. One implication of this *seignorage* extraction was the unequal distribution of the inflation burden. Societal groups with the capacity to engage in currency substitution have managed to externalise the cost of inflation onto others, mainly wage earners with little or no savings that can be held in foreign currency denominated accounts. The other, and more relevant, consequence has been the incentive for the government to maintain its discretionary policy and the high levels of inflation associated with it. Therefore, and irrespective of the private sector pressure for deviations from convergence, the government, too, has become motivated to deviate from its commitments implied by the EU-Turkey association.

Table 3.4 General government deficit, short-term borrowing and Central Bank credits

Year	I Budget deficit*	II Short-term borrowing*	III Central Bank credits*	(II / I) %	(III / II) %
1981	173	77	39	54	51
1982	151	106	32	70	30
1983	299	25	72	8	288
1984	979	474	190	48	40
1985	787	498	266	63	53
1986	1406	925	275	66	30
1987	2598	1268	355	49	28
1988	3860	1064	675	28	63
1989	7502	1452	457	19	31
1990	11954	2263	331	19	15
1991	33516	23509	10719	70	46
1992	47434	41372	17394	87	42
1993	129405	75252	53010	58	70

*: in billions of TL.

Source: Central Bank of the Republic of Turkey, *Annual Reports*, various years

Indicators of such deviations constitute a lengthy list. Soon after having signed the AP in 1970, Turkey demanded revisions that would allow for delay in its implementation in 1972. The main motive behind this demand was the divergence between the protectionist requirements of the Third Five-Year Development Plan covering the 1973-77 period and the AP obligations of gradual tariff dismantling, removal of quantitative restrictions, and adoption of the EU's common external tariff. In other words, the preferred policy of import substitution was invoked by the Turkish government as a reason for deviations from its commitment to converge towards EU norms.[12] Having failed to secure revisions, the government suspended the gradual tariff reduction unilaterally with the exception of two reductions over the 1970s. In addition, as EU countries began to explore alternatives to the Keynesian demand management policies in the second half of the 1970s, Turkey continued with heavy state intervention into the economy and tried to externalise the costs of this development strategy by demanding further concessions from the EU.

Also, over the 1980s, Turkey almost doubled the average rate of protection from 6.7% of the import value in 1981 to 12.2% in 1988. This protectionist drive was generated by private sector demands for protection as well as the state's own needs for extra revenue in the face of a deteriorating public sector deficit. The implications of increased protectionism for EU-Turkey relations are not difficult to anticipate. On the one hand, it clashed with the tendency in the EU to rely less on protectionist trade policy and more on supply-side friendly industrial policy measures since the mid-1980s onwards. On the other hand, it undermined the credibility of Turkey's membership bid. In other words, the nature of state-society interaction has once more forced the Turkish policy makers to deviate from convergence towards EU standards as the interests of either the state or societal groups have prevailed over the commitment to a European orientation. One particular factor that complicated these deviations was the arbitrariness of the protectionist instruments, which have taken the form of compulsory contributions to funds established by the government. Fund contributions did not exist in 1981, but they increased to about 6% of total import value in 1988. Another factor was the increase in the amount of investment subsidies that the government granted to private investors in the 1980s despite the announced policy of structural reform and liberalisation. Total investment subsidies extended to the private sector in the mid-1980s accounted for 57%

---

12 On the incompatibility between the import substitution policy and the AP, see Tekeli and İlkin (1993b), pp. 99-140. On Turkey's request for revision, see Birand (1986), pp. 301-306; and Ugur (1996a), pp. 307-308.

and 104% of the initial investment cost in developed and less-developed regions, respectively.[13]

Finally, the stance of the macroeconomic policy in Turkey has continued to diverge excessively from the EU norm. Whereas the EU member states have embarked on a supply-side policy of deregulation, fiscal consolidation and tight monetary policy, Turkey has followed a policy mix characterised by an activist fiscal and an accommodating monetary policy. Therefore, Turkish inflation rates have been 10-20 times higher than the EU average and higher than the inflation rates even in Central and Eastern European Countries. Similarly, public sector deficit and the debt/GDP ratio in Turkey has increased much faster than the EU average.[14]

3.2 Further Indicators of Non-credible Commitment to a European Orientation: The Limits to Democratisation in Turkey

The evidence examined above has been related to the aspects of state-society interaction inducing Turkish policy makers to engage in policy reversals mainly in the economic realm. Therefore, it cannot be treated as an adequate indicator of the wider credibility problem that Turkish policy makers are faced with. To appreciate the credibility problem more fully, we need to extend the analysis to the political domain and examine the way in which state-society interaction induced Turkish policy-makers to deviate from convergence towards EU standards in their democratisation reforms as well. Deviations from the commitment to democratisation have been so frequent that today Turkey is less democratic when compared not only with Mediterranean member states such as Spain, Portugal and Greece, but also with the post-1989 regimes in Central and Eastern Europe. This outcome has led a report commissioned by TUSİAD to note that countries 'which are not much better than Turkey in terms of economic conditions are now ahead of Turkey on the path of pluralistic-liberal democracy based on human rights and the supremacy of law. ... Most of these countries have now speeded up their march towards political modernisation or democratisation.'[15]

One factor that has contributed to this outcome has already been indicated above. Given the Turkish state's heavy involvement in the

---

[13] Figures from the Commission's Opinion on Turkey's membership application. Commission of the EC (1989), pp. 87.

[14] For a comparison of Turkey with other associated countries included in the final round of enlargement, see Apostolu (1998), pp. 6-10.

[15] TUSİAD (1997), p. 19.

economy, the legitimacy of the political regime has become dependent not on the extent to which it is democratic but on the extent to which it is able to satisfy externalisation demands. This type of state-society interaction has affected societal expectations accordingly, leading to a political culture that has tolerated the lack of democratisation in return for favouritism. It would be wrong, however, to suppose that societal forces in Turkey are not in favour democratisation. Rather, the context in which state-society interaction unfolds has made the attainment of favouritism relatively less costly than democratisation, especially for organised interests. As a result, societal forces in Turkey - depending on their organisational strength - have been induced to discount two factors in their interaction with the state: the negative consequences of the state's penetration of the civil society; and the decreasing returns on externalisation activities as the number of agents involved in such activities increases and the scope for satisfying such demands remains limited. Those societal groups that have opted otherwise because of weak organisational capacity or different preference ordering have incurred high costs in terms of repression, imprisonment, torture and marginalisation. Therefore, grass-root demands for democratisation have tended to follow a cycle of booms and busts depending on dissatisfaction with the existing regime and the cost of expressing democratisation demands.

It is necessary to indicate here that powerful interest groups in Turkey are becoming increasingly aware of this dilemma. Therefore, we see a tendency among some strong interest groups such as TUSİAD to adopt an increasingly critical stance against the deficiencies of the Turkish system - both in terms of economic instability and lack of democratisation. These criticisms, however, conceal more than they reveal. In a skilful manner, they ignore the contribution of the large corporations' externalisation activities to the credibility problem in Turkey. The credibility problem is presented as the outcome of 'bad government' rather than the result of state-society interaction that has produced bad government. In other words, the strength of the criticism levelled at the government is undermined by the lack of sanctions against individual corporations continuing to lobby for externalisation of private risks. Therefore, TUSİAD's criticism may remain ineffective not only because strategic behaviour of individual corporations is still conducive to such outcomes, but also the government will not take the criticism seriously as it is aware of the individual corporation's engagement in externalisation. Put simply, the large corporate sector represented by TUSİAD cannot have the cake and eat it at the same time because a commitment to democratisation also requires a commitment to give up the lucrative yet diminishing returns on the externalisation practice.

Given these conditions, the Turkish state may well declare a commitment to catch up with the 'contemporary civilisation' - interpreted by the political elite since Atatürk as the embodiment of a pluralist democracy. This commitment, however, can always be revoked as a result of either changes in the state's preferences or because of the absence of a bottom-up mechanism of checks and balances. A broad indicator of this credibility problem has been the overthrow of the civilian government by the military three times since 1960 and the civilian support that the military has enjoyed after each coup. Each of these major deviations from the democratisation programme has not only increased the probability of future deviations, but has also reflected the limits of the control-reliant mode of governance. Each of the military coups that took place in 1960, 1971 and 1980 was carried out on the grounds that democratic institutions ceased to function properly as a result of corruption, favouritism or excessive societal assertiveness against the state. In other words, the military coups were justified by arguing that the preceding mode of accommodating externalisation demands had run its course and become dysfunctional. This is in fact nothing but a confirmation of the argument pursued in this book: the nature of state-society interaction in Turkey is not only a source of non-credible commitments to democratisation but also a factor that facilitates the legitimation of major deviations from such commitments.

Additional factors exacerbating the non-credibility of the modernisation commitment can be appreciated by examining other aspects of the political domain. On the one hand, political parties in Turkey have increasingly acquired the characteristics of large interest groups trying to maximise support on the basis of favours that they promise to provide once they are in power. On the other hand, the state has given added impetus to this tendency by restricting the political parties' activities and closing them down when they go beyond the programmatic framework drawn by itself. Given this marginalisation of the political parties into interest groups, the state has increasingly become the sole authority that determines the way in which the national will or national interest should be defined and the political power should be organised. This control-reliant mode of governance has made the Turkish state unresponsive to societal demands concerning democratisation and stands as the mirror-image of its responsiveness to societal demands for externalisation of private risks.

That political parties tend to rely on clientelistic relations for support mobilisation is a well-known feature of political systems in developing countries with multi-party regimes. This type of clientelistic politics involves the distribution of favours in return for political support and is based on the appointment of economically powerful individuals as the party's representatives at provincial and local levels. Its incidence is negatively correlated with the level of economic development and the spread of market-based economic relations. Therefore, it is a phenomenon to be expected in Turkey given the country's economic development and its late industrialisation. However, this is only part of the reality. What distinguishes the political system in Turkey from others in, for example, Latin American countries is the fact that the incidence of clientelistic relations has remained high although the level of economic development increased over time. In fact, high rates of economic growth realised over the 1980s and 1990s went hand in hand with an increase in the incidence of clientelism as the basis for party politics in Turkey. With the exception of the Islamic party which currently controls the largest number of seats in the Grand National Assembly, programmatic differences cannot explain the fragmentation of centre-right and centre-left into various parties in today's Turkey. The dynamic sustaining this fragmentation is that the supporters of a particular party expect to gain at others' expense when the party they support comes to power. This dynamic, as indicated in the TUSİAD report, has led to fragmentation in political life and encouraged the development of extremist parties at the expense of the centre.[16]

In addition, the blurring of the distinction between political parties as traditional channels for interest aggregation on the one hand and interest group organisations trying to maintain loyalty by the supply of private goods on the other is a another source of the credibility problem with which Turkish policy makers are faced. First of all, Turkish political parties become less bound by their programmatic commitments when they come to power. Secondly, they come under intensive pressure from their constituents and organised interests seeking favouritism. The combination of these two dynamics creates a recipe for corruption and reduces the transparency in state administration. Therefore, and stated in the TUSİAD report, 'the triangle of politics-mafia-bureaucracy ... has been threatening to push the existing democracy even behind the positions' that it could have been able to reach.'[17] Given this non-transparent interaction between state and society, as mediated by political parties which are increasingly concerned with the supply of private goods to their supporters, the scope for credible commitments to democratisation is significantly reduced.

What makes the situation even worse is the apparent tendency on the part of the state to push the political parties further towards the status of interest groups and impose itself as the ultimate authority that determines the

16 TUSİAD (1997), p. 20.
17 TUSİAD (1997), p. 20.

way in which the 'political will of the nation' is defined. Indicators of this tendency can be seen clearly in the Law on Political Parties (LPP) of 1983. Article 4 of the LPP stipulates that political parties must operate in loyalty to the principles and reforms of Atatürk. In other words, political parties that dispute the relevance of these reforms and principles or interpret them differently may be declared illegal and banned from politics. Similarly, Article 78 states that political parties may not pursue the goal of changing the principles laid down in the preamble to the 1982 constitution. These principles include the provision that all thoughts and opinions contrary to Turkish national interests and Turkish historical and moral values shall not enjoy any protection under the law. Also, Article 97 provides that a political party 'may not engage in attitude, statement or action' against the military regime of 1980-83 and its acts or decisions.[18] It is obvious that these provisions severely restrict the scope for party competition on the basis of programmatic differences and force the political parties to compete on the basis of private goods that they can supply to their supporters when they come to power. Given this relegation of the political parties into interest groups, the scope for state - often military - intervention increases as the latter can present itself as the ultimate authority that saves the country from the negative externalities of competition between political parties pursuing their narrow interests at the expense of the society.

It is worth noting that such interventions have increased over time. Political parties were dissolved after the military interventions of 1960 and 1980; and they were tamed into supporting the military's programme in 1971-74. After 1982, however, this practice has become more widespread. Since then, the Constitutional Court has made eight decisions of dissolution based on violation of the ideological framework that the parties must conform to. Although constitutional amendments made in 1995 have provided for certain relaxations, these amendments have not been incorporated into the LPP yet and did not prevent the dissolution of the Islamic Welfare (Refah) Party in 1998. Under these conditions, members of parliament are induced to act as additional sources of non-credibility in Turkish policy-making. On the one hand, they tend to exercise influence on government bureaucracy in order to secure special treatment for their constituents. On the other, they engage in non-transparent deals in their contacts with corporate interests, contractors and civil servants. Both of these activities are additional sources of non-credible policy-making because of the non-transparent practices involved and the increased scope for civil servant discretion that they favour and require.

18 TUSİAD (1997), pp. 44-52.

In fact, the 1982 Constitution appears to be providing incentives for non-transparent deals between the MPs who are supposed to control the executive, the civil servants formulating policy decisions, and organised interests. Article 83 of the Constitution holds individual MPs responsible for their programmatic statements outside the Grand National Assembly (GNA), but does not restrict their parliamentary immunity in the case of certain crimes that bars a person from becoming an MP according to the same Article. In other words, Article 83 obliges MPs to toe the official ideological line and limits their criticism to platform speeches in the GNA, but provides them with the prospect of 'monopoly profits' on non-transparent deals during their terms of office. This is not only an arrangement that exacerbates the credibility problem discussed in this book, but a practice that runs counter to developments in EU countries. For example, France and the United Kingdom have actually limited parliamentary immunity to a function protecting their MPs against civil suits and not against criminal prosecutions. Also, it is no longer necessary to secure the assembly's lifting of parliamentary inviolability for starting judicial inquiries and hearings in connection with an MP's activities. In Turkey, however, the institution of immunity has been transferred into a mechanism of protection against criminal prosecution.[19]

The conclusions that can be derived from the preceding analysis can be summarised as follows. First, the Turkish state has imposed itself as the sole authority that not only defends, but also defines, the 'national interest'. The implication of this state of affairs for the credibility of the commitment to democratisation is obvious: the state can deviate from its commitment to policy reform at any time on the grounds that its actions are necessitated by the 'national interest' which it defines. Second, in their interaction with the state, societal forces are faced with a dilemma: the cost of societal assertiveness in terms of democratisation demands is high whereas the cost of externalisation demands is low. Therefore, societal forces (especially organised interests) are induced to be assertive with respect to the latter. The probability of such a choice is increased by the legal framework that forces political parties to emerge as interest groups rather than as interest aggregating institutions through which the state-society interaction is mediated. Finally, state-society interaction in Turkey unfolds under a high degree of non-transparency. Under this condition, the state is enabled to equate its preferences with the requirements of the 'national interest' that it defines, whereas societal forces are forced to take the state's definition as

19 TUSİAD (1997), p. 71.

given and not to question the legitimacy of deviations from the commitment to democratisation.

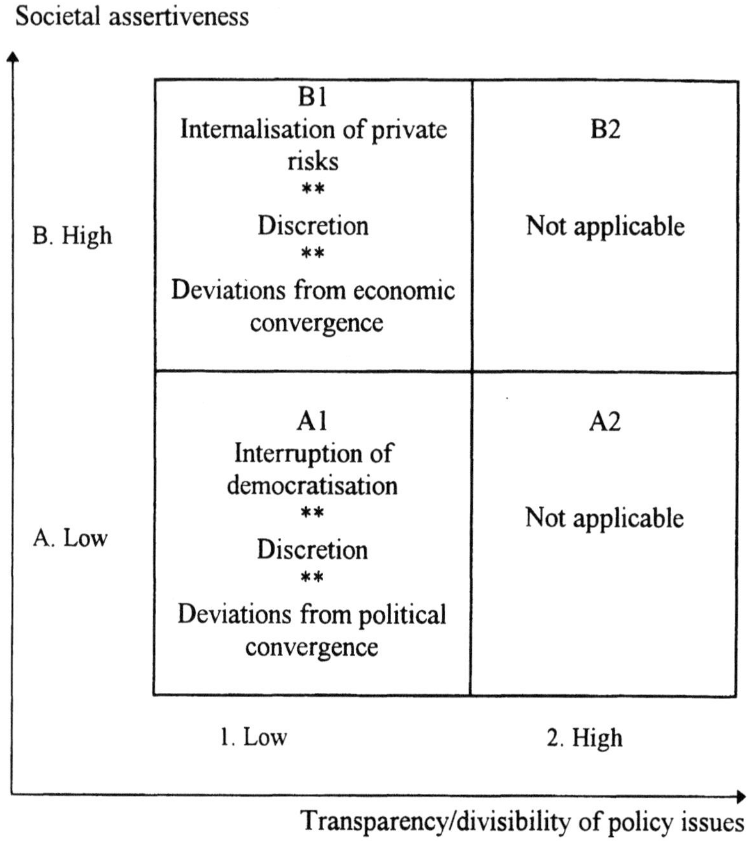

Figure 3.1 Policy convergence, discretion and non-credible policy commitments in Turkey

Having analysed the implications of the state-society interaction for the credibility of Turkey's policy commitments concerning economic and political issues, we can now use a diagrammatic representation similar to Figure 2.1 to summarise the possible outcomes concerning Turkey's convergence towards EU standards. Issue transparency/divisibility in Turkey tends to be low, whereas societal assertiveness fluctuates between high and low levels depending on whether the demands are related to externalisation or democratisation. Given this constellation, Figure 3.1 demonstrates that the policy-making process in Turkey will be characterised by a high degree of discretion and deviations from the convergence towards EU standards economically and politically.

State-society interaction in Turkey generates deviations from convergence towards EU standards because, depending on the organisational strength of the interest groups and the nature of the policy issues, it enables either the state or societal forces to equate partial/sectoral interests with an overarching national interest. Under this condition of reduced issue transparency/divisibility, high levels of societal assertiveness in the economic domain leads to internalisation of private risks, whereas low societal assertiveness in the political domain enables the state to limit the extent of democratisation. The probability of these outcomes is increased by the high degree of state discretion, which facilitates deviations from the commitment to convergence towards EU standards in the current period and sows the seeds of further deviations in the future. In addition, the discretion built into the policy-making process reduces the feasibility and desirability of policy convergence as a means of legitimation because discretion is compatible with either control-reliance or receptiveness to societal demands.

Under these conditions, the need equalising the returns on loyalty with returns in other countries diminishes and Turkish policy- makers would be induced to engage in policy differentiation rather than convergence as a means of legitimation. Therefore, the credibility of the commitment to policy reform and the declared intention to anchor the reform through closer ties with the EU becomes questionable. This result will obtain unless the existing contracts with the EU are likely to generate substantial gains and/or withdrawal costs that would render the maintenance of the commitment to policy reform the preferred option. Given that Turkey's policy reversals continued to be the norm under the AA and the AP, the next section will examine the extent to which the customs union established in 1996 is likely to imply such gains and/or withdrawal costs

3.3 The Customs Union and its Implications for the Anchor/Credibility Dilemma in EU-Turkey Relations

As a new contract, the customs union (CU) can be seen as an arrangement that might ameliorate the anchor/credibility dilemma in EU-Turkey relations. In fact, there are indications suggesting that it has been interpreted as a significant development that would encourage policy reform in Turkey and make the country's European orientation irreversible. For example, the Commission told the press in February 1995 that the formation of the CU would be a step that should anchor Turkey to Europe, while a failure to establish the CU would reinforce the anti-western and fundamentalist tendencies. The CU would also provide scope for pressuring the Turkish government to improve its human rights records and show greater respect for democracy.[20] That was why the Commission, referring to comprehensive documentation that it had prepared on various issues in EU-Turkey relations, urged the EP to approve the EU-Turkey CU even though the task of bringing Turkey into the fold of democratic countries has not been completed. Even European interest groups lobbied the EP with similar arguments. According to *Eurocommerce*, an EU-level interest group, the CU would be beneficial both to EU investors and the democratisation and liberalisation process in Turkey.[21] Mrs. Çiller, the then prime minister of Turkey, issued an open letter to the 'people of Europe' just before the EP was due to vote on the CU agreement and stated, *inter alia*, that 'through Europe, we will find new ways to upgrade and modernise all aspects of our economic, political and social life.'[22]

Although these statements confirm the relevance of the anchor/credibility dilemma as a metaphor for describing the evolution of EU-Turkey relations, they are cited here with a different purpose. Instead of taking these statements at face value, our aim is to examine the extent to which the CU can actually contribute to a resolution of the anchor/credibility dilemma that haunted EU-Turkey relations until 1996 - when the CU was established. To do this, we need to investigate the balance between the costs and benefits of the CU. This should give us an indication of the additional incentive that the CU may or may not provide for Turkish policy makers to engage in credible convergence towards EU norms. We then examine the reactions in Turkey to the CU with a view to highlight the current trends, and conclude with some tentative propositions about the anchoring potential of the CU for future policy reforms.

Assessing the costs and benefits of the CU involves taking into account the following factors. On the benefits side, we need to consider in particular the static effect of the CU on Turkey's national income, its impact resulting from structural and fiscal reforms it would bring about, the long-term dynamic effect that comes about as a result of improvement in the technological base, and the impact of direct foreign investment flows induced by the CU. On the cost side, the relevant factors include the short-term impacts of the CU on public finances, the current account balance, and the

20 *Agence Europe*, 3.2.1995, p. 8.

21 *Agence Europe*, 23.11.1995, p. 7; and 7.12.1995, p. 15.

22 *Agence Europe*, 11/12.12.1995, p. 3.

cost of adjustment (including sectoral adjustment by the private sector and policy reform by the government).

The most recent study on the welfare implications of the EU-Turkey CU estimates that it will increase Turkey's national income between 0.3% and 1.5% annually - depending on the extent of structural reform that Turkey undertakes. The findings of this study, which excludes the costs of short-run adjustment costs and the long-term dynamic gains, are given in Table 3.5.

Table 3.5 Welfare effects of the EU-Turkey customs union

Scenarios concerning the extent of integration and structural reform	Gains as % of 1990 GDP
1. Easier access to EU market as the EU removes quantitative restrictions on textiles & clothing and steel	0.3
2. Easier access to EU market as a result of product quality harmonisation	0.1
3. Impact of lowering Turkish tariffs on non-agricultural goods imported from the EU and implementing the EU's common Commercial policy (CCP)	0.1
4. Impact of negotiating reciprocal access to the markets of third countries to whom Turkey will grant preferential access in line with the CC P	0.5
5. Impact of eliminating export subsidies to exports destined to the EU market	--
6. The impact of reduced cost of trading between the EU and Turkey	0.1
7. Combined impact of scenarios 1-6	1.1

8. Impact of Turkey lowering its tariffs on agricultural imports from all countries by 50%	--
9. Impact of eliminating subsidies to exports destined for markets outside the EU	0.1
10. Impact of eliminating all tariffs, taxes and subsides except for VAT (the VAT is allowed to adjust in each sector so as to leave the fiscal deficit unchanged)	0.2
11. Impact of eliminating all distortions and using a uniform VAT rate across sectors	0.1
12. Combined impact of scenarios 8-11	0.4
13. Total impact (7 + 12)	1.5

Source: Compiled from Harrison et al. (1996), pp. 23-24.

One conclusion that can be derived from these figures is that the policy-independent welfare gain to Turkey from the CU is only 0.3% of the GDP in 1990 (scenario no. 1). This is equal to TL 904 billion in 1990 prices and net of the impact of increased taxation required to cover the fall in customs revenue after the establishment of the CU. Although this gain is independent of further policy reform in Turkey, it does not take into account the impact of short-term adjustment costs in terms of plant closures, unemployment, and restructuring. These adjustment costs are highly difficult to quantify and so are the long-term dynamic gains that result from increased investment and technological improvement due to the CU. Therefore, we can set the short-term adjustment costs against the long-term dynamic gains as unknowns and take this figure as a net, policy-independent gain.

The question that arises here is whether an improvement of 0.3% in Turkey's GDP is significant enough to act as an incentive inducing Turkey to view the CU as an anchor. In other words, to what extent can one take seriously the revealed expectation of both Turkey and the EU that the establishment of the CU would anchor Turkey to Europe? The answer may be positive only if non-quantifiable costs - such as ideological/cultural reservations about closer ties with the EU, the extent and impact of political pressure from uncompetitive sectors, and the perceived cost of reduced trade policy autonomy - are ignored. However, these additional and non-transparent costs are likely to prove significant for two reasons. First, the state and societal groups are likely to exaggerate such costs in order to justify their attempts to equate partial and sectoral interest with a non-negotiable national interest. Second, short-term costs are highly likely to induce both the state and societal groups to discount the long-term benefit of the CU. Under these conditions, it is very likely that either side may argue for withdrawal from the CU.

That this is not only a counter-factual assertion can be seen in the signals given by Mr. Erbakan in February 1996 - less than two months after the EU-Turkey CU had been established. While negotiating with Mr. Yılmaz (leader of the centre-right Motherland Party) on the distribution of ministerial portfolios in a coalition government, Mr. Erbakan (leader of the Islamic Welfare Party) told the press that his party would seek renegotiation of the CU agreement.[23] Although Erbakan retracted from the revision request when he became Turkey's prime minister in a coalition government with the centre-right True Path Party, he continued to campaign against the CU by arguing that the arrangement relegated Turkey to a second-class country. Therefore, it was not surprising to observe the beginning of deviations from the commitments under the CU agreement. In mid-1996, the Turkish government signalled that it was planning to introduce a 6% tax on imports of consumer goods from the EU. This was due to deterioration in Turkey's trade deficit and was put forward without exhausting the procedures of consultation with the EU, as envisaged in the CU agreement.[24]

Such indicators of reservations about the attractiveness of the CU as an anchor are not independent of the pressure from organised interest group trying to externalise their private risks associated with the CU. The completion of the CU will lead to decline in the import-weighted average rate of effective protection in Turkey from 18.44 to 1.12%. As a result, product groups experiencing a fall in the effective rate of protection will also experience a fall in their relative shares in the sectoral value added. Product groups likely to experience a fall of more than 10 percentage points in their relative shares of sectoral value added include: textile fabrics (26.6%); rubber and rubber products (32.66%); glass and glass products (24.28%); cement and earthenware products (45.37 and 25.49%); metal products (53.24%); and electrical machinery (14.87%). Also strategic product groups such as transport vehicles, chemicals and petrol refineries would experience a fall in their relative shares of value added by 44.24%, 11.16%, and

23 *Agence Europe*, 24.2.1986, p. 7.
24 *Agence Europe*, 23/24.7.1996, p. 7.

176.69%, respectively.[25] Given the costs that these figures entail and the ability of the interest groups to secure externalisation in Turkey, threats to revise the CU agreement or to introduce protectionist measures unilaterally cannot be treated as merely maverick acts. They are generated by the nature of the state-society interaction that induces Turkish policy makers to engage in policy reversals across policy areas.

Another conclusion to be derived from Table 3.5 is that further improvement in the welfare effect of the CU is dependent on two factors: policy reform in Turkey and Turkey's ability to secure reciprocal concessions from non-EU countries. Policy reforms that Turkey must carry out include: (i) lowering the level of tariff protection accorded to the agricultural sector against imports from the EU and non-EU countries; (ii) elimination of distortions in the form of export subsidies, fund contributions paid by importers, and other non-transparent measures; and (iii) increasing the rate of the VAT so as to leave the fiscal deficit unchanged. That Turkey has been reluctant to carry out these policy reforms can be seen in her limited progress towards introducing the necessary legislation.

According to the March 1995 AC decision on the CU, policy measures aimed at accepting the EU's common commercial policy in its entirety must be introduced by 2001. Although strict deadlines are not imposed with respect to some of the other measures, free circulation of goods within the EU market and the elimination of the EU's quantitative restrictions on textiles and clothing are conditional on Turkey's compliance with certain conditions. Irrespective of whether or not deadlines are imposed, Table 3.5 clearly indicates that it is in Turkey's interest to introduce the additional measures as soon as possible. What we observe, however, is a tendency reflecting clear reluctance to optimise the CU through additional measures. As of September 1996, Turkey appears to have slowed down the process of policy reform required for increasing the welfare gains from the CU.

For example, Turkey has consistently delayed the establishment of the Competition Board that would put into effect the competition laws introduced in 1994 with the aim of converging towards the EU competition policy. Second, Turkey has failed to modify its legislation on intellectual property rights in line with the Commission's demands. Third, some of the compulsory fund contributions by importers have been maintained (as in the case of the Mining Fund). Fourth, the introduction of the legislation that would ensure compatibility of Turkish trade policy instruments (such as anti-dumping regulations) with EU instruments is still incomplete. Although the commitment to introduce these measures dates back to the Association

25 Togan and Yılmaz (1995), p. 155.

Council decision of 6 March 1995 and the deadline for their introduction was the end of 1995, none of them was completed by September 1996. In addition, Turkey has not introduced other measures required by the CU agreement. Among these, the most important concern state aids to industry and technical harmonisation. The deadlines for the introduction of these reforms are 1998 and 2001, respectively. Again, as of September 1996, work in these areas was either stalled or behind schedule.[26]

A similar tendency can observed in Turkey's negotiation of reciprocal concessions with non-EU countries (mainly Mediterranean and Central and Eastern European countries) which are engaged in similar arrangements with the EU. As was shown in Table 3.5, concluding these agreements could contribute to Turkey's GDP by 0.5% - more than the 0.3% welfare gain associated with easier access to the EU market. Nevertheless, Turkey has not recorded significant progress in this area - with the exception of the free trade arrangement it has concluded with Israel. This is not an accidental outcome nor can it be explained mainly by the technical complexity of the negotiation process. It is also related to the fact that the competitiveness profiles of these countries are similar to that of Turkey. Finally, the increase required in VAT rates and coverage has inflationary consequences, making it an unattractive option given the already high levels of inflation in Turkey.

The evidence examined above suggests that the CU, over the last two years after it has been established, has not been an effective anchor for policy reform in Turkey. Nor has it contributed to the strengthening of the EU-Turkey relations. As will be demonstrated in chapters 6 and 7, Turkey's Cyprus policy has taken a definite turn towards further confrontation with the EU and the democratisation process has slowed down. This new period of uncertainty in EU-Turkey relations, coupled with the lack of macroeconomic stability in Turkey and the prospect of membership for Central and Eastern European countries, has had a negative effect on net foreign direct investment (FDI) flows into Turkey. Despite the establishment of the CU in 1996, the net FDI declined from US$772 million in 1995 to US$440 million in the first nine months of 1996. This tendency has generated further doubts about the benefits of the CU and fed into the government's reluctance to carry out the measures required by the CU.

Therefore, the CU is an arrangement that can cut both ways so far as the anchor/credibility dilemma in EU-Turkey relations is concerned. On the

---

[26] Türkiye-Avrupa Birliği Derneği (Turkey - European Union Association), *Bulletin*, nos. 14 and 15, July and September 1996. This apparent lack of commitment has caused frustration on the part of the Association - which is generally supportive of Turkey's arguments for membership.

one hand, it may lead to further economic integration between Turkey and the EU and further economic convergence towards EU standards. On the other hand, it can be used by either the state or societal groups in Turkey as a pretext to slow down the process of integration on the grounds that the burden it places on Turkey (i.e. compliance with the *acquis communautaire* without being able to participate in the EU's decision-making process) is greater than the potential benefits it offers. In addition, the EU, having locked Turkey into an arrangement that may serve as a substitute for membership, could well be prompted to exert less pressure on Turkey so far as democratisation is concerned.[27] The existing evidence suggests that the second implication of the CU tends to be the dominant trend at the moment. This can be seen not only in the slow-down of the required policy reforms, but also in frequent statements by Turkey's political elite indicating that 'Europe' is no longer a priority in Turkey's overall policy orientation.[28]

Conclusions

Two conclusions may be derived from the analysis above. The first concerns the credibility of policy commitments in Turkey. Turkey's non-credible commitment to a European orientation has its sources within the political economy of the country, where state-society interaction generates frequent policy reversals either because of the state discretion built into the system or due to the ability of private agents to secure internalisation of private risks. Both of these dynamics have reduced the ability of the Turkish government to maintain a time-consistent commitment to the declared policy choice of European orientation. These sources of frequent policy reversals are visible in both economic and political domains of the policy-making process and have fed into each other over time. Ironically, the vicious circle of state discretion, demands for externalisation, and further discretion has worsened as the Turkish economy has continued to grow. Therefore, economic growth in Turkey has both generated and required macroeconomic instability, because economic growth itself created scope for further externalisation demands but the ability of the state to internalise them remained constrained by a weak taxing power. Given these internal dynamics, it would be inappropriate to relate the policy reversals in Turkey to external factors such as the collapse of the Soviet bloc that, according to Eralp, has presented

27 Ugur (1996b), p. 22.

28 Such statements were made by Turkish officials after Turkey's exclusion from the next round of enlargement decided in the Luxembourg Summit of December 1997.

Turkey with a viable option of regional policy orientation.[29] These developments may increase the incidence of deviations from the convergence towards EU standards, but they cannot generate them.

The second conclusion is that the establishment of the CU is not necessarily a development that would ameliorate the anchor/credibility dilemma in EU-Turkey relations. Because factors generating the anchor/credibility dilemma are internal to the EU and Turkey, a new contract in the form of a CU cannot resolve the dilemma unless it provides for new rules and procedures that would address the dynamics generating policy reversals in Turkey and a weak anchoring capacity in the EU. The analysis above suggests that the CU agreement is designed to encourage economic reforms which may bring economic benefits in the long run but are costly in the short run. Although it may be argued that the long-run benefits should induce Turkey to accelerate the pace of policy reform, such an argument overlooks the credibility problem that has haunted successive Turkish governments because of their inability to trade off short-term costs with long-term benefits. In fact, the CU may exacerbate this credibility problem because it increases the short-term costs arising out of adjustment, increased import penetration, reduced policy choices, etc. In addition, the way in which the CU was rushed before Turkey could demonstrate a credible commitment to democratisation would leave the most contentious issue in EU-Turkey relations - i.e., Turkey's membership - unresolved. The conclusion of the CU agreement meant that Turkey would be left to determine the pace of democratisation and the EU would be able to reject Turkey's membership on the grounds that her political convergence towards EU standards is unsatisfactory. This is nothing but a continuation of the anchor/credibility dilemma that has preceded and is likely to outlive the conclusion of the CU.

---

29 Eralp (1993), p. 43.

4 The Anchor/Credibility Dilemma and Trade Policy

In chapters 2 and 3, we examined the dynamics generating a limited EU anchoring capacity and frequent policy reversals in Turkey. With this chapter, we begin to examine the way in which the EU's weak anchoring capacity has interacted with Turkey's non-credible commitment to policy reform to generate the anchor/credibility dilemma in EU-Turkey relations. We demonstrated in chapter 2 that the EU's anchoring capacity and the frequency of policy reversals in Turkey are determined by the level of issue transparency/divisibility and societal assertiveness. Therefore, these variables must be specified with respect to the policy issues to be examined in this chapter and the following three chapters. In other words, we need to establish the level of transparency/divisibility and societal assertiveness associated with each of the issues in EU-Turkey relations so that the policy options available to EU and Turkish policy-makers can be delineated.

The issue covered in this chapter, i.e., trade policy, is an area where issue transparency/divisibility and societal assertiveness are high. The divisibility of trade policy issues is high because policy decisions in this area affect different societal groups differently, depending on their positions as exporters, importers, consumers, or producers, etc. The level of transparency in the area of trade policy is also high because the negative or positive effects of policy decisions on a particular societal group can be more or less quantified. Finally, societal assertiveness in the area of trade policy is also high because of the distributional effect of the policy decisions on the consumers and producers. As shown in figure 2.1, this combination of high issue transparency/divisibility and societal assertiveness generates deep integration and a high EU anchoring capacity. Nevertheless, the EU 's anchoring capacity will be constrained by the need to undertake only partial commitments or risks that would be compatible with the construction of intra-EU package deals. The analysis in chapter 3, on the other hand, suggests that Turkish policy in this area would tend to be non-credible because of the low issue transparency/divisibility generated by the control-reliant mode of governance. Coupled with a high level of societal assertiveness (i.e., demands for externalisation), the low level of transparency/divisibility enables either the state or societal groups in Turkey to equate trade policy issues with an indivisible national interest that the policy-maker must defend. Therefore, Turkey's commitment to trade liberalisation envisaged in the AP will be non-credible as Turkish policy-makers accommodate the externalisation demands of the private sector and/or defend the interests of the public sector in the face of potential competition from EU exporters.

To probe the relevance of these propositions, this chapter is organised in three sections. In section 4.1, we provide a summary of the AP provisions regulating the movement of goods between the EU and Turkey during the transition to a customs union. This is a relevant starting point because it enables us to establish a benchmark against which the credibility of Turkey's policy commitments and the EU's anchoring capacity can be evaluated. The evidence presented in this section suggests that Turkey was not able to maintain a credible commitment to policy reform, which required progressive liberalisation. That was due to the control-reliant mode of governance that manifested itself in heavy state involvement in the economy and an import-substituting industrialisation strategy that worked against trade liberalisation. The negative impact of this mode of governance on the transparency/divisibility of trade policy issues was exacerbated by the receptiveness of the state to protectionist demands in a period of successive coalition governments.

The next two sections are devoted to the examination of the EU's anchoring capacity. Section 4.2 examines the extent to which the EU was able to act an anchor by granting Turkey unilateral concessions in the area of agricultural trade. The existing evidence suggests that the EU did indeed extend unilateral concessions despite the AP's reciprocity principle and Turkey's failure to align its agricultural policy with the Common Agricultural Policy (CAP). Nevertheless, the EU's anchoring capacity was limited to gradual and partial concessions, as the scope for intra-EU package deals was limited by the protectionist CAP regime. Section 4.3 examines the EU's anchoring capacity with respect to trade in textiles and clothing (T&C). The evidence concerning this issue is less straightforward not only because of the restrictions that the EU introduced since the mid-1970s, but also because of the *ad hoc* nature of the relatively lenient approach it adopted *vis-à-vis* Turkish exports. EU protectionism limited the access of Turkish exporters and might have had an adverse effect on investment decisions because of the uncertainty it generated. Nevertheless, EU restrictions on Turkish exports of T&C products must also be evaluated in the context of intensified protectionism from 1977-85 and compared with the treatment accorded to other associated countries. Taking these factors into account, section 4.3 will demonstrate that the EU was in fact less protectionist towards Turkey when compared not only with other associated countries but also with what would have happened had the EU invoked the safeguard clause (Article 60) of the AP unilaterally and over a long period. Therefore, this section also argues that the EU was capable of acting as an anchor, but its anchoring capacity remained limited because of the partial and gradual nature of the concessions granted and the uncertainty associated with the EU's discretion.

4.1 Trade Policy Provisions in the Additional Protocol and Turkey's Compliance

The AP provides that the EU would abolish unilaterally all tariffs, charges, and quantitative restrictions on Turkish exports of manufactured products from 1973 onwards. Against this, Turkey would abolish tariffs, charges having equivalent effects, and quantitative restrictions on EU exports of manufactured products over a period of 22 years, i.e., by 1995. This gradualism also applies to Turkey's adoption of the EU's common external tariff (CET). In addition, the AP differentiates between two categories of Turkish manufactures. With respect to relatively competitive sectors, tariffs and other restrictions would be dismantled over 12 years, i.e., by 1985. Heavily protected sectors, on the other hand, would be exposed to competition from the EU over a longer period of 22 years. The declared aim is to enable the Turkish industry to adjust and spread the cost of adjustment over a longer period. To lock in the policy reform, the AP provides that both Turkey and the EU will consolidate the liberalisation that they undertake. The binding effect of this principle, however, is relaxed by Article 60 which allows both parties to introduce temporary restrictions should they face a significant market disturbance or a serious balance of payments difficulty.

Although the AP envisages agricultural trade as part of the CU, it does not provide for free circulation of agricultural goods. Instead, Articles 33-35 of the AP provide for two processes. Under Articles 33 and 34, Turkey will align her agricultural policy with the CAP over the 22-year period and free circulation of agricultural goods will be established if, at the end of this period, Turkey has adopted the measures of the CAP. Article 35 provides for reciprocal preferential treatment, which will be reviewed every two years in the AC established under the AA. This arrangement constitutes an apparent contrast with that covering the industrial goods. Whereas provisions regulating the movement of industrial goods are based on unilateral and prior EU concessions, those regulating agricultural trade appear to make Turkey's convergence towards the CAP a pre-condition for EU concessions. In addition, the aim to either lock in Turkey's policy reform or specify the procedures for reciprocal concessions appears to be abandoned in the area of agriculture. Although Turkey's convergence towards the CAP is encouraged by the possibility of extending the free circulation to agriculture, the AP leaves it up to Turkey to determine the pace and the scope of the reform process. This tendency to avoid the establishment of clear-cut procedures that would reduce discretion on the part of both parties is made more apparent by the way in which by-annual reviews would be conducted. These reviews would be concluded within the AC, which is essentially an intergovernmental platform where either Turkey or the EU can veto a decision.

Given these aspects of the AP and the credibility problem faced by Turkish policy-makers, it is not surprising to observe that the AP has remained largely a non-binding contract so far as Turkey's compliance with her obligations are concerned. This non-binding nature of the AP can be seen from evidence in Table 4.1, which summarises Turkey's envisaged and actual compliance with tariff dismantling and adoption of the CET. As can seen from the table, Turkey fulfilled her tariff dismantling obligation only twice over the 12 year-period envisaged for the competitive sectors - in 1973 and 1976. In other words, Turkey failed to fulfil her obligation over a period of eight successive years from 1978-1985 in this area. Turkey also failed to undertake any of the tariff reductions that were due between 1973 and 1985. As far as adoption of the CET is concerned, Turkey failed to comply with any of the alignments due until 1988. Overall, with the exception of tariff dismantling in 1973 and 1976, Turkey did not comply with any AP provisions until the end of the 12-year transition in 1988.

Another conclusion that can be derived from Table 4.1 is that Turkey resumed fulfilling her obligations under the AP only after the membership application in 1987. This timing suggests that the accelerated implementation of the AP was designed to enhance the credibility of the membership bid. Nevertheless, this overdue policy change has in fact complicated the credibility problem that battered Turkish policy-making in the past. First of all, sudden policy changes based on ill-prepared initiatives had been a common aspect of Turkey's EU policy not only before but also after the conclusion of the AP.[1] Therefore, there was little reason for the EU to interpret the change in policy as a reflection of a time-consistent commitment. Second, the accelerated tariff dismantling and alignment with the CET after 1988 had been accompanied by the multiplication of non-tar-

---

1 On this aspect of Turkey's EU policy, see Birand (1986), pp. 55-94.

iff restrictions - fund contributions and surcharges on imports - that characterised Turkey's trade policy over the 1980s. Therefore, the credibility of the post-1988 convergence was impaired not only because of the history of non-credible commitments in the past but also because of further policy reversals after the membership application.

Table 4.1a Turkey's compliance with AP provisions on tariff dismantling

	12-Year List		22-Year List	
Year	AP provision (% redn.)	Turkey complies (% redn.)	AP provision (% redn.)	Turkey complies (% redn.)
1973	10	10	5	5
1976	10	10	5	5
1978	10	0	n.a.	n.a.
1979	10	0	5	0
1980	10	0	n.a.	n.a.
1981	10	0	n.a.	n.a.
1882	10	0	n.a.	n.a.
1983	10	0	5	0
1984	10	0	n.a.	n.a.
1985	10	0	10	0
1986	n.a.	n.a.	10	0
1987	n.a.	n.a.	n.a.	n.a.
1988	n.a.	10	10	10
1989	n.a.	10	n.a.	10
1990	n.a.	10	10	10
1991	n.a.	10	10	10
1992	n.a.	10	n.a.	10
1993	n.a.	10	10	10
1994	n.a.	10	10	10
1995	n.a.	10	10	10

Note: 0 : Turkey fails to comply
n.a. : not applicable for that year

Table 4.1b Turkey's compliance with AP provisions on the adoption of CET

	Adoption of CET			
	12-Year List		22-Year List	
Year	AP provision (% align)	Turkey complies (% align)	AP provision (% align)	Turkey complies (% align)
1973	n.a.	n.a.	n.a.	n.a.
1976	n.a.	n.a.	n.a.	n.a.
1978	15 0r 20*	0	15 or 20*	n.a.
1979	n.a.	n.a.	n.a.	0
1980	20	0	30	n.a.
1981	n.a.	n.a.	n.a.	n.a.
1882	20	0	20	0
1983	n.a.	n.a.	n.a.	n.a.
1984	20	0	n.a.	0
1985	20	0	n.a.	n.a.
1986	n.a.	n.a.	n.a.	n.a.
1987	n.a.	n.a.	n.a.	n.a.
1988	n.a.	20	n.a.	n.a.
1989	n.a.	n.a.	n.a.	20
1990	n.a.	20	n.a.	n.a.
1991	n.a.	n.a.	n.a.	n.a.
1992	n.a.	20	n.a.	20
1993	n.a.	20	n.a.	10
1994	n.a.	20	n.a.	20
1995	n.a.	10	30	15

Note: 0 : Turkey fails to comply
n.a. : not applicable for that year
* : 15% alignment if Turkish tariff deviates by 15% or less; 20% alignment otherwise

The question raised by Table 4.1 is obvious: why have successive Turkish governments failed to fulfil their obligations under the AP? We elaborate on this question by referring to three episodes in EU-Turkey relations: (i) reconciliation between demands for 'revision' and 'flexibility' concerning the implementation of the AP between 1972 and 1977; (ii) re-emergence of the 'revision' request in 1978; and (iii) the abortive attempt for membership in 1980. It will be argued that these policy reversals were due to the nature of state-society interaction in Turkey, where the Turkish state was either too strong or too weak *vis-à-vis* societal forces. As a result of this, Turkish policy tended to oscillate between bold commitments and failures to deliver as the preferences of either the state or societal forces prevailed in policy outcomes. It will also be argued that the same dynamic has impaired the credibility of the accelerated liberalisation from 1988 onwards.

The first episode concerns the emergence of the request to revise the AP in 1972 - two years after the AP was signed and one year before it entered into force. It must be indicated that the request for revising the AP did not emerge as a result of a sudden and significant deterioration in Turkey's balance of payments. In fact, the current account deficit declined in 1971-72 thanks to an increase in workers' remittances, especially from EU countries. Rather, the request for revision was related to preparations for the Third Five-Year Development Plan covering the 1973-77 period. Prior to 1972, and despite the entry into force of the AA in 1964, the implications of the EU-Turkey association were not examined either in the First Five-Year (1963-67) or the Second Five-Year (1968-72) Development Plans.[2] As if to compensate for this absurdity, the planners elevated the AP to the top of their agenda in 1971-72 while working on the third plan. The State Planning Organisation (SPO) argued that the AP was a serious obstacle to drawing a consistent development plan based on import-substitution. According to SPO, the AP '... is imposing a plan' upon Turkey. 'This is going to be even worse as the European Community expands. ... Therefore, the tariff dismantling rate must be reduced and Turkey should be allowed to decide when and how tariffs should be dismantled.'[3]

The policy reversal reflected by these statements was due to a constellation of various factors. First of all, the private sector was divided in its views on EU-Turkey association and eventual membership. Chambers of commerce and industry controlled by large enterprises around Istanbul were in favour of closer relations with the EU as a counter-weight to the inward-looking *étatist* economic policy. However, the small- and medium-sized companies, whose demands were articulated by the Eskisehir Chamber of Industry, were against integration on the grounds that tariff dismantling beyond a critical point would wipe out domestic producers. This view was shared by chambers of agriculture too - even though the concerns of the agricultural sector were voiced in less confrontational tones. Second, even

---

2 Although the Second Five-Year Development Plan mentioned the EU-Turkey association in passing, its projections did not incorporate the likely impacts of closer ties with the EU. On this, see Tekeli and İlkin (1993b), pp. 18-22.

3 Birand (1986), p. 301. See also, Tekeli and İlkin (1993b), pp. 124-40.

the enthusiasm of the large business sector was coloured with protectionist tendencies. The representatives of large enterprises were in favour of convergence towards European standards with respect to certain policies where *étatism* was seen as a burden: higher input prices attributed to the inefficiency of the public sector, public sector competition for limited funds, and the priority given to the public sector imports in the allocation of scarce foreign exchange. They were, however, in favour of deviations from European standards in areas of industrial relations and state subsidies. They argued for further limitations to union powers (which were severely limited anyway) and more effective ways of supporting the domestic industry.[4] The third factor contributing to the policy reversal was the increase in societal assertiveness in general as the interim regime established after the military coup of 1971 was on the way out. In this context, the prospect of elections in 1973 led to an increase in the significance of clientelism as a means of support mobilisation within an already fragmented party structure.

Given the constellation of these factors, the protectionist view of the SPO prevailed despite objections from the foreign ministry. A Turkish delegation, headed by the foreign minister himself, embarked on a tour of EU capitals to explore the possibility of revising the AP before it entered into force. Reactions to the 'revision' request were neutral at ministerial levels, but unequivocally negative at the level of EU officials dealing with the technical aspects of EU-Turkey trade. The latter reminded the Turkish delegation that there was neither scope nor justification for revising a highly complex agreement drawn up after a lengthy process of negotiations and still in the process of ratification by the member states.[5] Despite these signals, the SPO managed to side-line the foreign ministry and convince the government to submit a memorandum to the EU requesting a ten-year period during which Turkey could suspend tariff dismantling unilaterally and change the composition of the 12- and 22-year lists by more than what the AP provided for. The EU's reaction was highly critical. The Secretary General of the Commission, Mr. E. Noel, wrote later that Turkey's request had been quite unusual and amounted to asking the EU to write a blank cheque. In addition, it undermined the credibility of Turkey's commitment to maintain the association relationship. [6] Faced with these reactions, and given the conflict between the SPO and the foreign ministry, the Turkish government had to put the 'revision' issue on the back burner.

---

4 For the list of demands made by Vehbi Koç, the director of the largest holding group in the 1970s, see Tekeli and İlkin (1993b), pp. 105.

5 Birand (1986), pp. 305-306.

6 Tekeli and İlkin (1993b), p. 153.

This state of affairs lasted until a new coalition government, formed by the relatively pro-European Republican People's Party (RPP) and the pro-Islamic National Salvation Party (NSP), reiterated the revision request in March 1974. The Commission president Mr. Xavier Ortoli and the Secretary General Mr. E. Noel visited Turkey towards the end of April 1974 and asked the Turkish authorities, including the prime minister Mr. Bülent Ecevit, not to press ahead with the revision request. Mr. Ortoli told the Turkish press that problems encountered by Turkey should be tackled in relevant organs of the association rather than by changing the existing agreements. In addition, the AP was already allowing for concessions that could be improved.[7] Despite these warnings, the Turkish government did make a formal revision request during the AC meeting of 11 October 1974. Because of the unfavourable climate that followed Turkey's military intervention into Cyprus in July-August 1974, the request was made in general terms only and the EU was informed that the details would be submitted at a later date.

In the meantime, however, the government fell one month later in November 1974. A new coalition government was finally formed in March 1975, but the NSP was again one of the junior partners. Aware of the tendency in Turkey to deviate from the AP in the face of the difficulties raised by the import-substituting policy, the EU sent the vice-president of the Commission to Turkey to dampen the expectations about the revision of the protocol. Mr. Mugnozza told the Turkish press that it was necessary to be optimistic about the future of EU-Turkey relations. If pessimism prevailed and the conviction that Turkey's industrialisation would be jeopardised became widespread, Turkey's full membership prospect would be weakened.[8] In other words, the vice-president was giving the message that if Turkey continued to deviate from its obligations under the AP she could expect the EU to accommodate these reversals without re-assessing its own commitment to take Turkey in. Turkey's membership was conditional on credible commitment to the policy reforms specified in the AP. The Turkish foreign ministry was fully aware of this implication. In a report criticising new SPO proposals for suspending the implementation of the AP, the foreign ministry argued that their implementation would relegate Turkey to a third-class status in her economic, political and security relations with Europe.

Nevertheless, the SPO view gained the upper hand once more and led the Turkish government to demand 'flexibility' in the implementation of the AP rather than revision. This demand was presented formally in the AC

---

7 Tekeli and İlkin (1993b), p. 184.

8 Tekeli and İlkin (1993b), p. 189.

meeting of 16 September 1975. [9] Having been notified of this demand in advance, the Committee of Permanent Representatives (COREPER) had been trying to establish a common EU position in preparation for the AC meeting. The COREPER managed to hammer out a consensus on the need for concessions in order to strengthen the position of the pro-EU wing of the Turkish government, but it could not establish the details of these concessions. As a result, the EU delegation in the AC proposed the establishment of a working party that would investigate the impact of the AP on Turkey's deteriorating trade deficit with the EU and what measures could be taken to address it.

The source of these policy reversals in Turkey was closely related to the problems of the import-substituting industrialisation policy and the nature of the state-society interaction that underpinned it. First, the import-substituting industrialisation policy induced the Turkish government to provide excessive protection to import-competing industries where the state itself was the major actor. These included paper and paper products, fertilisers, petrol refineries, iron and steel, metal goods, and non-electrical machinery etc., where the effective rates of protection in 1973 were over 100%.[10] In other words, the state itself was a major player and was against the trade liberalisation envisaged by the AP. Second, increased societal assertiveness, coupled with the fragmented party structure, made successive coalition governments extremely receptive to electorate pressure. On the one hand, the junior partners in the coalition governments, the pro-Islamic National Salvation Party (NSP) and the pro-fascist National Movement Party (NMP), championed 'national industrialisation' and dictated their terms to larger parties. The larger centre-left and centre-right parties, on the other hand, accommodated some of these demands not only to secure the co-operation of the extremist parties, but also because of their own commitments to an import-substituting industrialisation policy. Third, large corporations - especially holding companies organised as horizontal conglomerates - were in favour of closer ties with the EU, but their support for the implementation of the AP was qualified. They would support its implementation in return for state subsidies that would enable them to externalise at least part of the adjustment costs.

Given the nature of the state-society interaction and the deepening crisis of the import-substituting industrialisation policy, it is not surprising to observe that Turkey went even further in its tendency to deviate from the policy reform envisaged in the AP. The calls for flexibility continued,

---

9 Birand (1986), p. 333.

10 Aktan and Baysan (1985), p. 70.

leading to a second full-blown demand for revision of the AP in 1978. This time the demand was more radical: not only should the AP be revised to provide Turkey with more scope for maintaining protectionism, but also there should be an end to the reciprocity principle embodied in the AP. It was thought that the prospect for securing these concessions was better in 1978 given that the extremist parties were not coalition partners. The leader of the RPP, Mr. Bülent Ecevit, formed a new government relying on the support of independent MPs only. The new government's first action was to suspend the 10% tariff reduction which had been due on 1 January 1978 and to confirm the suspension by the previous government of the first alignment with the CET. The EU responded by stating that it would not object to these actions when they were discussed in the relevant organs of the association.[11]

The next move by the new government was the prime minister's Brussels visit of 24-26 May 1978. Before the meeting with the president of the Commission, the Turkish prime-minister outlined two demands. First, he reiterated Turkey's intention to put an end to the reciprocity principle in EU-Turkey relations. Reciprocity had led to the erosion of the preferential treatment granted to Turkey, while enabling the EU to grant even fewer concessions on the grounds that Turkey was failing to comply with the AP.[12] Second, Turkey wanted a 'fundamental modification' in the AP in order to make it compatible with the needs of the import-substituting industrialisation policy.[13] After the meeting, however, statements by both sides reflected a moderation on Turkey's part. The Turkish prime minister, instead of emphasising the issue of 'modification', stressed the need for 'intensification of relations through adjustment'. Also, instead of 'denouncing' the AP, Turkey would like to see the association revived 'in the present context'. The president of the Commission, on the other hand, indicated satisfaction with the resumption of political-level contacts and pledged a 'sympathetic approach to Turkey's request for flexibility.'[14]

These statements were designed to reflect an air of optimism by playing down Turkey's demand for revising the AP. That this was the case was confirmed by Turkey's demand in July 1978 to freeze her obligations under the AP for five years. This demand was reiterated in October 1978 in another meeting with EU officials. It went beyond the calls for revision and flexibility by including not only tariff dismantling and alignment with the

---

11 Council of the EC, General Secretariat (1978), pp. 142-43.

12 The abandonment of reciprocity as a principle in trade relations with developing countries was formally accepted by the EU as a result of the Lomé I Convention signed on 28 February 1975. On this issue, see Grilli (1994), pp. 27 and 161-79.

13 *Agence Europe*, 26.5.1978, p. 8.

14 *Agence Europe*, 27.5.1978, p. 4.

CET, but also the approximation of economic policies provided for in Article 45 of the AP. The explanation given by Turkey was that the obligations under the AP were preventing the implementation of the Fourth Five-Year Development Plan and complicating the problems faced by the Turkish economy.[15]

The interesting point to note here is that Turkey's demand for freezing the implementation of the AP was made against a background of increased private sector demands for protection. Unlike the early 1970s when the opposition to integration with Europe came mainly from the small- and medium-sized enterprises, now larger corporations too were expressing doubts about the AP. In addition to the Eskisehir Chamber of Industry which had campaigned against it since the early 1970s, the Istanbul Chambers of Commerce and Industry as well as the IKV (the Economic Development Foundation, which favoured closer links with the EU) became increasingly concerned about European competition. These concerns were aggravated by the deepening crisis of the import-substituting policy that had reduced confidence for future investments as well as the amount of foreign exchange available for financing the imports of investment goods. As a result, these private sector organisations became critical of TUSIAD (the pressure group established by the business elite) for its advocacy of closer integration with Europe. They also began to argue that EU officials visiting Turkey should talk to them rather than TUSIAD in order to develop a more accurate view of the difficulties faced by Turkish industry.[16]

Although the chambers of industry and the IKV were not opposed to closer integration in principle, they were clearly in favour of negotiating with the EU for a better deal that would go beyond what the AP framework could allow for. That was why the chairman of the IKV, Mr. Ertuðrul Soysal, defended the prime minister's approach in Brussels as a positive step in line with the views of Turkish industrialists. Under these conditions, the transparency/divisibility of trade policy issues was undermined even further as both government and private sector views began to converge and the scope for politicising technical issues was increased. It was against this type of state-society interaction that Turkey's demands for revision and removal of the reciprocity principle were made in July 1978. This convergence between government and private sector views, however, lasted only until the autumn of that year. By then, it had become apparent that the EU would accept Turkey's demands only in return for pushing the prospect of membership into an unknown future. Because this signal came at a time

15 Tekeli and İlkin (1993b), pp. 222-23; State Planning Organisation (1990), p. 9.

16 Tekeli and İlkin (1993b), p. 222.

when the EU took a definite turning towards protectionism in general and the T&C sector in particular, the private sector broke ranks with the government and began to campaign for membership as a new strategy that would enable Turkey to obtain better concessions. The private sector believed that the membership threat, given the ongoing accession negotiations with Greece, would force the EU to be more flexible on the issue of trade concessions.

The rift between the government and the private sector on EU policy, coupled with the crisis of the import-substituting industrialisation policy, contributed to the fall of the government towards the end of 1979. A new government was formed with a programme of economic liberalisation and structural reforms. This development constituted the third episode in EU-Turkey relations, which was characterised by emphasis on membership rather than revision of the AP. Turkey's EU policy during this period was also non-credible because of the assumptions on which it was based. On the one hand, closer links with the EU were compatible with the programme of liberalisation and structural reforms. In fact, a pro-integration policy could emerge as an anchor and contribute to the credibility of the reform programme. On the other hand, however, the pro-integration policy was non-credible. It was assumed that the past failures to comply with the AP would have little or no impact on the EU's policy response. It was also assumed that the pending accession of Greece could be used as a factor that would force the EU to maintain an even-handed approach to Turkey. The following paragraphs will demonstrate why these assumptions were unrealistic and the credibility problem that haunted Turkey's policy remained a liability.

Soon after the new government was established, Turkey informed the Commission that the request for freezing her obligations under the AP would be withdrawn. In addition, Turkey began to signal her intention of applying for membership. In fact, this option suddenly became the central pillar of the 'new' approach to the EU because of the Turkish military's warning about intervention on 2 January 1980. The looming danger of military intervention induced not only the government, but also the private sector to perceive of EU membership as a political and economic anchor.[17]

Faced with this policy reversal, the EU began to focus on how Turkish membership could be delayed without alienating Turkey during a period of tension in East-West relations that followed the Afghan crisis. The AC meeting of 5 February 1980 was crucial in this context. The EU considered the meeting as a stock-taking exercise that would identify the need for further convergence - even though some concessions could be given to keep Turkey anchored to Europe. As a result, the communiqué at the end of the

---

17 *The Financial Times*, 21.1.1980.

meeting accepted the need for a 'new approach' to the problems of the association; but this 'new approach' fell short of giving a positive signal for membership. The communiqué stated that the two parties would try to ensure the development of the association in order to facilitate Turkey's membership, but this was an objective to be achieved at a later date.[18] The atmosphere of the AC meeting led the British journalist John Palmer to comment that EU ministers were torn between their anxiety to remain friendly with Turkey and a reluctance to encourage a Turkish application for membership. [19] This impression was later on confirmed by an EU diplomat who, after the AC meeting of 30 June 1980, told the press that the concessions were '... a way of telling the Turks that it [membership] is not on without actually kicking them on the teeth.'[20]

These reactions reflected the EU's limited anchoring capacity, but they were also predictable given Turkey's past performance. Turkey had failed to comply with the convergence requirements laid down by the AP and was going through a period of unprecedented economic and political turmoil. Given the risks of membership implied by this divergence from EU standards, the EU was even less prepared to accommodate Turkey than it could have been in the 1970s. Its reluctance to assume a fully-fledged anchoring role was exacerbated by new developments in Turkey, which confirmed that the credibility problem in Turkish policy-making was not only a matter of the past.

One indication of non-credibility was given immediately after the AC meeting of 5 February 1980. Negotiations at the Association Committee meeting of 27 February revealed that Turkey's interpretation of the membership was essentially the same as it had been in the 1970s. Membership was perceived as an arrangement that would enable Turkey to have her cake and eat it. On the one hand, membership was desirable as an economic and political anchor. On the other hand, however, convergence towards EU standards - both as a pre-requisite for membership and as a sign of credible commitment to policy reform domestically - was not acceptable. As a result of this approach, and in spite of her declared enthusiasm for

18 *Agence Europe*, 6.2.1980, p. 5. See also, Council of the EC, General Secretariat (1980), pp. 136-37.

19 *The Guardian*, 6.2.1980.

20 *The Times*, 2.7.1980. On the speculation in Ankara that Turkey could postpone the membership application, see *The Guardian*, 1.7.1980. For the link established by the EU between the concessions and the membership issue, see also *The Financial Times*, 1.7.1980; *The Guardian*, 2.7.1980; and *Le Monde*, 3.7.1980.

membership, Turkey demanded permission to use the safeguard clause of the AP and introduce unilateral restrictions to trade.[21]

The membership application itself was another indicator of non-credibility. Following the AC meeting of 30 June 1980, the Turkish government accelerated its preparations for membership application. Being a minority government, however, it relied on the support of other parties including the anti-European NSP. Given this parliamentary arithmetic, the NSP demanded a vote of confidence on the government's EU policy, which was attributed to the pro-European foreign ministry. The NSP motion, which accused the foreign minister of 'selling Turkey to the EU', gathered enough support and led to his resignation in the first week of September 1980. The prime-minister, Mr. Demirel, did not come out in support of his foreign minister because he did not want the government to collapse and the liberalisation programme derailed. One week later, however, the military coup of 12 September 1980 sealed the fate of the membership application in a dramatic fashion.

The conclusion to be drawn from these episodes is a fairly straightforward one: the credibility of Turkey's commitment to convergence towards EU trade policy was consistently undermined by policy reversals between 'revision', 'flexibility, and 'membership threat'. Although the indicators of policy reversals fluctuated between these poles, the underlying cause was the same. Irrespective of the composition and ideological orientation of successive governments over the 1970s, Turkish governments engaged in sudden policy shifts as a result of the discretion built into the control-reliant mode of governance. These policy shifts were also facilitated and sometimes dictated by the protectionist demands of the private sector which, despite general declarations in favour of integration with the EU, was essentially unsure of its capacity to compete without protectionist measures.

Although Turkey speeded up the process of dismantling tariffs after 1988, the credibility of this policy reform was questionable. Despite the decline in the nominal rate of protection implied by the post-1988 tariff dismantling, the effective rate of protection enjoyed by the manufacturing industry in 1994 was still around 18%. In addition, the effective rate of protection in the same year was more than 20% for about half of the product groups within the manufacturing sector - with peaks reaching 30%-50% in certain industries such as beverages, clothing, plastics, cement, petrol refineries, and transport vehicles.[22] Given that Turkey, by 1994, had dismantled nominal tariffs by 90% (see Table 4.1), effective rates of

---

21 *Agence Europe*, 28.2.1980, p. 5.

22 Togan and Yılmaz (1995), pp. 155.

protection higher than 10% can be explained only by the existence of non-tariff protection which tended to be in the form non-transparent state aids and subsidies. This was a clear indication of the half-heartedness of the trade liberalisation that Turkey embarked upon to enhance the credibility of her membership bid in 1987.

4.2 EU Concessions in Agricultural Trade: Gradualism and Limitations

As indicated in section 4.1 above, the AP did not provide for free movement of agricultural products between Turkey and the EU. Trade in these products remained subject to the EU's CET and/or variable levies, depending on whether or not a specific product was protected by the CAP. Article 35 of the AP provides that preferential treatment in the area of agriculture would be reciprocal and reviewed in the AC every two years. Nevertheless, the AP did not revoke the preferential treatment accorded under the AA to four Turkish export staples (tobacco, raisins, hazelnuts, and dried figs) and a number of other products including fresh grapes, oranges, wines, and some fish varieties. In these products, Turkey enjoyed non-reciprocal preferential treatment in the form of tariff-free access or reduced-tariff entry - subject to quota limitations. Obviously, the AP provisions on agriculture were designed to protect EU farmers. Turkey consented to the protectionist implications of this arrangement for various reasons. First, as far as trade in industrial goods was concerned, the AP committed Turkey to undertake a gradual tariff dismantling over a period of 22 years whereas it provided for immediate tariff removal by the EU. Second, the quotas for export staples specified in the AA were generally set at generous levels. In fact, from 1964 to early 1970s, Turkey had not been able to exhaust her quota allowances for these products. Third, agriculture was not a priority in the import-substituting industrialisation policy, even though it was supported through minimum purchase prices and subsidised inputs. Finally, Turkey was reluctant to reform her agricultural policy and adopt the CAP because low agricultural prices were necessary to keep wages down and, thereby, reduce the cost of production in the manufacturing sector.

Within a relatively short period, however, the conditions that underpinned this consent began to change. Turkey's trade deficit with the EU began to increase at faster rates than that with the rest of the world.[23]

---

[23] Between 1971 and 1973, Turkey's trade deficit with the EU increased by 132% against an 89% increase in the deficit with rest of the world.

This deterioration, coupled with the import-substitution policy of the period, forced Turkey not only to seek ways of revising its obligations under the AP as indicated above, but also to put pressure on the EU to improve the coverage as well as the level of preferential treatment accorded to the agricultural sector. Also, from the mid-1970s onwards, the essentially inward-looking Turkish T&C industry began to search for external markets as protected domestic output began to increase faster than domestic consumption. Finally, the EU's commitment to gradual concessions in agriculture and further liberalisation in the T&C sector proved difficult to realise as a period of lower growth rates and higher levels of unemployment set in from early 1970s onwards.[24] Under these conditions, the EU became more resistant to Turkish demands for agricultural concessions and began to put pressure on Turkey to voluntarily restrict its exports of textiles and clothing products.

Despite the emergence of such a protectionist tendency in the EU's commercial policy, however, the first agricultural review provided for in the AP took place in 1973. This review followed the preferential treatment accorded to exports of some developing countries (the Group of 77) through the generalised system of preferences (GSP).[25] The EU, through Council regulation of 30 March 1971, granted unilateral preferential treatment to the exports of the GSP countries from 1 July 1971 onwards. Because this arrangement eroded the preference margins enjoyed by Turkey, the latter demanded an automatic extension of the GSP preferences to Turkish export of agricultural products. In the AC meeting of 2 April 1971, the EU responded by indicating that the preferential treatment extended to developing countries under the GSP did not prejudge the extension of similar preferences to other countries, including Turkey. In fact, the Commission was asked to prepare a report on the possible impact of the GSP preferences on Turkey's exports to the EU.[26]

Following these opening gestures, Turkey made a formal request for inclusion in the GSP list during the AC meeting of 20 July 1972. During that meeting, Turkey also asked the EU to take into account the negative impact of the United Kingdom's accession as the latter's average tariff rate on

---

24 The annual growth rates of the gross domestic product (GDP) in the EU(12) declined from 4.8% between 1961-70 to 2.9% between 1971-80. The level of unemployment, on the other hand, increased from 2.4% to 4.4% respectively. Somers (1991), pp. 253-255.

25 On the EU's generalised system of preferences, see Tulloch (1975), pp. 54-75; Weston et al. (1980), pp. 21-55; Grilli (1993), pp. 250-54.

26 *Bulletin of the EC*, no. 6-1971, p. 75 and no. 7-1971, p. 79. Turkey raised the issue of inclusion into the GSP list again in July 1971. *Bulletin of the EC*, no. 9/10-1971, p. 132.

agricultural imports was lower than the CET.[27] In contrast to the accommodating tones of the response given in 1971, the EU rejected the automatic extension of the GSP treatment to Turkey on the grounds that this would constitute a precedent and could lead to similar demands by other associated countries. Instead, the EU offered to extend gradual and discreet concessions within the review mechanism provided for in the AP and agreed to bring the first agricultural review forward by two years. Negotiations between July 1972 and June 1973 ended up with the AC decision of 30 June 1973, which extended preferential treatment to an additional 9 agricultural products from Turkey. This was a non-reciprocal treatment and became effective from 1974 onwards through Regulation 3375/73 and Regulation 3574/73.[28] This first agricultural review established a precedent whereby the EU would grant agricultural concessions in a non-reciprocal manner.

As a result of the concessions granted in the first review, Turkey began to enjoy a zero tariff rate on 37%, and partial tariff concessions on 33% of its agricultural exports to the EU. Although this meant that 70% of Turkey's agricultural exports to the EU enjoyed some sort of preferential treatment, Turkey's concern was about the relative preference margin *vis-à-vis* GSP countries rather than the percentage of its exports enjoying preferential treatment. According to the Commission's Ankara Office, Turkey had a positive margin compared to GSP countries only for 42% of its exports to the EU. Of the remaining 58% of the exports, 38% was enjoying similar preferences and about 20% was subject to worse treatment.[29] Given this situation and the worsening of the trade deficit, the first agricultural review was not successful in arresting Turkey's push for inclusion into the GSP list.

Although both the Commission and the European Parliament were in favour of granting a GSP status to Turkey, the Council was opposed to such an arrangement mainly because of resistance from France and Italy, whose Mediterranean products were likely to be affected not only by Turkish exports but also by the exports of other Mediterranean countries with which the EU was in the process of negotiating preferential agreements. Both France and Italy were aware that once Turkey was granted a GSP status automatically, it would be politically more difficult to (i) invoke the safeguard clause of the AP to protect their farmers when necessary and/or (ii) resist pressure from other Mediterranean countries for similar treatment. Therefore, both member states were trying to ensure that agricultural

---

27 *Bulletin of the EC*, no. 9-1972, pp. 96-97; and Council of the EC, General Secretariat (1972), p. 157.

28 *Official Journal of the EC*, no. L345, 15.12. 1973, p. 1; no. L359, 28.12.1973, p. 17.

29 Commission of the EC, Ankara Office (1977), pp. 70, 74.

concessions to Turkey were selective and limited. In order to secure the support of France and Italy for the conclusion of the ongoing negotiations with Mediterranean countries, other member states, the Commission and the European Parliament began to adopt a similar stance too.

As a result, the EU began to negotiate with Turkey for the second agricultural review in the light of a new consensus that excluded the possibility of Turkey's inclusion into the GSP list. However, inclusion was now even more important for Turkey as the EU was inching towards a 'global' Mediterranean policy. As it turned out, the objective of establishing a 'free trade area' in the Mediterranean had to be scaled down to bilateral trade and co-operation agreements with Mediterranean countries. Nevertheless, the prospect of having to compete with Mediterranean countries such as Israel and the Magreb countries was more than enough reason for Turkey to ensure that its preferential status was not undermined.[30] Therefore, as discussions about the second agricultural review took off in 1974, Turkey asked not only for inclusion in the GSP list but also for automatic entitlement to any preferential treatment to be granted to other Mediterranean countries. As a means of strengthening its case against the EU and improving access to the US market, Turkey had also tried to secure inclusion into the GSP list of the United States, who agreed to this demand at the end of 1975.

During 1975, the EU position became more rigid. Turkey was informed that the EU would not establish an automatic link between its Mediterranean or GSP commitments on the one hand and preferences to be extended to Turkish agricultural products on the other. Nonetheless, the EU would consider concessions for products with an export potential. Because of the need to satisfy the demands of the NSP in the coalition government, this offer was unacceptable for the Turkish government. The latter began to politicise the issue of agricultural concessions and argued that any alternative to automatic extension of GSP or Mediterranean concessions was incompatible with Turkey's special status as an associated country. From this point of view, the association agreement was a special arrangement that should provide Turkey with some scope to reduce the cost of adjustment. Although such demands may be justified given the erosion of Turkey's preferences, they were not compatible with the realities of the EU system that required issue dissection and linkage as a pre-requisite for the construction of package deals. As a result, the AC meeting of 16 September 1975 ended with no decision on the second agricultural review.

---

30 On the negotiations leading to second-generation Mediterranean agreements, see Grilli (1993), pp. 181-191.

Following the failure of the AC to reach a decision, the Commission continued to tread along a path that aimed at securing improvement in EU concessions on the one hand and convincing Turkey about the value of agreeing to improved access for a number of agricultural products on the other. As part of this strategy, the Commissioner responsible for agriculture, Mr. Gundelach, told the Turkish press in November 1975 that the agricultural review was delayed because of objections from some member states, especially France. He added that further delay would lead to the politicisation of the issue and have negative consequences for EU-Turkey relations.[31] In other words, the Commission was in favour of presenting an improved package of concessions to Turkey even though this would fall short of extending GSP and Mediterranean concessions automatically. This intervention by the Commission struck a chord with the Italian Presidency which, although opposed to automatic extension of preferences to Turkey, was keen to have the agricultural issue resolved during their term of office for two reasons. First, the prospect of securing some compensation in return for concessions would be better under an Italian Presidency. Second, it was desirable for the Italian government to have the issue resolved as early as possible and preferably before the Italian elections, due to take place in the second half of 1976.

Consequently, the COREPER worked intensively on the Commission proposal that had been submitted to it before September 1975. Following a lengthy process of bargaining that ironed out the differences between national representatives, the Council was able to arrive at an intra-EU package deal in early December. There were three aspects to this compromise. First, the concessions to be granted to Turkey were linked to the 'Global Mediterranean Policy' and the intra-EU compensation mechanism that this policy would necessitate. In fact, the Italian delegation managed to have a resolution drafted on how the consequences of opening the EU to the Mediterranean countries would be dealt with.[32] Second, the package was constructed with a view to minimise French objections. Third, it was presented as an opening offer to Turkey that could be improved during the course of negotiations. Whilst the first two aspects contributed to the acceptability of the package for France and Italy, the third aspect was

---

31 For Mr. Gundelach's statement, see Tekeli and İlkin (1993b), p. 193.

32 The resolution asked the Commission to establish, before the end of 1976, a balance sheet for the Mediterranean policy and to present proposals about what was required to address the concerns expressed in that context. See Council of the EC General Secretariat (1976), p. 126.

expected to induce Turkey to take part in negotiations that did not involve an automatic extension of the preferences.[33]

The package failed to cause a change in Turkey's position, but it enabled the EU to develop an assertive and common position on the issue. As a result of this assertiveness, the EU was able to tell the Turkish foreign minister during the AC meeting of March 1976 that Turkey should effectively relinquish any hope about automatic concessions. The Council president, Mr. G. Thorn, told his Turkish counterpart that this was what the EU council concluded after having discussed the issue at length.[34] Because Turkey continued to reject the offer as a basis for negotiations, the Council tried to improve the offer by increasing the number of products to be granted a preferential treatment. The initial offer, which identified 20 products, was improved slightly to include 26 products in the Council meeting of 24 July 1976. This was possible to attain only after Italian representatives in COREPER were assured that farmers likely to be affected by Turkish exports would be compensated. The EU rushed the offer to the Association Committee to avoid the postponement of another AC meeting scheduled for 27 July. This was not possible as the Turkish delegation indicated that they could not formulate their response at such short notice.[35] Although the postponement of the AC meeting meant that the issue would continue to haunt EU-Turkey relations, the reason given by the Turkish delegation was encouraging. By not rejecting the offer totally, the Turkish delegation signalled some change in Turkey's position that had been to reject anything less than automatic extension of GSP and Mediterranean concessions.

The AC meeting had to be postponed twice between July and December 1976 amid remarks as to whether or not the EU-Turkey association was dying. By December 1976, however, Turkey gave up its demands for automatic extension of preferences granted to other countries, and the EU agreed to increase the number of products with preferential treatment from 26 to 33. With these concessions, Turkey secured tariff reductions that varied between 30-80% of the CET for products not covered by the CAP. In this context, the EU provided better access for some fish varieties, tomato concentrate, apricot pulp, grapefruits and citrus fruits. For products protected under the CAP - such as durum wheat, olive oil and sardines - levies were reduced by 40-50%. Although these concessions went some way to meet Turkey's demands, their value in terms of increasing the attractiveness of the association link with the EU was reduced by quota

33 On this, see European Parliament (1976), pp. 39-40.

34 Birand (1986), pp. 345-46.

35 Council of the EC, General Secretariat (1976), p. 127.

limitations, voluntary export restraints, or seasonal restrictions that Turkey must observe.[36]

Results of the 1976 agricultural review confirmed two aspects of the EU's anchoring capacity in transparent/divisible policy areas. On the one hand, the EU was capable to grant Turkey unilateral concessions that went beyond what some of the member states were prepared to accept. On the other hand, these concessions were kept partial and conditional so that the member states likely to lose were compensated through intra-EU package deals. These aspects of the EU's anchoring capacity were confirmed by a report of the EP Committee on Agriculture. In its report evaluating the concessions granted to Turkey, the Committee argued that the product-by-product approach was essentially correct. An automatic approach would involve the risk of ignoring the implications of the concessions for the CAP.[37] In other words, the EP Committee in close contacts with the agricultural lobby was in favour of extending selective concessions to Turkey as the cost of such concessions could be managed within the EU, but it was against general and automatic concessions requiring comprehensive CAP reforms, which were both unfeasible and undesirable.[38]

The Commission interpreted the conclusion of the second agricultural review as a welcome development that would stabilise the EU-Turkey relations. Speaking in the plenary session, the Commissioner in charge of external relations told the EP that its agreement with the Commission on the overall stance of the policy towards Turkey should enable them to persuade the Council to pursue a 'dynamic policy' that the circumstances might demand in the future.[39] The celebratory tone of the Commission's statement, however, should not conceal the issues that needed to be resolved before a claim to success in anchoring Turkey could be made. For Turkey, the second review was nothing more than a temporary compromise which she had to accept because of the weakness in her bargaining position. That was why the Turkish minister for agriculture, soon after the AC meeting of December 1976, made it clear that Turkey would not accept less favourable treatment compared to other countries.[40] In addition, agreement by France and Italy to the concessions was conditional on setting up an intra-EU compensation

---

36 For the list of products and concessions, see *Agence Europe*, 3.3. 1977, pp. 5-6. See also, *Official Journal of the EC*, no. L331, 23.12.1977 and no. L319, 14.12.1977.

37 European Parliament (1976), pp. 41-42.

38 This view of the *Rapporteur* was reiterated in the EP debate on Council Regulations putting the second agricultural review into effect. See *Agence Europe*, 23.4.1977, p. 11.

39 *Official Journal of the EC - Debates of the EP*, no. 212 (February 1977), pp. 238-39.

40 *Agence Europe*, 3.3.1977, p. 5.

mechanism that would take into account the impact of the concessions extended not only to Turkey but also to other Mediterranean countries.

Negotiations on a compensation mechanism continued until the end of 1977. The first round concerned COREPER deliberations on a Commission proposal prepared in early June. The permanent representatives, as a result of pressure from French and Italian delegations, criticised the Commission proposals for being too vague and incomplete. According to COREPER, there was a lack of balance between the EU's external commitments and the rate of internal developments aimed at dealing with their consequences for domestic producers. Therefore, it was necessary to take into account internal priorities before envisaging further external concessions. During discussions in the Council, the French and Italian delegations adopted a common position that emphasised the need to tilt the CAP towards Mediterranean countries. The French foreign minister asked for market regulations that would provide income security for Mediterranean farmers. His Italian counterpart, on the other hand, asked for an arrangement that would channel funds to Mediterranean farmers from the European Regional Development Fund (ERDF) and the guidance section of the European Agricultural Guarantee and Guidance Fund (EAGF). These views, however, were received cautiously by Northern member states, which argued that the EU should not encourage new agricultural surpluses. Given this north/south divide, the Council meeting of 20 July 1977 ended with no decision.[41]

The third round of intra-EU negotiations took place within the Economic and Social Committee (ESC). The report drafted on the basis of these negotiations recommended an active structural and regional policy as well as adaptation of the CAP in favour of the Mediterranean regions. The ESC report stated that such measures would ensure an equitable sharing of the short-term costs resulting form the EU's opening towards the Mediterranean countries until the medium- to long-term advantages of that opening could be enjoyed.[42] Partly because of the lack of direct competition between northern and southern agriculture and partly because of the overall EU interest in the Mediterranean basin, the Commission was able to submit its revised proposal in December 1977. In its proposal, the Commission charted a line that aimed to reconcile the reluctance of the northern member states with the demands of France and Italy. It proposed higher rates of price increases for Mediterranean agricultural products within the CAP and recommended restructuring measures through extensive irrigation projects that would encourage product differentiation, i.e. shifting into products less

---

41 *Agence Europe*, 23.6. 1977, pp. 6-8; 21.7.1977, p. 7.

42 *Agence Europe*, 9.11.1977, p. 11.

vulnerable to competition from Mediterranean countries.[43] This package was linked to the annual review of the CAP prices and agreed by the Council before the end of 1977.

In the meantime, Turkey failed to comply with the 10% tariff reduction due in 1976. Also, she made no attempt to align her agricultural policy with the CAP. Given the EU's threat in 1976 that further concessions to Turkey would be conditional on Turkey's fulfilment of its obligations under the AP, the prospect for automatic entitlement to GSP or Mediterranean concessions became dimmer compared to the early 1970s. In fact, the Commission signalled in 1978 that the EU was in no position to accommodate new demands even if these were limited to partial concessions. According to Commission calculations, by 1978, 93% of Turkey's agricultural export to the EU was already receiving preferential treatment in one way or the other.[44] Despite this signal, the Turkish government demanded not only automatic concessions but also an end to the reciprocity principle of the AP. Although the EU did not invoke this principle against Turkey with respect to agricultural trade, the Turkish government felt that the reciprocity principle in general was limiting her ability to suspend trade liberalisation without giving the EU a pretext to be less receptive to Turkish demands. In addition, the Turkish government demanded better access for T&C products, financial aid/credits of US$ 8 billion, and a Five-Year freeze on Turkey's obligations under the AP. On the basis of the feedback received from Mr. E. Noel and Mr. Duchateau after their visit to Ankara in November 1978, the Commission decided to respond to Turkish demands positively. The Commission president, Mr. Jenkins, intervened personally and tried to bring to the Council's attention the serious economic difficulties that Turkey was experiencing.[45] In addition, the Commission prepared a draft proposal on 21 December 1978 and argued in favour of granting better access to Turkish textiles as well as agricultural products.[46]

The proposal was prepared at a time when the EU was trying to share the burden of helping Turkey out of its difficulties with other western countries. For this purpose, Germany asked the Organisation of Economic Cooperation and Development (OECD) to extend financial assistance to Turkey. The Secretary General of the OECD, Mr. van Lennep, responded on 6 February 1979 by indicating that the OECD would play an active role and

---

43 *Agence Europe*, 7.12.1977, p. 9.

44 *Agence Europe*, 26.5.1978, p. 8.

45 On Mr. Jenkins' letter to the foreign ministers' meeting on the fringe of the European Council, see *Agence Europe*, 6.12.1978, p. 7; and no. 2577, 9.1.21978, p. 5.

46 On the Commission proposal, see *Agence Europe*, 22.12.1978, p. 7.

had already established contacts with the International Monetary Fund (IMF) on this issue.[47] Another motive behind the German initiative was to use the OECD package as a bargaining chip and limit the extent of agricultural or other concessions to Turkey. Having observed this tendency, the Commission decided to postpone the finalisation of its initial proposal until after the Council meeting of 5 February 1979. As the Council did not signal any enthusiasm for agricultural concessions in that meeting, the balance between the commissioners in favour of extending further concessions to Turkey and those who objected to such treatment was tipped in favour of the latter. Therefore, the Commission meeting of 7 February 1979 did not endorse the recommendation that Turkey should be granted a most favoured nation status in the Mediterranean context - a status that would have enabled Turkey to benefit from any existing or future concessions granted to Mediterranean countries. In another meeting one week later, the conflict between the German commissioner Mr. Haferkamp who was in favour of granting agricultural concessions in order to dampen Turkey's pressure on free movement and the French Commissioner Mr. Gundelach who was against was resolved in favour of the latter. As a result, the Commission decided to postpone the issue of agricultural concessions until after the Five-Year freeze of Turkey's obligations under the AP.[48]

The shift in the Commission's stance was in stark contrast to the optimistic expectations that Mr. Davignon had appeared to entertain in early 1977 regarding an alliance between the Commission and the EP to persuade the Council to adopt a dynamic EU external policy. The EP, therefore, was right in criticising the EU institutions, including the Commission, for pushing the onus of assisting Turkey on to other international organisations such as the OECD. As far as the EU proposal was concerned, the EP stated in its resolution that the member states were not prepared to make even limited concessions in order to counteract the negative political developments in Turkey.[49] Notwithstanding this criticism, the Council maintained its insistence on excluding agricultural concessions from the EU offer. The Council president Mr. O'Kennedy and the Commission vice-president Mr. Haferkamp conveyed this position to Turkey during their visit to Ankara in September 1979.[50] Neither the deteriorating political situation nor Turkey's overture towards the Soviet Union were effective in changing this stance.

---

47 *Agence Europe*, 7.2.1979, p. 13.

48 On the conflict between Haferkamp and Gundelach, see *Agence Europe*, 1.2.1979, p. 5. On the gradual move towards Mr. Gundelach's position and final decision, see *Agence Europe*, 9.2. 1979, p. 5; and 15.2.1979, p. 4.

49 European Parliament (1979b), p. 14.

50 *Agence Europe*, 17/18.9. 1979, p. 8; and 22.9. 1979, p. 6.

When, however, a new Turkish government declared its intention of applying for membership in early 1980, the Council's rigid approach was swiftly replaced by an accommodating one in which agricultural concessions were the most important element. Although developments in Iran and Afghanistan could have influenced this change, it was obvious that the prospect of Turkish membership was the most significant factor.

Therefore, the Commission proposal of December 1978 offering Turkey agricultural concessions was dusted off the shelf and the possibility of granting tariff-free entry to Turkish agricultural products over a period of six years began to be considered. There were, however, two difficulties in securing an intra-EU compromise on this issue. On the one hand, Turkey was demanding the removal of both tariffs and levies imposed under the CAP within a period of four rather than six years as suggested by the Commission. The second difficulty related to intra-EU bargaining. The previous tilting of the CAP towards the Mediterranean regions was not enough for securing another agreement by the Italian and French representatives even to the six-year period of tariff removal let alone the four-year period demanded by Turkey. This reluctance on the part of Italy and France was in complete contradiction with the German position which favoured extending generous agricultural concessions to Turkey as a means of reducing Turkish pressure on the issue of free movement. Under these circumstances, the EU needed a new package deal that would replace the 1977 compromise.

The new compromise was facilitated by three factors. First, Italy, for whom agricultural concessions were a contentious issue, was holding the Presidency again. It was more desirable for the Italian government to resolve the issue during their terms of office as the Presidency could be used to inject a greater Italian input for shaping the package deal. Therefore, the Italian foreign minister appealed to the national delegations in COREPER to come forward with a constructive package that would be compatible with Turkish expectations.[51] Second, Germany realised during the negotiations in the Association Committee that a generous level of agricultural concessions would not be enough to convince Turkey to accept a revision of the AP with respect to free movement of workers. It might, however, be effective in forcing Turkey to agree to a delay in introducing the implementing measures envisaged in the AP. As a result, Germany changed its stance of pushing the onus on its partners and agreed to partial improvements in the conditions of Turkish workers residing in the EU. Third, because of the risks involved in refusing a Turkish membership bid against the background of the Afghan

---

[51] *Agence Europe*, 23.4.1980, p. 6; and 24.4.1980, p. 6.

crisis and the increased tension in East-West relations, all member states came to realise that a further round of concessions across the board was inevitable.[52] As a result of these factors, a series of Association Committee meetings between 25 February and 20 June 1980 ended with the acceptance of a four-point package on agriculture, freedom of movement, financial aid and economic cooperation.[53]

Following the negotiations both with Turkey and within the EU itself, the AC meeting of 30 June 1980 decided to abolish existing tariffs on imports of agricultural products originating in Turkey over a six-year period, as the EU had been demanding. Non-tariff barriers such as seasonal restrictions, levies and reference prices, however, would have to be observed by Turkish exporters.[54] Despite these limitations, the Turkish government considered the AC decision as the achievement of a goal that had been pursued since early 1970s: the automatic extension of preferences granted to GSP or Mediterranean countries in order to avoid the erosion of the preferential treatment accorded to Turkish agriculture. In fact, the AC decision went even beyond that provision by committing the EU to remove all tariffs, and placed Turkey at a more advantageous position compared with Greece, which had just concluded the accession negotiations.[55]

On the face of it, the AC decision of June 1980 was in conflict with the earlier EU position that concessions could be granted only partially and on a product-by-product basis. Therefore, it raises the question as to whether the argument that the EU's anchoring capacity is limited should be revised. A close examination, however, would indicate that the AC decision of 30 June 1980 was but a different manifestation of the EU's limited anchoring capacity. Although the 1980 concessions seemed to go beyond the principle

---

52 On EU concerns that affected the outcome of the Association Council meeting of February 1980, see *The Financial Times*, 21.1.1980; *Agence Europe*, 6.2.1980, p. 5; and 7.2.1980, p. 6; *The Guardian*, 6&7.2.1980; *The Times*, 6&7.2.1980.

53 On the Association Committee meetings, see *Agence Europe*, 28.2.1980, p. 5; 26.3.1980, p. 11; 30.5.1980, p. 7; 31.5.1980, p. 9; and 21.6.1980, p. 5. On intra-EU negotiations, see *Agence Europe*, 23.4.1980, p. 6; 24.4.1980, p. 6; and 7.5.1980, p. 5.

54 On the Association Council decision, see *Agence Europe*, 2.7.1980, p. 7. See also, Council of the EC, General Secretariat (1980), p. 138. The first tariff reduction was provided for by the Council Regulation 562/81 of 11 March 1981. See *Official Journal of the EC*, no. L65, 11.3.1981, pp. 1-36. Following this, three more Council regulations - 3590/82, 3721/84, and 4115/86 - provided for following reductions. See *Official Journal of the EC*, no. L375, 31.12.1982, pp. 1-26; no. L343, 31.12.1984, pp. 6-32; and no. L380, 31.12.1986, pp. 16-20.

55 The EU defended the concessions to Turkey by indicating that complications could occur when transitional arrangements were involved in the accession process. On this, see *Agence Europe*, 3.9.1980, p. 6.

of partial preferences, there were significant conditions that minimised the exposure of EU farmers to Turkish export as a result of: (i) the gradualism involved in the elimination of tariff duties; (ii) seasonal restrictions; and (iii) minimum price thresholds that Turkish exporters must observe. In addition, the EU extended these concessions with the aim of securing a delay in Turkey's membership - an eventuality that was perceived to be more costly than what the third agricultural review would imply. In other words, the 1980 concessions must, in fact, be interpreted as yet another indication of the anchor/credibility dilemma in EU-Turkey relations.

4.3 Trade in Textiles & Clothing: Further Evidence on EU's Limited Anchoring Capacity

Developed countries have protected their textiles and clothing (T&C) industry not only during the Short and Long Term Agreements of 1961-73, but also under the Multifibre Arrangement (MFA) of 1973-94. Over this period, EU policy went through low-level of protectionism until 1976, strict protectionism from 1977-85 and gradual liberalisation after 1986. The reversal of the policy in 1986 led to the elimination of national quotas in 1993 and the conclusion of the 1994 Agreement on Textiles and Clothing (ATC) as part of the Uruguay Round conclusions.

This circular evolution of the EU's T&C policy has naturally affected its relations with Turkey. In fact, the controversy concerning T&C trade from mid-1970s onwards led many students of EU-Turkey relations to focus on the extent of protectionism in EU policy and the negative consequences of this stance for Turkey's perception of the association.[56] Although this focus is justified to some extent by the EU's strict protectionism from 1977-85, it tends to miss three significant details. First, it does not take into account the fact that EU protectionism against Turkish T&C products was relatively lenient compared to protectionism against other countries. Second, the EU did not invoke the safeguard clause (Article 60 of the AP) until 1984 in an attempt to avoid confrontation with Turkey.[57] Finally, the EU adopted a permissive stance against Turkey's continuous rejection to sign *formal* restraint agreements under the MFA regime despite the fact similar

56 See for example, Balkır (1993), pp. 123-25; Kılınç (1990), pp. 96-98; and Tekeli and İlkin (1993b), pp. 251-63.

57 As a Commission Official with insider information about this issue, Cendrowicz is aware of this fine detail. See Cendrowicz (1992), p. 12

agreements were concluded with other Mediterranean countries, including Greece and Portugal.

We raise these issues here not to justify EU restrictions on Turkish T&C export, but with the aim of pointing to the possibility that the EU could assume a limited anchoring role in transparent/divisible policy areas even if the general stance of its trade policy is protectionist. The protectionist drive in the EU's T&C trade policy began at the end of first Multi-Fibre Arrangement (MFAI) in 1976. Between 1973 and 1976, the German and Dutch perspective envisaging an international division of labour and overseas processing dominated the EU's T&C trade policy, which emphasised restructuring the T&C industry rather than protectionism. From 1977 onwards, however, the French, Italian and British approach gained the upper hand as slower growth rates set in and unemployment increased. Therefore, under MFAII and MFAIII (1977-85), the stance of the EU's T&C trade policy was more protectionist not only when compared to its policy under MFAI, but also in comparison to the United States.[58] Given this policy shift, the EU's capacity to maintain the concessions under the AP was reduced significantly. To avoid Turkey's alienation, however, it charted a way between strict protectionism and free trade. This strategy was based on selective restrictions and a regime of monitoring by exporters. It is true that selective protectionism increased the uncertainty for Turkish producers and, therefore, had an adverse effect on investment decisions. However, it also allowed ample scope for Turkish exporters to make inroads into the EU market during a period of strict protectionism against other suppliers.

Signs of a lenient approach towards Turkish T&C export began to emerge in 1976 when it became apparent that the EU was preparing for a more restrictive MFAII. In 1976, the EU introduced quantitative restrictions on cotton yarn exports from Brazil, Pakistan, Mexico and Colombia, but not Turkey. As a result, Turkey's share in the EU market increased from 19.2% in 1975 to 34.5% in 1976. This increase was due partly to trade deflection caused by EU restrictions on Turkey's competitors. Another factor that enabled Turkey to increase its share of the EU market, however, was a 25% subsidy granted to cotton yarn exporters. The EU threatened Turkey with quantitative restrictions unless the export subsidy was abolished. The Turkish government first resisted the EU threat, but she reduced the export subsidy by 15% in March 1977. Also, exporters agreed to raise their prices

[58] For detailed studies of EU T&C policy until early 1980s, see Dolan (1983); Aggarwal (1983); and Farrands (1979). For studies on post-1986 liberalisation, see Pelkmans (1993); and Ugur (1998).

by 10% in order to neutralise the effect of the remaining 10% subsidy.[59] However, Turkey did not implement this agreement strictly. Therefore Turkey's export of cotton yarn to the EU market increased by 10% in 1977, compared to an increase of 6% or lower in the export of other countries which had to conclude restraint agreements under the MFAII.

In May 1977, however, the French government decided to introduce national restrictions on the imports of some clothing products originating in both associated and non-associated countries. This demand was made under Article 115 of the Treaty of Rome that allowed for national restrictions subject to *ex post* approval by the EU. As far as Turkish products were concerned, such restrictions must also be based on Article 60 of the AP. Before Article 60 could be invoked, however, a national decision must be converted into an EU measure in accordance with Regulation 1842/71 of 26 August 1971.[60] The 'conversion' was duly completed and Turkey was included among other countries whose exports would be restricted under Regulation 1566/77 of the Commission. Turkey's inclusion in the regulation, however, was only nominal as the Commission could not get the Turkish government to sign a voluntary restraint agreement. Therefore, Turkey was excluded from the quota restrictions that the Commission Regulation imposed on imports of cotton yarns and some clothing products from Mediterranean countries. The regulation provided that importers of Turkish products would be issued with authorisation certificates without limitation until an agreement could be concluded with the Turkish government.[61]

These were the initial signs of the EU's relative willingness to treat the import of Turkish T&C products as a special case to avoid rupture in EU-Turkey relations. This special treatment provided the Turkish government with a precedent upon which it could maintain its policy of rejecting any formal restraint agreement with the EU. Restraint agreements were considered by the Turkish government to be in conflict with Turkey's special status as an associated country. The same argument was also made against undertaking any commitment to ensure the exporters' compliance with the terms of informal agreements that they might conclude with the Commission on their own initiatives. Despite the risk of setting a precedent that could be exploited by other Mediterranean countries in the future, the EU did not retaliate by invoking Article 60 of the AP. On the contrary, both the

59 Council of the EC, General Secretariat (1977), p. 141; *Agence Europe*, 23.2.1977, p. 5; and Tekeli and İlkin (1993b), pp. 255-56.

60 See Regulation 1842/71, *Official Journal of the EC*, no. L192, 26.8.1971, pp. 14-15.

61 On the introduction of quantitative restrictions on imports from Mediterranean countries, see *Agence Europe*, 7.7.1977, p. 9. For Regulation 1566/77 and the special arrangement for Turkey, see *Official Journal of the EC*, no. L174, 14.7.1977, pp. 9-12.

Commission and the Council appeared to be in agreement on treating the situation as a special case and imposing quantitative restrictions only as a last resort on the basis of requests by member states. As a result of this consensus, the decision not to impose unilateral restrictions on the imports of Turkish textiles was extended to 1978 too.[62]

The special treatment accorded to Turkish T&C exports must be set against the EU policy of constructing a pyramid of differentiated preferential treatment through association and cooperation agreements. At the top of this pyramid were the GSP countries enjoying unilateral concessions in the form of tariff-free entry into the EU market. Because, however, the export capacity of the GSP countries was very limited, the most significant category was the Mediterranean countries that occupied the next section of the pyramid. Among these countries, Turkey - together with Greece - enjoyed a special status in that their export capacities were significant and provisions of their association agreements were relatively generous as tariffs were applicable only to a few number of products. In fact, the EU-Greece Association Agreement did not even contain a safeguard clause that could be invoked. Then there were the MFA countries, the export of which was subject to bilateral agreements that became more restrictive from 1977 onwards. Turkey's special position in this context becomes clearer when compared with Mediterranean countries linked to the EU with association or cooperation agreements. The EU secured voluntary restraint agreements with these countries, including Greece, but accommodated Turkey's opposition to either sign such agreements or monitor the implementation of the agreements that might be signed with Turkish exporters.

The next time producer pressure on the EU proved to be too intense to exempt Turkey from restrictions was in the second half of 1978 when Turkish export of cotton yarn and some clothing products to the United Kingdom in the first six months proved to be more than the nominal quota envisaged for the whole year. Having observed this increase, the UK government decided to impose quantitative restrictions on the import of Turkish cotton yarn without waiting for the results of talks to be held in the Association Committee.[63] The Commission obliged and approved the UK's restriction on the basis of Regulation 1842/71. In order to avoid an open clash with the Turkish government, however, the EU delegation to the Association Committee played down the significance of the restriction by

62 See *Agence Europe*, 26.11.1977, p. 5; and Council of the EC, General Secretariat (1977), p. 141.

63 *Agence Europe*, 14.9.1978, p. 12. On initial UK complaint, see *Agence Europe*, 31.8.1978, p. 3.

indicating that it was limited to one product, one member state and for a short period only - from mid-September until 31 December 1978.[64]

Despite the attempt de-dramatise the situation, the Commission was caught up between two imperatives. On the one hand, the UK was pressing for the extension of the 1978 quantitative restrictions into 1979. In addition, France and Italy were also pressing for a restraint agreement with Turkey. On the other hand, the Turkish government had already asked in May 1978 for a radical improvement in the EU's concessions to Turkey - including an increase in the tariff-free quota for cotton yarns and cotton fabrics. Faced with this situation, the Commission tried to get the Council to agree to a lenient approach towards Turkey. The commission's preference for treating the Turkish T&C export as a special case could be seen from the letter that the Commission president, Mr. Jenkins, sent to the Council in early December 1978. In that letter and during his meeting with the Turkish foreign minister, Mr. Jenkins indicated that the EU should be able to provide some concessions to Turkey.[65]

As a result, the Commission's first draft proposal on the EU's common position (December 1978) called for a 'cautious assessment of possible measures' that would ensure better access to the EU market of Turkish agricultural and textile products. Apparently, this was too much for the member states in favour of protectionism. Therefore, the second document finalised on 24 January 1979 did not mention the possibility of better access.[66] Nevertheless, Commission attempts to limit the disaffection of the Turkish government continued. For example, even though Turkey continued to object to voluntary export restraint agreements, the Commission refrained from invoking Article 60 of the AP despite hints by some member states about the inevitability of such a measure. The Commission justified its position by arguing that it would be unwise for the EU to single out textiles in a period when the EU-Turkey association was being discussed at a 'global' level.[67] In line with this tendency, the Commission turned down a complaint by the lobby group EUROCOTON that Turkish exporters were dumping cotton yarn on the EU market with a dumping margin of 15-30%.[68]

---

64 Council of the EC, General Secretariat (1978), p. 144.

65 On Mr. Jenkins' attempts to influence the Council, see *Agence Europe*, 6.12.1978, p. 7; and 9.12.1978, p. 5.

66 On the change in the Commission opinion, compare *Agence Europe*, 22.12.1978, p. 7 with *Agence Europe*, 26.1.1979, p. 5.

67 On this, see *Agence Europe*, 17.1.1979, p. 5. On UK demands for restrictions against Turkish textiles, see *Agence Europe*, 29/30.1.1979, p. 5. On the Commission's objections to unilateral quotas, see *Agence Europe*, 24.2.1979, p. 5.

68 *Agence Europe*, 13.7.1979, p. 11.

This aversion to unilateral restrictions continued until November 1979 when, upon a request from the UK government, the Commission had to eventually restrict Turkish cotton yarns destined to the British market to 428 tonnes between November-December 1979. This was both a belated and ineffective restriction given the fact that Turkish exports in the first 8 months of 1979 already exceeded the annual quota envisaged for the UK market by 55%.[69]

Due largely to this lenient approach, the annual rate of growth in Turkey's export of cotton yarn to the EU between 1978-79 was 15.0% - more than four times above the annual increase of 3.5% that the Council accepted for cotton yarn originating in all other developing countries, including those benefiting from GSP treatment. Therefore, it was not surprising to observe that, by the end of 1979, Turkey became the largest supplier of cotton yarn to the EU market - supplying one-third of total EU imports and leaving behind the traditional suppliers such as Hong Kong and Taiwan.[70] The special treatment accorded to Turkey was also obvious when compared with other Mediterranean countries. By 1980, the EU had managed to secure formal restraint agreements with other Mediterranean countries, including Greece and Portugal.[71] These agreements provided for two major undertakings by exporting countries: quantitative restrictions on the export of T&C products; and co-operation in implementing those restrictions through issuing export licenses. Despite these examples of voluntary restraint agreements concluded directly with governments, the EU was still unable to get the Turkish government to co-operate even on the implementation of an agreement that would be signed with the private sector, let alone conclude a formal agreement.[72]

As heavy producer pressure began to build up in 1980, the Commission had to respond positively to a new dumping complaint lodged by EUROCOTON in early 1981. Following extensive inspections carried out in Turkey, the Commission decided to impose an anti-dumping duty of 16% on imports of Turkish cotton yarn in December 1981.[73] Turkey called on the EU to discuss the anti-dumping duty in the Association Committee. The EU

---

69 In the briefing given to the press, the Commission was once more anxious to play down the significance of the restrictions by pointing to the fact that Turkish exports should have been banned altogether until the end of the year. See *Agence Europe*, 9.11.1979, p. 5; and 12/13.11.1979, p. 7.

70 See *Agence Europe*, 12/13.11.1979, p. 7; and 19.1.1980, p. 13.

71 See *Agence Europe*, 19.1. 1980, p. 14.

72 For EU negotiations with Turkish exporters of textiles, see *Agence Europe*, 2/3.1.1980, p. 7; and 19.1.1980, p. 14.

73 See Commission Regulation 3453/81, *Official Journal of the EC*, no. L347, 3.1.21981, pp. 19-21.

agreed, but set the time of the meeting as late as possible to allow enough time for discussing the issue internally in the Council. Therefore, when the Association Committee met on 2 April 1982, the EU Council had already discussed the issue and decided to reduce the anti-dumping duty from 16% to 12%. In fact, the Council Regulation to that effect was completed and ready to be published. As Turkey continued its objections to any restriction on the grounds that this would not be compatible with the AA, the Association Committee meeting ended without agreement and the Council regulation was published the next day.[74]

In response, the Turkish government retaliated by imposing a 15% surcharge on the imports of 45 tariff headings of iron and steel products originating in the EU. Following Turkey's retaliation, a meeting of the Association Committee was sought again - but this time by the EU. After two meetings of the Committee on 26 April and 26 May, a deal was struck on 30 July 1982 between the EU and Turkey. According to the deal, both sides would revoke the duties that they imposed. Although the Turkish government was still adamant not to sign a restraint agreement with the EU, it agreed to collaborate on ensuring compliance of the exporters with certain price levels that they would negotiate with the EU. In return for this concession by Turkey, the EU had to give up the demand for definite quantitative ceilings and agreed to a dual monitoring system aimed at avoiding sudden surges in Turkish exports.[75] The deal in 1982 was clearly favourable to Turkey. First of all, Turkey continued to be the only country that did not sign a formal restraint agreement with the EU. The Turkish government undertook only to collaborate on the monitoring of the voluntary restraint agreement to be concluded between the EU and Turkish exporters. Second, this voluntary restraint agreement covered only the *textiles* sector.[76] The clothing sector, which was beginning to surpass textiles in terms of export earnings, was not included. As will be demonstrated below, a similar agreement with Turkish exporters of clothing would be signed only in 1986.

Negotiations with respect to the *clothing* sector followed a similar pattern. As negotiations concerning Turkey's export of textiles were continuing, the Commission introduced quantitative restrictions on Turkey's export of T-shirts and shirts on 29 June 1982. In response, the Turkish government re-introduced the 15% surcharge on iron and steel products

---

74 See Council Regulation 789/82, *Official Journal of the EC*, no. L90, 3.4.1982, p. 1.

75 See *Bulletin of the EC*, no. 4-1982 (May 1982), p. 44. On the meetings of the Association Committee, see Council of the EC, General Secretariat (1982), pp. 148-49.

76 On the agreement between the EU and Turkish exporters of textiles, see *Agence Europe*, 9.7.1980, p. 14.

originating in the EU towards the end of 1982. Before that, the Turkish government had also introduced special checks and delaying tactics against French exports as France was highly active in pressurising the Commission to introduce quantitative restrictions.[77] Although the EU's restrictions were valid only until the end of 1982, Turkey maintained the surcharge and the delaying procedures well into 1983. An AC meeting at ambassadorial level was held on 28 March 1983 to deal with this issue, but no agreement was reached.[78] As trade skirmishes between the two sides continued along these lines, Turkey became the largest supplier to the EU market of not only textiles but also of clothing products.[79]

As the EU began to negotiate for MFA IV in 1985, domestic producers of textiles and clothing products initiated a new campaign for protectionism not only in the context of the MFA but also against Turkey. On two occasions in 1985 (May and July), COMITEXTIL sought and obtained assurances from the Commission that the EU was aware of the difficulties caused by Turkish exports. In order to assure the producers, the Commission pointed to partial measures introduced in the form of either anti-dumping duties or quantitative restrictions.[80] In fact, one such measure was taken against trousers and T-shirts, and was valid until the end of June 1985. Although COMITEXTIL tried to press the Commission to extend the restriction for another period on the grounds that the Turkish government was subsidising export by about 17%, the Commission refrained from renewing the restrictions as negotiations with the Turkish exporters were still going on. However, three rounds of negotiations with Turkish exporters ended with no agreement. To force the hand of the Turkish exporters, the Commission invoked the safeguard clause and adopted Regulation 2662/85 on 21 September 1985. The restrictions imposed by this regulation were EU-wide for T-shirts, pullovers, trousers and shirts; and at national levels for underwear and dresses (UK), socks and underwear (Germany) and dresses (France).[81] By that time, the import of clothing products from Turkey

---

77 For Turkish government's delaying tactics, see *Bulletin of the EC*, 6-1982 (June 1982), p. 59. On Turkey's re-introduction of the 15% tax on iron and steel products, see Council of the EC, General Secretariat (1982), p. 149.

78 *Bulletin of the EC*, 3-1983 (March 1983), p. 63; and Council of the EC, General Secretariat (1983), p. 141.

79 Turkey's export to the EC in 1984 was 147,000 tons, compared with 117,000 tons from Hong-Kong and 115,000 tons from Portugal. *Agence Europe*, 30.5.1985, p. 13.

80 See *Agence Europe*, 5.6.1985, p. 10; and 6.7.1985, p. 10.

81 On the last round of talks, see *The Financial Times*, 14.9.1985 and *Le Monde*, 15.9.1985. For the quantitative restrictions, see Regulation 2662/85 in *Official Journal of the EC*, no. L252, 21.9.1985, pp. 15-19; *The Financial Times*, 23.9.1985; and *Agence Europe*, 21.9.1985, p. 8.

exceeded the envisaged nominal quota for 1984 by 107% to 600% percent, depending on the product. The clash involving clothing products, however, did not affect the functioning of the informal agreement concluded for textiles, which was renewed for another two years at the end of 1985.[82]

Following the introduction of quantitative restrictions on clothing products, the EU continued to explore the possibility of arriving at an informal agreement with Turkish exporters. In other words, the EU was still reluctant about the use of unilateral restrictions because such measures were open to political exploitation by Turkey and would not provide a stable regime enabling EU producers to plan accordingly. For that reason, an EU delegation visited Ankara in February 1986 and held extensive talks with Turkish officials. The delegation returned with the impression that the Turkish government was less reluctant to: (i) accept a supervisory role in the implementation of an informal agreement to be concluded with clothing exporters; and (ii) abolish the subsidies it had been providing to the sector.[83] The change in Turkey's position was related to the re-activation of the strategy first developed in 1980: membership application should be used as weapon to circumvent not only the restrictions on textiles but also the EU's objections to free movement of workers.[84] This new approach on the part of the Turkish government coincided with the EU's gradual move towards liberalisation under MFA IV and Uruguay Round negotiations. As a result, the Commission was able to agree to concessions concerning quota levels.[85] Consequently, an agreement was reached between the EU delegation and Turkish exporters of clothing products on 11 April 1986. The Turkish government agreed to supervise the agreement and ensure exporters' compliance with its terms. According to the agreement, there would be EU-wide quotas for seven and national quotas for five categories of clothing products. The annual growth rates for quotas were set at 3% - 6%, whilst the level of quotas was determined at quantities acceptable for Turkey.[86]

As a result of the *ad hoc* yet relatively less protectionist EU stance towards Turkey, the latter's share of the EU market in textiles and clothing began to increase at fast rates from 1981 onwards. As can be seen from Table 4.2 below, Turkey's share in the EU market increased from 2.96% in

---

82 Council of the EC, General Secretariat (1985), p. 143.

83 *Agence Europe*, 15.2.1986, p. 10.

84 *Agence Europe*, 12.4.1986, p. 10.

85 *Agence Europe*, 10.4.1986, p. 6.

86 On the conclusion of the agreement, see *Agence Europe*, 10.4.1986, p. 6; and 12.4.1986, p. 10. On quota growth rates, see *The Financial Times*, 29.4.1986. On the removal of unilateral restrictions introduced in September 1985, see Regulation 1770/86 in *Official Journal of the EC*, no. L153, 7.6.1986, p. 31.

1981 to 12.7% in 1992. Although this performance was also related to the increase in the competitiveness of the Turkish T&C industry, the positive impact of the relatively lenient EU stance cannot be ignored. The significance of the EU's relatively lenient approach to Turkish T&C exports can be inferred from the slow down in the increase of Turkey's share since 1989, when other suppliers began to make inroads into the EU market as a result of the EU's gradual return to liberalisation.

Table 4.2 Turkey's export of T&C products to the EU market

Year	Value (Mn ECUs)	Share of EU market (%)
1976	372	3.59
1977	268	2.47
1978	330	2.86
1979	346	2.46
1980	313	2.01
1981	498	2.96
1982	655	3.71
1983	747	3.93
1984	1,040	4.34
1985	1,289	5.00
1986	1,546	6.47
1987	1,814	6.87
1989	2,482	10.76
1990	2,697	11.61
1991	2,901	11.31
1992	3,296	12.70

Source: EUROSTAT Foreign Trade Database (1994).

Another conclusion that can be derived from Table 4.2 is that Turkey's share in the EU market increased at faster rates during the 1980s, i.e. after the conclusion of the informal agreements with Turkish exporters. This tendency suggests that the conclusion of these agreements did not prohibit Turkish exporters from securing increased market shares. If anything, it suggests that Turkish exporters managed to make further inroads into the EU market as a result of favourable quota and price levels, increased certainty, and gradual liberalisation in the EU's T&C trade policy after 1986. Obviously an additional factor could be the increased competitiveness of the Turkish T&C industry. Existing evidence, however, suggests that increased competitiveness alone cannot account for the increase in market shares because the competitiveness of the Turkish T&C industry increased at lower rates in comparison to major competitors. That was why, as of 1994, T&C products were still shielded against foreign competition with nominal protection rates of 24.16% and 17.71%, respectively.[87]

Finally, Table 4.2 also suggests that the decline in Turkey's share of the EU market over the 1970s cannot be attributed to EU restrictions only. The analysis above demonstrates that EU restrictions in the 1970s were partial, product-based and time-limited. Also, Turkish exporters displaced their major competitors in certain products such as cotton yarn where Turkey's comparative advantage was high. Although the uncertainty created by *ad hoc* protectionism might have reduced the ability of Turkish exporters to make further inroads into the EU market, Turkey's declining market share in the 1970s must also be related to the adverse effect of her foreign exchange policy in that period. In an attempt to reduce the cost of importing investment and intermediate goods required by import-competing industries, the Turkish currency was kept over-valued throughout the 1970s, leading to a decline in the purchasing parity adjusted exchange rate from 10.28 in 1970 to 4.12 in 1978.[88] This meant that the Turkish currency, in terms of purchasing parity standards, appreciated by 60% and the adverse effect of this appreciation on Turkey's export to the EU market cannot be ignored.

In the light of the evidence examined above, we would argue that EU restrictions against Turkish T&C exports were less damaging than: (i) those imposed against other countries, and (ii) what could have been the case had the EU invoked Article 60 of the AP from 1976 onwards, when its T&C policy took a definite turn towards strict protectionism. Nevertheless, the introduction of these restrictions reduced the effectiveness of the EU as an anchor for policy reform in Turkey. This limited anchoring capacity, however, does not justify the Turkish argument that the EU acted in contravention to the AP and did not take into account Turkey's special status as an associated country. Although the restrictions on Turkish T&C export was in contravention of Article 24 of the AP which provided for the elimination of quantitative restrictions and the consolidation of liberalisation in favour of Turkey, they were compatible with Article 60 which provided

87 Togan and Yılmaz (1995), p. 155.

88 Krueger (1978), p. 26. The purchasing power parity adjusted exchange rate take into account the inflation rates in Turkey and seven of its major trading partners - mainly European countries. Therefore, it is a fairly reliable indicator of the competitiveness loss that the Turkish T&C industry was faced with.

for protective measures. Therefore, the argument that EU restrictions were in contravention to the AP should be considered as suspect. Second, the EU Commission has consistently tried to limit the use of Article 60 of the AP and was sometimes successful in checking the protectionist tendencies of both EU producers and EU member states. This was done with the frequently stated intention of avoiding a rupture in EU-Turkey relations. Therefore, we would make the counter-factual argument that Turkey could have secured an even better treatment for her T&C exports had she tried to strike an alliance with the Commission from the beginning - before the web of non-transparent relations between the Commission bureaucracy and EU producers had become too complex.

Conclusions

The evidence examined above suggests that the EU agreed to extend to Turkey agricultural concessions that were more generous than what the review procedure and the reciprocity principle of the AP would have implied. Therefore, it is safe to argue that the EU was capable to act as an anchor for Turkey's policy reform by providing some incentives that would reduce the cost of convergence towards European standards. Nevertheless, these incentives remained partial and were introduced in a gradual manner. In addition, some of these incentives were actually provided as side payments designed to secure a delay in Turkey's accession, which was considered as highly risky in the face of Turkey's non-credible commitment to convergence. Given these aspects, a critical assessment of the trade issues in EU-Turkey relations would suggest that the EU's limited anchoring capacity was not a result of its failure to comply with the AP (as Turkey would maintain) but because of the way in which the AP was rafted. The AP was designed not as a contract that would resolve the anchor/credibility dilemma in EU-Turkey relations but as a document that would relieve the EU of the obligation to play an effective anchoring role. As a mirror image of this, the AP was also drafted with a view to allow Turkey to avoid her obligations without facing significant sanctions - apart from the pretext she would provide to the EU to argue that Turkey's failure to comply with the AP must be considered as a significant concession in itself.

Therefore, trade issues in EU-Turkey relations must be interpreted differently than what EU-centric or Turkey-centric views would suggest. One dimension of the new interpretation is that the EU's partial anchoring capacity in this policy area must be set against Turkey's non-credible commitment to trade liberalisation. As demonstrated in section 4.1, the

Turkish government deviated from its obligations under the AP not only during the 1970s and 1980s but also in the 1990s - despite the membership application of 1987. These deviations were closely related to the type of state-society interaction in Turkey, which enabled either the state or the private agents to present partial interests as reflections of an indivisible national interest that the policy-maker must protect in the context of EU-Turkey association. Obviously, this credibility problem interacted with the EU's limited anchoring capacity and enabled the EU to justify the limited nature of the agricultural concessions as well as the *ad hoc* protection against Turkish T&C export on the grounds that the flexibility that Turkey enjoyed in the implementation of the AP was in itself a major concession. Therefore, the anchor/credibility dilemma in this policy area demonstrated that the mere existence of a formal contract such as the AP might not be a sufficient condition for either reducing the probability of policy reversals in Turkey or inducing the EU to play an effective anchoring role. In addition, the anchor/credibility dilemma in this policy area produced sub-optimal results for both Turkey and the EU, which could have been avoided had both sides been willing to conclude a more transparent contract with less scope for discretion.

A second dimension of the new interpretation is that Turkey's criticism of the EU's trade policy has been essentially misguided and self-defeating. It has been misguided because it relied on the assumption that Turkey was eligible for special treatment because of her association link with the EU. This assumption was too simplistic because it ignored the fact that any concession that the EU could grant was bound to be partial and gradual because of the need to construct intra-EU package deals that would distribute the cost of concessions among the member-sates. It also ignored the fact that the extent of the 'special treatment' that Turkey could secure would be dependent on the 'access fee' it was prepared to pay in terms of economic policy reform in both the agricultural and industrial sectors. Turkey's criticism of the EU's trade policy was also self-defeating because it overlooked the fact that the argument for special treatment was enabling the EU to argue that Turkey's failure to comply with the AP was a special treatment in its own right. Consequently, Turkey has failed not only to secure the special treatment she argued for but also to make the trade issues part of a negotiation package aimed at closer integration with the EU.

A third dimension of the new interpretation is that the EU's lenient stance in the area of T&C trade was significant enough to contribute to the increase in Turkey's share of the EU market. The significance of this finding is twofold. First, it indicates that Turkey's criticism of EU protectionism should not be taken at face value. Rather, it should also be considered in the light of Turkey's failure to converge towards EU standards by failing to comply with the AP and protecting her T&C industry through non-transparent measures such as subsidise and tax rebates. Second, this finding indicates that the existing arrangements regulating EU-Turkey trade, despite their shortcomings, could provide Turkish exporters with the opportunity to make inroads into the EU market if the sectors involved were competitive. This possibility is confirmed not only by the evidence on the export performance of the T&C sector but also by the failure of the agricultural sector to make inroads into the EU market despite the fact that Turkey had obtained almost tariff-free access in 1980. Although quantitative and seasonal restrictions imposed on Turkish export of agricultural products have affected the export performance of this sector, the other factor at work has been the structural weaknesses of Turkish agriculture which reduced its competitiveness. It was due to this weakness that the share of agriculture (including the agro-industry) in Turkey's export has declined from 72.2% in 1978 to 25.31% in 1989. In retrospect, this evidence suggests that Turkey's emphasis on generalised preferences over the 1970s was a misguided strategy that was bound to fail in terms of improving Turkey's trade balance with the EU.

5 The Anchor/Credibility Dilemma and Free Movement

Unlike movement of goods where EU competence is exclusive, movement of people is regulated by the EU and the member states. While intra-EU free movement is regulated by EU legislation, movement of people from outside the EU is subject to national legislations. In addition, policy-making in the area of intra-EU movement of people is generally integrationist and the policy stance is liberal/inclusionist. The integrative nature of the policy-making can be seen in the delegation of competence to the EU under Articles 48-51 of the Treaty of Rome, the extension of the qualified majority voting to intra-EU free movement of workers in the Single European Act (SEA), and the greater role given to the European Parliament (EP) after the Treaty on European Union (TEU). The liberal/inclusionist stance of the policy can be seen in provisions concerning equal access to the labour market, equal treatment, and participation in local and European elections. On the other hand, extra-EU immigration is still subject to national legislation and the stance of the policy in this area is exclusionist. Since 1973, the Commission's attempts to establish implied competence have failed and the convergence among national policies has been towards exclusion.

Explanations for this anomaly tend to focus on state sovereignty. It is argued that the state's ability to decide on who is 'national' and what range of privileges are associated with nationality is a critical power that derives from state sovereignty. Writing back in 1905, Oppenheim argued that 'Just as a state is competent to refuse admittance to a foreigner, so it is ... competent to expel at any moment a foreigner who has been admitted into its territory.'[1] This is by no means a view held only by a past generation of international lawyers. As recently as 1966, H. Kelsen argued that '... every sovereign nation had the power to admit aliens only in such cases and upon such conditions as it might see fit to prescribe, and to expel them at any time and for any reason.'[2] Similarly, a realist/neo-realist approach to international relations would argue that international regulatory frameworks

1 Oppenheim (1905), p. 378.

2 Kelsen (1966), p. 366; quoted in Plender (1988), p. 1.

dealing with immigration issues will be difficult to establish as states tend to regulate international migration in accordance with their national interests.[3]

Similar arguments can be seen in the writings of what may be described as the critical school in social sciences. Although scholars in this tradition are aware of the xenophobic societal tendencies underpinning government policies, they concentrate their attention mainly on how political elite try to manipulate certain cultural or political tendencies in order to exclude non-nationals. According to Pieterse, such attempts were evident in many cases, including Europe's experience with Nazism and fascism.[4] Webber, on the other hand, argues that developments in the European migration policy reflect a move from 'ethnocentric' to 'Eurocentric' racism. This move, according to Bunyan, is orchestrated by the political elite with a view to justify the construction of an authoritarian European state.[5]

Although these arguments could explain the intergovernmental and exclusionist aspects of the EU's immigration policy *vis-à-vis* third countries, they cannot be applied to its policy concerning intra-EU free movement. Therefore, other students of immigration suggest that sovereignty should not be taken as a fixed given. It is argued that factors affecting the state's capacity to deploy its powers must also be examined in order to explain the existence of different regimes of immigration management. For example, Hollifield points to the need for opening-up the state concept and examining the impact of the domestic regime's attributes on the discrepancy between the restrictive tones of the European immigration policy and the liberal outcomes it has generated.[6] While Heisler recognises the fact that immigration is simultaneously a domestic and international issue, Grete focuses on the exclusionist consequences of the European welfare regimes for the making of extra-EU immigration policy.[7] There are also various contributions pointing to the interaction between emerging xenophobic societal tendencies and political elite strategies aimed at marshalling political support. These strategies are described as 'racecraft' by Layton-Henry and as 'political use of xenophobia' by Thrandart.[8]

In this chapter, we attempt to capture the partially relevant aspects of these perspectives by arguing that the exercise of sovereignty is mediated through state-society interaction that generates different policy outcomes depending on the transparency/divisibility of the policy issue and the level of societal assertiveness. We argue that the ability to decide on who is national and what

---

3 Weiner (1985), pp. 441-55.

4 Pieterse (1991), pp. 3-10.

5 Webber (1991), pp. 11-17; and Bunyan (1991), pp. 19-27.

6 Hollifield (1992a and 1992b).

7 Heisler (1992) and Grete (1993).

8 Layton-Henry (1992); and Thrandart (1992).

privileges are associated with nationality makes the state both powerful and weak *vis-à-vis* its constituents. On the one hand, the state is empowered to decide on who the members of the 'nationality club' are and what kind of club services should be provided in return for loyalty. On the other hand, however, it is constrained by the club dynamic in such a way that its ability to treat the demands of the membership as partial or sectional is reduced. In other words, members of the nationality club are enabled to present their partial or sectional demands as reflections of an indivisible national interest that the state must uphold and defend against non-members.

This constellation implies that the transparency/divisibility of the policy issues will be blurred as either the state or societal forces are enabled to equate the issue of immigration with an undivided national interest. Once the transparency/divisibility of the policy issue is blurred in this manner, the stance of the policy would tend to be exclusionist and the method of international policy co-ordination would remain intergovernmental. While exclusion is implied by the need to provide services exclusive to club members only, intergovernmentalism is implied by the need to allow for discretion that the state can draw upon when faced with constituent demands that cannot be traded off with positive gains in other areas of policy co-ordination. One way out of this intergovernmentalist and exclusionist dynamic is to redefine the domain over which the 'nationality club' is based. The state may be induced to do this either because it reaches a point where the satisfaction of the demands for exclusive club services becomes very difficult or the cost of exclusion outweighs the benefits derived from loyalty maintenance due, for example, to rampant xenophobia that strains relations with third countries. To the extent that the 'nationality club' is regionalised to include a certain number of sub-clubs, the issue of immigration may acquire a certain degree of transparency/divisibility as the larger club leads to approximation of the returns on loyalty and thereby reduces the attractiveness of loyalty shifts. Under this condition, policy integration among a certain number of states becomes a desirable method of dampening societal assertiveness and an inclusionist policy stance becomes feasible as the ability of the nationals to equate immigration with an undivided national interest is reduced.

When applied to EU policy-making, this perspective enables us not only to explain the contrast between intra-EU and extra-EU immigration policies, but also to anticipate a limited EU anchoring capacity in the context of the EU-Turkey association. The contrast between intra-EU and extra-EU movement of people can be explained by the way in which the concept of nationality is invoked. The mixed-scanning type of governance in EU member-sates have enabled the policy-makers to invoke the concept of nationality in a way that enhances the transparency/divisibility of the intra-EU movement of people. This is done by reciprocal recognition of nationality and, thereby, redefining the domain where privileges associated with one's nationality can be enjoyed. The shortcoming of the sovereignty thesis outlined above is to suggest that this necessarily implies a dilution of sovereignty. As the following paragraphs will demonstrate, however, this is not necessarily the case. Although EU member states may have to compromise their sovereignty by sharing it, they can also enhance it by increasing their capacity to regulate the intra-EU movement of people at lower costs and check xenophobic tendencies.

Due to high levels of disparity between EU member states and Turkey in terms of employment opportunities, wage levels, and democratisation, such a redefinition of the 'nationality domain' is highly difficult if not impossible. Therefore, free movement between the EU and Turkey could not be introduced despite the fact that Article 36 of the AP contained explicit provisions to that effect. The solution to this problem requires the satisfaction of two conditions. On the one hand, Turkey must approximate its standards towards the EU to narrow the gap between the 'push' and 'pull' factors that affect the level of outmigration from Turkey. On the other hand, however, the EU must be prepared to act as an effective anchor to the policy reform in Turkey by absorbing part of the adjustment costs. Evidence presented below suggests that these conditions have not been met. Consequently, the anchor/credibility dilemma in this area has been more pronounced compared to the area of trade policy examined in chapter 4 - making the issue of free movement the most contentious issue in EU-Turkey relations until 1986.

To elucidate these arguments, section 5.1 examines the way in which issue transparency/divisibility has been effective in generating the contrast between EU policies on intra-EU free movement and extra-EU immigration. This section will demonstrate that the redefinition of the nationality domain in order to create a 'European club' has enabled the EU and its member states to establish a integrationist and inclusionist intra-EU regime on the one hand, and an intergovernmental and exclusionist extra-EU regime on the other. Because intra-EU free movement is based on reciprocal recognition of member state nationalities, policy co-ordination in this area ceased to be a zero-sum-game. However, the creation of European 'nationality domain' has necessarily led to the exclusion of non-EU nationals against whom this domain is defined. Section 5.2 builds on this analysis to examine the unfolding of the anchor/credibility dilemma in the area of free movement, where the limited anchoring capacity of the EU has been the critical factor. Here, we will demonstrate that the EU's anchoring capacity had to remain highly limited as the club mentality implied by the intra-EU regime of free movement has reduced the scope for concessions to Turkish immigrants considerably. It is true that this anchoring problem has been exacerbated by the divergence between the strength of the push factors that induced out-migration from Turkey and the weakness of the pull factors that reduced the demand for labour in the EU. Nevertheless, the perceived risk of Turkish immigration and the threat that this is expected to pose to the privileges associated with the membership of the European club are essentially related to the way in which intra-EU free movement has required and generated the exclusion of third country nationals - whether Turkish or not.

5.1 Intra-EU Freedom of Movement: Inclusion *vs.* Exclusion and the EU's Anchoring Capacity

The Treaty of Rome provides for intra-EU free movement with the following rights: (i) the right to accept offers of employment, (ii) the right to move freely for the purpose of securing employment, (iii) the right to remain in a member state for the purposes of performing a paid work, and (iv) the right to remain in a member state after having been employed there. Eligibility to benefit from these rights appears to be dependent on whether or not the European constituent is a *worker* of a member state. Obviously, the concept of 'worker' was more inclusive than that of 'national' given the larger number of foreign workers recruited by the member states since early 1960s. Therefore, a 'nationality principle' was quickly introduced through secondary legislations in order to limit the right to free movement only to the nationals of the member states.[9] The first step in this direction was Regulation No. 15/61 of the Council, the French text of which used the term *ressortissant d'un Etat membre* - implying that the 'worker' must be a 'national' of a member state.[10] Regulations 38/64 and 1612/68 adhered to the same interpretation and national courts began to throw their support behind it.[11] Consequently, by the time the free movement of workers was established in 1968, it became clear that the right to free movement would be granted to EU nationals only, excluding third country workers residing in a member state. In addition, the nationality principle enabled the member states to minimise the cost of policy integration regarding intra-EU free movement, and to avoid policy co-ordination with respect to extra-EU immigration.

As the gradual transition toward intra-EU free movement was completed in 1968, Regulation 1612/68 stated that 'Any national of a member state, ..., would have the right to take up' employment and 'to pursue such activity within the territory of another member state...' This acceptance of the nationality

9 See Goodwin-Gill (1978), p. 172; and Bohning (1973), p. 81.

10 *Journal Officiel des Communautés Européennes*, no. 57, 26.9.961, p. 1075. See also, Dummett and Nicol (1990), p. 9.

11 For Regulations 38/64 and 1612/68, respectively, see *Journal Officiel des Communautés Européennes*, no. 62, 17.4.1964, p. 965; and *Official Journal of the EC*, no. L257, 19.10. 1968, p. 1.

principle as the basis for eligibility to move within the EU led to the creation of 'insiders' and 'outsiders'. A clear indication of this can be seen in Article 3(2) of the Regulation, which stated that national legislation restricting access to the national labour market may remain in force against non-EU nationals, but can no longer be applicable to EU nationals. As a result, nationals of EU member states were spared not only from pre-employment restrictions such as quotas, medical checks, possession of work permits, restrictions to employment type, etc., but also from post-employment restrictions applicable to occupational mobility, security of employment, union membership, etc. Under these conditions, non-EU nationals faced double discrimination: they were to compete on an unequal footing under given labour market conditions and they were the ones who would be denied access should these conditions deteriorate - as Article 16(2) of Regulation 1612/68 confirmed. According to this Article, vacancies would be offered to non-EU nationals only if they could not be filled by EU nationals. Finally, the principles of nationality and reciprocal recognition were complemented by the principle of equal treatment. Article 1 of the Regulation stated that EU nationals would be subject to the employment legislation of the member state where they are employed and enjoy the same priority as the nationals of that state.

The Commission described this arrangement as a step towards the emergence of 'an incipient form of European Citizenship'.[12] It is true that the redefinition of the nationality domain has put an end to the strict correspondence between the territory of a member state and the territory over which its nationals can enjoy rights that derive from their nationality. Therefore, and irrespective of how limited the nationality-based rights that can be enjoyed outside one's country are, the reciprocal recognition of nationality as a basis for intra-EU free movement can be seen as a step towards breaking the link between state territory and citizenship rights. Under this new form of citizenship, the regulation of citizenship rights (which concern mainly employment rights in this context) would tend to be a transparent/divisible policy issue. This is because the ability of the member states to link the policy decisions with a territorially-defined national interest declines and the nationals are forced to dampen their claims to priority *vis-à-vis* other EU nationals. Therefore, the delegation of competence to the EU in the area of intra-EU free movement was both feasible and desirable for the member states.

Nevertheless, the fact that the enjoyment of rights outside one's country was still derived from his/her status as a national of a member state meant that nationals of non-EU countries would necessarily be excluded from these rights. Therefore, and contrary to what some students of migration would argue, the

---

12 *Bulletin of the EC*, no. 11/68, November 1968, pp. 5-6.

foundation of 'fortress Europe' was laid down in 1968 and not in 1992 when the Single Market was established.[13] The Single Market has only exacerbated the divide between the insiders and outsiders as the rights granted to the former were extended to cover all individuals and the territorial barriers to other forms of free movement were reduced. In other words, the more intra-EU freedom of movement became consolidated, the more the exclusion of non-EU national became more obvious. Under these conditions, the regulation of extra-EU immigration became an increasingly non-transparent/non-divisible policy issue as member state governments played the 'immigration card' for electoral purposes and EU nationals emerged as a veto group whose demands for nationality-based privileges could not be ignored. Again, that is why EU policy in this area has remained exclusionist and the policy-making process has been intergovernmental with little competence granted to EU institutions, including the Commission, the Parliament and the European Court of Justice.

Having established that 'fortress Europe' was actually established in 1968 on the basis of nationality, reciprocal recognition and equal treatment, we now examine the implications of this arrangement for the making of EU policy on intra-EU free movement. First, we discuss the way in which free movement has actually stabilised intra-EU migratory flows as the latter becomes a function of demand for labour in the country of destination rather than the supply of labour in the country of origin. Second, we examine the indicators of the way in which intra-EU free movement has induced EU nationals to define their 'insider' status against non-EU nationals. Finally, we demonstrate that the nationality and equal treatment principles have enabled the member states to avoid policy integration in the area of extra-EU immigration and maintain an exclusionist stance against non-EU nationals. Although these implications are inter-related, they are treated separately to provide an easy-to-follow account - with references to their inter-connectedness being made where relevant and necessary.

The major implication of the equal treatment principle was to make employment-related movement between EU countries dependent on the demand for labour in the country of destination. There might be incentives for workers to move from an EU member state with low wages and social protection and/or high unemployment, but potential emigrants would find it highly difficult to do so unless there is a shortage of labour in the country of destination. First of all, the principle of equal treatment reduces the scope for competitive wage bidding. Second, under the condition of equal treatment, recruitment decisions of the employers would tend to be biased in favour of the national labour force due to factors such as compatible training, cultural compatibility, lack of language

13 On the association between 'fortress Europe' and the Single Market, see Pieterse (1991), p. 5.

barriers, etc. Third, even if emigrant workers do tend to accept lower wages to price out the national workers, employers have to also take into account the likely reactions from national trades unions, governments, and EU institutions. [14] Finally, the 'menu costs' associated with the recruitment of other EU nationals are in addition to and not a substitute for the cost of recruiting national workers as vacancies must be advertised both nationally and EU-wide. Therefore, the principle of equal treatment has made the intra-EU movement of labour a function of the demand for labour in the country of destination and not the supply of labour in the country of origin.

As intra-EU free movement became a function of the demand for labour in the country of destination, migratory flows between member states were stabilised and made easier to manage. For example, following the establishment of the right for free movement in 1968, there was no unexpected or large-scale increase in the number of Italian workers who, until the early 1970s, had constituted the largest migrant community within the EU. The trend towards stabilisation is also evident when we look at the figures for intra-EU migration in general. EU nationals moving within the Union over the 1960s and 1970s have increased at lower rates compared to third country nationals entering the European Union. This was in spite of the protectionist policies introduced by almost all member states against third country nationals from 1973 onwards.

More recent accessions have also been accompanied by similar results. For example, the number of Greek nationals (the second largest source of migrant labour in the EU) seeking employment in other EU member sates did not increase after January 1989 when they became entitled to free movement. It is worth noting that this result was not due to high levels of performance in the Greek economy - which can be expected to reduce the push factor - but due to deficient demand in countries of destination, whose unemployment rates were on the increase. Nor did the number of Portuguese or Spanish migrants increase as they became entitled to free movement in 1992. Consequently, and in spite of the increasingly restrictive policies imposed on immigration from third countries, the number of EU nationals moving in the EU is still lower than that of immigrants from third countries. The proportion of EU nationals to total number of migrants in the EU has remained at 39.2% when all residents (workers and their families) are taken into account and at 43.7% when only workers are considered.[15]

As a result, labour market disturbances likely to be caused by sudden surges in intra-EU migratory flows were avoided and the risk of xenophobic backlash was reduced. By relegating the solution of the problems associated with intra-EU

---

14 Attempts during the mid-1990s by employers to employ British workers at lower wages in Belgium have led to strong reactions from all of these actors.

15 International Labour Organisation (1990), pp. 4, 31-32.

movement of workers to the market, EU member states were no longer faced with excessive pressure from their own nationals to protect 'national' jobs by restricting the movement of other EU nationals. Also, the scope for free movement on the basis of the demand for labour in countries of destination have been limited but significant enough to make the EU-wide nationality domain relevant at least for the upper end of the labour market where mobility is high due to lower adjustment and compatibility costs. The combination of these factors has enhanced the transparency/divisibility of intra-EU free movement. Therefore, policy integration on the basis of quantifiable and controllable costs/benefits has proved feasible and the stance of the policy tended to be inclusionist. This outcome, however, was at the expense of non-EU nationals (those already residing in the EU as well as potential immigrants) for two reasons: (i) the 'insider' identity fostered by the EU-wide nationality domain led to the exclusion of non-EU nationals, against whom the European nationality club was defined; and (ii) the reciprocal recognition of member state nationalities as a criteria for eligibility to free movement reduced the need for integrating national immigration policies *vis-à-vis* third countries.

As intra-EU movement of workers was stabilised, the increase in European unemployment led to the emergence of new attitudes among EU nationals. A *Eurobarometer* survey in 1988 reported that the majority of the respondents, when asked to identify people of other nationalities, tended to single out third country nationals rather than nationals of EU member states residing in their countries. The survey also found out that the number of third country nationals in a member state was a good predictor of its nationals' tendency to equate them with 'otherness'.[16] Results obtained from other surveys also indicated that EU nationals tend to be in favour of restricting the rights of non-EU immigrants as high levels of unemployment persisted. Responses to a question on whether the rights of immigrants should be restricted or extended showed that those in favour of restriction increased from 18% to 33% while the proportion of those in favour of extension declined from 30% to 19% between 1988 and 1991.[17] Replies to another question on how the respondents felt about the presence of non-EU nationals reflected a similar tendency: those who think that there are too many non-EU nationals increased from 37% to 50% over the same period. Also, in contrast to the high levels of support for a common foreign policy (69% according to a survey in 1991), the support for EU competence in the area of third country immigration was only 39%. This compares poorly with the 51%

---

16 *Eurobarometer,* November 1989, p. 3.

17 *Eurobarometer (Special issue)*, November 1989, p. 7; and no. 35, June 1991, p. A3.

who were in favour of either purely national or intergovernmental policy-making with respect to third country immigration.[18]

What is observed here is similar to the attitudes of club members. In a club environment, club members demand exclusion of non-members from the services supplied by the club. Such attitudes are generated by the perception that returns on club membership are an increasing function of excluding non-members. In the context of intra-EU free movement club, EU nationals tend to discount the cost of exclusion and expect their governments to increase the restrictions against non-EU nationals. As managers of the club, national governments area aware of the fact that exclusion is not costless. Nevertheless, they respond to the demands of the nationals in an accommodating manner because the priority of the insiders is the principle on which the club is based. The result of this state-society interaction is the blurring of the transparency/divisibility of the immigration issue. Therefore, it is not surprising to observe that EU member states have pursued an increasingly restrictive policy against non-EU nationals and insisted on an intergovernmental mode of policy co-ordination.

The link between restricting extra-EU immigration and the realisation of intra-EU free movement can be seen in a large number of EU documents prepared by the Commission and the Council. For example, one of the initial Commission communications to the Council, forwarded in 1978, stated that illegal employment of non-EU labour was prejudicial to the employment of all workers and therefore it constituted an obstacle to the achievement of intra-EU free movement.[19] In 1979, the Commission tried to convince the Council about the need for policy co-ordination *vis-à-vis* non-EU nationals on the grounds that national policy autonomy must be weighed against the obligation to ensure that EU nationals could exercise their rights to have priority in the access to the labour market.[20] Also, in its Resolution of 9 February 1976, the Council stated that it was important to '… strengthen co-operation between member states in the campaign against illegal immigration of workers who are nationals of third countries…'[21] In 1980, the Council's determination to exclude non-EU nationals became even more pronounced. It was of the opinion that the EU labour market should be integrated further, but only by '… taking into account the employment priority to be afforded to nationals of member states and of the need to contain access to the Community labour market from third countries…'[22]

---

18 *Eurobarometer*, no. 34, December 1990, p. A59; no. 35, June 1991, p. 155; and no. 36, December 1991, p. A36.

19 Commission of the EC (1978), Annex, pp. 1-2

20 Commission of the EC (1979b), p. 3

21 *Bulletin of the EC*, Supplement 3/76, March 1976, p. 8.

22 *Official Journal of the EC*, no. C168, 8.7.1980), p. 4.

That these exclusionist tendencies were not limited to the 1970s and early 1980s can be seen in further policy documents and developments that characterised the late 1980s and 1990s too. [23] The Schengen Agreement and the Implementing Convention were signed in 1985 and 1990, respectively. Schengen was an arrangement outside the EU framework, but its impact on the EU's immigration policy was so significant that it '... proved to be the very realisation' of the member states' objective of finding an intergovernmental method for control third country immigration.[24] In 1986, the London Summit of the European Council instructed the interior ministers to explore ways of harmonising the member states' visa policy and 'intensify cooperation on measures to prevent illegal immigration.'[25] The result was the establishment of the intergovernmental *ad hoc Immigration* group and the gradual harmonisation of national visa policies that intensified the exclusionist stance of the immigration policy across the EU. The most detrimental consequence of these developments for extra-EU immigrants was the further blurring of the transparency/divisibility of the immigration issue by linking it with terrorism and drug trafficking.

Resistance by member states to EU competence in the area of extra-EU immigration was equally clear and durable. When EU member states began to suspend recruitment of foreign workers unilaterally in 1973, the Commission argued for the co-ordination of national immigration policies *vis-à-vis* third country immigration.[26] The Council responded by adopting a resolution on 21 January 1974, which made it clear that the member-sates were determined to treat third country immigration as a matter of national rather than EU policy-making. Following calls from the EP in 1974 for a Migrant Workers' Charter,[27] the Commission submitted a new communication in 1976. Aware of the Council's reluctance, the Commission tried to secure some relaxation in the opposition to an integrated policy by emphasising the need for restricting further flows of non-EU nationals in order to enable EU nationals to enjoy the benefits associated with the priority principle of free movement.[28] Although the EP Committee on Social Affairs and Employment criticised the Commission's communication for being non-committal towards non-EU nationals,[29] the Council adopted an even more exclusionist stance and issued the Directive of 28

23 For a more detailed account of the post-1985 period, see Ugur (1995).
24 Schutte (1991), p. 568. See also, Pastore (1992).
25 *Agence Europe*, 7.12.1986, p. 5.
26 *Bulletin of the EC*, no. 2/74, February 1974, pp. 18-36
27 *Official Journal of the EC*, no. C76, 3.7.1974, pp. 25-26.
28 *Bulletin of the EC*, Supplement 3/76, March 1976, p. 21.
29 *Official Journal of the EC - Debates of the EP*, no. 194, September 1974, pp. 177-81.

June 1977 on the education of migrant workers' children, which covered only EU the children of EU nationals.[30]

A similar resistance to EU competence in the area of extra-EU immigration was observed once more following the Commission proposal of 1978, which called for the approximation of member state legislation on illegal immigration. Although the Commission was supported by the EP, its communication did not even secure a response from the Council. Therefore, it had to submit a new communication in March 1979. It invited the Council to engage in exchange of views with the Commission and to enable the latter to 'organise, within the existing Community institutions, ..., consultation with and between member states.'[31] When asked about its opinion, the Economic and Social Committee (ESC) approved the Commission's communication in October of the same year.[32] The Council responded to this communication on 22 November 1979 by adopting a Resolution calling for consultation on matters concerning (i) priority of EU nationals and (ii) immigrant labour from third countries in the context of the Union's external relations.[33] Although this move seemed to be in line with the Commission's requests, in reality it constituted a fatal blow to the latter's attempts at establishing competence in this area. The minutes of the Council meeting contained an explicit indication of why this was the case. According to the Council, the aim of the consultation was '... to facilitate the adoption *not of Community instruments, but of a common attitude of the member states.*[34]

It must be indicated here that the Commission's strategy was, in fact, self-defeating. By making the intra-EU free movement and the priority of EU nationals conditional on restrictions to extra-EU immigration, the Commission exacerbated the non-transparency/non-divisibility of the extra-EU immigration and enhanced the ability of the member states or their nationals to act as veto groups against policy integration. In addition, it made the extra-EU immigration issue a 'hot potato' reflecting a political rather than a technical logic needed to identify and solve important problems - as it had to confess later in a 1990 report.[35] Of course, the Commission also pointed to the externalities associated with uncoordinated national policies. This argument, however, was also problematic for two reasons. First, the externality risk was minimised as a result of the nationality principle on which intra-EU free movement was based. As long as eligibility to free movement was conditional on the nationality of a member state, the risk of migration deflection within the EU was reduced. In other words,

30 *Official Journal of the EC - Debates of the EP*, no. 220, September 1977, p. 170.
31 Commission of the EC (1979), 23 March 1979.
32 *Bulletin of the EC*, no. 10/79, October 1979, p. 112.
33 *Bulletin of the EC*, no. 11/79, November 1979, p. 45.
34 Mancini (1988), p. 23. (Emphasis added).
35 Quoted in Matheson (1991), p. 56.

free movement of non-EU nationals from relatively less to relatively more protectionist member states was excluded and the spill-over effects of uncoordinated policies were reduced. Second, even if externalities do arise, they could be internalised by essentially intergovernmental policy co-ordination and, therefore, the argument for policy integration with supranational inputs could be criticised easily as bureaucratic encroachment. Such criticism would be more influential in terms of deterring the Commission from new initiatives when the transparency/divisibility of the issues at hand is blurred - as was the case with third country immigration.

Therefore, it was not surprising to observe a period of silence on the Commission's part until 1985, when it came forward with two new initiatives. In the first, it indicated the areas on which consultations should be held with respect to extra-EU immigration. It also asked the Council to recognise the need for cooperation and consultation between member states and the Commission within the EU framework.[36] Although these demands were beyond what the Council were prepared to accept, the latter, paradoxically, recognised the desirability of promoting cooperation and consultation and noted the Commission's intention for drawing up an appropriate procedure to that end.[37]

The paradox, however, disappeared when the Commission took the next step and adopted a Decision to overcome the inertia that had lasted for more than a decade. According to Article 1, the member states must give the Commission advance information on all draft measures and agreements that they intended to conclude with respect to extra-EU immigration. Article 2, on the other hand, provided for consultation meetings following a request by the Commission itself or by a member state. Article 3 of the Decision stated that the consultation procedure was aimed to ensure that draft measures and agreements mentioned in Article 1 were in conformity with EU policies, particularly those concerning the EU labour market.[38] This Decision proved to be the last straw that broke the camel's back: five member states, Denmark, France, Germany, the Netherlands and the United Kingdom challenged the Decision in the Court of Justice.

The Court ruled that the Decision was void, because it extended the scope of communication and consultation procedure to cover matters (such as cultural integration of workers from non-member states and their families) which were beyond the provisions of Article 118 of the Treaty of Rome providing for cooperation in the social field. Undoubtedly, the Court's ruling dealt a major blow to the Commission attempts to establish implied competence. More importantly, however, the Court of Justice - the institution which was renowned

36 Commission of the EC, (1985a).

37 *Official Journal of the EC*, no. C186, 26.7.1985, p. 4; Mancini (1988), p. 25.

38 *Official Journal of the EC*, no. L217, 14.8.1985, pp. 25-26.

for the implied competence it had established in the areas of commercial and competition policies - felt it necessary to refrain from establishing such a competence in the area of immigration, which, in view of the Advocate General, was both inescapable and conceded by the Council various times.[39]

Mancini suggested that the main reason for member states' resistance to EU competence was related to the Single Market. The Declaration on Articles 13-19 of the Single European Act (SEA), whilst confirming the right of the member states to take necessary measures for controlling immigration and combating terrorism, it left open the framework within which such measures would be taken. That was why, according to Mancini, the member states decided to act in a pro-active manner and took the opportunity provided by the SEA to 'bring things out into the open' and secure themselves against Commission incursions.[40] In other words, the member states became convinced about the need for policy co-ordination in view of the SEA which extended the right to free movement to include not only workers but also ordinary citizens and service providers. This extension was likely to increase the risk of externalities and required a higher level of policy co-ordination. The non-transparency/non-divisibility injected into the issue of extra-EU immigration, however, made it incompatible with an integrative procedure. As Mancini has observed, there were significant 'political and public policy ramifications' that an integrated policy towards third country immigration would entail.[41]

The Court's decision and the subsequent dominance of intergovernmentalism have inevitably undermined the capacity of the Commission to play an effective role. The Commission participated in the meetings of the *ad hoc Immigration* group, but without the right for policy initiation. Its input was mostly advisory on the implications of harmonised policies for the EU's relations with third countries, especially for those linked to the EU with association agreements. Although its participation in those meetings enabled it to have access to valuable information, this was a far cry away from the role that it had been pushing for until 1985. Also, this downgraded role caused a deterioration in the Commission's relations with the Parliament. Because of its tacit agreement to the secrecy surrounding the intergovernmental procedures, it led some MEPs to argue that it '... plays double towards the Parliament and there are constant doubts as to whether it was looking after the Community's interests.'[42]

---

[39] According to Simmonds (1988), p. 200, 'The belated attention paid in recent years to the position of migrants from non-member countries received a major setback with this judgement - and from an unexpected source.'

[40] Mancini (1988) . Mancini developed this argument in his capacity as the Advocate General of the European Court of Justice.

[41] Mancini (1988), p. 27.

[42] van Outrive (1992).

It is important to point out that the TEU has, to some extent, tried to introduce coherence to the intergovernmentalist tendencies examined above. First of all, the TEU provided the Commission with a shared right of initiative that would enable it to submit proposals on some aspects of extra-EU immigration such as asylum and external border crossing. Second, Article K3 of the TEU stipulated that the ECJ might have jurisdiction with respect to the interpretation of the immigration-related conventions adopted by the Council. Although these provisions can be seen as an attempt to check the bias towards intergovernmentalism, the scope for optimism remains limited. The Council could adopt 'conventions and measures' related to extra-EU immigration on the basis of a two-thirds majority, but its decision would only serve as a *recommendation* to member states who then might adopt it 'in accordance with their constitutional requirements.' In addition, ECJ jurisdiction was provided for in Article K3(c), but this was made conditional on whether or not the 'conventions and measures' adopted by the Council have provided for such jurisdiction.[43] These new provisions imply that the intergovernmental nature of the policy-making in this area would continue as the member states are able to determine whether Council recommendations should be incorporated into the national legislation and whether the ECJ should have jurisdiction over the recommendations adopted by the Council.

Two Council recommendations adopted under the TEU confirm not only the intergovernmentalist nature of the policy-making but also the tightening of the exclusionist policy stance. The recommendation on harmonising the methods of combating illegal employment introduces identity checks, residence permit controls, checks by providers of welfare services, etc. In addition, it aims to establish a reporting system whereby central and local authorities dispensing benefits to foreign nationals inform the 'competent authorities' of any illegal claimants. Even 'marriages of convenience' did not escape the attention of the Council: authorities issuing residence permits should pay attention to the risk of such arrangements before granting a residence permit.[44] Another recommendation adopted on 27 September 1996 resolves an old-standing dispute between the UK and the rest of the member states. The UK government has always been against imposing criminal or administrative penalties on employers hiring foreign nationals illegally on the grounds that this arrangement was not compatible with the national practice. With the 1996 recommendation, work place checks and penalties become part of the UK legislation. In addition, all member-sates are expected to co-ordinate their activities, including joint

---

43 See Council of the EC (1992), pp. 131-33.

44 *Official Journal of the EC*, no. C5/1, 10.1.1996, pp. 1-3.

operations in particular sectors or regions where illegal employment of foreign nationals is suspected.[45]

The consolation for the Commission in the face of this intergovernmentalist trend was the lessons it derived with respect to linkage politics. Jacques Delors' failure in May 1992 to overcome British objections to the Commission's interpretation of Article 8(A) on the removal of internal border controls proved to be the turning point in this process. From then onwards, the Commission began to adopt the view that linkage politics would not be effective in forcing the member states to adopt an integrated policy as '... public attitudes on immigration are based on feelings rather than facts.' As a result, the Commission concluded that the way forward would be to review national legislations with a view to '... remove conditions of nationality for the exercise of rights or granting of benefits which are not justified by objective conditions.'[46] In other words, the Commission had to accept that the factor which enabled the member states to resist policy integration was the non-transparency/non-divisibility of the extra-EU immigration, which was exacerbated by the nationality principle of the intra-EU freedom of movement. Whether or not this new approach would be developed further and lead to different outcomes remains to be seen.

Having examined the inclusion/exclusion dichotomy characterising the EU's policy on intra-EU and extra-EU movement of people, we conclude this section by general observations on the EU's ability to act as an anchor. The analysis above suggests that the EU's anchoring capacity in the area of extra-EU movement of people would be highly limited for two reasons. The first relates to the dynamics unleashed by the creation of a European nationality domain based on reciprocal recognition of nationality. As a result of this club environment, EU nationals are both induced and enabled to argue for and secure the exclusion of non-members, i.e., non-EU nationals. The manifestation of this type of state-society interaction in EU policy outcomes has been in the form of emphasising the need to adopt co-ordinated policies that restrict extra-EU immigration as a pre-requisite for the consolidation of the intra-EU freedom of movement. The irony here is that the more the EU and its member states try to satisfy the demands of the club insiders, the more costly it becomes to exclude non-members and therefore the less is the supply of club services. This, in turn, generates further insider demands for exclusion of non-nationals that the EU and its member states find it even more difficult to satisfy. Given this vicious circle, the ability of the EU to extend concessions in this area as a means of inducing third countries to undertake policy reform and converge towards EU standards would necessarily remain limited.

---

45 *Official Journal of the EC*, no. C304, 14.10.96, pp. 1-2.

46 Commission of the EC (1994), pp. 4 and 43.

Another factor constraining the EU's anchoring capacity is the intergovernmental nature of policy co-ordination in the area of extra-EU immigration. As indicated in the preceding analysis, the nationality criteria has excluded non-EU nationals from free movement and has reduced the risk of spill-over effects likely to arise out of different national immigration regimes. Under this condition, the member states have been able to resist Commission and EP initiatives aimed at securing implied competence in the area of extra-EU immigration. The resulting intergovernmental co-ordination has reduced the EU's anchoring capacity further because of the tendency towards: (i) lowest-common-denominator outcomes of intergovernmentalism; and (ii) sub-optimal level of legislation in the absence of a policy initiator such as the Commission.

Section 5.2 below will examine the specific case of the EU-Turkey association with a view to ascertain the extent to which these dynamics have been at work. Specifically, it will investigate whether the EU has been capable of extending concessions in the area of free movement in order to make the anchor link attractive for Turkey. The analysis below will differentiate between two issues in the free movement between Turkey and the EU: the gradual introduction of free movement as envisaged in the AP, and the improvement of the rights of Turkish workers and their families already residing in EU member states. This distinction is based on the transparency/divisibility of these issues, which tends to be low in the case of the former due to the insider-outsider dynamic explained above, and relatively high in the case of the latter as the consequences of policy decisions can be quantified and/or divided between the member states.

5.2 The Anchor Problem in the Area of Free Movement Between the EU and Turkey

One aspect of the EU-Turkey association is the absence of an explicit commitment by Turkey to converge towards EU standards before free movement can be introduced. Neither the Association Agreement (AA) nor the AP provides for any prior convergence in this area. Article 12 of the AA states that the gradual introduction of free movement between Turkey and the EU will be guided by Articles 48, 49 and 51 of the Treaty of Rome, i.e., by the principles of nationality and equal treatment. Article 36 of the AP reiterates this principle and provides for the gradual establishment of free movement by 1986. Although this gradual process is to be managed by the decisions of the Association Council (AC), there is no provision indicating the criteria that the latter would apply to sanction the transition from one stage to the other. Therefore, it is impossible to relate the EU's performance in this area to the credibility Turkey's policy commitments. In other words, any limitation to the EU's anchoring capacity as defined in this book must be analysed in the light of factors internal to the EU.

The second aspect to be pointed out is that provisions concerning the removal of restrictions on free movement are general, whilst those concerning the rights of Turkish immigrants residing in a member state are specific. For free movement between Turkey and the EU, the modalities would decided by the Association Council - without specific guidance apart from the provisions of the Treaty of Rome. The improvement of rights, however, is regulated by three specific mechanisms: equal treatment of Turkish workers with respect to working and remuneration conditions prevailing in the member state where they are employed; introduction of social security measures for Turkish workers and their families; and arrangements for the aggregation of insurance premia as well as working periods in the case of movement between member states. Given this contrast, one cannot but suspect that the EU may well have left the arrangement for free movement vague to cover itself against unpredictable risks. Therefore, even at this level of generality, it is possible to anticipate EU deviations from the commitment to free movement on the grounds that the AC (which decides by unanimity) could not agree on specific modalities of the transition.

Having presented these stylised facts, we will now examine the unfolding of the events in more details. We start by providing some figures indicating the significance of the free movement for Turkey. Table 5.1 clearly shows that six member states (EU6) were the largest market for immigrant labour from Turkey. The percentage shares of the EU6 in the annual number of workers emigrating from Turkey, was 97.5% in 1964, declined to 81.8% in 1967 due to the recession in Europe, and reached another high of 92% in 1973 - just before the unilateral suspension of recruitment by EU member states. Also, with the exception of 1967, the number of workers absorbed by EU6 each year continued to increase in terms of magnitude until 1973.

As a result, annual emigration to EU6 was nearly doubled from 65 thousand in 1964 to 124 thousand in 1973. If the trend until 1973 highlights the significance of the EU market for emigrant Turkish workers, the figures after 1973 demonstrate their vulnerability to changes in the EU demand for labour. After the first oil shock of 1973, Germany led other EU member states by unilaterally suspending foreign labour recruitment. As a result, the number of Turkish workers emigrating to EU6 in 1976 declined dramatically to less th in one-tenth of the peak number in 1973. In addition, the share of the EU6 in the annual number of emigration also declined and became insignificant by the end of 1970s. Because of Turkey's dependence on the EU market for foreign labour, the number of workers sent abroad continued to remain very low until early 1980s when Turkish workers began to move into the Middle-Eastern market which was experiencing a boom following the second increase in oil prices.

Table 5.1 Turkish workers sent to the EU and abroad through Turkish employment services

	Total sent to EU6	Total sent abroad	% share of EU6
1964	64,536	66,176	97.5
1967	7,247	8,855	81.8
1970	115,316	129,575	89.0
1973	123,712	135,820	92.0
1976	2,137	10,558	22.0
1979	1,077	23,630	4.5
1982	99	49,388	0.2
1985	74	47,353	0.16
1987	73	40,807	0.18

EU6: Belgium, Denmark, Germany, France, The Netherlands, and the UK

Source: Martin (1991), pp. 22-23.

The unilateral suspension of recruitment by EU countries led to a fall in workers' remittances against the background of a dramatic deterioration in Turkey's trade deficit. As can be seen in Table 5.2, workers' remittances were more than enough to cover the trade deficit between 1971-73. After 1973, not only did Turkey's trade deficit quadruple, but the rate of increase in workers' remittances slowed down. As a result, the remittances/trade deficit ratio declined from 135.6% between 1971-73 to 44% between 1974-76. The decline was mainly due to the suspension of recruitment by EU member states as other receiving countries were either less significant in total or did not reduce their absorption of Turkish workers to the same extent.

Obviously, the impact of labour emigration on the sending country's economic development is not limited to the balance of payments effect captured in table 5.2. Initial non-quantitative remarks in this area suggested that the overall effect is positive as emigration can be seen as a way of recovering at least part of the sunk costs incurred in educating and training the excess supply of labour which is either unemployed or under-employed in the sending country.[47] A more recent study, however, suggests that the overall impact on the growth of national output has not been significantly different from zero for a group of Southern European countries including Turkey. In fact, the overall effect for Turkey between 1961-1973 is found to be the most insignificant compared to Greece, Italy, Portugal and Spain. With respect to the partial effect on the labour market of the sending countries, the same study suggests that Turkey has been able to export only 3% of her unemployed to receiving countries in the same period.[48] Nevertheless, the deterioration in Turkey's trade deficit and the tendency of the State Planning Organisation to perceive of this deterioration as a major constraint on economic development have forced successive Turkish governments to discount other effects in favour of the balance of payments effect. In fact, as indicated in chapter 4, balance of payments considerations were the main factor that forced Turkey to demand 'revision' and 'flexibility' in the implementation of the AP until the end of 1970s.

Table 5.2 Workers remittances to Turkey, 1967-88: Average values and as percentages of trade deficit

Year	Av. remitts. (AR)*	Av. trade def. (ATD)*	AR/ATD (%)
1967-70	153.5	234.5	65.46
1971-73	798.3	588.7	135.60
1974-76	1240.0	2818.0	44.00
1977-79	1189.7	2939.0	40.48
1980-82	2233.7	3909.7	57.13
1983-85	1678.0	3319.3	50.55
1986-88	1820.3	2967.7	61.44

*: In Millions of US Dollar

Source: Martin (1991), p. 34.

Turkey's tendency to perceive of free movement as an essentially economic issue clashed head on with the emerging tendency among EU member states to discount the economic cost/benefit analysis in favour of weighing the social-

47 Kindleberger (1967), p. 69.
48 Schraubhaar (1985), pp. 16-18.

political costs of foreign labour recruitment against its likely economic benefits. It is true that the economic argument was not discarded altogether. In fact, the unilateral suspension of foreign labour recruitment was related to the increase in oil prices and the following rise in European unemployment. EU unemployment rates increased from an average rate of about 2.3% between 1964-70 to 3.0% in 1974 and 5.2% in 1978. The economic downturn, however, was by no means the most significant factor that led to the suspension of foreign labour recruitment. The Organisation for Economic Cooperation and Development (OECD) pointed to the political factors that were also at work. In its *Report on Migration* of 1974, the OECD stated that the decisions to suspend recruitment '... which may have appeared at the time to be related to the energy crisis ... are in fact the result of essentially political considerations.' According to the OECD, reports received from member countries in 1974 reflected a clear tendency to argue that the social and political drawbacks of immigration have become greater than its economic advantages. That was why labour-importing OECD members stopped recruitment before any downswing in the economic cycle was in sight.[49]

It was against this asymmetrical interpretations that Turkey raised the issue of free movement for the first time in 1975. Faced with pressure on the domestic labour market and a deteriorating trade deficit, the Turkish government stated that '... the progressive achievement of freedom of movement for workers constituted one of the basic principles of the Ankara Agreement' and demanded that the AC should initiate the transition towards free movement. This request was justified given the fact that Article 36 of the AP provided for the transition to free movement to begin in 1976. To be able to respond, the EU Council asked for a communication from the Commission upon which member states could negotiate and arrive at a common position. Although the Commission communication was submitted on 3 May 1976, the Council was unable to finalise the EU's common position before the AC meeting scheduled for the second half of July 1976. Consequently, the EU delegation was able to make only a draft statement at the Association Committee meeting of 20 July 1976.[50]

The draft statement was based on three arguments: (i) any solution to the issue could not ignore 'the very difficult situation' in the EU's labour markets; (ii) efforts must be focused on the consolidation of the *status quo* concerning the position of the existing Turkish workers; and (iii) measures must be limited to improving the access to the labour markets of the Turkish workers who are already in the EU, but only '... within the capacity of the employment markets and of social structures' of the member states.[51] This statement was a clear

49 OECD (1974), pp. 4-6.
50 EC-Turkey Association Council (1976), p. 34.
51 EC-Turkey Association Council (1976), p. 35.

indication of the member states' emerging approach to free movement. First, it confirmed the tendency among member states to focus on the socio-political implications of immigration. Second, it was in line with the exclusionist implications of the nationality principle underpinning the intra-EU freedom of movement. Finally, by signalling willingness to improve the rights of the existing migrants, it confirmed the argument in this study that the EU could assume an anchoring function only with respect to transparent/divisible issues.

On its part, Turkey responded to this draft statement on 23 July 1976 by stating that it did not contain new commitments, which should have been in accordance with Articles 48-50 of the Treaty of Rome. In other words, Turkey interpreted the EU position rightly as a move to avoid the introduction of free movement. The weakness in Turkey's argument, however, was twofold. On the one hand, it was underpinned by balance of payments difficulties rather than a coherent vision that might have enabled Turkey to take into account the fact that free movement could no longer be discussed as a legal matter and in terms of its economic implications only. On the other hand, it was made against the absence of any credible Turkish vision about the future of EU-Turkey association within which the gradual transition to free movement could be negotiated.

As a result of this wide gap between the two positions, the scheduled meeting of the AC was cancelled and a new time was fixed for 16 October 1976. Aware of the importance of the issues involved, the Council of Ministers, in its meeting on 27 July 1976 (i.e., only three days after Turkey's position was made clear), decided to send the president of the Council and the vice-president of the Commission to Turkey '... to explain and comment upon the Community's position.'[52] Results of the negotiations between the EU delegation and Turkish authorities during the visit in Early September could be detected from subsequent developments. Soon after the visit of the EU delegation, the EU reiterated the same offer mentioned above. Turkey's reaction was surprisingly moderate: she appreciated the '... difficult situation in the employment markets of the member states' and requested the 'adoption of liberalisation measures which should give Turkish workers priority over workers from third countries.'[53]

Given this moderation, the following two meetings of the Association Committee resulted in the cobbling up of the final package. The AC meeting, however, had to be postponed once more to allow for further negotiations on two issues. One concerned the duration over which the provisions of the package were to apply. This issue was resolved by Turkey's acceptance of the EU recommendation that the package should not be reviewed for four years. The other issue concerned the codification of the priority to be extended to Turkish

---

52 Council of the EC, General Secretariat (1976), p. 126.

53 EC-Turkey Association Council (1976), pp. 35-36.

migrants *vis-à-vis* other non-EU nationals. The EU was in favour of codifying its commitment as a statement rather than a formal AC decision that the European Court of Justice could invoke against the member states. Faced with Turkey's objections, however, the EU agreed to relinquish this demand at the end of the last Association Committee meeting on 14 December 1976. This compromise finally enabled the AC to meet on 20 December and to formally sign Decision 2/76, which provided for priority to Turkish workers against other third country nationals under certain conditions.[54]

For example, the preamble of the decision stated that the priority principle envisaged by the decision would be applied only if there was no '... serious danger to the standard of living and the level of employment in the various regions and branches of activity' in the member states of the EU and '... without prejudice to the application between member states of the Community provisions governing the freedom of movement.'[55] It was clear from this statement that the priority granted to Turkish immigrants could always be suspended on the grounds of surges in sectoral or regional unemployment. Also, Turkish immigrants within the EU would be excluded from the benefits that might be enjoyed by EU nationals as a result of consolidating the intra-EU freedom of movement. As if these qualifications were not strict enough, Article 2 of the decision provided that Turkish workers would be entitled to second priority subject to limitations in terms of occupational mobility. In other words, Turkish workers would be able to respond to vacancies and benefit from the priority against other non-EU nationals, only if they had been employed for at least 5 years in that member state - without taking into account the periods of sickness and involuntary unemployment. Finally, Article 6 provided that any member state can refrain from complying with the second priority principle without prior consultation in the AC.

These provisions clearly support the argument that the EU's anchoring capacity would be highly limited when policy issues are non-transparent/non-divisible. The nationality principle on which intra-EU freedom of movement was based has led to the creation of an insiders club that enabled EU nationals to act as a 'veto group' and forced the EU member states to maintain their nationality-based privileges at the expense of Turkish immigrants. Therefore, the AC decision confirmed not only the EU's deviation from the principle of free movement for Turkish workers, but also the limited nature of the concessions it could grant in a transparent/divisible area. The limited nature of the second priority was clearly designed to protect the interest of EU nationals in the labour market at the EU, national and regional levels. This was done by limiting

54 Council of the EC, General Secretariat (1976), p. 37.

55 EC-Turkey Association Council (1976), p. 94.

mobility to the member state where a worker was employed and to regions where no serious danger to 'standards of living and employment levels' was involved.

Not surprisingly, this exclusionist stance was championed by Germany which had the largest number of Turkish immigrants. Therefore, during negotiations in 1978 on the OECD aid package to Turkey, Germany asked the EU to link Turkey's demand for freezing its obligations under the AP with a freeze on the gradual introduction of free movement. This was, according to Germany, necessary to 'provide a better balance of commitments and advantages, and to take account of the situation in the labour market.'[56] Clearly, this was a call to revise the AP - just as Turkey had done in 1972. The Commission intervened and objected to the German demand, arguing that Germany's approach would have been justified under normal circumstances, but not at that particular moment when the EU was discussing exceptional aid for exceptional conditions in Turkey. The EU must wait until the negotiations on the second phase of free movement, i.e., 1980, when it will be in a more favourable position given its contribution to the OECD package and concessions in other areas - mainly trade and a new financial protocol.[57]

Indeed, Germany waited until the second review of the free movement between the EU and Turkey. In intra-EU deliberations, some member states were in favour of relaxing the restrictions on Turkish workers' free movement '... within the limits of job availability.' Germany, however, argued that this approach would be too generous and the EU, if necessary, should be prepared to re-negotiate the question of free movement.[58] Apparently, Germany was not able to secure the support of other member states and the Commission to present the revision request as a common EU position. Nevertheless, the German government ensured that its unilateral demand for revision was submitted to the Association Committee, scheduled to meet on 30 May 1980. This tactic proved effective from the EU's point view as it alerted Turkey to the seriousness of the German position. Faced with the options of either no Association Council meeting or a meeting that would secure some improvement in the rights of the Turkish workers and some agricultural concessions, Turkey opted for the latter. In the preparatory meeting of the Association Committee, the Turkish delegation stated that the Turkish government recognised the difficulty '... to introduce free movement for workers and has therefore accepted some measures to improve the present situation.'[59]

---

56 *Agence Europe*, 9.3.1979, p. 10.
57 *Agence Europe*, 9.3.1979, p. 11.
58 *Agence Europe*, 30.5.1980, p. 7.
59 *Agence Europe*, 31.5.1980, p. 9.

Following Turkey's approval of the EU's partial concessions, the Association Council met on 30 June and adopted Decision 1/80. The decision provided Turkey with some concessions in agricultural trade (see, chapter 4); 75 million Units of Account of exceptional aid; a fourth financial protocol of 600 million Units of Account; an economic and technical co-operation package; and some improvements to the rights of Turkish workers. Concessions concerning the rights of the Turkish workers were in two areas: (i) reduction in the time limit to full occupational and regional mobility within a member state from 5 to 4 years, and (ii) the provision for the right to full occupational and regional mobility for the families of the workers after 5 years of residence. Given the fact that labour recruitment had virtually stopped in 1974, the decision implied real improvements only for family members who tended to follow the workers with a time lag. Other improvements provided for in Decision 1/80 were: access of Turkish workers' children to the labour market, provided that they have completed a course of vocational training in the host country; encouragement of employment services to fill vacancies with unemployed Turkish workers on the basis of second priority; and admission of Turkish workers' children to courses of apprenticeship and vocational training.

Although social security issues were also part of the negotiations in the run up to the AC meeting of 30 June, no agreement could be reached by then. Therefore, the matter had to be dealt with in a later meeting in September. Decision 3/80 of the AC provided for equal treatment of Turkish workers in the area of social security, including sickness, maternity, invalidity, unemployment, family and industrial injury benefits, and old-age pensions. One aspect of these provisions is that entitlement to most of these benefits is derived from compulsory insurance and not residence. The aim here is to exclude illegal workers and encourage return to Turkey after retirement or disability. Another concerns the aggregation of insurance premia in cases of movement between member states or between the host country and Turkey. Given these aspects, this Decision can be seen as a clear and substantial confirmation of the tendency to grant concessions in return for the exclusion of new arrivals.

Why did Turkey accept this deal? One of the reasons was Germany's intention to revise the terms of the freedom of movement or at least to re-interpret them. In fact, on 26 June 1980, just four days before the AC meeting, Germany informed Turkey at a meeting at the fringe of the NATO Council in Ankara that it decided to introduce compulsory visa for Turkish nationals. This decision, however, was not to be imposed yet. The Turkish foreign minister asked for details and was reported to be '... hopeful that some solution to the compulsory visa can be found.'[60] The Turkish foreign minister must have been trying to

60 *Agence Europe*, 27.6.1980, p. 7.

contain the problem through bilateral negotiations before other EU members followed suit. This strategy implied that Turkey should be highly flexible at the Association Council meeting.

Another reason which could explain why Turkey agreed to the EU offer was the change of tactics by the Turkish foreign ministry. Turkey had a new government towards the end of 1979 and the new foreign minister was eager to submit a membership application as soon as possible.[61] The foreign minister was planning to tackle the free movement problem as part of the negotiations on accession. This was the first time that Turkey began to move away from the legalistic approach to free movement and place it in the context of her wider relations with the EU. The developments of the Autumn of 1980, however, were quite swift and unexpected. The foreign minister lost his seat as a result of a censor motion on 5 September 1980. A week later, on 12 September 1980, the military took over. These developments put an end to the strategy of linking the issue of free movement with accession negotiations, and enabled Germany and other member states to avoid any further moves towards free movement.

Following the military coup of 12 September 1980, Germany's visa policy for Turkish nationals was put into effect on 5 October 1980. This move was quickly followed by France in order to avoid the likely deflection of migratory flows. Other member states, Belgium, the Netherlands and Luxembourg joined in on 23 October 1980, stating that their decision '... was taken after consultation with Turkey in order to control the social and economic effects which might result from a possible increase in Turkish immigrants.'[62] The Parliamentary Assembly of the Council of Europe asked Germany and France to reconsider their decisions two days before the visa restrictions were imposed, but the request was rejected. Later on, the Parliamentary Assembly adopted a resolution stressing the discriminatory nature of the restrictions implied by the visa for nationals of a member of the Council. This resolution was vetoed at the intergovernmental level by 'one or more of the countries involved.'[63] Consequently, by the end of 1980 not only did the EU avoid granting any substantial improvements to the freedom of movement for Turkish workers, but also managed to push the issue further to the bottom of its agenda as a result of the German initiative, followed by other member states.

After the military coup in Turkey, negotiations on the issue of free movement had to be conducted through bilateral contacts between Turkey and Germany. The first significant development in this process was the visit of the Turkish prime minister, Mr. Turgut Özal, to Bonn in September 1984. Germany

---

61 Birand (1986), pp. 388-94

62 *Agence Europe*, 24.10. 1980, p. 6.

63 *The New York Times*, 5.11.1980.

made it clear that freedom of movement was not possible because of the increase in the number of Turkish immigrants it was expected to generate. In effect, Germany was reiterating its request for revising Article 36 of the AP. Because the Turkish government was aware of the fact that freedom of movement for Turkish workers would remain impossible unless Germany was prepared to move in that direction, the Turkish prime minister's reaction was moderate: Turkey would not give up her right for free movement due to be effected by the end of 1986, but would recognise the need to take into Germany's concerns.

Another occasion on which the issue of free movement was covered in bilateral negotiations between Turkey and Germany was Chancellor Kohl's visit to Turkey on 9 July 1985. This was the first visit to Turkey by a Western head of government since the military coup of 1980. Some German commentators considered this as a benevolent move by Germany - constituting 'a first climax' in German attempts to promote the rehabilitation of Turkey's image in the west, especially in the EU. Schlegel argued that Germany had been in the vanguard so far as normalisation of Turkey's relations with the West was concerned.[64] This argument, however, begs the question as to why German-Turkish relations have deteriorated after 1985. The answer to this question can be derived from the developments that preceded and followed Chancellor Kohl's visit. German concerns about Turkish immigration were made public by the German government spokesman, Mr. Friedhelm Ost, in a press conference just before Kohl's visit to Turkey. Ost referred to a 'paper' that had been prepared by the German government on the issue of free movement of Turkish workers. According to *Le Monde*, the paper was a startling shock for Turkish officials. In that paper, Germany was subscribing to a re-interpretation of the free movement - a move 'totally incompatible with Ankara's approach.'[65] The importance of the paper was due to the fact that it was not an accidental leak and that it reflected the amount of work carried out in relation to free movement of Turkish workers both in Germany *and* between Germany and the European Union.

First, the paper re-interpreted Article 12 of the Association Agreement and argued that the phrase 'to be guided' did not imply free movement in the form that was established within the EU. Second, it re-interpreted the definition of the labour market by arguing that the market should be considered as a collection of many sub-sectors and regions and therefore freedom of movement could only be considered in relation to each sector or region - an argument that reflected the concerns of the German *Lander*. Finally, the paper argued that '... freedom of movement is composed of several elements and that free access to the job markets was only one of them.' This implied that improvement of conditions for

64 Schlegel (1986), p. 292.

65 *Le Monde*, 12.7.1985.

Turkish workers in Germany must replace the free movement provision of Article 36.[66] As a result of this tough line, Kohl's visit to Turkey ended with no solution to the problem despite the financial, technical and military aid package proposed to Turkey as a side payment.[67]

The German paper also stated that the Commission's view on the issue of free movement was similar to that of Germany. Because the Commission did not take any action to deny such allegations, it is only safe to accept that the German approach had the tacit approval of the Commission. Later developments indicate that this statement is a reasonably correct reflection of the convergence between the positions of Germany and the Commission over the five-year period between September 1980 and July 1985. This convergence was also noticeable in the Commission's formal proposals made to the Council as a basis for a common EU position - to be defended in the coming meeting of the AC, which was planned for September 1986 and constituted the first ministerial level meeting after the 1980 military coup in Turkey.

The Commission began work on the draft proposal in January 1986. Its overall strategy was in line with that of Germany: granting Turkey some concessions regarding the rights of Turkish migrants residing in the EU in return for the postponement of the free movement due to be implemented at the end of 1986. Also, initial work reflected the fact that the Commission was aware of the need to allow member states to take national measures that would enable them to avoid domestic political problems.[68] As a result, the Commission argued against the introduction of free movement for Turkish workers on the grounds that unemployment levels in the EU were high and free movement for Turkish workers could not be introduced before Greek, Spanish and Portuguese nationals were able to enjoy the same right - envisaged for 1987 in the case of Greece and 1992 in the case of Spain and Portugal.[69] When the final draft was made public on 15 July 1986, it clearly demonstrated the extent to which the Commission was moving towards Germany's position on the issue of Turkish workers' freedom of movement. The Commission was against freedom of movement because, '... a further influx of workers from non-EU countries is unfeasible due to changes in economic and social framework conditions since the conclusion of the Association Treaty.'[70]

Essentially, the Commission proposal envisaged some measures that would improve the conditions of Turkish workers who were already in the EU. For

---

66 This information is based on Schlegel (1986), pp. 293-295.
67 On Germany's offer, see *The Guardian*, 11.7.1985.
68 *The Financial Times*, 7.3.1986.
69 *Agence Europe*, 7.3.1986.
70 Schlegel (1986), p. 295.

example, the Commission proposed that the limits on occupational and geographical mobility should be abolished, equal treatment should be extended to include training and re-adaptation, family re-unification should include children under 15 years of age, permanent residence after 5 years of uninterrupted stay in a member state, etc.[71] These measures, however, were essentially those which Germany was prepared to accept. The only aspect of the Commission proposal which went beyond the German position was its provision for second priority to Turkish workers who were not residing in the EU. According to the Commission's second priority proposal, the EU should inform Turkish authorities of vacant positions that could not be filled by EU nationals before it informs third countries. This would be done only if the EU was sure that the 'arrival of new Turkish workers would not cause difficulties.' This meant that vacant positions would be reported after 'it is seen that there is no grave danger to the standard of living and employment in EU regions and industries and that the policies for integrating immigrants were not jeopardised by new Turkish workers.'[72] This was not only a far cry from what Turkey expected of free movement, but also allowed the member states to derogate from commitments by invoking the conditions of the labour market and the cost of integrating the existing immigrants.

Germany was not prepared to approve even the so-called second priority for Turkish workers. In addition to Germany, Greece added a new dimension to the debate on free movement of Turkish workers: Turkish nationals could not be allowed into the Greek labour market for reasons of 'national security'. Therefore, the issue could not be discussed in the EU-Turkey Association Council meeting of 16 September 1986 because of the Council's failure to agree on a common EU position. Due to German and Greek resistance, the common EU position could not be formalised until the EU Council meeting on 25 November. The Council agreed on a decision granting improvement to Turkish workers already in the EU, with a derogation for Greece. It was also agreed to convey the EU position to Turkey 'discreetly', i.e. outside the formal channels of the association.[73] For that purpose, it was agreed that the president of the Council, Sir Geoffrey Howe, should write a letter to the Turkish government informing them that the EU's interpretation of the freedom of movement differed from that of Ankara. The Commission's Ankara representative, Mr. Gwyn Morgan, met with the Turkish minister responsible for relations with the EU and suggested that Turkey should 'produce a considered, not a hasty reply'. He also

---

[71] *Agence Europe*, 16.7.1986, p. 9.

[72] *Agence Europe*, 16.7.1986, p. 10.

[73] Council of the EC, General Secretariat (1986), p. 126. On the decision to negotiate with Turkey discreetly, see *Agence Europe*, 26.11.1986, p. 6.

added that talks at ministerial level between Turkey and the EU could not begin until after the German elections in January 1987.[74]

At the end of the 1986 negotiations with Turkey, EU member states scored two goals: they managed to secure an exclusionist position against immigration from Turkey and pulled the Commission towards their position. Being aware of these results, the Turkish government revisited the old strategy of linking the issue of free movement to full membership as was the case in the Autumn of 1980. It made it clear that an application was being prepared for this purpose, which would be submitted to the Belgian Presidency due to take over in January 1987.[75] Another option which Turkey was exploring was to explore the possibility of place individual applications for free movement before the Court of Justice by Turkish nationals living in the EU.[76] This, however, proved to be an unfounded optimism. A case before the ECJ would highlight the limitations facing the EU derived competence in relation to non-transparent/non-divisible issues was concerned.

The involvement of the ECJ in the issue of free movement for Turkish immigrants was due to a request made by a German court, *Verwaltungsgereicht Stuttgart*. The German court asked the ECJ to give its opinion on the rules of the Association Agreement providing for freedom of movement. The request was made in relation to a case brought by Meryem Demirel, a Turkish national against whom the *Land* authorities of Stadt Schwabisch-Gmund issued an expulsion order. The order was issued on the grounds that Mrs. Demirel's husband had not been residing in Germany for at least eight years - the minimum period required by German Aliens Law for family re-unification. The ECJ ruling of 30 September 1987 was of two parts. First, it concluded that the ECJ was competent to deliver a ruling on this matter because the Association Agreement was concluded on the basis of Article 238 of the Treaty of Rome. This was something that has been established before in relation to other cases: if a mixed agreement like the EU-Turkey Association Agreement implied an obligation for a member state under EU Law, the Court is then competent to determine the extent of this obligation.[77] The second part of the ruling concerned the substantive issue at hand: did the decision of the *Land* authorities contradict the provisions of the Association Agreement on freedom of movement? The Court ruled that it did not. This was due to the fact that the gradual establishment of free movement envisaged in the Association Agreement and the AP was to be accomplished as a result of implementing decisions to be taken by the AC. Since the AC failed to do

74 *International Herald Tribune*, 29.11.1986.

75 *International Herald Tribune*, 29.11.1986.

76 *The Financial Times*, 1.12. 1986; and *Agence Europe*, 1/2.12.1986, p. 6.

77 Nolte (1988).

so it was not possible to determine what obligations there were for the member state in question, i.e. Germany.[78]

This was the second ruling by the Court of Justice in 1987 on issues concerning third country immigrants. The first, mentioned in section 5.1 above, declared null and void the Commission's 1985 decision requesting the member states to provide advance information on all draft measures and agreements concerning third country immigration and to engage in policy co-ordination. The ruling in *Demirel v Stadt Schwabisch Gmund* case declared that no obligation could be assigned for the member state concerned because the member states and Turkey had not yet agreed on rules and principles governing the transition to free movement. What was important about these judgements was not their coincidence in terms of time, but the way in which they closed the circle around a the contentious issue of EU competence in the area of extra-EU immigration. The two rulings implied that the EU, without an *a priori* commitment by the member states, could neither assign obligations for them nor could it force them to fulfil any such obligation which they might have undertaken in agreements with third countries unless they had already agreed to details of implementation.

To its credit, the European Parliament was aware of the chicken-and-egg problem involved here: on the one hand, Article 36 of the AP could not have direct effect as the member states and Turkey had not yet agreed on details of its implementation; on the other hand, the necessary details could not be worked out as the member states were under no obligation to co-ordinate their policies on extra-EU immigration. Therefore, in its resolution adopted on the basis of the Pimenta Report, the Parliament accepted the need for discussing the details of implementation. Although this was a step that pointed the way out of the impasse, the Parliament's position suffered from an obvious contradiction: discussions on implementation measures, according to the EP, should be conducted with a view to avoid aggravation of the 'social problems' already experienced by the EU.[79] This qualification indicated that the EP was essentially playing the same tune with other EU institutions. Given the constituency considerations of the MEPs, this was not something difficult to anticipate.

What was more difficult to anticipate was the Commission's opinion on Mrs. Demirel's case. In its opinion submitted to the Court, the Commission stated unequivocally that neither Article 12 of the AA nor Article 36 of the AP were directly applicable. This interpretation, according to Nolte, was almost as restrictive as that of the German government.[80] It was evident that this opinion was in contradiction with the way in which the Commission had been defending

---

78 Nolte (1988), p. 414. See also, Wornham (1994), pp. 72-75.

79 *Official Journal of the EC*, no. C96, 17.4.1989, p. 213.

80 Nolte (1988), p. 413.

its Decision of 1985 against the member states : the Commission argued against Germany and other member states that they had to agree to a procedure of notification and consultation aimed at approximating national legislations concerning third country immigrants. In the *Demirel* case, however, it was justifying a restrictive measure against those immigrants on the grounds that the member states had not yet agreed to such approximation.

A similar tendency was also reflected in its Opinion on Turkey's membership application. In developing its argument against Turkey's accession, the Commission stated that 'Access of Turkish labour to the EU labour market, which would eventually come about ..., gives rise to fears, particularly while unemployment remains at high levels within the Community.'[81] This statement both reflected and re-enforced the non-transparent nature of the policy issue at hand. The Commission's detailed report on Turkey - which served as a basis for its Opinion - provided a good deal of information on Turkey's labour market and demographic trends, but it never attempted to provide estimates of the likely migratory pressures that those trends would imply and how those pressures could be managed through a gradual phasing in of the free movement. The Commission did not only fail to take such a step that would make discussion on this issue more transparent, it also committed the 'sin' of exacerbating the non-transparency surrounding the free movement of Turkish workers by adopting a populist and scare mongering approach.

Faced with these developments, the Turkish government became increasingly resigned to the idea that a legalistic approach was an ineffective way of securing the free movement of Turkish workers. Therefore, it began to indicate willingness to give up its claims for free movement in return for improvements in its relations with the EU. This was stated clearly during the preparation of a report by the British Presidency in 1992 on the strengthening of EU-Turkey relations.[82] The EU responded to this approach positively. Following the Association Council meeting of 9 November 1992, the Commission told Turkey that Turkish workers residing in a Schengen country could be allowed to travel within the EU without a visa. In terms of their access to jobs in the EU, however, all the Commission could suggest was a study on the implications of such a right.[83] However, even these promises proved to be too optimistic. After the TEU, the Council has concentrated on consolidating the restrictions against the employment of third country nationals. As indicated in section 5.1 above, the post-TEU Council recommendations dealt with harmonising the means of combating illegal immigration and illegal employment - without any

---

81 Commission of the EC (1989b), p. 7.

82 *Agence Europe*, 21.5.1992, p. 5.

83 *Agence Europe*, 4.2.1993, p. 6.

improvements to the rights of existing third country nationals to travel or seek employment outside the member state in which they are employed.[84]

Conclusions

We can conclude from the analysis above that the contrast between intra-EU freedom of movement and the exclusionist EU policy *vis-à-vis* third country immigrants has been closely related to issue transparency/divisibility. While intra-EU free movement was rendered transparent/divisible by redefining the nationality domain, the transparency/divisibility of third country immigration was blurred as a result of creating an 'insider' - 'outsider' divide. The redefinition of the nationality domain meant that EU nationals were granted the right to enjoy privileges associated with nationality beyond the territories of their respective states in return for sharing the nationality-based privileges with nationals of other member states within their own countries. As a result, the demands of nationals for special treatment were dampened and the issue of intra-EU movement became compatible with package deals as a basis for policy integration. In contrast, however, the redefinition of the nationality domain required perpetual exclusion of third country nationals against whom the 'insider' status was defined. This arrangement meant that the demands of EU nationals for exclusive club services had to be satisfied by excluding non-members. Therefore, EU policy concerning third country immigration has been formed through intergovernmental co-ordination and its stance has remained exclusionist.

Another conclusion is that the 'insider' - 'outsider' divide was actually created in 1968 when intra-EU free movement was introduced on the basis of member state nationality and not in 1992 when the transition to the Single Market was completed. Therefore, the tightening of restrictions after 1992 should be considered as an 'exclusionist surge' waiting to transpire rather than a new dynamic. The only novelty in the post-1992 exclusionist drive was due to the fact that it was designed under a new type of migratory pressures in the form of increased refugee movements at a time when intra-EU free movement was being consolidated. Although this new context has led to an acceleration in the intergovernmental process of policy co-ordination, the principles generating exclusionist policy outcomes as well as the emphasis on excluding non-EU

[84] See *Official Journal of the EC*, no. C274, 19.9.1996 for Council Resolutions of 20.6.1994 and 30.11.1994, restricting the admission of third country nationals for employment or self-employment purposes; *Official Journal of the EC*, no. C5, 10.1.1996 for Council Recommendation of 22.12.1995 on harmonising the means of combating illegal employment in general; and *Official Journal of the EC*, no. C304, 14.10.1996 for Council Recommendation of 27.9.1996 on combating illegal employment of third country nationals.

nationals as a precondition for consolidating intra-EU free movement go back to the late 1960s and early 1970s.

Given these aspects of the EU's policy on movement of people in general, one would think that the specific context of EU-Turkey relations is not likely to generate different results. To some extent, this expectation is confirmed by the EU's deviation from its commitment to introduce free movement by 1986. The process leading to this outcome has led to the suspension of free movement as the member state hosting the largest section of the Turkish migrants, Germany, resisted any relaxation of the restrictions on new entries. Therefore, a third conclusion that can be derived from the analysis above is that the EU cannot act as an anchor when the policy issue is non-transparent/non-divisible. This result was due to the way in which the redefinition of the nationality domain created an 'insider' group who could equate its interests (employment opportunities) with an undivided national interest that cannot be negotiated with non-nationals, including both existing and potential Turkish immigrants.

Finally, the EU's policy *vis-à-vis* Turkey also displayed some novelty in that it conceded some concessions to Turkish migrants within the EU by improving their rights. In fact, these concessions constituted not only a contrast to the EU's failure to introduce free movement by 1986, but also reflected an attempt to achieve two objectives. First, the EU and its member states agreed to grant these concessions as a side payment for securing a delay in the introduction of free movement. Put differently, the EU displayed a tendency to trade off concessions in transparent/divisible areas such as limited occupational and regional mobility, second priority, incorporation of the migrant workers' families into the labour market, and social security benefits, etc. with non-transparent/non-divisible issues such as free movement where the 'veto group' capacity of the 'insiders' impeded any significant concession. Second, the EU wanted to reduce the risks associated with anchoring Turkey's European orientation. The relatively transparent/divisible issues concerning the rights of existing Turkish workers proved compatible with this risk-minimising strategy - as the analytical framework underpinning the anchor/credibility dilemma would suggest.

6 The Anchor/Credibility Dilemma and the Cyprus Problem

Introduction

This chapter examines the EU's response to the *de facto* division of Cyprus following the Turkish military intervention of 1974. The existing evidence suggests that the EU failed to play a significant role in resolving the Cyprus problem not only during the Sampson coup and Turkey's military intervention in July 1974, but also throughout the 1970s and 1980s.[1] This failure confirms the predictions of Figure 2.1, which suggest that intergovernmentalism and a low anchoring capacity would tend to be the norm in EU policy-making when policy issues are non-transparent/non-divisible and societal assertiveness is low. The transparency/divisibility of a foreign policy issue such as the Cyprus problem is low because information about member state objectives is imperfect, costs of policy decisions are difficult to quantify, and policy preferences are presented as reflections of an undivided national interest that cannot be made subject to compromises and package deals. In addition, societal assertiveness concerning foreign policy issues is low as the definition of national interest in this area is assumed to be the prerogative of the government.

Nevertheless, developments in the 1990s indicate that the EU's detached involvement in the Cyprus problem has been replaced by gradual activism following membership applications of Turkey and Cyprus in 1987 and 990, respectively. Because of the change in the European orientation of both countries, even the United Nations (UN) came to the conclusion in 1989 that Cyprus' EU membership should be considered as a new context in which a settlement of the Cyprus problem could be pursued more effectively. From a state-centric perspective, the emergence of the EU as a significant actor can be explained by referring to the end of the Cold War or to Greek membership. While the end of the Cold War may be presented as a factor that increased the scope for 'European' initiatives on Cyprus, Greek membership may be invoked as a

[1] See, for example, Tsakaloyannis, (1980); and Stephanou and Tsardanidis, (1991).

development that enabled the Greek government to 'Europeanise' the Cyprus problem by using its veto power in other policy areas requiring unanimous decisions. However, the explanatory power of a state-centric analysis is weakened by the tendency to: (i) over-estimate the effect of the 'Greek factor' on the EU's Cyprus policy, and (ii) ignore the impact of policy choices in Cyprus as well as Turkey on the EU's involvement in the Cyprus problem.

To address these shortcomings, this chapter examines the EU's Cyprus policy in the light of state-society interaction and issue transparency/divisibility. The aim here is to establish the extent to which the EU has been capable to develop a package of incentives and sanctions that would induce Turkey to converge towards declared EU standards in foreign policy - namely respect for international law, other countries' sovereignty, integrity of external borders, and a commitment to the settlement of territorial disputes by peaceful means. The analysis below suggests that the EU has not been capable of playing such an anchoring role towards Turkey. Although deviations from declared EU foreign policy standards and the EU-wide consensus on the sovereignty and territorial integrity of the Cypriot state have been generated by the non-credible nature of Turkey's commitment to a European orientation, the EU's failure to act as an effective anchor has exacerbated this credibility problem.

Viewed from this perspective, the Cyprus issue in EU-Turkey relations constitutes yet another policy area where the anchor/credibility dilemma has been at work. In terms of imposing sanctions and undertaking risks designed to reduce the probability of Turkey's deviations from a European orientation, the EU lacked an anchoring capacity from 1974 until the late 1980s and could play only a limited anchoring role in the 1990s. Therefore, Turkish policy-makers found it less costly to deviate further from the EU's preferred solution to the Cyprus problem by moving from the relatively justifiable argument concerning the security of the Turkish-Cypriot community through consolidating Turkey's military presence to gradual integration of Northern Cyprus. In addition, Turkey misinterpreted the EU's detached involvement in the Cyprus problem as a success of her policy, which was geared towards securing an even-handed EU approach to Turkey and Greece. The change in EU stance in the 1990s was also misinterpreted as a reversal caused by the EU's submission to Greek pressure rather than the change in Turkey's and Cyprus' European orientation. As a result, the legacy of Turkey's divergent approach began to haunt Turkish policy-makers in the 1990s, when it became evident that Turkey's Cyprus policy was incompatible with her declared European orientation and constituted a failure even if only Turkey's objectives on Cyprus are taken into account. Therefore, the Cyprus issue has been and remains to be a liability for Turkey, irrespective of whether or not EU membership is maintained as an objective and whatever the nature of Turkey's relations with North Cyprus would be.

To work out these arguments, this chapter is organised in four sections. Section 6.1 provides a summary of the developments leading to the 1974 crisis. We demonstrate here that the lack of a Cypriot political identity added to the complexity of the Cyprus problem. Under this condition, the risks associated with a possible EU intervention aiming to contribute to or impose a solution to the Cyprus problem tended to be high whereas the returns on such a venture tended to be uncertain. Therefore, in the absence of societal assertiveness compelling the member states to take an active stance, neither the incentives nor the constraints were strong enough to induce the EU to develop a co-ordinated policy response. Section 6.2 explains the EU's detached involvement in the Cyprus problem from this perspective and identifies some developments that would force the EU in the 1990s to adopt a relatively activist stance. These developments included the accession of Greece to the EU, the denouncement by the Greek-Cypriot political elite of the unification with Greece (*enosis*) as a policy goal, and the gradual consolidation of the Turkish-Cypriot administration into a separate state in Northern Cyprus.

Although these developments were significant enough to challenge the relevance of the EU's detached involvement, the decisive factor that led to gradual activism in EU's Cyprus policy were the membership applications of Turkey and Cyprus. The EU's Cyprus policy after these developments is examined in section 6.3, where we demonstrate that the declared European orientation of Turkey and Cyprus have induced the EU to engage in policy co-ordination to minimise and manage the risks associated with their respective applications. This increased activism made the EU an indispensable actor even though its anchoring function *vis-à-vis* Turkey and Cyprus remained limited because of the dominant intergovernmentalism in the policy-making process.

Section 4 brings together the findings of the preceding sections and evaluates the credibility as well as effectiveness of Turkey's Cyprus policy. In this final section, we will question the relevance of the Turkish thesis that the EU's Cyprus policy has been shaped by the 'Greek factor', i.e., the ability of Greece to influence the EU's approach towards Turkey by 'Europeanising' the Cyprus problem. We also take issue with the Turkish argument that the Cyprus problem was invented by the EU as a pretext to reject Turkey's membership application. Instead, we will argue that the emergence of the Cyprus problem as an obstacle to Turkish membership dates back to Turkey's second military intervention in August 1974, when it became evident that Turkey's objective was not only to ensure the security of the Turkish-Cypriots, but also to establish a military presence that would be difficult to challenge. In addition, the EU's detached involvement as well as Turkey's capitalisation on the EU's failure to assume an anchoring role until late 1980s were not indicators of success in

Turkey's Cyprus policy, but a clear manifestation of the anchor/credibility dilemma that kept Turkey outside the post-Luxembourg enlargement process.

6.1 Cyprus as a Non-transparent/Non-divisible Policy Issue in EU-Turkey Relations

The literature reflects a clear consensus on two aspects of the process leading to the 1974 crisis in Cyprus: the lack of a Cypriot national identity; and the role of external actors including Greece, Turkey, the United Kingdom (UK), the United States (US), and the Soviet Union. The negative consequences of these factors for the viability of an independent Cypriot state were exacerbated by the US-led containment strategy against the Soviet Union, which raised the stakes for both sides to exercise influence in the eastern Mediterranean. Given this constellation, one can only agree with the description of the Cyprus problem as an ethno-religious conflict that has been exacerbated by intensive external involvement.[2]

The lack of national identity has been confirmed by both Greek- and Turkish-Cypriot leaders. For example, upon his election as the Archbishop of the Greek-Cypriots in 1950, Makarios took oath that he 'shall never waiver' from the policy of 'annexing Cyprus to mother Greece.'[3] Even after independence, Makarios stated that '… no Greek who knows me can ever believe that I would wish to work for the creation of a Cypriot national awareness. The Agreements have created a State but not a Nation.'[4] Statements made by the Turkish-Cypriot leadership afterwards were not different. The vice-president of the Cypriot state and the leader of the Turkish-Cypriot community, Dr Fazil Küçük, stated on 31 December 1963 that the 'Cyprus Constitution is dead' and that there was no possibility of the Turkish and Greek communities living together on the Island. Asked whether his statement implied partition of the Island between Greece and Turkey, his reply was short-cut: 'call it partition if you like'.[5]

Therefore, Cyprus remained divided not only vertically along socio-economic lines but also horizontally along ethnic and religious loyalties. The implication of the horizontal division for the viability of a Cypriot state comprising the two communities is not difficult to detect. The functioning of the state organisation established in 1960 came to an end by 1964 when the Turkish-Cypriot leadership pulled out of the central government on the grounds that they were marginalised by the Greek-Cypriot leadership. Following this

---

2 Yavuz (Fall 1992), p. 1.

3 Ertekün (1981), p. 3.

4 Published in *Cyprus Mail*, 28.3.1963, quoted in Ertekün (1981), p. 8

5 Quoted in Republic of Cyprus, Press and Information Office (1984), pp. 10-11.

disintegration, state-society interaction in both sides entered a new phase where the state became the ultimate means through which ethno-religious identities could be asserted and the collective good of security can be enjoyed. Although this increased the ability of the political elite to present themselves as the representatives of their communities' interests, it also set in motion a societal penetration of the state and forced the latter to become a centre for the distribution of private goods. In other words, the difference between a state (or a political entity) organised to provide collective goods and an ethno-religious network facilitating access to private goods was blurred.

The division of Cyprus along ethnic and religious lines was exacerbated in 1882 when the British colonial administration introduced proportional representation for Greek- and Turkish-Cypriots. This arrangement induced the leaders of both communities to transform the latent ethno-religious divisions into formalised frameworks of identity building. By encouraging a rapid expansion of schools along ethno-religious lines, the British added a new dimension to this process by inducing both communities to turn to their respective 'motherlands' to obtain teaching material and personnel.[6] Another legacy of the British colonial rule was the introduction of Turkey into the Cyprus equation in the early 1950s as a counter-balance to the Greek-Cypriot's drive for *enosis*. Although the evidence is mixed about Turkey's interest in Cyprus after 1945, it is safe to argue that the Turkish government did not have a well-defined Cyprus until the early 1950s.[7] In part, this was due to the legacy of the inward-looking Turkish foreign policy that emphasised the protection of national borders as codified under the Lausanne Treaty of 1923. Another reason was the need to avoid negative reactions from the West at a time when integration into post-war Western institutions (including NATO) was an urgent priority.[8]

After 1954, the Turkish policy on Cyprus was based on the right of the Turkish-Cypriots for self-determination. For the Greek-Cypriot leadership and the Orthodox church, this was a flagrant attack on the struggle for emancipation - the aim of which was the overthrow of the British rule as a step towards *enosis*. Therefore, both Turkish- and Greek-Cypriot paramilitary organisations began to engage in violent clashes sustained by security arguments on the part of the former and anti-collaborationist struggle on the part of the latter. One of the obvious and inevitable consequences of this positioning was the re-enforcement of the ethno-religious divide that cut across class and other socio-economic divisions in both communities. Therefore, the disintegration of the Cypriot state in 1964 was only an 'accident' waiting to happen.

---

6 Anthias (1987), p. 188.

7 Gürel (1985), pp. 133-37; Sönmezoğlu (1991).

8 On this, see Armaoğlu (1963).

Given this history behind the disintegration of the Cypriot state in 1964, attempts by the Greek-Cypriot leadership to revive and consolidate it thereafter added new dimensions to the Cyprus problem. On the one hand, a solid commitment to *enosis* would undermine the legitimacy of Greek-Cypriot because of UK and US opposition to a change in the independent status of the Cypriot state, and Turkey's threat that the Island would be partitioned if the Greek-Cypriots pushed for unification with Greece. On the other hand, giving up *enosis* as an objective was not a feasible option because of the societal penetration of the Cypriot state as well as the likely reactions from Greece. Therefore, the Greek-Cypriot political elite, under the leadership of Makarios, pursued a two-track strategy of emphasising the legitimacy of the Cypriot state that they had denounced in 1960, and preparing the Greek as well as Greek-Cypriot public opinion for a delay in *enosis* until 'the time was right'. The instruments to be used were the establishment of close relations with the Non-Aligned Movement (NAM) and the exploitation of the East-West rivalry. This strategy enhanced the viability of the Cypriot state but at the cost of alienating not only NATO and Turkish-Cypriots, but also the Greek government - especially the military Junta from 1967-74.

In fact, the conflict between Makarios and the Greek Junta was the main reason behind the coup which ousted the Makarios regime and precipitated the Turkish military intervention in July 1974. The conflict reached its climax in early July when Makarios wrote to General Gizikis an open letter, stating that there had been reliable indications that Greece was supporting the EOKA-B (the armed organisation fighting for *enosis*) to overthrow his regime since 1971; that Athens supplied money and advice to the opposition press supporting the EOKA-B; that various attempts to assassinate him were directed from Greece; and that Greek officers in the Cypriot National Guard were involved in all these activities. In addition, Makarios gave an indication about the rift between his approach and that of the Junta to *enosis*: although the Cypriot state could be abolished in the event of *enosis*, it must be strengthened as long as this option was not feasible. He also made it clear that he was not '... an appointed prefect or locum tenens of the Greek government in Cyprus, but an elected leader of a large section of Hellenism' and should be treated by Greece accordingly.[9] Although preparations for the overthrow of the Makarios government had preceded this letter, there were clear signs that its publication was influential on the timing of the coup, which was decided at a meeting of the Greek Junta on 13-14 July 1974.[10]

The coup of 15 July 1974, which brought Nicos Sampson to the presidency of Cyprus, clearly indicated the limited scope for consolidating the Cypriot state.

---

9 For the full text of the letter, see Ertekün (1981), pp. 243-46.

10 *The Economist*, 20.7.1974, p. 11.

Nationalists in Greece and Cyprus were not prepared to allow the flourishing of an independent Cypriot state because such an objective conflicted with *enosis*. Another limitation to the viability of an independent Cypriot state was the US hostility towards Makarios' orientation towards the NAM and his friendly relations with the Soviet Union. Since the early 1970s, the US had been describing Makarios as the 'Castro of the Mediterranean' and did not view his overthrow with much concern.[11] The main US concern was to avoid the escalation of the crisis into an armed conflict between Turkey and Greece at a time when the control of the eastern Mediterranean was essential for the effectiveness of the containment strategy.

The consolidation of the Cypriot state was also constrained by the EU's perspective on Cyprus. The EU, including the UK who had sovereign rights on 3% of the Island and military bases, was in favour of an independent Cypriot state under Makarios. However, the European commitment to defend its independence was less than complete under normal conditions and mostly lacking when it came to face high levels of risks. This tendency could be seen clearly in the statements of the British Foreign Secretary to the House of Commons Select Committee. According to Mr. Callaghan, British bases on the Island were '... more of a NATO interest today than when we first went there.' Also, 'British power and influence in the Middle East are clearly not as great now and have been replaced by the United States.' In addition, the UK government had to take into account NATO interests even after Turkey's intervention because the withdrawal of Greece from the military command under the Junta '... placed a very high premium on the Turkish role in the eastern flank of NATO.'[12] Under those circumstances, the UK government was not in a position to risk confrontation either with Turkey or with the US who was deeply suspicious of Makarios' active role in the NAM.

With respect to the risks associated with an involvement in the Cyprus problem, the Foreign Office Minister, Mr. Hattersley, indicated that the history of British involvement in Cyprus pointed out that the UK government would have only one option: diplomatic activity on various international platforms. That was because '... imposed solutions ... from the time of Derby and Disraeli onwards have not proved a Great success.' Therefore, British efforts 'have been concentrated on giving support to the inter-communal talks in the belief that they offer the best prospect of a lasting success.'[13] This point of view was also shared by *The Economist*, who argued that Britain saw much of the same in Northern Ireland. Just as attempts to contrive a solution from outside failed there, they

11 On this, see Laipson (1991), p. 165.
12 Select Committee (1976), pp. 63-64.
13 Select Committee (1975), p. 14.

would also fail in Cyprus. Therefore, the antagonists should be left to work out their own alternative.[14]

Given that these factors forced the UK (as the only EU member state with a military presence on the Island and a right to intervene) to abstain from an active intervention into the Cyprus problem, it was natural that the EU (as an entity suffering from a yawning gap between the role it was expected to play and the means it had at its disposal) should be even more reluctant to assume an active role. The tendency of the EU to adopt a policy of detached involvement in the Cyprus problem was both a reflection and a result of the non-transparency of the foreign policy issues that have generated the power-capability gap described by Hill.[15] As a foreign policy issue, the Cyprus problem was even less transparent because of the limitations to viability of the Cypriot state. That was why EU attempts in 1974 at contributing to the resolution of the Cyprus problem had to be short-lived - as the analysis in the next section demonstrates.

6.2 Reaction to the Crisis and the Aftermath: The EU's Failure to Emerge as an Anchor and Turkey's Policy Drift

The 1974 Cyprus crisis was not the only issue of concern for the EU during the first half of the 1970s. Still trying to come to terms with the first oil shock, the EU was faced with a 'Southern Europe' problem which contained elements of both hope and anxiety. The dictatorial regime in Portugal had collapsed in April 1974, but the future of the new regime was by no means certain. In Spain, General Franco was in a 'biological struggle' for survival, but the answer to the question of 'what happens after Franco' was unclear. Moreover, of the two associated countries, Greece had been under a military regime since 1967, and Turkey had been finding it difficult to comply with the requirements of the Additional Protocol. Finally, Italy was also a source anxiety for the EU because of the country's vulnerability to political instability - as could be seen from the purge in 1974 of senior army officers for their neo-fascist connections.[16]

Against this background, the Sampson coup of 15 July 1974 constituted an additional shock for the EU. Therefore an urgent (and preferably effective) response to the Cyprus crisis was considered as a litmus test that would indicate whether or not the EU could rise to challenges it was facing in Southern Europe. The feasibility of a quick response was increased by the fact that France, a member always anxious about countervailing the US with an externally active

14 *The Economist*, 20.7.1974, p. 12.

15 Hill (1993).

16 *The Economist*, 10.8.1974, pp. 14-15.

EU, was holding the presidency. While the EU had been worried about the relative deterioration in the relations between itself and the US, France was experiencing a revival in the Gaullist approach to cross-Atlantic relations. Therefore, the French President, Mr. d'Estaing, instructed the French foreign minister 'to ensure that EU member states took an active part in the solution of the Cyprus crisis' and he suggested that 'they should use all the means available to them - in particular economic pressure - to promote the restoration of peace.'[17]

Combined with the fact that Cyprus, Greece and Turkey were associates, French activism precipitated a rapid EU reaction. On 15 July 1974, the day of the Sampson coup, the French foreign minister called for an urgent meeting of the European Political Cooperation (EPC).[18] The meeting took place on 16 July and declared that EU member states were deeply concerned by the events affecting the 'stability in the Eastern Mediterranean.' The Nine also 'reaffirmed their attachment to Cyprus' independence and territorial integrity.'[19] A statement made on the same day by the Commission reflected a similar approach. Pointing out that the EU-Cyprus Association was based on the independence and territorial integrity of the Island, the statement added that the Agreement was based 'on the principle that the whole of the Island's population is to benefit from the advantages of the Association. Any development questioning this principle cannot but have consequences on the Association itself and on the prospects for its further development.'[20]

These statements reflected two elements of the consensus among the EU member states. One explicit element was the member states' common aim to avoid further escalation of the Cyprus crisis as a result of either a Turkish intervention or an *enosis* declaration by the Sampson regime. The confirmation of the EU's attachment to the independence and territorial integrity of the Island and the warning that any change in this status may jeopardise the EU-Cyprus association can be interpreted as reflections of this consensus. Although implicit, a second element could also be detected. The UK was in favour of reinstituting the constitutional order, including the return of Makarios as the legitimate president of Cyprus. However, the EPC and the Commission were careful enough to draw attention only to negative consequences of changing the status of the Cypriot state. The reason why the EU did not make an explicit statement on the legitimacy of the Sampson regime was its desire to avoid an open clash with the US, whose inclination was to recognise the Sampson regime provided that it did not push for *enosis*. That was why the French foreign minister, while

---

17 *The Times*, 22.7.1974.

18 *Agence Europe*, 17.7.1974, p. 3.

19 *Agence Europe*, 18 .7.1974, p. 4.

20 *Agence Europe*, 18.7.1974, p. 4.

declaring satisfaction with the EU's energetic involvement, was careful enough to assure the US Secretary of State that the EU's activity was 'convergent' with that of the United States.[21]

However, neither the statements on behalf of the EU nor US efforts were effective in changing the course of events. Talks between Britain and Turkey from 17-18 July concerning intervention by the former as a guarantor power ended without a result. Turkish troops landed on the Island on 20 July 1974 and by 22 July, when a cease-fire was declared, they established an important stronghold in Cyprus. At the time of the cease-fire, Turkey was in control of a triangle with a 5-mile base along the beach of Kyrenia on the north coast and a peak around Boghaz down the road to Nicosia, the Island's capital. They also controlled a corridor along the main road from Kyrenia to Nicosia, together with the northern part of Nicosia.

From 20-22 July, the EPC met twice and the French foreign minister, Mr. Sauvagnargues, had several telephone conversations with the US Secretary of State, Dr. Kissinger. If one aim of those conversations was to ensure parallel action, the other was to allay American concerns about EU activity and diffuse the tension that had arisen because of the EU's divergent approach to the coup in Cyprus. Although the EU had initially adopted a non-committal approach to the reinstitution of Makarios, the vagueness was gradually replaced by a clear emphasis on his recognition as the legitimate leader. This was an outcome of the negotiations in the EPC, which were concluded with an announcement on 20 July 1974 by the French Ambassador to the United Nations. Mr. D.E. Giringaud stated that the EU was in favour of restoring the constitutional order in Cyprus and could not 'consider the maintenance ... of the present *de facto* regime in keeping that order.'[22]

While the US was inclined to accept the coup as a *fait accompli* and prepare public opinion in favour of recognising the Sampson regime, the EU made it public that it would not subscribe to this approach. The difference between the EU and the US positions with respect to the regime in Cyprus was hailed by an editorial in *Agence Europe* as the first example of how a European perspective could contribute to peace and democracy without necessarily having to follow the US lead.[23] According to an editorial reflecting the views of those eager to see an active EU presence in world politics, the EU's approach 'has allowed the United States to realise that its initial attitude was not the most likely way to lead to a both speedy and fair outcome.' The editorial continued by indicating that '... at a given moment, it was feared that this outcome would emerge through devious

21 *Agence Europe*, 22/23.7.1974, p. 3; *The Times*, 22.7.1974.

22 Quoted in Tsardanidis (1983), p. 219.

23 See *Agence Europe*, 24.7.1974, p. 1.

channels, that is to say that the solution would be sought not in its natural context, which is both that of NATO, …, and that of Europe … but in that of the interests of the superpowers.'[24]

Although it is justified to emphasise the difference between the EU and US positions on the constitutional future of Cyprus, it is also necessary to point out that the EU was incapable of rising to the challenge and coming up with a coherent framework which would induce Turkey to act in line with the European perspective on Cyprus. The gravity of this failure becomes more obvious when it is taken together with Turkey's strategic considerations that preceded the military intervention of 20 July 1974. According to Birand, the military operation was decided in the National Security Council meeting of 15 July 1974, before the Turkish prime minister's visit to London. From the official accounts given to Birand, it was obvious that the London visit was designed to gain time and give the impression that Turkey was keen to exhaust the legal procedure implied by the Treaty of Guarantee. In fact, the military operation was decided on the assumption that the interests of the superpowers in maintaining the *détente* process had brought about '… a significant change in the international community's reactions to crisis situations.' This change meant that the superpowers would resort to 'crisis containment' rather than 'military intervention.' Therefore, the crisis-initiating party 'would always be in an advantageous position.'[25] It must also be added that the decision for a military intervention was taken without prior consultations with the Turkish-Cypriot leadership. This was clear from Mr. Denktaş's statement of 16 July that the crisis was essentially a Greek affair, to which Turkey responded by sending encrypted telegrams instructing him that the crisis was not an internal Greek affair and that Turkey was preparing for a strong reaction.[26]

Despite Turkey's tendency to create a *de facto* situation in Cyprus, all the EU could do was to block the delivery of 5,000 tonnes of food assistance which had been decided previously.[27] At the EPC level, on the other hand, all that could be done was to remind the parties of the fact that their association with the EU could be affected if they did not refrain from provocative actions. Because this threat was not spelled out in detail and no credible measure could be taken against Turkey's military intervention, Turkey went ahead with the implementation of the previously determined strategy. Obviously, Turkey's military intervention was also facilitated by the US policy of crisis containment, which was designed mainly for the prevention of war between Greece and

24 *Agence Europe*, 22/23.7.1974, p. 1.
25 Birand (1984), pp. 25-66.
26 Birand (1984), p. 52.
27 *The Economist*, 3.8.1974, p. 45.

Turkey. Therefore, the cease-fire agreed on 22 July 1974 under US pressure proved to be only an interregnum during which Turkish troops continued to advance and pave the way for the second intervention on 14 August 1974.[28]

After the cease-fire, the EU began to pursue a less marked involvement in the Cyprus issue for two reasons. First, Turkey and Greece agreed to take part in the Geneva talks following EU and US calls to that effect. Given that the danger of an imminent conflict between Greece and Turkey was avoided, the EU was only happy to limit its involvement to supporting the UK's efforts for convening and leading the Geneva talks. The crisis containment policy was deemed sufficient despite the continued advancement of the Turkish troops. As a result, the area under Turkish control was more than doubled and the number of troops increased from 7,000 on 20 July to 23,000 on 30 July, when the first round of Geneva talks ended.[29] The second round of talks produced even a worse situation: Turkey pulled out of the talks and launched its second military operation that enabled it to control 38% of the Island. Second, the collapse of the Sampson regime in Cyprus and the military Junta in Greece created a new situation, forcing the member states to re-assess their policies. The combination of these factors implied that the precarious consensus that had been based on a critical stance against the Sampson coup and the Greek military Junta could no longer be maintained. As a result, the common EU approach that underlay the activism of the early days began to fade.

Ironically, it was France who initiated this process of disintegration. Following the fall of the Greek Junta, the French government began to reflect a markedly sympathetic position towards the new Karamanlis government. The shift in French policy began on 24 July, when the French President Giscard d'Estaing stressed the importance of the EU's role in the Cyprus crisis and went further than his partners by expressing an unqualified support for the Greek people 'who invented the language and institutions of democracy.' The Commission, although welcoming the return to democracy, found it necessary to indicate that the new government would be judged by its actions, including the government's contribution to resolving the Cyprus problem.[30] That the difference between France and the EU was not only about semantics became obvious when the French government decided to accelerate the delivery of Mirage fighter-bombers, gunboats, and tanks which had been ordered by the Junta.[31] This was a

---

28 On this, see Tsakaloyannis (1980), pp. 35-54. See also, Birand (1984), p. 232.

29 *The Economist*, 3.8.1974, p. 24.

30 *Agence Europe*, 25.7.1974, p. 3.

31 *The Observer, Foreign News Service*, no. 32623, 28.8.1974; and *The Guardian*, 29.9.1974.

clear move away from the British and German policies of pursuing an even-handed approach in order to avoid Turkey's alienation.

Furthermore, France was also anxious to project the EU as an alternative to the United States. In a televised speech on 27 August 1974, d'Estaing stated that '... there are all kinds of alibis not to construct a political Europe. But there will be no alibi for those who have been summoned to a *rendezvous* with history ... and ... turn empty-handed.'[32] This activist call was largely an anathema for the British government who was concerned with the approaching elections. Therefore, the British government was quick to express scepticism about the French statement. In fact, the conservative press dismissed it as 'a Gaullist look across the Atlantic'. Germany - in order not to jeopardise the Franco-German rapprochement at the time - declared interest, but she also signalled lack of enthusiasm by indicating that it was waiting for the details to come from Paris. The smaller members of the community assumed a cautious approach and suspected that d'Estaing's new initiative was based on a French-German collusion which they considered as a manoeuvre designed to disregard them.[33]

As can be seen from the account above, the EU was able to respond with a common approach to the crisis in Cyprus. However, as soon as the crisis was contained, the divergence among national policies surfaced and limited the EU's ability to develop a common approach that either marked its difference from that of the US or enabled it to assume an active role. When a new consensus emerged in September 1974, it was bearing the mark of the lowest common denominator determined by the divergence among member state policies. Therefore, the EPC meeting of 16 September reflected a clear move towards a detached EU involvement in the Cyprus problem. This tendency could be clearly seen in the text that the EPC meeting adopted on Cyprus. On the one hand, the text reflected a tendency to focus attention on post-crisis issues such as aid and the future of refugees. It pointed to the Commission decision to provide food aid, which would be distributed by the United Nations High Commission for Refugees (UNHCR) and not through a separate European channel. On the other hand, the EPC reaffirmed its commitment to the independence and territorial integrity of Cyprus, but they also made it clear that the EU's role would be limited to the encouragement of inter-communal talks to be conducted with the 'support of other parties concerned.'[34]

This approach was reflected in the replies given to Parliamentary questions during the EP's plenary session of 26 September 1974. The president-in-office of the Council urged caution and added that there might be 'snags in a premature

---

32 *The Daily Telegraph*, 28.8.1974.

33 See *The Guardian; The Financial Times;* and *The Daily Telegraph*, 29.8.1974.

34 *Agence Europe*, 18.9.1974, p. 3.

intervention on the part of the Nine, leading to failure. … We must avoid anything that could be prejudicial to any party involved.' Following an intense debate calling for a dynamic EU approach, the president-in-office did not hesitate to rule out the possibility of a more active EU involvement once more. He emphasised the importance of impartiality in the EU's approach and rejected the idea that some sort of sanctions or censure measures could contribute to finding a solution. '… [I]t is not permissible to resort to levers or bargaining counters to pave the way for negotiation,' he said, and added that '… an impartial approach offers the best chance of promoting a lasting harmony and understanding between the two communities.'[35]

The new EU approach failed to satisfy the parties involved in the Cyprus problem as well as those who would have liked to see a more assertive EU policy. The approach was unsatisfactory for the Greek-Cypriots because, in their view, it encouraged the Turkish-Cypriots to maintain the *de facto* division of the Island. It was not acceptable for the Turkish-Cypriots either because it was based on the recognition of the Cypriot state as the representative of Cyprus. Those in favour of an active EU involvement were also disappointed and criticised the approach for lack of assertiveness. This criticism was evident in the Parliamentary Debate mentioned above. The spokesperson for the Socialist Group stated that 'the question that arises is whether Washington must always be ... the policeman standing at every corner of the world or whether Europe feels strong enough to make an independent, improved and stronger contribution.'[36]

More relevant to our purposes in this book, however, is the compatibility of the emerging EU policy with the analytically derived conclusion concerning intergovernmentalism and the absence of an anchoring capacity when policy issues are non-transparent/non-divisible. Given the non-transparent nature of the Cyprus issue and the risks involved, it was not surprising that the relative activism induced by the crisis was quickly replaced by an arms-length approach dictated by the lowest common denominator. Therefore, neither the expectation that the EU could have played a more active role nor the boasting of the French government about a 'European' alternative to the US had a realistic foundation. That is because of the incompatibility of the EU system with the undertaking of major risks that are difficult to estimate and/or to share among its member states. This lack of anchoring capacity sowed the seeds of further lethargy that continued until membership applications by Turkey and Cyprus were perceived as developments that could reduce the risks and enhance the effectiveness of an EU involvement in the Cyprus problem.

35 *Official Journal of the EC - Debates*, no. 181, September 1974, pp. 123-132.
36 *Official Journal of the EC - Debates*, no. 181, September 1974, p. 128.

Against this anchor failure, the Turkish policy on Cyprus constituted the other side of the anchor/credibility dilemma. Having established a stronghold by 30 July, the Turkish government began to make its ambitions in Cyprus clearer. It became obvious during the Geneva talks that Turkey's overriding objective was to carve out a significant part of the Island to secure a military advantage rather than reinstitute the constitutional order or ensure the security of the Turkish-Cypriots. The priority for Turkey was to ensure that Turkish troops deployed on the Island were not in a vulnerable position in the long run. The security of the Turkish-Cypriots was a secondary objective that was presented as the function of the former. It was this aspect of the Turkish policy that prompted the Foreign Affairs Committee of the House of Commons in 1987 to argue that while the first Turkish intervention could have been regarded as a legitimate exercise of Turkey's Guarantor rights the intervention in August was an attempt to impose partition.[37] From our perspective, the second intervention as a clear indication of the extent to which the Turkish government was prepared to discount closer relations with the EU which, despite its lethargy, was clearly in favour of a unified and independent Cypriot state. This deviation from the European consensus constituted not only a clear signal of Turkey's non-credible European orientation, but also a significant step that locked Turkey's Cyprus policy into a path of continued and increasing divergence from future policy developments in the EU.

This particular manifestation of the anchor/credibility dilemma in EU-Turkey relations set in motion a prolonged process of inactivisim on the EU's part and further attempts by Turkey and the Turkish-Cypriots to consolidate the Turkish Federated State of Cyprus, established on 13 February 1975. EU's inactivisim took the form of hiding behind UN sponsored inter-communal talks. This policy was defended by various EPC statements made either at UN General Assembly meetings, or on separate occasions following the interruption or resumption of the inter-communal negotiations. The common themes in those statements were (i) respect for UN resolutions affirming the independence, sovereignty and territorial integrity of Cyprus; and (ii) adherence to inter-communal talks as the most promising way of finding a solution.[38]

Only on one occasion did the EU venture to propose an alternative to the UN-sponsored talks. This proposition was made at the Dublin meeting of the EPC on 13 February 1975 - the day when the Turkish Federated State of Cyprus

---

37 Foreign Affairs Committee (1987), p. xiv.

38 See, for example, the Italian foreign minister's statement at the UN General Assembly on 24 September 1975 (Verbatim Service, 24.9.1975); the Danish foreign affairs minister' statement on 15 January 1976 (Danish Embassy Press Release, London, 15.1.1976); the Irish foreign minister's statement on 26 September 1979; Lord Carrington's statement on 22 September 1981 in Euroconsult Ltd (1991), pp. 127-128.

was established. In a *communiqué* issued at the end of the meeting, the EPC stated that they would, through the presidency, contact the governments of Cyprus, Greece and Turkey to indicate that the EU was prepared to hold discussions with all the interested parties in order to facilitate a negotiated solution.[39] This call, however, was rejected by the parties to which it was addressed. In his reply to Parliamentary Questions, the president-in-office of the Council, Mr. FitzGerald, admitted the failure of the EU initiative and reiterated support for UN-sponsored negotiations. He stated that the EU was not prepared to insist on a separate European platform for inter-communal negotiations on the grounds that Cyprus was an issue 'where the mere taking of initiative by the EU does not of itself resolve the problem and may in certain circumstances complicate it.'[40] Not only that, a proposition by a member of the European Parliament, Mr. Jahn, that the EU should prepare a 'generous development plan' linked to a political settlement in Cyprus was ruled out.[41]

EU support for the UN-sponsored talks, however, was a problematic policy even when considered in the light of the narrow objective it aimed to achieve. The policy could neither penalise nor induce the parties to maintain the inter-communal talks let alone agree on a solution. It was backed neither with a package of incentives nor by credible threats. In fact, the EU did not only reject Mr. Jahn's economic aid package, but also another proposal put forward by the EP's External Relations Committee in 1988. A similar tendency was also evident with respect to the imposition of sanctions. A House of Commons Select Committee recommended as early as 1976 that the EU should impose sanctions against Turkey and revise the association agreement. This recommendation fell on deaf ears not only in the EU but also the UK, despite the fact that the Select Committee was careful enough to sweeten it by signalling that such an initiative would enable the UK government to play a leading role. Given this reluctance, the declared EU support for inter-communal talks was in effect a strategy that reduced the chance for a solution. It allowed the Turkish- and Greek-Cypriots to engage in face-saving exercises and withdraw from the talks as and when they deemed necessary.

In addition, the policy of supporting inter-communal talks was nothing but a blank cheque for the member states to adopt go-it-alone policies when necessary or to refrain from any serious commitment to ensure that the talks were conducive to a solution. Table 6.1 below demonstrates that such tendencies did

39 Euroconsult Ltd (1991), p. 124.

40 *Official Journal of the EC - Debates*, no. 191, May 1975, p. 86.

41 Mr. Jahn's proposal was based on the argument that non-intervention 'would not help the EC, but would have the opposite effect.' See *Official Journal of the EC - Debates*, no. 191, p. 85.

actually characterise the attitudes of the member states. From 1976 onwards, the majority of EU member states abstained from supporting General Assembly resolutions urging the Security Council to exert pressure on the parties involved.

Table 6.1 Voting pattern of EU member states in the UN General Assembly

Country	Res. 75	Res. 76	Res. '77	Par.* 5	Res. 78	Par.* 8	Res. '79	Pars.*1 3-15	Res. 83
USA	A	A	A	N	A	N	A	N	N
Belgium	Y	A	A	A	A	A	A	N	N
Denmark	Y	A	A	A	A	A	A	N	N
Germany	Y	A	A	A	A	A	A	N	N
Italy	Y	A	A	A	A	A	A	N	N
Luxemb.	Y	A	A	A	A	A	A	N	N
Nethe'ld.	Y	A	A	A	A	A	A	N	N
UK	Y	A	A	A	A	A	A	N	N
Ireland	Y	A	Y	A	Y	A	A	N	Y
France	Y	Y	Y	A	Y	A	A	A	Y

* Paragraph(s) voted separately
Y = Approval **A** = Abstention **N** = Against

Source: United Nations (1975-83).

Res. '75: Resolution 3212(30) of 20.11.1975. Calls upon all states to respect the sovereignty, independence and territorial integrity of Cyprus; demands for withdrawal of foreign armed forces and resumption of inter-communal talks.

Res. '76: Resolution 32/12 of 12.11.1976. In addition to the above, it 'expressed the hope' that the Security Council will consider the appropriate measures for ensuring the implementation of previous Council decisions.

Res. '77: Resolution 32/15 of 9.11.1977. Same as Resolution 32/12 of 12.11.1976, with the exception of a slight change in paragraph 5 outlined below.

Par. 5: Paragraph 5 of Resolution 32/15. *Recommends* that the Security Council '... should adopt all practical means to promote effective implementation' of previous Council decision.

Res. '78: Resolution 33/15 of 9.11.1978. Same as Res. '77 outlined above.

Par. 8: Paragraph 8 of Resolution 33/15. Reiterates the demand for adoption of effective measures for ensuring implementation.

Res. '79: Resolution 34/30 of 20.11.1979. Same as previous resolutions, with the exception of paragraphs 13-15 outlined below.

Pars. 13-15: Paragraphs 13-15 of Resolution 34/30. Calls for the establishment of an *ad hoc* committee that would liaise with the Secretary-General and recommend measures for the implementation of the relevant General Assembly resolutions on Cyprus.

Res. '83: Resolution 37/253 of 13.5.1983. Calls for immediate implementation of previous resolutions and withdrawal of 'occupation forces'.

One reason for this tendency was the reluctance to exert pressure on Turkey and the Turkish-Cypriot leadership. Another was the reluctance of the Security Council members, such as the UK, to tie their hands by supporting a resolution calling for action. These considerations were summed up by the UK representative, who stated during the 1977 General Assembly session that it 'would be a mistake ... to coerce the parties or to prejudge the separate discussions of the problem in the Security Council.'[42] A third reason related to concerns about avoiding a confrontation with the US, who was opposed not only to exerting pressure on Turkey, but also to the Non-Aligned Movement that sponsored these resolutions. Overall, the resulting tendency to avoid any serious commitment to the implementation of the Security Council decisions deprived the EU of a possible influence on the parties involved, especially Turkey.

Finally, divergent Irish and French votes on the 1977, 1978 and 1983 resolutions reflected the lack of a common EU policy and undermined the credibility of the EU's calls on Greek- and Turkish-Cypriots to maintain the inter-communal talks. Capitalising on these weaknesses, Turkey and the Turkish-Cypriot leadership began to take further steps aimed at consolidating the division of the Island. It must be added that the EU's signal in 1976 that the accession of Greece would not lead to the 'Europeanisation' of the Greco-Turkish conflict made Turkey's drive towards consolidating the division more feasible. Following the membership application of Greece, both the Council and the Commission assured the Turkish government that the EU would hold consultations with Turkey to ensure that the accession of Greece did not have an adverse effect on

42 United Nations (1977), p. 359.

Turkish interests.[43] Given these assurances and the revealed lethargy, the Turkish Federated State of Cyprus was upgraded into an independent state called the Turkish Republic of Northern Cyprus (TRNC) in November 1983, a referendum on the constitution of the TRNC was held in May 1985, and presidential elections took place in June of the same year.

It is true that the EU expressed its disapproval of these developments. For example, the EPC meeting of 16 November 1983 expressed deep concerns about the declaration of the TRNC and called upon all interested parties not to recognise it.[44] Also, the UK called for a Security Council meeting and supported the Security Council resolution of 18 November 1983, which deplored the 'purported secession of part of the Republic of Cyprus' and called on all states not to recognise the TRNC.[45] In 1985, the EPC reiterated the EU's non-recognition of the TRNC and criticised the referendum as well as the presidential elections held in northern Cyprus.[46] These initiatives, however, were not backed by any credible and consistent EU strategy that would either induce or compel Turkey and the Turkish-Cypriot leadership to heed the calls made either by the EU or by the UN. In addition, they were taken against a background of division in the EU's Cyprus policy at the UN and were accompanied by a clear reluctance to undertake any substantial risks. For example, the UK's rush for a Security Council meeting in November 1983 had been preceded by the UK's rejection of the General Assembly Resolution in May of the same year, mainly because it called for the withdrawal of Turkish troops. The French and Irish votes for the 1983 General Assembly Resolution as well as the French support to the Security Council Resolution were essentially indicative of these countries' foreign policy orientation rather than a sign of EU assertiveness. Therefore, their impact was to put the division in the EU's Cyprus policy under the spot lights and encourage Turkey to maintain the assumption that the 'Europeanisation' of the Cyprus problem was not an imminent danger.

Nevertheless, indications about the unrealistic nature of Turkey's assumption began to emerge since 1981 when Greece joined the EU. Ironically, however, the way in which Greek membership contributed to the 'Europeanisation' of the Cyprus problem was different from what Turkey suspected to be the case and successive Turkish governments tried to avoid. Of course, since 1981, the Greek government and Greek MEPs have consistently raised the issue of Cyprus at various levels in the EU. One indication of these efforts was the increase in the number of Cyprus-related parliamentary questions

---

43 *Agence Europe*, 5.3.1976, p. 8, and 10.3.1976, p. 6.

44 Euroconsult Ltd. (1991), p. 125.

45 Republic of Cyprus, Press and Information Office (1991), pp. 85-86.

46 Euroconsult Ltd. (1991), pp. 125-26.

directed to the Commission, the Council and the EPC. Another was the Greek government's attempts to block the normalisation of EU-Turkey relations from the mid-1980s onwards. Until late 1988, however, these attempts remained essentially ineffective in terms of either influencing the EU's stance on Cyprus or blocking the normalisation of EU-Turkey relations. The EU's Cyprus policy continued to be characterised by inactivism and EU-Turkey were normalised despite Greek opposition. Also, as indicated above, any surge in EU criticism of Turkey's Cyprus policy was caused by deliberate Turkish and Turkish-Cypriot attempts to consolidate the division of the Island rather than by Greek or Greek-Cypriot pressure as such.

What, then, was the impact of Greek membership on the 'Europeanisation' of the Cyprus problem? We argue that Greek membership contributed to the 'Europeanisation' of the Cyprus problem not because it enabled Greece to drag the EU into an activist stance, but because it made *enosis* a redundant option and, thereby, enhanced the viability of the Cypriot state. This paradox has been ignored not only by Turkish policy-makers who have been only keen to criticise the EU for giving in to Greek pressure, but also by students of EU-Turkey relations who have rightly detected a trend towards EU activism on Cyprus following the accession of Greece in 1981.[47] What is missing in such accounts, however, is the fact that the scope for consolidating the Cypriot state and integrating it within the EU was increased as *enosis* became a less likely option after 1981. The reason why *enosis* became a less feasible option after the accession of Greece lay in the unpleasant fact that the annexation of Cyprus would be tantamount to violating the sovereignty of an associated country by a member state and any EU objection to such annexation would be more damaging for Greece compared to pre-1981 when the latter had not been a member yet. Given this constellation, the pro-*enosis* camps in Greece and Cyprus were weakened and the scope for resolving the *enosis*/independence dilemma that had haunted the Greek-Cypriot leadership since the early 1950s was increased. In addition, the Greek-Cypriot leadership began to perceive of the EU as a new platform for consolidating the Cypriot state not only with the support of Greece as a Hellenistic ally within the EU but also by borrowing credibility from closer integration. Therefore, the first action of the Greek-Cypriot leadership after the accession of Greece was to renounce *enosis* as a future goal in November 1981.

That this was not only a public relations exercise can be seen in evidence given to the Foreign Affairs Committee of the House of Commons in 1986-87. The Greek-Cypriot foreign minister told the Committee that the idea of *enosis*

---

[47] For arguments that the accession of Greece has contributed to the deterioration of EU-Turkey relations, see Kohlhase (1981), pp. 128-31; Meinardus (1991), pp. 161-62; and Mango (1990), p. 99. An exception is Esche (1990).

was a matter of the past. In addition, Cyprus was an independent state and the Greek-Cypriots cherished their independence , which they would strive to maintain. The Foreign Affairs Committee was of the view that this was a genuine position given the fact that the Greek-Cypriot political elite had been in control of an internationally recognised state, and had no 'great hankering to become mere provincial legislators and officials' in a Greek province.[48] Given this change in the position of Greek-Cypriot political elite, it was not surprising that the EU became an attractive platform where the objective of consolidating the Cypriot state could be pursued.

It was this change of attitude towards *enosis* rather than the Greek pressure that forced the EU to gradually increase its involvement in the Cyprus problem. As the European orientation of the Greek-Cypriot leadership began to take shape, the EU had to respond by exploring ways through which the risks associated with closer integration of Cyprus could be reduced. The first step in this direction was taken in July 1983, when the EU Council, after prolonged intra-EU negotiations, decided to upgrade the EU-Cyprus association with an additional protocol that granted partial concessions for agricultural and industrial products originating in Cyprus. This protocol was extended from 1984 to 1987, when the EU-Cyprus customs union (CU) agreement was signed. The CU agreement provided for a gradual removal of tariff and non-tariff barriers by Cyprus at a rate of 9% per year in return for preferential EU treatment for 43 agricultural products and tariff-free entry for industrial products, provided that Cyprus complied with rules of origin. As a result, Cyprus became the most favoured country *vis-à-vis* the EU when compared with other associated countries, including Turkey.[49]

Despite these changes in the parameters of the Cyprus problem, Turkish policy on Cyprus continued to be based on the assumption that Turkey's significance as a bulwark against the Soviet Union would prevent the EU from taking an active and critical stance. As late as 1987, the Turkish foreign minister referred to a 1973 speech by Kissinger and reminded his audience that 'the political, military and economic issues in Atlantic relations are linked by reality, not by our choice nor for the tactical purpose of trading off one against the other.' Adhering to this 'realist' view, the foreign minister stated categorically that 'Turkey has no intention of paying any political price for full membership, especially on issues of national interest.'[50] This was a telling indicator of the essentially flawed basis of Turkey's policy not only on Cyprus as an 'issue of

---

48 Foreign Affairs Committee (1987), p. xxvi.

49 Euroconsult Ltd. (1991), p. 61.

50 This is from Mr. Halefoğlu's speech of 8 July 1987 at the Royal Institute of International Affairs, (Mimeograph).

national interest', but also on EU-Turkey relations which, by implication, were considered as less than a matter of national interest. In other words, Turkey once more demonstrated her desire to have the cake and eat it. On the one hand, she was prepared to clash with the emerging EU activism on Cyprus regardless of the implications for her membership application. On the other hand, it wanted the EU to accommodate this policy deviation on the grounds that Turkey's place in Europe was dictated by reality and not by choice. This was a recipe for disaster so far as the credibility of Turkey's European orientation was concerned.

In the light of the analysis above, we reiterate the argument that the gradually increasing EU involvement in the Cyprus problem from late the 1980s onwards was a result of the Greek-Cypriots' European orientation to which Turkey responded by an obsolete and non-credible policy, rather than the veto power of the Greek government within the Council. This dynamic was rightly picked up in the report of the Foreign Affairs Committee of the House of Commons mentioned above. According to the Committee, since 1974, Turkey had placed itself into an awkward position: not only did she violate the rule of law in dispute resolution but she also became less able to secure support to her objective, i.e. a sort of *de facto* partition of the Island. Therefore, the Committee, which in fact was sympathetic to partition had there been no Turkish occupation, recommended that the EU Council and the European Council should make it absolutely clear to Turkey that reactivating the association as well as any further consideration of Turkey's membership application would be frozen until significant moves were made towards a settlement in Cyprus.[51]

6.3 The Cyprus Problem in EU-Turkey Relations in the 1990s: Relative EU Activism and Further Policy Deviations by Turkey

As a result of the developments examined above, it became evident in the late 1980s that the EU was on a sliding scale towards a more active involvement in the Cyprus problem. One indicator of this tendency was the hardening of the EP's approach towards Turkey. The EP proposal of 1988 for a comprehensive aid package conditioned on a solution to the Cyprus problem was ineffective in generating a response from either the Commission or the Council. However, the EP made it clear in that report that it would use the new powers acquired under the Single European Act (the assent procedure) and, unless Turkey was prepared to change her stance on Cyprus, would veto further normalisation of the EU-Turkey association. Again in 1988, and for the first time after the 1974 crisis, the Rhodes Summit issued a statement and made it clear that the Cyprus problem

51 Foreign Affairs Committee (1987), p. xxxv.

was affecting EU-Turkey relations. A year later, it became public that the UK, France, Germany and Italy had been engaged in discussions on the Cyprus problem outside the formal context of the EPC.[52] Finally, at the end of 1989, the Strasbourg Summit added a new dimension to the EU's announcements on Cyprus by emphasising the European vocation of the country just at a time when the Commission was about to reject Turkey's membership application.

It has been indicated in section 6.2 that these developments in the EU's Cyprus policy were related to the Greek-Cypriots' European orientation as a means of enhancing the viability of the Cypriot state rather than the veto power of Greece within the EU. From 1990 onwards, the relationship between the Greek-Cypriots' European orientation and EU activism acquired a new dimension with the application of Cyprus for membership. It is true that the European orientation of the Greek-Cypriot leadership has been evident since the early 1960s when Britain made the first attempt to join the EU. Although, at that time, Commonwealth members belonging to the Non-Aligned Movement viewed the EU as 'a capitalistic, monopolistic Western bloc that would dominate the Third World and be a tool of the United States', the Cypriot government took a different view without breaking ranks with its allies in the NAM.[53] In spite of the political instability that prevailed from 1963 onwards, the Cypriot government set in motion a gradual process that led to the Association Agreement of 1972. This European orientation was only to be expected given the fact that 40% of Cypriot exports in 1972 were absorbed by the UK. The Cypriot government was concerned that the UK's accession to the EU would increase the rate of protection and, therefore, it wanted to circumvent the impact of the common external tariff on the UK market by signing an association agreement that would provide for preferential treatment.

The 1974 crisis and the anti-American attitudes it precipitated were also effective in inducing the Greek-Cypriot leadership to take further steps towards strengthening the relations with the EU. Those attempts, however, remained tentative and economic in nature. The EU's response was to avoid any significant opening by arguing that the political situation on the Island was limiting the scope for upgrading the EU-Cyprus association agreement.[54] As this negative approach pushed the Greek-Cypriot leadership towards the establishment of stronger links with the NAM, the EU found it even easier to reject the upgrading of the association agreement. The Greek accession of 1981 constituted a watershed and enabled the Greek-Cypriot leadership to redefine their approach to Cyprus' relations with the EU. As a result, the European orientation of the

---

52 *Agence Europe*, 26.1.1989, p. 3.

53 Agathocleous (1993).

54 On this, see Tsardanidis (1983); and (1984).

Greek-Cypriot leadership began to be marked by a political dimension in addition to the essentially economic concerns of the 1970s. Two developments in the late 1980s confirmed not only the change in the Greek-Cypriot leaderships' European orientation, but also the consequences of this change in terms of closer links with the EU. These were the signing of the Customs Union Agreement in October 1987 and the election of George Vassiliou to the presidency in early 1988 on a pro-European ticket. While negotiations on the CU enabled the Greek-Cypriot leadership to engage in a formal dialogue with the EU, the election of Mr. Vassiliou signalled the beginning of a new policy geared towards membership.[55]

Underlying this politically motivated European orientation was the expectation that closer links with the EU would enable the Greek-Cypriot leadership to exert more pressure on Turkey; and a Cyprus within the EU could induce the Turkish-Cypriot leadership to discount the security considerations in return for economic gains. The collapse of the Soviet bloc and the EU's attempt to establish closer links with the Central and Eastern European countries made this policy choice even more necessary as an 'eastern' EU orientation might well leave Cyprus isolated in the post-Soviet international order.[56] These considerations could be detected in statements made by the Greek-Cypriot leadership at various platforms. For example, in his speech on the occasion of the membership application, Mr. Vassiliou stated that '... the accession of Cyprus to the EU will provide the best possible guarantee of the political future of the country and that of all Cypriots in conditions of stability and security.'[57] Similar statements were also made both by the president and other officials of the Cypriot government in their lobbying of the EU member states.[58] As a result, the EU found itself in a position where the strengthening of its 'eastern' ties would inevitably require a parallel, but less enthusiastic, opening towards the Mediterranean associates, including Cyprus. Under this condition, the EU was forced to accelerate the search for a solution to the Cyprus problem in order to reduce the risks associated with closer ties with a *de facto* divided country.

As the EU began to adopt an activist stance, Turkey's Cyprus policy became less compatible with a negotiated settlement. The twist in Turkish policy became evident in June 1989, when the Turkish-Cypriot leadership rejected the federal solution on the grounds that a federation would not ensure the security

55 Republic of Cyprus, Press and Information Office, *Press Release*, 29.11.1989.

56 For a summary of these developments, see Redmond (1993), pp. 1-15.

57 *Cyprus Bulletin*, 4 .7.1990, p. 4.

58 For Mr. Vassiliou's speech to the Royal Institute of International Affairs in London, see *Agence Europe*, 3.3.1989, p. 3. For the foreign minister's speech to the Institute of Directors on 29 November 1989, see Republic of Cyprus, Press and Information Office, *Press Release*, no. 14, 29.11.1989. Finally, for Vassiliou's welcoming statement to the EU's first Ambassador to Cyprus, see *Cyprus News*, no. 12, May 1990, p. 1.

and equality of the Turkish-Cypriot community. The Turkish-Cypriot leadership pulled out of the UN-sponsored inter-communal talks, arguing that a solution to the Cyprus problem must be based on two separate states connected with a weak confederal link. In addition, Mr. Denktaş invited the Bulgarian Muslims who had fled to Turkey as a result of oppression in Bulgaria to come and settle in Northern Cyprus. He also secured a TRNC Assembly decision in August 1989 that instructed him to reject the UN proposals of 1989 and not to participate in future inter-communal talks as long as 'confederation' was not accepted as a basis for negotiations.[59] This development signalled clearly that Turkey would step up the campaign for consolidating the TRNC as a separate state which could be part of a Cypriot confederation but would remain closely integrated with Turkey economically, politically and militarily. Set against evident indications that the EU was moving towards a relatively activist stance and the EU's support for a unitary Cypriot state, this policy choice indicated that Turkey was prepared to deviate from her European orientation (as declared in her membership bid) because of her interests in Cyprus.

Under this condition, the Cyprus problem in EU-Turkey relations over the 1990s constituted yet another manifestation of the anchor/credibility dilemma, characterised by the EU's limited capacity to anchor Turkey's policy on Cyprus and the Turkey's deviations from her declared European orientation. Although the EU became increasingly involved in the Cyprus problem, this involvement lacked a coherent structure of incentives and sanctions that would increase the cost of Turkey's deviations from the declared European orientation. Instead, the EU has gradually moved towards embracing the inevitability of a permanent division of the Island. Turkey, on the other hand, indicated by words and by actions that her European orientation was not a credible commitment and EU membership could not be traded off with concessions on Cyprus. In the following paragraphs, we examine the unfolding of the events in the 1990s with a view to highlight the shortcomings of the EU's Cyprus policy and Turkey's continued reluctance to relinquish the military superiority it has enjoyed since 1974.

The limitation to the EU's anchoring capacity was not due to its reluctance to impose sanctions in the form of delaying Turkey's membership. In Fact, the EU indicated on a number of occasions in the 1990s took further steps in the 1990s that the Cyprus problem would be a stumbling block for Turkey's membership. In its Opinion of December 1989 on Turkey's application, the Commission stated for the first time that the Cyprus problem, together with the dispute between Turkey and Greece, was affecting the EU-Turkey Association negatively.[60] In an Internal Working Document leaked to the press, the

59 *Agence Europe*, 19/20.6.1989, p. 17; and 24.8.1989, p. 2.

60 Commission of the EC (1989).

Commission went beyond this diplomatic wording and held Turkey responsible for the occupation of half of Cyprus since 1974, for '... blocking all efforts for reunification', and for intending to create an 'independent vassal state.'[61] The president of the EP also stated during his visit to Cyprus at the beginning of December 1989 that 'one of the conditions for full normalisation of relations between the EU and Turkey would have to be the end of Turkish occupation.'[62]

When Mr. Denktaş made it clear on 28 February 1990 that the Turkish-Cypriots would not accept anything less than a right for self-determination, the EP adopted a resolution on 15 March 1990 and condemned the announcement as 'spoiling tactics.' The EP also called on the EU foreign ministers '... to consider how to give support to those progressive Turkish-Cypriot leaders who are prepared to negotiate honestly with the Cyprus government under the auspices of the UN.'[63] This was a radical step that dared to suggest interference with the internal affairs of the Northern Cyprus. The Commission did not come forward with its own statement, but it used a special occasion to express its position indirectly. The EU's first ambassador to Cyprus held a press conference on 24 May 1990 and stated that 'when countries are coming together all over the world, Cyprus cannot be the orphan of Europe.' Having also hinted at Turkey's concerns about remaining isolated in the post Cold War European system, the ambassador stated that this situation would enable the EU to hold the key for a solution to the Cyprus problem.'[64] These statements were followed by others from the European Council. At the end of the first Dublin Summit of 28 April 1990, the European Council expressed concern over the impasse in inter-communal talks and called for urgent resumption of talks in accordance with Resolution 649/90 of the Security Council.[65] At the end of the second Dublin Summit of 25-26 June 1990, it reaffirmed the previous declarations and stated that the Cyprus problem was affecting the EU-Turkey relations.[66]

The momentum continued with the Italian proposal of December 1990 calling for a four-party conference. Following the UN Secretary-General's appeal for more European support in November 1990, the Italian presidency proposed a parallel platform to that of the UN where Turkey, Greece, Cyprus and the EU would discuss the Cyprus problem. The proposal was made with an explicit signal to Turkey indicating that failure to move towards a solution would

61 *Agence Europe*, 2.12.1989, p. 8.

62 *Agence Europe*, 20.4.1989, p. 3.

63 *Official Journal of the EC*, no. C 96 (17.4.1990), p. 252.

64 *Cyprus News*, no. 12 (May 1990), p. 1.

65 Resolution 649/90 was adopted on 12 March 1990, and called on the parties to resume their talks to achieve a solution based on a bi-zonal, bi-communal federal structure.

66 Euroconsult Ltd. (1991), p. 127. Turkey blamed Greece for the critical tone of the second Dublin Summit declaration. See *The Financial Times*, 17.7.1990.

'constitute an obstacle to EU-Turkey relations.'[67] Although this was a significant move that constituted the first EU attempt at proposing an alternative platform, its significance was undermined by the reluctance of other member states to endorse it. Neither the large members (especially Germany and Britain) nor the small members such as Belgium, Luxembourg and the Netherlands were prepared to underwrite the risks associated with a full blown Europeanisation of the Cyprus problem. As a result, the Luxembourg presidency that followed in January 1991 was forced to scale down the Italian initiative by returning to the old policy of supporting the UN. Turkey rejected even this watered down version of the EU initiative on the grounds that EU intervention could jeopardise the attempts to find a solution through the UN. Mr. Denktaş, on the other hand, responded by calling on the EU to stop recognising the Greek Cypriot administration as the legitimate government of Cyprus.[68]

Following the failure of the Luxembourg initiative, Britain brought the Cyprus problem to the G7 platform on 16 July 1991. Although the British approach was still marked with caution, the move was important as Turkey was becoming increasingly eager to attract direct foreign investment. British pressure continued after the G7 meeting, when the British Foreign Secretary visited Turkey. The Cyprus issue in Anglo-Turkish talks assumed an even higher profile as a result of a letter written to the Foreign Secretary by 39 British MPs, urging the British government to take a more active role in finding a solution to the Cyprus problem.[69] In November 1991, the Foreign Secretary told the House of Commons that 'a heavy responsibility' for the deadlock in the inter-communal talks fell upon Mr. Denktaş.[70]

In order to maintain the pressure on Turkey, the Cypriot government took further steps in its policy of 'Europeanising' the Cyprus problem. In March 1992, the Greek-Cypriot delegation to the EU-Cyprus Joint Parliamentary Committee (JPC) managed to secure a joint declaration that urged the EU to provide a positive answer to the country's membership application. The JPC also promised to play an active role in 'encouraging and supporting' Cyprus' accession to the EU.[71] In May of the same year, the Cypriot government decided to link the Cypriot pound to the European Currency Unit (ECU). This was presented as a politically and economically significant step in the policy of

---

67 *Cyprus News*, no. 19, December 1990, p. 1.

68 Cyprus News, no. 21, February 1991, pp. 1, 2.

69 See *Cyprus News*, no. 26, July 1991, p. 2.

70 *Cyprus News*, no. 30, November 1991. p. 1. A stronger statement was made by the Shadow Foreign Secretary, who stated that the Cyprus problem 'is an illegal Turkish invasion', and that '... as long as Turkish troops are in Cyprus, the British government will oppose Turkish admission to the EU.' *Cyprus News*, no. 30, November 1991, p. 1.

71 *Agence Europe*, 18.3.1992, p. 10.

preparing Cyprus for EU membership through policy harmonisation.[72] These moves were undertaken with a clear objective of exerting a positive influence on the EU's reply to the membership application. This objective was maintained by the new president, Mr. Clerides, who stated that the EU membership would facilitate the settlement of the Cyprus problem because it could effectively guarantee the security of both communities.[73]

These efforts *did* bear fruit: the EU became increasingly inclined not only to make the improvement of its relations with Turkey conditional on the solution of the Cyprus problem, but also to signal that Cyprus might be included in the round of enlargement by the end of the century. The first signal to that effect was given by the Commissioner for external political relations, Mr. van den Broek, who in May 1993, indicated that the Commission's opinion on Cyprus' membership application would unambiguously confirm the country's 'European credentials.'[74] A month later, the Commission published its Opinion on Cyprus' membership application and stated that, as far as the Greek-Cypriot part of the Island was concerned, Cyprus was capable of complying with the *acquis communautaire*. Although the Opinion did not recommend the opening of accession negotiations, it made it clear that the decision Cyprus' membership should not be made conditional on a solution to the Cyprus problem. In addition, the Commission disregarded the Turkish-Cypriot argument that the 1960 Guarantee Treaty required the consent of both communities. The Commission argued against this thesis by stating that the application was made by the Cypriot government as the only legitimate representative of Cyprus.[75]

In 1993, Mr. van den Broek conceded that the division of Cyprus would complicate the accession negotiations. Nonetheless, he stated that Turkey, as the party blocking the settlement of the Cyprus problem, should not be able to determine the EU's decision. Therefore, the EU could negotiate only with the Greek-Cypriots if no progress was achieved by January 1995.[76] This position was confirmed by the Council when it instructed the Commission to open 'substantive talks with the government of Cyprus' to prepare for the accession negotiations that would follow.[77] The last EU initiative along this line was the appointment of an EU observer to the UN-sponsored inter-communal talks. Although this issue was discussed in the Council meeting of 4/5 October 1993, a

---

72 *Agence Europe*, 1.5.1992, p. 13; and 9.5.1992, p. 12. Later on, the Central Bank of Cyprus set the parity at C£ 1.00 = ECU 1.7086, with a fluctuation margin of +/- 2.25%. *Agence Europe*, 20.6.1992, p. 16.

73 *Agence Europe*, 4.3.1993, p. 4.

74 *Agence Europe*, 10/11.5.1993, pp. 9-10.

75 Commission of the EC (1993).

76 *Agence Europe*, 1.7.1993, pp. 7-8.

77 *Agence Europe*, 4/5.10.1993, p. 7.

decision could not be taken because of British objections. Following pressure from the Cypriot government, however, the UK lifted her objections and an observer was appointed in December 1993. The observer would be in close liaison with the UN Secretary-General and report to the EU Council on the development of the talks.[78]

It is clear from the evidence above that the EU's increased involvement in the Cyprus problem was closely related to the Greek-Cypriot leadership's European orientation, which took the concrete form of a preference for membership. Faced with this policy choice, the EU needed to reduce the risks associated with Cyprus' membership by ensuring that the Cyprus problem was either resolved or the probability of resolving it was increased beforehand. Nevertheless, the essentially intergovernmental nature of the EU's policy-making process in the area of foreign policy and the lack of constituent pressure on the member states combined to make the EU unable to come to terms with three issues: (i) the credibility and effectiveness of the threat to delay Turkey's membership given the EU's detached involvement until the late 1980s; (ii) the construction of a comprehensive package of incentives and sanctions towards Turkey and the two communities in Cyprus; and (iii) the way in which the Cyprus problem should be linked with Turkey's EU membership application. The EU's failure to come to terms with these issues, as we demonstrate below, has reduced the effectiveness of the EU's input into the resolution of the Cyprus problem and encouraged Turkey to take further steps towards consolidating the Island's division.

The EU may well declare that the Cyprus problem would block the normalisation of the relations with Turkey. The effectiveness of such declarations, however, was undermined by the EU's inherent tendency to avoid the risks associated with anchoring Turkey's convergence towards Europe. As indicated in chapters 2, 4 and 5, the EU was able to undertake only limited and quantifiable risks or commitments towards Turkey. In addition, these limited risks or commitments were undertaken partly to avoid the higher risks associated with Turkish membership rather than as part of a coherent strategy designed to reduce the probability of policy reversals in Turkey. Therefore, the threat that the Cyprus problem would affect EU-Turkey relations negatively was interpreted by Turkey as reflection of a European reluctance to take Turkey into Europe. Combined with Turkey's tendency to externalise the cost of convergence towards EU standards, the EU threat to delay membership led mainly to further divergence in the form of consolidating the division of Cyprus. A possible solution to this anchor/credibility dilemma would require a comprehensive policy

[78] On this development, see *Agence Europe*, 7.10.1993, p. 3; and 22.12.1993, p. 5. See also, *Cyprus News*, no. 51, November 1993, p. 2; and no. 52, December 1993, p. 1.

package consisting of two elements: a set of performance-related incentives for both communities in Cyprus; and a set of conditions that would require both Turkey and Cyprus to accept *ex ante* that negotiations on the wider issues in their relations with the EU would proceed in parallel to their contributions to the settlement of the Cyprus problem. As will be demonstrated below, the EU's approach to the Cyprus problem failed on both counts.

The EU failed to devise a set of transparent and performance-related incentives and sanctions for both communities in Cyprus on three occasions: the Third Financial protocol of 1989; the Commission's reply to Cyprus' membership application in 1993; and the Luxembourg Summit of December 1997. It failed on the occasion of the Third Protocol because neither the magnitude of the financial aid and credits was a large enough incentive nor was the link between the incentive and the solution to the Cyprus problem was explicit. Although the Third Protocol provided for a 55% increase in aid and credits compared to the Second Protocol, the amount of financial injection amounted only to US$ 62 million, an amount hardly compatible with what the EP had had in mind when it proposed in 1988 that the EU should come up with a comprehensive package. In addition, the Third Protocol differed from the previous two by targeting the 'convergence of the markets of Cyprus and Europe in domains covered by the Customs Union Agreement' instead of infra-structure projects with direct benefits for both communities. Therefore, it could be interpreted as a signal to the Turkish-Cypriot leadership that they would stand to lose unless they co-operated towards a solution to the Cyprus problem. The implied threat, however, was compromised by the lack of a common EU position on the details of a possible solution to the Cyprus problem, against which the performance of both Greek- and Turkish-Cypriot leaderships could be judged.

A similar failure was also evident in the Commission's *Opinion* on Cyprus' membership application.[79] The Commission acknowledged the European vocation of Cyprus and confirmed that Cyprus as a whole could be eligible for Objective I regional assistance which, together with other structural assistance, would amount to ECU 120 million per year. In addition, Cyprus would benefit from the Common Agricultural Policy by an amount of ECU 60 million. In return, Cyprus would contribute to the EU budget ECU 100 million in customs duties, farm levies, and VAT and national income based contributions. On balance, Cyprus would be a net beneficiary of the EU budget at a rate of ECU 80 million per year. Bearing in mind that the Third Protocol had provided only for US$ 62 million of financial assistance over a period of five years, it could be seen that the premium on a solution to the Cyprus problem was much higher in 1993. Once again, however, the EU failed to use this incentive as part of a wider

79 Commission of the EC (1993).

package on Cyprus for various reasons. First, differences between the member states prevented the EU from setting up a specialised unit within the Council to monitor developments in Cyprus and produce policy recommendations. Second, the Commission confirmed that Cyprus would be considered as a single region for the purpose of regional assistance, but left the distribution of that assistance between the North and the South unresolved. Third, it did not specify how freedom of movement would be established between the North and the South should Cyprus accede as a unified country. Finally, the Commission was convinced that Cyprus' accession would provide security and prosperity for the two communities. However, it assumed that the benefits of EU membership would be the crowning of an agreement between the Greek- and Turkish-Cypriots rather than a part of a package designed to induce as well as force them to agree on a settlement. Therefore, the Commission's *Opinion*, instead of contributing to the capacity of the EU to emerge as a powerful broker, it confirmed its reluctance to assume such a role.

The third occasion on which the EU failed to link the benefits of EU membership with the settlement of the settlement of the Cyprus problem was the Luxembourg summit of December 1997.[80] The enlargement framework agreed in Luxembourg was based on two pillars: accession partnerships and increased pre-accession aid. Accession partnerships would mobilise financial assistance for the applicant countries and lock the latter into an incentive-sanction structure where the level of assistance and the prospect for membership are linked to the applicant country's progress in complying with the *acquis communautaire*. Once an accession partnership is established by a unanimous decision, the EU Council would decide by qualified majority on the principles, priorities and intermediate objectives of each partnership, and on measures to be taken when an element essential for the pre-accession partnership is missing. This framework, however, is designed specifically for the Central and Eastern European Countries (CEECs), with Cyprus being treated as a special case under a separate paragraph. Although the presidency Conclusions indicated that Cyprus would participate in targeted projects and EU programmes, neither sanctions similar to hose built into the accession partnerships were defined nor the special nature of the Cyprus problem was dealt with. In addition, detailed review procedures were specified for assessing the CEECs convergence towards the *acquis*, but no review procedures were envisaged for Cyprus in relation to either compliance with the *acquis* or progress in the settlement of the Cyprus problem. As a result, one is left with the impression that the Luxembourg Summit was not committed either to develop a comprehensive package of incentives and sanctions or to link such a package with the settlement of the Cyprus problem.

---

80 *Bulletin of the EU*, no. 12-1997.

As if these failures were not enough, the EU, in 1995, complicated the settlement of the Cyprus problem by linking the Cypriot accession with the agreement on the EU-Turkey customs union. Partly under Greek pressure and partly as an attempt to signal to Turkey that the latter could not mortgage the EU's policy on Cyprus, the EU Council decided on 6 March 1995 to link the EU-Turkey customs union with the beginning of the negotiations on Cyprus' accession. According to this linkage, Greece would lift her veto on the EU's financial assistance to Turkey; Turkey would be upgrade its links with the EU; and Cyprus would be given the green light for membership by Committing the EU to start accession negotiations six months after the end of the Intergovernmental Conference.[81] The EU would gain as a result of: (i) getting the EU-Turkey customs union off the ground subject to EP approval, and (ii) signalling to Turkey as well as the Turkish-Cypriot leadership that it would be in their interests to co-operate on the settlement of the Cyprus problem. However, the linkage was so badly designed that its component concerning the settlement of the Cyprus issue failed instantly. The Turkish foreign minister stated on 6 March 1995 (the day on which the customs union agreement was signed) that Turkey would integrate North if the EU decided to take Cyprus, in whole or in part, as a member. He also argued that Cyprus' membership was impossible before Turkey, as a guarantor power, could accede to the EU.[82]

A similar challenge to the linkage was made by the Greek-Cypriot leadership in March 1996 when the EU reminded Greece that her attempts to block the financial aid to Turkey might affect the negotiations on Cyprus' accession. According to Mr. van den Broek, the beginning of the negotiations on Cyprus' accession was part of the package that also included the EU-Turkey customs union, which Greece threatened to block in the wake of the *Imia* crisis in the Aegean. The Cypriot foreign minister was quick to reject this interpretation and argued that Cyprus 'cannot be called upon to pay for the consequences' of the Greco-Turkish dispute.[83] So, one year after the package had been designed, it became evident that the EU's linkage policy was counter-productive. This outcome was not surprising because the linkage was established in an attempt to please the parties involved rather than to supply a coherent and transparent framework of incentives and sanctions that would cover a solution to the Cyprus problem, accession of Cyprus, and a solution to the anchor/credibility dilemma in EU-Turkey relations. Underlying this weakness was the EU's limited capacity to

---

[81] For the Council decision of 6 March 1995, and the preceding developments, see *Agence Europe*, 8.2.1995, p. 6; 13/14/2/1995, p. 5; 15.2.1995, p. 10; 27/28.2.1995, p. 4; 4.3.1995, p. 4; and 8.3.1995, p. 5.

[82] *Agence Europe*, 8.3.1995, p. 5.

[83] Agence Europe, 8.3.1996, p. 8.

act as an anchor for associated countries when the risks associated with the anchoring function are perceived to be high. It was due to this anchor failure that the EU, despite its increased involvement in the Cyprus problem, has failed on two counts. On the one hand, it failed to emerge as a broker that could contribute to the settlement of the Cyprus problem either on a European platform or as part of the ongoing UN efforts. On the other hand, it filed to induce Turkey to think twice before attempting to consolidate the division of the Island and deviating further from the European stance on Cyprus.

6.4 The Cyprus Problem, the Greek Factor and the Credibility of Turkey's European Orientation: An Assessment

Having examined the evolution of the EU's policy on Cyprus, we now examine the impact of the so-called Greek factor on the EU's Cyprus policy and on EU-Turkey relations. Favoured by Turkish policy-makers, the Greek factor thesis basically amounts to the following: EU policy-makers gradually became receptive to Greek pressure as Turkey tried to establish closer links with the EU. This argument is counter-productive and does not hold water for three reasons. First, it is self-defeating because it accords Greece with a degree of influence that she neither deserves nor is capable of wielding within the EU. Second, it ignores the fact that the EU has been reluctant to take Turkey as a member both before and after the accession of Greece. Finally, it allows not only Turkey, but also the EU to evade the anchor/credibility dilemma in EU-Turkey relations by presenting Greece as a scapegoat.

It is clear from the existing evidence that Greece has used all opportunities to raise obstacles to the normalisation of the EU-Turkey relations. For example, in the first EU-Turkey Association Council (AC) meeting after the Turkish military coup of 1980, the Greek foreign minister raised the Cyprus issue and stated that Greece would block the implementation of the EU-Turkey association unless Turkish troops were withdrawn.[84] In the AC meeting of April 1988, Greece insisted on, and secured the introduction of, a statement into the EU's joint *communiqué* that the Cyprus problem was affecting the EU-Turkey relations.[85] Greece also succeeded in ensuring that a similar statement was included in the declaration of the Rhodes Summit in 1988. These diplomatic activities of the late 1980s were accompanied by the Greek veto on the release of the Fourth Financial protocol, which provided for a package of aid and credits

---

[84] *The Financial Times*, 17.9.1986.

[85] See the note issued by the Commission to National Bureaus, BIO(88)133, 26.4.1988. See also, *The Guardian*, 25.4.1988; and *The Financial Times*, 26.4.1988.

totalling ECU 600 million. In addition, Greek officials made it clear on various occasions that Greece would veto Turkey's membership application and lobbied the Commission heavily to come up with a negative reply.

Nevertheless, the impact of the Greek pressure remained limited only to the suspension of the financial protocol. In other words, Greece was unable to block either the revival of the EU-Turkey association or the political dialogue that followed. In fact, Greece had to accept the Commission's proposal of 1990 (the Matutes Package) that envisaged: (i) completion of the customs union by 1995; (ii) financial co-operation; (iii) technological co-operation; and (iv) re-enforcement of cultural and political links with Turkey.[86] Although Greece continued to block the release of the financial aid, the Matutes Package was *de facto* implemented and its major component, the customs union, was established in 1996. This result was not accidental - rather it reflected the EU's resolve to keep Turkey attached to the EU despite Greek pressure, but without accepting her membership. Therefore, the end result confirmed that Greece was able to score some diplomatic points against Turkey, but could not alter the EU's policy line which dated back to the 1980s when the EU reflected its desire to maintain the EU-Turkey association without underwriting Turkey's membership. In that sense, the rejection of Turkey's bid for membership in 1989 was a result of the EU's tendency to avoid substantial risks rather than Greek pressure.

If a 'Greek factor' ever existed in EU-Turkey relations, it was in the form of presenting Greece as a scapegoat by both Turkey and the EU. Turkey, in an attempt to justify her deviations from the EU's declared preference for a settlement of the Cyprus problem and a resolution of the Greco-Turkish dispute, criticised the EU for giving in to Greek pressure. This argument has been invoked not only in relation to Greek initiatives on Cyprus but also with respect to the tension arising out of the Greco-Turkish conflict in the Aegean. Against this, the EU limited its reaction to signalling to Turkey that the Cyprus problem as well as other issues between Turkey and Greece must be resolved before Turkish accession could be possible. This linkage, however, was dictated by the EU's need to avoid the internalisation of the Greco-Turkish conflict rather than Greek pressure *per se*. Although the EU is justified in imposing the resolution of the Greco-Turkish dispute (including the Cyprus problem) as a precondition for Turkey's membership, its reluctance to emerge as a broker that would increase the probability of the settlement by undertaking risks and providing incentives has been a gross failure. Just as Turkey tried to externalise the cost of converging towards the EU, the latter was concerned about avoiding the risks that an effective anchoring role would necessarily entail.

86 For the Commission's proposal, see Commission of the EC (1990a).

The EU's reluctance to act as an effective anchor preceded the accession of Greece and was closely related to Turkey's non-credible commitment to a European orientation. In addition to the steps taken towards consolidating the division of Cyprus, Turkey categorically stated that Cyprus was an issue of national interest that could not be traded off as part of a package involving closer links with the EU. This policy line was evident not only before but also after the membership application in 1987. For example, in 1988, when the Commission was still working on its *Opinion*, the press reported that the Turkish military was strongly against the idea of troop withdrawal; the Turkish foreign ministry told the German presidency of the EU that Turkey would not participate in the AC meeting unless all references to Cyprus were excluded from the agenda; the prime minister behind the membership application, Mr. Özal, stated that Turkey had no policy of acceding to the EU at all costs; and President Evren, the leader of the 1980 coup, stated during his London visit that Turkey would not accept any linkage between her membership application and the settlement of the Cyprus problem.[87] Given these signals, the German presidency suspended its efforts to hold an AC meeting in May 1988 and, in the same month, the Commission told the Turkish prime minister that Turkey would have to accept the rules of the game and recognise the Cypriot government if she wanted closer relations with the EU.[88]

These signals set the tone of the EU's policy towards Turkey in the 1990s. On the one hand, the EU embarked on a more critical policy against Turkey with respect to the Cyprus problem. On the other hand, the EU's critical stance remained strong in words but soft in actions. As would be expected, this combination has only exacerbated the anchor/credibility dilemma in EU-Turkey relations. Although the EU's threat that Turkey's Cyprus policy would affect her membership application adversely was confirmed by later developments, this confirmation was only superficial and, therefore, the threat could not be interpreted as credible. After all, the EU's reluctance to take Turkey in had preceded the emergence of EU activism concerning the Cyprus problem and had been known to Turkey since 1980. In addition, the EU's most comprehensive package in the 1990s (the Matutes Package approved in 1992) was designed not only to secure a delay in Turkey's membership, but also to signal to Turkey that closer relations (provided that they fell short of membership) were feasible even if no progress was achieved in the settlement of the Cyprus problem.

Consequently, Turkey became even less concerned about converging towards the EU's Cyprus policy, which supported the UN's proposal for a bi-

[87] For these statements, see *The Independent*, 27.4.1988; *The Financial Times*, 28.4.1988; 14.6.1988; and 14.7.1988.

[88] *The Independent*, 21.5.1988; and *Agence Europe* 30/31.5.1988, p. 6.

zonal, bi-communal federal state. The first indication in this direction came in 1992, when the EU and Turkey concluded the Matutes package with the aim of strengthening the association. In that year, the inter-communal talks broke down once again as Mr. Denktaş rejected the UN proposal for a bi-zonal, bi-communal federation on the grounds that this solution did not recognise the TRNC as a sovereign state. This policy was followed by a number of steps that intensified the integration of the north Cyprus with Turkey. In September 1994, Turkey signed the 13th joint economic protocol with the TRNC to circumvent the European Court of Justice ruling which required the exports from the North to be certified by the internationally recognised Cypriot government. According to this protocol, the TRNC would use the Turkish Lira as the national currency and apply the Turkish foreign exchange regime; the Cyprus Turkish Airlines would become a Cyprus-based rather than Turkey-based company; and Turkey would provide extra funds to address the liquidity problem of the TRNC economy. In addition, the TRNC declared that the traffic system would be changed to comply with the right lane driving in Turkey and the incorporation of the TRNC into Turkey's telecommunications code was completed.[89]

The integration of the TRNC with Turkey gathered a new momentum after 1995, following the EU's declaration that negotiations on Cyprus' accession would begin six months after the end of the Intergovernmental Conference. The joint declaration of 28 December 1995 tied the hands of the Turkish-Cypriot leadership by stating that Cyprus should join the EU only simultaneously with Turkey and set up an association council that would take measures to achieve 'partial integration' of the north in the areas of economic, financial, security, defence and foreign policy.[90] As this process unfolded, two joint declarations (between Turkey and the TRNC) were made on 20 January and 20 July 1997 with the aim of increasing the viability of the TRNC economically and militarily. Then, in early 1998, Turkish president, Mr. Demirel, declared on the TRT (the Turkish Radio and Television Network) that one could no longer speak of a single Cyprus as there were two nations and two states on the island. Also, the deputy prime minister, Mr. Ecevit, reiterated that the Turkish Cypriot had a separate state and initiated a plan to encourage Turkish entrepreneurs in Gaziantep, a south-eastern province, to invest in the TRNC. Encouraged by these developments, Denktaş told the Turkish Press that he was wrong in the past to uphold the concept of federation and participate in the inter-communal talks. He added that now 'two states' must hold talks to solve the Cyprus problem.[91]

---

89 The Economist Intelligence Unit (1994), pp. 24-25.

90 Kyle (1997), p. 31.

91 *Sabah* (Turkish Daily), 23.2.1998.

Another joint declaration by Mr. Demirel and Mr. Denktaş was made on 23 April 1998, stating, *inter alia*, that the continuation of the TRNC as an independent state was an essential goal to be achieved in line with previous declarations. Also, the joint economic area between Turkey and the TRNC will include free movement goods, services and capital.[92] The escalation of the tension after the decision of the Cypriot government to purchase S-300 missiles from Russia led not only to military muscle flexing but also to the questioning of the presence of the UN peace keeping force (the UNFICYP) in Cyprus. According to Anatolia Agency (1.7.1998, 12.13 pm), the TRNC announced that the UN Security Council repeated the mistake of referring to the Cyprus Republic in its resolution that extended the term of office of the UNFICYP for another six-moth period. The implication of this announcement is that the TRNC 'will determine the conditions valid for the existence and activities' of the UNFICYP within its borders.

The consequences of this integrationist policy for the future of Cyprus are not difficult to anticipate. An informed and long-time observer of the Cyprus problem, Mr. Sami Kohen of the *Milliyet* newspaper, states that even the revival of the dialogue with the Greek-Cypriot leadership will be difficult and the integration of the TRNC with Turkey will become irreversible.[93] This is a realistic assessment because the integration process is generating new obstacles to the re-unification of Cyprus. On the one hand, the TRNC has been extending its patronage network by adopting the Turkish model of state-owned economic enterprises (SOEs) and using them for the distribution of favours such as employment in return for political support. On the other hand, the TRNC has become a centre of attraction for non-productive economic activities (such as gambling), which were deflected into north Cyprus after Turkey's decision to ban the establishment of casinos. This mixture of patron-client relations and shadowy business activities are highly likely to undermine any effective Turkish-Cypriot opposition to the integrationist drive and would continue to prevent the Turkish-Cypriots from realising their potentials within alternative arrangements, including EU membership.

In addition to confirming our argument that Turkish policy on Cyprus has been non-credible, these recent developments also confirm the argument that this policy has been inefficient even if Turkey's European orientation is ignored. Although it is difficult to obtain reliable data, it is estimated that Turkey has supplied 90% of all external aid to Cyprus and financed at least 20% of the TRNC's budget deficit between 1974-93. These amounts do not include

---

92 Transcribed and translated from the announcement of 23 April 1998, 3.30 pm, on the Turkish-Cypriot Bayrak radio.

93 *Milliyet* (Turkish daily), 17.2.1998.

investment and developments spending directly undertaken by the Turkish government or the military.[94] Despite these injections, as of 1997, the income per head in the North was about US$ 3,800 - less than a third of the South; the rate of inflation mirrored that of Turkey at 87.5% compared to 3% in the South; and the budget deficit constituted 15% of the GDP compared to 3.4% in the South.[95] Irrespective of what Turkey's future relations with the TRNC or the EU turns out to be, the widening gap between the North and the South is very likely to remain a liability that Turkish policy-makers will have to come to terms with. In other words, Turkey will be haunted by the legacy of her military presence and its support for a puppet administration that 'transformed the economy of [north] Cyprus from a productive to a lethargic and parasitic entity.'[96]

94 Economist Intelligence Unit (1994-95), p. 35.
95 McDonald (1998), p. 10.
96 Quoted from a businessman in *Sabah* (Turkish daily), 18.4.1998.

7 The Anchor/Credibility Dilemma and Human Rights

Introduction

Human rights policy issues are relatively more transparent than standard foreign policy issues due to the existence of a body of principles codified in the Universal Declaration of Human Rights, the European Convention for the Protection of Human Rights and Fundamental Freedoms (European Convention), and the Human Dimension of the Organisation for Security and Co-operation in Europe (OSCE). In addition, policy decisions in this area generate different societal reactions depending on one's commitment to the promotion and defence of human rights in third countries. Therefore, the exogenously-given level of transparency/divisibility associated with human rights issues is high as there is scope for the proponents and opponents of an activist human rights policy to argue their case in public. The endogenously-determined level of transparency/divisibility, however, may be blurred due to the fact that member states can submerge human rights issues under an indivisible national interest, presented as economic, security or defence priorities that must be observed when a third country's human rights record is questioned. Consequently, the overall level of transparency/divisibility associated with human rights issues tends to be low. Against this, societal assertiveness may fluctuate between high and low levels depending on the level of the constituents' human right awareness and the strength of the non-governmental organisations. Given this combination of issue transparency/divisibility and societal assertiveness, the EU's human rights policy will be characterised by the outcomes summarised in cells A1 and B1 of Figure 2.1. When low levels of transparency/divisibility are combined with low levels of societal assertiveness, the policy outcomes will be determined by the lowest common denominator and the EU will lack an anchoring capacity. When, however, societal assertiveness increases, the EU might acquire a degree of anchoring capacity as the scope for policy co-ordination and supranational inputs increases.

A factor that may enhance this anchoring capacity is the functionality of a high profile human rights policy for legitimating the EU system. As indicated in chapter 2, the EU policy-making process is executive-driven and technocratic because of the need for issue dissection and aggregation as a basis for package deals. That is why the EU system has been criticised for its heavy reliance on technocratic bargaining within committees (the so-called 'comitology' problem) and lack of democratic control.[1] In this system, an activist human rights policy *vis-à-vis* third countries may become functional as a means of making the technocratic image of the EU machinery less visible and granting the EP certain powers that may be less contentious for the member states. In other words, human rights may become a policy area where Therefore, the EP may emerge as a significant actor influencing the development of an EU human rights policy *vis-à-vis* third countries. To the extent that this is the case, the Turkish policy-makers' tendency to ignore the EP or to criticise the EU in general for using the EP as a pretext for avoiding Turkey's closer integration may be a self-defeating strategy. This approach overlooks the dynamic that enables the EP to assume a significant role in the promotion of human rights in an associated country and gives further signals about the non-credibility of Turkey's commitment to policy reform as a precondition for closer ties with the EU.

These aspects of the EU's human rights policy are examined in section 7.1, where we demonstrate that EU member states have been induced to co-ordinate their human right policies as a result of societal assertiveness and concerns about legitimating the EU system. We also observe that convergent policy choices have been codified through political declarations, resolutions and, eventually, treaty provisions. Three principles are embodied in these texts: respect for human rights is an essential element in the EU's relations with third countries; EU interventions aimed at promoting and safeguarding human rights in a third country cannot be considered as interference in internal affairs; and cultural relativism cannot be invoked as a reason to derogate from the principles established by the Universal Declaration of Human Rights. For third countries wishing to join or establish close links with the EU, these principles imply higher convergence and/or withdrawal costs compared to UN or Council of Europe membership. The convergence cost is higher in the EU context because EU membership requires the incorporation of the *acquis communautaire* (including provisions on human rights) into the national legislation whereas the Universal Declaration or the European Convention has to balance ambitious objectives with a high degree of flexibility required by the concept of state sovereignty.[2] In that sense, it

---

1 See Williams (1991); and Siedentopf and Hauschild (1988).

2 On the tensions arising out of this contradiction in UN regime and the European Convention, see Farer (1992) and Weston et al. (1992), respectively.

can be used as a 'filter' to avoid close relations with or membership of third countries. The withdrawal cost is also higher in the EU context because failure to comply with the Universal Declaration or the European Convention implies only 'status costs' in terms of isolation or exclusion; whereas failure to comply with EU human rights standards implies both 'status costs' and 'economic costs', which include loss of preferential access to markets, financial aid, and the benefits of economic cooperation.

Nevertheless, the EU's human rights regime is lop-sided so far as the distribution of the convergence costs and benefits is concerned. As we have indicated in chapter 1, convergence is a special case of policy co-ordination the success of which depends not only on the existence of a corpus of principles towards which the third country should converge but also on the extent to which transparent rules and procedures for distribution are established. The EU regime is strong in terms of setting minimum standards that must be met, but it is severely limited in terms of specifying the rules and procedures for the distribution of the short-term costs and long-terms benefits associated with a third country's convergence towards those standards. In fact, the EU regime is designed to make the third country bear the short-term costs of convergence in return for long-terms benefits that closer links with the EU might produce. It is because of this lop-sidedness that neither the EU nor Turkey could escape the anchor/credibility dilemma specified in this book. The EU's human rights regime may exclude cultural relativism or transcend the principle of non-intervention into domestic affairs, but the anchoring function that this regime can deploy is fully effective only if the third country with a poor human rights record is already prepared to bear the cost of convergence towards EU standards.

When, however, the third country does not fit into this category, a different set of incentives and sanctions is required in order to ensure that its convergence towards EU standards is encouraged or its deviations from those standards are deterred. In Section 7.2, we shall demonstrate that this dimension is missing in the EU's human rights policy and, therefore, Turkey has found it either less attractive to converge towards EU standards or less costly to deviate from them. Although this missing dimension should not be used as a pretext to conceal the non-credible nature of Turkey's commitment to converge towards EU standards, the weakening effect it has on the EU's anchoring capacity should not be ignored either. The EU has failed on a number of occasions to act as an effective anchor either as a result of non-transparent considerations by the member states or because of the EU's failure to devise performance related criteria that would link the progress in the area of human rights policy reform with the eventual target of membership. When considered in conjunction with Turkey's non-credible commitment to converge towards EU standards, these failures have changed the cost/incentive structure faced by Turkey in a way that has been conducive to further policy reversals which, in turn, has induced the EU to be even more reluctant to play an anchoring role.

7.1 The Evolution of the EU's Human Rights Policy: Theory and Evidence

International relations literature on the scope for a human rights dimension in foreign policy tends to draw attention to the tension between the assumption of an international society composed of sovereign states and the moral urge that policy-makers cannot be indifferent to the way in which those states tend to treat their constituents.[3] This tension is especially obvious in a state-centric approach to international law, which ascribes rights and obligations to states as sovereign entities. Once such a view is adopted, the division of the international public space along the lines of territorial sovereignty leaves only a limited scope for other states or international organisations to raise a particular state's human rights record as a legitimate concern in their relations. This limited scope enables the 'sovereign states' usually to avoid their obligations under international conventions related to human rights issues.[4] This tension could be seen in the field of foreign policy analysis too. As Vincent has indicated, human rights and foreign policy have different constituencies: the society of all humankind stands in contrast to the society of states. Under this condition, foreign policy-makers would tend either to reflect a reluctance to be concerned with human rights issues or to use them as a means of leverage in relations with their counterparts. Such tendencies, then, would be justified on the grounds that the international system implies rights and obligations for states which, by definition, require pluralism and diversity as common assumptions.[5]

Of course most students of international relations, including Vincent, would not conclude that human rights issues should play no part in a country's external relations. What is implied from this state-centric analysis is that states would tend to invoke their sovereign rights and resist intervention from outside or they would invoke human rights issues as a convenient tool for achieving power-political goals. Therefore, foreign

---

3 See, for example, Coplin (1965); Henkin (1990); Pease and Forsythe (1993).

4 Therefore, critics of the state-centric view consider the concept of sovereignty as a license for genocide. See Kuper (1992).

5 Vincent (1986), p. 129.

policy-makers should be aware of this constraint and try to balance the moral argument with the realism that the international state system would require. Their analysis should be seen as a warning against cosmopolitan policy recommendations which assume that state boundaries are superficial and should not override the need to be concerned with the fate of human beings across boundaries.[6]

A refinement of this state-centric approach is provided by the international regimes theory and the English School in international relations.[7] While the former points out the constraints imposed on states because of interdependence and negative externalities, the latter emphasises the need for common rules and values that states must develop as members of an international society. In some ways, these approaches can be seen as attempts to strike a balance between the cosmopolitan view that envisages a large scope for intervention in the field of human rights, and the realist/neo-realist perspective which tends to highlight the limits to such intervention. The international regimes theory or the English School suggests that states should learn to live with rules for basic individual rights without necessarily having to do away with the principle of sovereignty.

The relevance of the cosmopolitan or interdependence perspectives for the study of international institution building in the field of human rights cannot be overlooked. In contrast to strictly state-centric approaches, they can explain the proliferation of both governmental and non-governmental organisations in this field, especially after the end of World War II. They can also generate legitimate research programmes within which the significance of cosmopolitan identity or interdependence can be tested. They may, however, be faced with certain difficulties when it comes to (i) account for different levels of policy co-ordination and/or integration to which different groups of states would subscribe under a given level of interdependence, and (ii) explaining the development of international institutions in which aspects of both intergovernmentalism and supranationalism are observed simultaneously. While an attempt may be made to overcome the first difficulty by referring to differences in national preference formation, the concept of preference formation remains problematic as it is detached from state-society interaction. The second difficulty is even more difficult to resolve as the cosmopolitan approach

---

6 For the cosmopolitan approach to human rights, see Beitz (1979), pp. 63-66, 88-89, 143-53; Linklater (1993); and Falk (1992). On the application of the cosmopolitan perspective to wider issues, see Falk (1971), pp. 1-16 and 296-312.

7 For approaches within an international regimes or English School tradition, see Donnelly (1985), pp. 57-97. See also, Vincent (1986). For a comparison of international regimes theory and the English School, see Evans and Wilson (1992).

envisages supranationalism to be the norm while the international regimes theory or the English School predicts intergovernmentalism to prevail.

To address these shortcomings, this section analyses the EU's human rights policy *vis-à-vis* third countries as an endogenous outcome of the interaction between the state and society. In this perspective, the development of an EU human rights policy is related to the level of societal assertiveness about human rights issues and the extent to which EU member states can blur the transparency/divisibility of these issues by linking them with an undivided national interest. While societal assertiveness induces the member states to approximate their policies in an attempt to approximate the rates of returns on loyalty and thereby legitimate the political system; the extent of policy approximation and the procedures through which the convergent policies are codified will be checked by the ability of the member states to blur the transparency/divisibility of the human rights issues. The evidence examined below lends support to this analysis and provides some indications about the extent to which the EU could emerge as an effective anchor that would enable Turkish policy-makers to overcome the credibility problem which permeated the area of human rights too.

The EU's human rights policy has evolved through two phases: an essentially inward looking phase until 1985 and an outward-looking phase from 1986 onwards. During the first phase, the EU's involvement in human rights issues was triggered off by internal developments to which the European Court of Justice had to respond. Beginning in mid-1960s, the Court delivered judgements on various human rights cases and referred to constitutional traditions of the member states as 'considerations of fundamental relevance' to its judgements.[8] From mid-1970s onwards, the EP also began to push for an EU human rights catalogue that would provide redress for individuals affected by EU legislation.[9] The outcomes of this phase, however, remained limited to the Copenhagen Summit statement of 14 December 1973, which declared that the 'European identity' was characterised by '... the principles of representative democracy and respect for human rights'; and the inter-institutional declaration of 1977, which called for the protection of fundamental rights as derived from the constitutions of the member states and the European Convention.[10]

During the second phase, not only did the policy become more outward looking, but also more active. Beginning with the publication of EP reports from 1983 onwards, the second half of the 1980s witnessed various

8 See Duparc (1992), p. 13.
9 Mower, Jr. (1980), p.50.
10 Duparc (1992), pp. 30, 35.

developments. First, the Single European Act (SEA) provided that human rights issues should be an essential element in the conduct of the EU's external relations. In addition, Articles 8 and 9 of the SEA amended Articles 237 and 238 of the Treaty of Rome and made the conclusion of accession as well as association agreements conditional on the EP's assent. The EP made it immediately clear that it would 'make the most of the political opportunities offered by the SEA' and pointed to 'the advances that can be made towards achieving a true European identity in external policy'.[11] Second, various statements and joint declarations were made between 1986-91 at various levels where the link between human rights and external relations was made explicit.[12] Finally, the EU has introduced human rights clauses into the association agreements with the African Caribbean and Pacific (ACP) countries from 1989 onwards. Finally, Article J(2) of the TEU provided that one of the objectives of the EU's common foreign and security policy is to develop and consolidate respect for human rights, defined in Article F of the Common Provisions as fundamental rights guaranteed by the European Convention.

As a result, the number of declarations issued and *demarches* made in the context of the European Political Cooperation (EPC) until 1992 and the Common Foreign and Security Policy (CFSP) thereafter increased significantly. As can be seen in Table 7.1, the number of declarations increased from less than ten in the first half of the 1980s to an average of 22 in the second half and 82 in the 1990s. The number of *demarches*, on the other hand, increased from less than ten per year to 70 and 90 over the same periods. In addition, EU member states began to engage in intensive policy co-ordination with a view to adopt a common position on UN General Assembly resolutions concerning human rights issues. Unlike the pattern of voting on Cyprus we highlighted in chapter 6, EU member states were able to vote in unison and the level of uniformity increased from about 50 percent in the first half of the 1980s to about 60 percent in the second half and over 80 percent in the 1990s.

Irrespective of the effectiveness of the increased activity, the trend examined above raises two questions: (i) has the increased activism been related to societal assertiveness or external factors? (ii) what is the relationship between increased activism and the functionality of a high-profile human rights policy for legitimating the EU system? Elaboration on these questions is necessary not only to probe the relevance of the argument that the EU's human rights policy is an endogenous outcome of societal

11 European Parliament (1988), p. 5.

12 See Duparc (1992). See also, de Gucht (1988); and Coates (1992).

assertiveness and issue transparency/divisibility, but also to detect the extent to which the EU can act as an anchor for policy reform in third countries.

Table 7.1 Indicators of EU human rights activity, 1981-96

Year	Number of declarations issued	Number of demarches made	% UN resolutions on which EU member states voted alike
1981-85	4	20	n.a.
1986	8	n.a.	54%
1987	n.a.	n.a.	57%
1988	15	50	60%
1989	27	70	55%
1990	60	100	70%
1991	110	75	n.a.
1992	60	140	n.a.
1993	n.a.	n.a.	89%
1994	89	50	90%
1995	85	83	76%
1996	67	102	92%

n.a.: not available

Source: Fouwels (1997), pp. 306-307.

7.1.1 External Factors vs. Societal Assertiveness in the Making of the EU's Human Rights Policy

Two external factors might have affected the EU's human rights policy *vis-à-vis* third countries: the increased emphasis on human rights issues in the US foreign policy from 1976 onwards; and the transformation of the Central and Eastern European countries (CEECs) after 1989. The shift in the US policy had a bearing upon the EU's human rights policy because of its wider implications for East-West relations. The transformation of the CEECs also had a bearing because it required a fundamental reconsideration of the assumptions upon which the EU's policy towards the CEECs was based. Having acknowledged that, however, the following discussion will demonstrate that these external factors cannot be taken as explanatory variables for the evolution of the EU's human rights policy. Instead, one needs to examine the way in which these external developments have been mediated through state-society interaction within the EU and its members.

The change in US human rights policy, according to Forsythe, was due to the lack of morality in the 'realist' foreign policy pursued under the Nixon Administration in the first half of the 1970s.[13] This 'realist' orientation clashed with the 'reality' of the Vietnam trauma that caused a significant change in the 'composite American psyche' and induced Jimmy Carter to respond by according a high profile to human rights issues.[14] Encouraged by the favourable results of the 1976 primaries, the Carter campaign strengthened the emphasis on human rights as an essential element in the US foreign policy. Although the question as to whether or not this campaign rhetoric led to a radically different human rights policy after 1977 remained unresolved, research findings demonstrate unequivocally that human rights issues occupied a larger place on the new administration's agenda.[15] The impact of this development on the EU, however, was in contrast to what an interdependence based approach to human rights would suggest. As the content of the policy documents that emerged during the 1970s would indicate, the EU was not pushed to imitate the US administration and assign a high profile to human rights issues in its foreign policy. On the contrary, some members of the EU, especially Germany and France, signalled explicit discontent with the negative implications of the US activism for *détente*. France and Germany were concerned that the US administration's emphasis on human rights issues within the Soviet bloc might provoke Soviet reactions that could jeopardise their commercial and political relations with the Soviet Union and other Warsaw Pact countries.[16] These considerations can be taken as a significant factor that shaped the reluctance of the Council and the member states during the second half of the 1970s and early 1980s to respond positively to the EP's requests for a more active human rights policy commitment in foreign policy.

In contrast, the EU responded to the collapse of the Soviet bloc by adopting an activist human rights policy stance *vis-à-vis* the post-communist regimes. The first step in that direction was taken on 30 May 1989, when the Spanish foreign minister, Mr. Ordonez, made a joint EU statement in the first session of the Conference on Human Dimension (CHD) of the

---

13 Forsythe (1984), p. 270.
14 Mower, Jr. (1987), p. 13.
15 See, for example, Mower (1987); Carleton and Stohl (1985); and Forsythe (1988).
16 See Ludlow (1982), pp. 66-67.

Conference on Security and Co-operation in Europe (CSCE).[17] The statement on behalf of the Twelve was made for the first time by a foreign minister instead of a permanent representative. Mr. Ordonez stated that the Twelve would like to see the CHD 'as a dynamic instrument' that would increase the effectiveness of the CSCE human dimension. The link between events in Eastern Europe and the EU's active involvement was made explicit in the statement: the Twelve attributed the significance of the occasion to developments internal to participating states and the resulting conditions that marked the Conference.[18] A similar link was indicated by the Irish Foreign Affairs Minister, Mr. Gerard Collins, in his statement to the 46th Session of the United Nations Commission on Human Rights (UNCHR) on 2 February 1990. Mr. Collins stated that his focus on Eastern and Central Europe was due to the fact that '... what is happening there has far reaching implications for strengthening peace and security in the world'.[19]

Although these statements point to a link between increased EU human rights activity and developments in Eastern Europe, this link was not a straightforward one for two reasons: (i) the human rights record of the CEECs was quickly submerged under non-transparent/non-divisible foreign policy considerations, and (ii) the EU's tendency to accord a high profile to human rights issues in its relations with third countries both preceded and survived the increased activity between 1989-91. Signs reflecting the short-termism of the EU's human right policy towards the CEECs began to emerge in the November 1991 Paris Summit of the CSCE. A year later, the EU member states began to adopt a clearly negative attitude. This was apparent in the Fourth Follow-Up Meeting of the CSCE in Helsinki in 1992 - known as the Helsinki II. As Amnesty International pointed out, human rights had to fight for survival at Helsinki II.[20] Almost all participating states were concerned with security issues and it was only due to US insistence that a separate working group could be established on human rights issues. Moreover, most states either did not participate in the human rights working group or sent only junior diplomats.

In contrast to their statement of 30 May 1989 that called for the CHD to be made a dynamic instrument for strengthening the effectiveness of the CSCE, the EU member states voted in favour of scrapping the mechanism. The new mechanism, the Human Dimension Implementation Meeting

17 The CHD was established by the Vienna Concluding Document of the CSCE, which was negotiated from 1986-89. The CHD was established for following-up implementation and adoption of new measures. On this, see Buergenthal (1992), pp. 184-88.

18 European Political Cooperation (1989).

19 European Political Cooperation (1990).

20 Amnesty International (1993).

(HDIM), had neither the power to conclude documents nor the authority to draft human rights standards. In retrospect, this outcome was not surprising: external developments that generated assertiveness in the EU's human rights policy have also led to a shift of attention away from human rights considerations towards concerns about security as well as other foreign policy priorities such as potential commercial and political links. Once linked with such non-transparent issues, human rights ceased to be a policy issue upon which the member states could develop a consensus. Therefore, as Lehne has suggested, the scope for 'normative work' was reduced after the transformation of Eastern and Central Europe.[21]

Evidence concerning the impact of societal assertiveness on the EU's human rights policy can be found in both independent research and EU documents. For example, a case study undertaken in 1977 in various EU countries reveals that about 70-80 percent of the respondents in Germany and France supported the definition of an extensive catalogue of human rights that went beyond state-granted privileges. Analysis of data on British and Italian attitudes reflected similar results. In the case of Germany and France, it was clearly evident that the level of education was the most significant variable that affected human rights awareness. Increase in education was found to be associated not only with increased human rights awareness, but also with increased support for an activist policy towards third countries.[22]

Similar trends could be detected in a survey conducted by the Commission in 1989. Between 60 and 94 per cent of respondents stated that human rights should be respected under all circumstances. Interestingly, the level of support was higher for social rights (87-94 per cent) when compared with some first generation human rights such as religious freedom or freedom of speech (60-84 per cent). The same survey's results also indicated that education and strong leadership attributes were correlated with higher levels of human rights awareness and more pronounced criticism of the EU's human rights policy. For example, on average, 48 per cent of the respondents indicated that the EU's human rights policy was not sufficiently active. This rate increased to 58% among respondents with advanced educational levels or strong leadership attributes.[23]

It was against this societal assertiveness that EU member states were induced to approximate their human rights policy as a means of loyalty maintenance. In fact, this concern was mentioned explicitly in various EU

---

21 Lehne (1991), p. 85-94.

22 Szabo (1979a); and Szabo (1979b).

23 *Eurobarometer* (November 1989), pp. 21-33.

documents and policy statements. For example, in the 1988 report on human rights, the EP *rapporteur* stated that the first direct elections in 1979 led to a dramatic increase in the EP's human rights activity. This was related to the combined effect of direct election and increased concerns of ordinary citizens as well as human rights activists. As a result of these developments, according to de Gucht, those MEPs who felt that the EP should not concern itself with human rights issues had to change their positions as a result of representations from individuals and organisations.[24] In another report, Ken Coates indicated the EP's high level of activity in the area of human rights was '... largely *a response to the concerns of the electorate*, and the internationalisation of human rights movement, which is essentially sustained by the concerns of individual citizens'.[25]

The analysis above would suggest that the degree of societal assertiveness can provide a useful starting point in explaining the EU's human rights policy. In fact, the relevance of this factor will be even more evident if we take into account the fact that the EU's human rights policy had first begun as an inward-looking process prompted by a specific manifestation of the EU's democratic deficit, i.e., the fact that EU institutions are not subject to the direct supervision of the European Court of Human Rights. This said, however, such an account will remain simplistic if it does not take into account the fact that EU member states, both before and during the policy co-ordination process, can blur the transparency/divisibility of human rights issues by linking them with the concept of national interest. At a given level of societal assertiveness, blurring the transparency/divisibility of the human rights issues enables the member states to deploy the monopoly power associated with territorial competence and diminish the scope for shifts in constituent loyalty. As the scope for loyalty shifts is reduced in this manner, societal assertiveness becomes less effective. Therefore, the extent of policy convergence and codification will be determined not only by societal assertiveness but also by the manner in which the member states react to that assertiveness. In other words, the emergence of a co-ordinated EU human rights policy must be examined as an endogenously determined outcome of state-society interaction at different levels of issue transparency/divisibility and societal assertiveness. Under this condition, external factors such as the collapse of the Soviet regimes in Central and Eastern Europe, may act as a shift variable but can neither generate nor sustain a long-term EU human rights policy.

---

24 de Gucht (1988), pp. 21-22.

25 Coates (1992), p. 54.

7.1.2 Legitimating the EU System as an Additional Factor in the Making of the EU's Human Rights Policy

Formally, as an element of external policy, human rights matters have been dealt with by the EPC until 1992 and the CFSP thereafter. It can be argued that the EPC/CFSP framework is an intergovernmental forum that should be studied within a state-centric perspective.[26] As a result, the EU's human rights policy can well be examined with reference to the concepts of sovereignty and national interests, and the power politics associated with them. This, however, would be a simplistic rendering and overlook the complexity of the EU's policy-making process, in which the EP and the Commission are involved and the EPC/CFSP framework is locked into a symbiotic relationship between intergovernmentalism and supranationalism. Although the convergence of the member states' human rights policy is primordial to supranational inputs, the latter is far from being insignificant. In fact, all major policy announcements made by the Council, the EPC or the CFSP had been preceded by intense activity within both the EP and the Commission. The latter played a significant role not only in terms of exerting pressure on the intergovernmental actors of the EU, but also in terms of guarding the codified policy outcomes and limiting the scope for policy reversals.

Existing evidence suggests that the EP has played a pro-active role in the development of the EU's human rights policy either by forcing the issues into the agenda of the Council and the Commission or by arguing for policy actions that went beyond what the Council and the Commission was prepared to do at a given time. Although these pro-active attempts have failed to achieve concrete results on many occasions, they were influential in maintaining a gradual momentum that, over time, has led to cumulative results. For example, the first Inter-institutional Declaration of April 1977 was influenced significantly by the EP's pressure.[27] The inclusion of references to human rights into Lomé Conventions was also influenced by the EP. Following the first EP recommendation to this effect in 1983, such references were included in Lomé III in 1985 as general statements, and as binding articles in Lomé IV of December 1989. Similarly, the call for incorporation of human rights as an element of external relations was made by the EP in its resolution of 17 May 1983. Although the EPC had stated in its replies to various parliamentary questions that member states are

---

26 See, for example, Pijpers (1991).

27 Mower, Jr. (1980), p. 58.

concerned about human rights violations in third countries, the first formal statement that linked human rights with external relations came three years later, with the EPC Statement of 21 July 1986.[28] The EP stated in almost all of its resolutions that expressions of concerns about human rights could not be considered as interference in domestic affairs. This principle was announced by the EPC only in 1986 in the above-mentioned statement. The European Council's pronouncement on this principle came even later, in the Luxembourg Declaration of 29 June 1991. Finally, the significance of EP resolutions for joint action in the EPC framework was acknowledged by the latter, when it stated in its first annual memorandum that the views of the EP '... are increasingly referred to when preparing the positions which the Twelve try to adopt jointly'.[29]

A similar trend can be observed in the institutionalisation of the human rights policy process. For example, the EP first established a Working Group on Human Rights within its Political Affairs Committee in October 1980. This group was later upgraded to a Sub-committee on Human Rights in 1984. In 1986, it requested the appointment of a commissioner charged with the human rights portfolio. The Commission did not go so far, but first it decided to allocate human rights matters to the president's portfolio. Then, in May 1988, it created a 'Directorate F' within the general secretariat responsible for monitoring intergovernmental co-ordination between the member states. This Directorate, which was renamed as 'Directorate A' and relocated into Directorate General IA in 1993. This unit was charged with the task of assisting in the co-ordination of human rights policy among different services of the Commission, consulting with the EPC and the CFSP platforms, and disseminating information.[30] A similar EP contribution could be observed in the establishment of working group within the EPC framework. The EPC's Working Group on Human Rights was established in 1987 in response to the EP's 1986 resolution urging the EPC to take a step in that direction. This EPC's working group was charged with the task of liasing with human rights groups co-ordinating the EU's policy at the UN and the Organisation for Security and Cooperation in Europe (OSCE).

Another input from the EP was related to the submission of reports and memoranda on the EU's human rights policy. Initially, the Commission rejected the EP's request for formal dialogue. From 1986 onwards, however,

28 For the EP Resolution see *Official Journal of the EC*, no. C161, 20.6.1983, p. 64. For the foreign ministers' Statement see Doc. no. 86/230 in *EPC Documentation Bulletin*, vol. 2, no. 2, 1986, pp. 57-58.

29 *EPC Documentation Bulletin*, vol. 2, no. 1, 1986, p. 157.

30 *Official Journal of the EC*, no. C99, 13.4.1987, p. 162; de Gucht (1988), p. 26; and Fouwels (1997), p. 316.

it began to devote part of its annual report to EU human rights policy *vis-à-vis* third countries. Similarly, the EPC first refused to enter into a written dialogue with the EP's Working Group on Human Rights when this was established in 1980, but later on it began to submit annual memoranda to the EP from 1986 onwards and the practice was maintained after the introduction of the CFSP in the TEU. Although they contained only little information on what the EPC did and what results were achieved, these reports served as a reference point for the EP and formed part of the EU's institutional memory in the field of human rights. Although the list above seems impressive, the EP's activism and the accommodating responses from other institutions should be taken neither as an indicator of an enlightened and benevolent approach to the protection of human rights nor as a proof of that the EU's human rights policy is essentially driven by supranational actors. With its executive-driven and technocratic structure, the EU responded to the EP's activism positively because the latter was functional for legitimating the EU system in the face of increasing concerns about its democratic deficit. The positive response was also useful in providing the EP with a channel of 'voice' and dissipating its resentment against the executive-driven legislative process.

This experience has certain parallelism with some nation-state experiences where the EP's powers are limited, but its functionality for legitimating of the political system is important. For example, in the Canadian case, where the EP was weakened as a result of the concentration of power within the cabinet, the former retained a significant degree of power in influencing the Canadian government's human rights policy. According to Nolan, the most important reason for this has been the Canadian EP's status as a legitimate part of Canada's history, culture and government, which, in turn, has added to its legitimation role - a fact that governments could not ignore.[31] Similarly, human rights had to be part of the process of building an EU, which '... is able to function with authority, and as something more than an association of states retaining all attributes of sovereignty as traditionally defined'.[32] That was why the EP was able to instigate debate between various EU institutions, request clarification of official positions through parliamentary questions/debates, and adopt resolutions that from time to time went beyond what the Council or the Commission would prefer.

Although high levels of societal assertiveness and concerns raised by the EU's democratic deficit have allowed for significant inputs from the EP as a

---

31 Nolan (1985).

32 Mower, Jr. (1980), p. 46.

supranational actor, the effectiveness of those inputs has been checked by the interaction between supranational and intergovernmental dimensions of the EU system. For example, the agenda of the EP's Sub-committee on Human Rights was largely independent, but it was also associated with that of the other groups for two reasons: (i) the agenda of other groups would signal to the EP the issue areas over which it could try to exercise some influence, and (ii) particular issues on that agenda could explicitly require EP inputs, especially if they were related to co-operation, association or accession agreements. A similar interaction exists in the case of the Commission's Directorate A. Although this Directorate could propose a specific human rights policy issue to be debated in the EPC framework, its agenda is mostly determined by issues already under discussion within that framework. That is because the Directorate's main responsibility was not policy initiation, but acting as an impartial broker between governments in order to facilitate the adoption of joint positions.

The EPC (CFSP) Working Group on Human Rights acts as a platform for policy coordination between the member states and as a centre towards which information would flow from various sources.[33] In formulating its recommendations, the Working Group makes use of the information compiled by member state embassies about human rights violations in various countries, takes into account the inputs from the EP and the Commission, and consults with other EPC Working Groups dealing with the UN or the OSCE in order to assess the implications of any likely decision. After this process is exhausted, a recommendation would be formulated and submitted to the Political Committee (PoCo). The Commission would be represented in PoCo meetings, where it would try to put its case and draw attention to the EP's views on the issue under discussion. Then the PoCo could either arrive at a decision about what action would be taken or pass a recommendation to the EPC (or CFSP) meetings where a final decision would be taken. The decision could be in the form of undertaking a *demarche*, making a public statement, approaching the country concerned privately, or agreeing on a common position at international fora.

Given complexity of the interaction between supranational and intergovernmental actors of the EU system and the process of intergovernmental bargaining at the ECP (CFSP) level, the limits to the effectiveness of the EU's human rights policy should not be difficult to detect. At the end of the day, it is obvious that the member states, through

---

33 This information is based on the first memorandum submitted by the Dutch presidency for the years 1981-86. See *EPC Documentation Bulletin*, vol. 2, no. 1, 1986, pp. 157-160.

their representatives in the EPC (CFSP) Working Group or at ministerial level, have the final say about what action should be taken on behalf of the EU. Taken together with the fact that decisions concerning human rights are taken unanimously, it can be seen that there is ample scope for blurring the transparency/divisibility of the human rights issues by linking them with a national interest that cannot be traded off as part of a package deal facilitating the adoption of common positions. Therefore, the EU's anchoring capacity (i.e., its ability to undertake risks and/or to impose sanctions aimed at securing improvement in third country's human rights record) will be limited even if societal assertiveness is high - as suggested in cell B1 of figure 2.1. Obviously, the limitation will be more severe if societal assertiveness is low - as indicated in cell A1 of figure 2.1.

Given this limited anchoring capacity, the EU can be expected to adopt an activist human rights policy towards a third country only if the latter's European orientation is credible. That is because the third country's credible European orientation implies a change in risk/incentive structure faced by the EU and the member states. The risk of adopting an activist stance will be reduced while the incentive will be increased as the third country with a credible European orientation signals its willingness to bear the short-term costs of converging towards EU standards. To the extent that this is the case, the change in the risk/incentive structure may induce the EU and the member states to 'redefine' the national (or European) interest in the light of the new information. Ironically, then, the EU's capacity to emerge as an anchor for policy reform in third countries will be higher when these countries are already prepared to pay the 'access fee', i.e., to bear the cost of convergence towards the EU's human rights standards in return for closer relations. This type of anchoring is a far cry away from the effective anchor conceptualised in this book, i.e., the ability to undertake risks and impose sanctions that would distribute the costs and benefits of the policy co-ordination and, thereby, reduce the probability of policy reversals in third countries. As we demonstrate in section 7.2 below, the reluctance of the EU to assume such an anchoring role will interact with Turkey's non-credible commitment to policy reform and exacerbate the anchor/credibility dilemma that characterised the EU-Turkey relations.

7.2 Turkey's Human Rights Record and the EU: Reciprocal Failure

As explained in chapter three, state-society interaction in Turkey is conducive to limited democratisation and frequent deviations from the political convergence required by closer integration within the EU. This is mainly because the control-reliant mode of governance in Turkey encourages demands for externalisation of private risks but discourages demands for democratisation. Therefore, it is not surprising to observe that Turkey's human rights record has been divergent from the EU standards and violations of human rights have been the rule rather than the exception. Although the human cost of these violations are extremely difficult to establish, the existing information suggests that they are substantial. According to unofficial estimates of the Amnesty International, the number of people killed under torture in Turkey since 1980 is around 400. The number of disappearances and political killings amounts to 200 and 2,500, respectively. The number of casualties in the armed conflict in the Kurdish-speaking provinces is estimated to be over 30,000, including civilians. To these figures, one must also add the suffering of the tens of thousands of people who have been imprisoned following the drastic measures introduced after the military of 1980.[34]

Despite the fact that violations of human rights were evident in the 1970s, the EU's interest in Turkey's human rights record began only in 1980. One reason for this belated interest was strategic considerations. The withdrawal of Greece from NATO's military command in 1974 increased the premium on Turkey's role in the containment of the Soviet Union and induced the EU to subordinate human rights issues to strategic considerations. Another reason was political instability and wide-spread political violence in Turkey. Under this condition, societal pressure on the EU and the member states was limited as the European public opinion was preoccupied with images of political turbulence rather than poor human rights record. Finally, the EU's human rights policy until mid-1980s was essentially inward looking and lacked an institutional framework through which the member states' human rights policy could be co-ordinated.

These factors delayed the EU's reaction to human rights violations in Turkey until June 1980 - three months before the military coup of 12 September 1980. Referring to an Amnesty International (AI) Report published on 9 June 1980, the Socialist Group of the EP stated that their members of the EU-Turkey Joint Parliamentary Committee (JPC) would raise the issue of human rights violations in the next JPC meeting, scheduled for 20 October 1980.[35] Although the meeting did not take place because of the military coup in September, the president of the EP delegation, Mr. Fellermaier, contacted the Turkish authorities and asked for an examination

---

[34] I would like to thank Jonathan Sugden of the Amnesty International for drawing my attention to these figures.

[35] *Agence Europe*, 16/17.6.1980, p. 4.

of the allegations contained in the AI report.[36] This was the first EU initiative that reflected the fact that the EP would be more vocal in its criticism of human rights violations in third countries (especially associated countries) after the first direct elections in 1979.

After the military coup, the EU's human rights policy *vis-à-vis* Turkey went through two phases. During the first phase from 1980-85, there was a marked contrast between the EP's tendency to be vocal in its criticisms and that of the member states to adopt a 'wait-and-see' policy within the EU framework but a relatively more critical stance within the Council of Europe. As we explain in section 7.2.1 below, this divergence made the EU's human rights policy towards Turkey both incoherent and ineffective. The EU's failure to emerge as an anchor during this phase was due to two factors. First, the military coup of 12 September 1980 put an end to Turkey's membership initiative that the Turkish government had launched in early 1980. Therefore, the EU was relieved of the need to engage in the policy co-ordination that would have been required by Turkey's push for membership. Second, the escalation of the tension between NATO and the Warsaw Pact increased the scope for submerging human rights issues under non-transparent security and defence arguments. This non-transparent approach to the military regime's human rights record reduced the scope for policy co-ordination among the member states and introduced a power political dimension to any initiative that the EU had to take in the face of systematic human rights violations. The combination of these factors meant that the EU's human rights policy towards Turkey would reflect the outcomes of cell A1 in figure 2.1, i.e., intergovernmentalism and lack of an anchoring capacity.

The second phase, from 1986 up to the present, has been characterised by a relative increase in the EU's criticism of Turkey's human rights record. Although this increase was partly due (or in parallel to) to the developments in the EU's human rights policy in general, it was also related to factors specific to EU-Turkey relations. If one reason for this change in the policy stance was increased European concerns about Turkey's human rights record in the face of continued human rights violations and increased number of asylum seekers, the other was Turkey's preparations for a membership application which changed the cost/incentive structure faced by the EU. As this change took place approximately at a time when the EU was set to pursue a high-profile human rights policy towards third countries in general, the question of whether the EU could act as an anchor for policy reform in Turkey became even more relevant. As we demonstrate in section 7.2, the

36 *Agence Europe*, 2.7.1980, p. 4.

answer to this question is largely negative. Despite increased activism and attempts at establishing a link between Turkey's human rights reform and the development of EU-Turkey relations, the EU's policy towards Turkey remained torn between two tendencies. On the one hand, the EU was forced to develop an activist stance against Turkey's poor human rights record because of increased societal assertiveness and the change in the risk structure implied by Turkey's bid for membership. On the other hand, however, the EU was also reluctant to assume a full anchoring role because of the history of Turkey's non-credible commitment to policy reform. As a result, the EU's human rights policy reflected the outcomes of cell B1 of Figure 2.1, where high levels of societal assertiveness and low levels of transparency/divisibility lead to shallow policy integration and limited anchoring capacity. As one would expect, this result undermined not only the effectiveness of the increased EU activism but also the quality of the human rights policy reforms carried out by Turkey.

7.2.1 The EU's 'Wait-and-See' Policy Towards Human Rights Violations in Turkey until 1985: Reluctance to Impose Sanctions

The first EU response to the military coup came from the Commission on 13 September 1980. Due to security considerations fuelled by the developments in Iran and the Afghan crisis, the Commission's reaction to the military coup in Turkey was couched in general terms. The Commission stated that it '... is following the developments in Turkey with the greatest concern' and that the EU 'hopes to see human rights will be fully respected'.[37] In addition, the Commission's statement did not contain any indication about what implications the military coup would have for the future of the EU-Turkey Association. This tone was maintained in the statement of the foreign ministers on 15 September. The EPC expressed 'concern' about the developments in Turkey and 'took note' of the assurances given by the military regime concerning the 'rapid re-establishment of democratic institutions and observance of human rights'. The EPC was 'deeply anxious' that those assurances were put into practice as soon as possible.[38]

These statements were significant not for their content as such, but for the future implications of the 'wait-and-see' policy stance that they had reflected. They signalled that the EU would take the assurances of the

[37] *Agence Europe*, 13.9.1980, p. 3.

[38] *Agence Europe*, 17.9.1980, p. 3. See also, *Official Journal of the EC - Debates*, no. 1-263, 19.11.1980, p. 116.

National Security Council as given and use the EU-Turkey Association as a modest means of leverage for accelerating the return to democracy and ensuring respect for human rights. This was a typical lowest common denominator outcome determined by the divergence between the preferences of the member states. On the one hand, it provided those who were anxious about not alienating Turkey (e.g., Germany, the UK and to some extent Italy) with the assurance that the EU-Turkey association would not be suspended in a period of instability in Iran and Afghanistan. On the other hand, it provided those concerned with either Turkey's human rights records (e.g., Denmark, The Netherlands) or with counter-balancing the US influence on the EU's approach to Turkey (e.g., France) with some scope to wield a stick against Turkey if the military regime failed to keep its promises. Overall, this compromise was acceptable to the Commission too as the military coup itself put an end to Turkey's membership for the foreseeable future.

As would be expected, however, this compromise had nothing to offer to the EP which, after the direct elections of 1979, was keen to carve a niche for itself in the executive-driven EU system. Therefore, the EP's reaction was stronger and implied a threat. The Chairman of the EP delegation to the EU-Turkey JPC made a statement on 15 September and called for immediate steps towards restoration of democratic institutions and freeing of all political prisoners. He also indicated that parliamentary democracy was '... a fundamental pre-condition for the full application' of the EU-Turkey Association.[39] Two days later, during the plenary meeting of 17 September 1980, the EP adopted a resolution which stated that the current situation in Turkey was incompatible either with Turkey's commitments under the European Convention or with its association with the EU. Suspension of relations would be considered if Turkey did not return to democratic rule as soon as possible.[40] In addition, a large number of MEPs asked for an immediate suspension of the EU-Turkey association and criticised both the Commission and the Council for being lenient on the military regime. The Council defended the 'wait-and-see' policy by arguing that the suspension of the association would serve the interests of the military rulers rather than the Turkish people. On its part, the Commission stated that the best policy would be 'to maintain the association relations with the anticipation that democracy would be restored as quickly as possible'.[41]

---

39 *Agence Europe*, 15/16.9.1980, p. 3.

40 *Agence Europe*, 18.9.1980, p. 7, See also, Info-Türk (1986), pp. 342-343.

41 *Agence Europe*, 19.9.1980, p. 6.

The link between this lenient approach and the reduced probability of Turkey's membership can be detected by contrasting the EU's approach with that of the Council of Europe. Only two weeks after the statements above were made in the plenary session of the EP, the Council of Europe declared on 1 October 1980 that Turkey 'cannot remain a member unless it returns to democracy as soon as possible'.[42] Interestingly enough, this statement was supported by EU member states which had just decided not to suspend the EU-Turkey association. Speaking on behalf of the EU Council, Mr. Thorn asked the EP on 19 November 1980 to appreciate the member states' 'realist' approach to Turkey and indicated that the EPC was trying to exert pressure on the Turkish military regime - as could be seen from the Council of Europe meeting.[43] Apparently, the EU Council and the member states were inclined to exert pressure on Turkey in a discrete manner and outside the formal platforms of the EU. Therefore, a delegation of the Commission met with Turkish officials in November 1980 to discuss ways in which the emergency aid of 75 million units of account would be utilised by Turkey, but the issue of human rights was not raised.[44] Also, even though at an ambassadorial level, the EU-Turkey Association Council (AC) met in early December to discuss the imposition of visa by the Benelux countries, Germany and France. Once more, human rights were not on the agenda.[45] More importantly, the EU decided to invite Turkey for consultations within the EPC mechanism in order to alleviate its concerns about the accession of Greece in 1981.[46]

Aware of the permissiveness implicit in this approach, the Turkish military regime continued to avoid any undertaking about the time table for the restoration of democracy and refrained from any commitment about the quality of the democratisation it had in mind. As a result, the EP began to assume a more critical stance. During the plenary meeting of 10-11 April 1981, the EP discussed and adopted a resolution that called on the Commission, the Council and the member states to 'take up their responsibilities' and request Turkey to present a definite list of measures for the protection of human rights. The resolution also asked the EU and its member states to notify Turkey that the association agreement would be immediately suspended if Turkey did not return to democracy 'within two

42 *Agence Europe*, 2.10.1980, p. 4.

43 *Official Journal of the EC - Debates*, no. 1-263, 19.11.1980, p. 136.

44 The emergency aid had been granted in 1979 when Turkey was faced with a balance of payments crisis. *Agence Europe*, 28.11.1980, p. 11.

45 *Agence Europe*, 4.12.1980, p. 10; and Council of the EU (1980), p. 141.

46 *Agence Europe*, 10.12.1980, p. 4.

months'.[47] Faced with intense criticism, the Commission had to concede to the EP's recommendations to (i) send an EP mission to investigate human rights violations in Turkey and (ii) call for a definite time table for the restoration of democracy.[48] In another action on 5 December 1981, the EP indicated that the Budget Committee would block the release of part of the emergency aid that had been decided before the coup. The Commission tried to circumvent the EP by proposing to the Council on 7 December 1981 that funds could be paid through the European Investment Bank (EIB). The Council did not agree to this proposal partly because it did not want to confront the EP and partly because such an action would be resisted by some member states - especially Greece, Denmark and The Netherlands.[49] While the Council and the Commission were still concerned about appeasing the Turkish military regime, the EP stepped up its pressure by dissolving the EP delegation to the JPC on 22 January 1982.

As can be seen from these developments, the EU was still unable to develop a consistent policy towards Turkey despite the fact that fifteen months had passed after the coup. The implications of this failure to assume an anchoring role are not difficult to detect. First of all, the military regime found it less difficult to impose a highly restricted democratisation project. Second, the EU's failure to formulate a transparent and detailed list of conditions for the maintenance of the EU-Turkey relations meant that the credibility and effectiveness of future EU criticism were undermined. Finally, the compromise that had been established in September 1980 among EU member states became difficult to maintain. This difficulty was exacerbated by negative constituent reactions to the double standards in the EU's human rights policy, which was highly critical of the military coup in Poland but lenient towards the Turkish military regime. Therefore, by 1982, it became evident that the EU's human rights policy *vis-à-vis* Turkey was heading towards further disarray. On the one hand, Germany began preparations to release the German financial aid to Turkey in late 1981 and she finally lifted the ban on 2 December 1982. The German government also stated that it was in favour of releasing the ECU 600 million EU assistance approved in the fourth financial protocol of 1980. [50] On the other hand, however, three EU member states (Denmark, France and The Netherlands) stepped up their preparations for taking an action against Turkey before the European Commission of Human Rights (ECHR). Their complaint against

---

47 Info-Türk (1986), pp. 344-345.
48 *Official Journal of the EC - Debates*, 10.4.1981, p. 277.
49 *Official Journal of the EC - Debates*, no. 1-279, January 1982, p. 58.
50 *Official Journal of the EC - Debates*, no. 1-294, February 1983, p. 70.

Turkey was finally placed on 1 July 1982, on the grounds that a 'public emergency' did not exist in Turkey that would allow her to derogate from her commitments under the European Convention.[51]

To cover up the rift and avert the criticism about the EU's double standards, the EU Council had to inform the Turkish foreign minister in January 1982 that Turkey must fulfil various conditions if she wanted to maintain its association with the EU.[52] Also, on 23 February 1982, the EPC arranged a visit to Turkey and provided the information that formed a basis for a European Council *communiqué* on 30 March 1982, which stated that human rights violations in Turkey were of considerable concern and stressed that the country should return to democracy as soon as possible.[53] These initiatives, however, were too little and too late. The Turkish military regime brushed them aside by threatening to distance Turkey from Europe and appointed a Consultative Assembly with instructions to draft a highly restrictive constitution. The brief given to this assembly envisaged a constitution which would protect the state against the individual, ensure the continuity of the National Security Council, and shield the military rulers against any legal action in the future. The constitution was duly drafted in September 1982 and approved in a referendum in November 1982, when Turkish citizens were threatened with a ban from future elections if they failed to vote.[54] Following the approval of the Constitution by a majority of 91.37%, the National Security Council adopted an electoral law that allowed only 'approved' political parties to participate in the elections. The elections were held in November 1983 and a new civilian government was formed by the prime minister Turgut Özal, under the tutelage of the military.

The defiance of the National Security Council, coupled with increasing pressure from human rights activists, forced the EU to maintain some pressure on Turkey. For example, the German presidency assured the MEPs in March 1983 that the EU was not turning a blind eye to the developments in Turkey and referred to the inter-institutional declaration of April 1977 on human rights to which the Council and the EPC were committed.[55] The EP, on the other hand, described the so-called democratisation process as a farce and adopted a resolution on 13 October 1983, stating that the elections to be held in November were far from being a true indicator of democracy.[56]

---

51 See Council of Europe (1982), p. 11; and Info-Türk (1986), p. 352.

52 *Official Journal of the EC - Debates*, no. 1-279, January 1982, p. 58.

53 *Official Journal of the EC - Debates*, no. 1-287, July 1982, p. 140.

54 Info-Türk (1986), pp. 114-132.

55 For the EP debate and Genscher's replies, see *Official Journal of the EC - Debates*, no. 1-296, March 1983, pp. 38-45.

56 Info-Türk (1986), p. 146.

These reactions, however, remained ineffective in the face of the division between the member states. Although the member states who had taken action against Turkey in the Council of Europe maintained their critical position until the end of 1984,[57] the British and German governments stated on 22 November 1984 that they were not against Turkey's assumption of the Council of Europe presidency - a prestigious post that Turkey had to give up in May 1981 in the face of mounting criticism.[58] In addition, the Dublin meeting of the EPC in September 1984 discussed the situation in Turkey, but failed to take a decision.[59]

Developments in 1985 did not lead to a significant change in the EU's human rights policy towards Turkey. It became evident that the member states were in favour of gradually reviving the association which, unlike the EU-Greece association during the Greek junta, had not been suspended. During the EP session of 17 April 1985, the UK stated that it was in favour of lifting the ban on financial aid to Turkey.[60] Also, Denmark, France and The Netherlands began to explore the possibility of a 'friendly settlement' to their complaint against Turkey. They made proposals for a settlement on 22 February 1985, to which Turkey replied on 4 March. The negotiations continued until December, when Turkey finally agreed to observe its obligations implied by Article 3 of the European Convention and to report to the ECHR regularly in 1986.[61] Germany and Belgium went even further. The German Chancellor became the first head of government to visit Turkey after the coup. During his visit between 10-12 July 1985, he tried to trade off German influence on the EU with Turkish concessions on the right of Turkish workers for free movement - envisaged to become effective from end of 1986 onwards.[62] Belgium, on the other hand, signed a state-to-state loan agreement for BF 250 million on 15 July 1985.[63]

One reason for these overtures was the race between the member states to capture some share in the lucrative trade and investment opportunities generated by Turkey's high growth rates, rapidly increasing foreign trade,

---

57 The applicants rejected Turkey's proposal for a negotiated settlement on 30 November 1984. See Council of Europe (1985), p. 155.

58 Info-Türk, (1986), p. 370. British and German support did not enable Turkey to take the presidency, but was a significant indicator of the division within the EU.

59 *Official Journal of the EC - Debates*, no. 2-325, April 1985, p. 158.

60 *Official Journal of the EC - Debates,* no. 2-325, April 1985, pp. 158 and 205.

61 Council of Europe (1985), p. 157. Turkey also agreed to respond to the Commission's comments on those reports, with a view to ensure that the terms of the settlement were adhered to.

62 On this visit, see Schlegel (1986), p. 293. See also, *Agence Europe*, 11.7.1985, p. 8; *Le Monde*, 12.7.1985; and *The Guardian*, 11.7.1985.

63 Info-Türk (1986), p. 380.

and even higher rates of increase in military expenditures. The Turkish press, most probably with encouragement from the Turkish government, began to publicise the stakes involved. For example, the daily paper *Hürriyet* stated that the award of contract for the construction of the second Bosphorous bridge to the Japanese was closely related to Turkey's annoyance with the Europeans. Another Turkish paper commented that the friendly settlement of the case in the ECHR was a result of the applicant countries' failure to get their share in Turkish investment projects that totalled US$ 3 billion in 1985.[64] The member states, however, were facing difficulties in justifying their overtures towards Turkey. They had to try to neutralise domestic pressure by pointing to the progress made by Turkey in the field of human rights and democratisation. In the case of Germany, an additional factor was also called upon: adopting a soft approach towards Turkey was presented as the cost of avoiding further immigration - a sensitive issue that would affect constituent attitudes.

Despite these gestures, two developments in 1985 indicated that human rights would remain a contentious issue in EU-Turkey relations. One of these was related to the EP's attempt to distance itself from the lenient approach of the Council and the EPC. In its resolution of 23 October 1985, the EP put forward five conditions for restoring its relations with Turkey: the abolition of death penalty, putting an end to torture and prosecution of all torturers, ending of mass trials, granting the individual right of petition to the ECHR, and removal of all restrictions on the freedom of opinion.[65] This resolution constituted a significant step in the EP's policy for two reasons. First, it reflected determination to block normalisation of relations with Turkey in spite of the signals from the member states to the contrary. Second, but more importantly, it was the first document that moved away from general references to human rights by identifying specific targets as minimum conditions for the establishment of normal relations with Turkey. Not surprisingly, this resolution led to a hysterical reaction from Turkey. It was perceived by the Turkish government not only as a dangerous document that would keep the spotlight on Turkey's human rights record for some time to come, but also as a move that could spoil the tentative steps that the member states were taking towards normalisation of relations. Therefore, the Turkish foreign ministry took issue with the EP and stated that the report was based on a 'pre-conceived idea' and that it dealt a blow to the 'prestige and credibility' of the EP in Turkey.[66] Even the prime minister, Mr. Özal,

64 *Hürriyet*, 28.10.1985; and *Milliyet*, 17.12.1985.
65 *Info-Türk: Monthly Bulletin*, no. 108, October 1985, p. 1
66 *Milliyet*, 25.10.1985; and *Agence Europe*, 26.10.1985, p. 3.

felt it necessary to respond to the resolution during his visit to the US. He told Turkish journalists that the EP's rapporteur, Richard Balfe, was a 'crook' and that Turkey did not need the ECU 600 million that the fourth financial protocol had provided for.[67]

The other development concerned the Commission. The EP resolution mentioned above was based on information supplied by the Commission's representative in Turkey, Mr. Gwyn Morgan. In addition to the information he provided on Turkey's human rights record, Mr. Morgan was vocal in his criticism. A statement he made in June 1985 was interpreted as interference in domestic affairs as he indicated that Turkey's relations with the EU would be set back for a decade if the Turkish National Assembly enacted the draft bill granting new powers to the police force.[68] An incident in November 1985 appeared to be the right moment to ask for his withdrawal, although unofficially through the press. Information compiled by Mr. Morgan on Turkey's human rights records was sent to John Taylor, the director general of research in the EP. However, the file was accidentally placed in the pigeonhole of another John Taylor - an Ulster Unionist MEP. When the Unionist John Taylor passed the file to the Turkish authorities instead of its true addressee, the Turkish governments initiated a campaign against Mr. Morgan. Although the British, West German and Dutch embassy officials signalled publicly that Mr. Morgan's position was no longer tenable, the Commission overruled these criticisms and kept Mr. Morgan as representative after a short withdrawal on safety grounds.[69]

By the end of 1985, it was clear that the EU's human rights policy towards Turkey had been far from being compatible with an anchoring role which required a clear commitment to undertake risks and willingness to impose sanctions with a view to ensure respect for human rights in an associated country. In other words, the EU, despite EP criticism, made it clear that it was prepared to act only as a 'passive anchor' that Turkey might use for securing the irrevocability of the policy reform and not as an 'effective anchor' that would reduce the scope for Turkey's deviations from European standards on the basis of transparent incentives and sanctions. Therefore, the member states, the Council and the Commission sidelined the EP, adopted a lenient approach towards the Turkish military regime, and reduced the cost for Turkey to engage in a highly limited return to democracy. Underlying this policy stance was the fact that the military

---

67 *Hürriyet*, 28.10.1985.

68 *The Financial Times*, 10.6.1985.

69 *The Financial Times*, 27.11.1985. In his defence of Mr. Morgan, the Commissioner Mr. Cheysson stated that he had done his job. *Info-Türk*, no. 110, December 1985, p. 4.

regime constituted an undesirable yet objectively functional development which enabled the EU to avoid the risks associated with a Turkish bid for membership. As indicated in chapter 4, the EU made it clear in 1980 that it was not prepared to take Turkey in because of the high levels of risk associated with the latter's divergent policy choices and the non-credible nature of her European orientation. In fact, the economic concessions granted in 1980 were closely related to the objective of securing a delay in Turkey's membership application. In that sense, the EU's human rights policy from 1980-85 constituted yet another telling manifestation of the anchor/credibility dilemma in EU-Turkey relations. While Turkey's non-credible European orientation induced the EU to be even more risk averse; the latter's failure to undertake risks and its unwillingness to impose sanctions made it easier for the Turkish military to deviate from EU standards and impose a highly restrictive regime.

This outcome is consistent with the observation made at the end of section 7.1.2: the EU is more likely to act as an effective anchor when a third country with a poor human rights record decides to commit to a credible European orientation. That is because the credible commitment of the third country reduces the risks perceived by the EU and induces the latter to develop a common response to the management of reduced risks. In contrast, Turkey's European orientation had been not only non-credible, but was practically suspended as a result of the military regime. Under this condition, the EU's response was bound to be incoherent and ineffective as the incentive for developing a co-ordinated response was weak and the risks of an activist policy were perceived to be high. Therefore, the EU and the member states resorted to 'realist' tactics and blurred the transparency/divisibility of the human rights issues by subordinating them to security considerations or lucrative economic stakes. As a result of either institutional competition or the need for system legitimation, the EP was able to pursue an activist human rights policy, but its effect on the overall policy stance remained limited.

7.2.2 Revival in Turkey's European Orientation and the EU's Human Rights Policy after 1985

From 1986 onwards, Turkey's human rights record became the most contentious issue in EU-Turkey relations because of Turkey's membership bid and the EU's increased activism that followed. The evidence examined in this section suggests that the EU has moved away from the 'wait-and-see' policy of the 1980-85 period by specifying the areas where reform was necessary and by linking the strengthening of the EU-Turkey relations with human rights reforms in Turkey. Specific areas of reforms identified by the EU included the death penalty, the penal code and the code of criminal procedures, the anti-terror law, the treatment of the Kurdish minority, and the anti-democratic provisions of the 1982 constitution. Linkages between Turkey's human rights reform and the development of EU-Turkey relations were made in a large number of EP, Council and Commission statements/reports; on the occasion of responding to Turkey's membership application, and during the negotiations leading to the conclusion of the customs union agreement.

Nevertheless, the change in the EU's human rights policy towards Turkey fell short of making the EU an effective anchor for a number of reasons. First of all, the linkage politics was based on the assumption that a gradual strengthening of the link with Turkey would induce the latter to accelerate the pace of policy reform. In other words, the EU put the cart before the horse and ignored the credibility problem that made policy reversals in Turkey a recurrent outcome. This assumption was hardly compatible with what an effective anchoring function would require as it left the pace of policy reform to be determined by Turkey, whose commitment to policy reform was essentially time-inconsistent. Second, the effectiveness of EU criticism was compromised because of the EU's failure to devise and insist on a package of incentives and sanctions triggered by transparent criteria reflecting the extent of the policy reform undertaken by Turkey and the level of integration that the EU prepared to offer. In the absence of such a package, neither the incentive for convergence towards nor the cost of deviations from EU standards was significant enough to induce Turkey to improve its human rights record. Third, the EU refrained from establishing a specialised unit that would monitor progress in Turkey's human rights policy reform either with or without the participation of Turkish representatives. The EP did try to use the JPC platform after 1988 for this purpose, but this initiative remained inadequate because of the Commission's and the Council's failure to use the AC in a similar way or to supplement it with an additional platform dedicated to human rights issues. As a result, the EU failed to act as an anchor for Turkey's human rights policy reform on three significant occasions: the revival of the association in 1986; immediately before and after Turkey's membership application in 1987; and the conclusion of the customs union agreement in 1995.

The EU's failure to act as an anchor during the revival of the association could be seen in the preparation for the first AC meeting after the coup. The Council justified the convention of the AC on the grounds that it was necessary to reflect 'the progress that Turkey has made in restoring democracy and the wish of the Council to encourage further reform'.[70] This reasoning was questioned by the EP and the Commission with respect to its timing. Having discovered that the Council was set to convene the EU-Turkey AC, 100 MEPs sent a letter to the Council on 25 March 1986 and indicated not only their objections to the envisaged meeting but also their resolve to block the normalisation of EU-Turkey relations in the future. Also, the Commissioner, Mr. Claude Cheysson, told the press in June 1986 that 'the European people do not consider that fundamental rights are respected in Turkey ... [and] ... more progress is expected by every one.[71] Despite these warnings, the AC meeting was held in September 1986 without any prior planning about how the normalisation of EU-Turkey relations would be linked with Turkey's human rights policy reform and what the EU would do if Turkey failed to improve her human rights record. This lack of a transparent linkage and sanction strategy was a major failure because it made the EU miss the opportunity of exercising some influence on Turkey at a time when the latter's European orientation was gathering new momentum after the interruption caused by the military regime.

It quickly transpired that the Council's decision to convene the AC was based on the assumption that closer relations with Turkey would induce the latter to deliver in the area of human rights reform. This assumption, however, was not only unrealistic but also self-defeating. It was unrealistic because it ignored the inability of Turkish policy-makers to undertake a time-consistent commitment to policy reform and treated the recurrence of policy reversals as a non-problem. The assumption was also self-defeating because it was bound to weaken the credibility of any future attempt by the EU to link the further strengthening of the EU-Turkey relations with progress in Turkey's human rights policy reform. Undoubtedly, these negative aspects of the emerging EU approach towards Turkey were not accidental. On the contrary, they reflected a well designed strategy of reciprocal discretion whereby Turkey was given an almost free hand for determining the pace as well as the quality of the policy reform process, and the EU was given the opportunity to use discreet diplomacy for raising its concerns about Turkey's human rights record mainly when and to the extent that it saw fit. The preference for discreet (and essentially non-transparent) interventions was spelled out by the Council on the grounds that this strategy had made Turkey well aware of the EU's expectations. The Commission lent support for this strategy by citing the Turkish government's decision to

70 *Official Journal of the EC - Debates*, no. 2-341, July 1986, p. 95.

71 *The International Herald Tribune*, 21 June 1986. See also, *The Financial Times*, 21 June 1986.

establish a Parliamentary Committee for monitoring human rights developments as a 'concrete' achievement that.[72] During the plenary session of June 1987, it became apparent that the EPC had been discussing the Kurdish issue since 1986 but its deliberations were kept secret.[73]

Given the credibility problem that had made policy reversals a recurrent outcome in Turkish policy-making, it was not surprising to observe that Turkey's policy reform remained limited both before and after the membership application of 1987. Before the membership application, Turkey took three partial steps towards human rights policy reform. First, she declared that the 1964 decree that had frozen the assets of the Greek minority in Turkey since the first Cyprus crisis of 1963 would be repealed. In another move, Turkey agreed, on 23 January 1987, to grant Turkish citizens the right of individual petition before the ECHR for a period of three years.[74] Finally, a Parliamentary Committee was established within the National Assembly to monitor developments in the field of human rights. One of the steps taken after the membership application of April 1987 was the amendment of the electoral law that had banned Turkish citizens from voting in the 1983 elections on the grounds that they failed to vote in the constitutional referendum of 1982. Although this amendment did re-institute a fundamental right for 2.4 million voters, the grossly undemocratic nature of the electoral law remained unchanged.[75] Another step was to repeal the 1964 decree on 5 February 1988. The timing of this step was designed to circumvent Greece in the AC meeting, due to be held in April 1988. Finally, the Turkish government decided to sign the European Convention on the Prevention of Torture in January 1988. In fact, Turkey became the first country to ratify it in February of the same year.[76] Diplomats in Ankara interpreted this move as a sign of Turkey's realisation that 'she must improve her human rights image as she tries to become a full member of the EU'.[77] Although there was an element of truth in this assessment, Amnesty International reports indicated that torture had actually increased and was

---

72 *Official Journal of the EC - Debates*, no. 2-350, March 1987, p. 123; and no. 2-353, June 1987, p. 87.

73 *Official Journal of the EC - Debates*, no. 2-353, June 1987, p. 169.

74 *Le Monde*, 28.4.1987. See also, *Info-Türk*, no. 123, January 1987, p. 2.

75 The EP pointed out to the undemocratic nature of the electoral law before and after the Turkish elections of December 1987. See *Agence Europe*, 3.12.1987, p. 3.

76 *Agence Europe*, no. 4733, 29 February/1 January 1988, p. 4. The Convention provided for the investigation complaints about torture by independent experts and allowed for visits to prisons as well as police stations.

77 *The Guardian*, 12.1.1988.

complemented with extra-judicial executions and 'disappearances' from late 1980s onwards.[78]

It is true that these limited reforms were introduced against increased EU criticism of Turkey's human rights record. The EU, however, played only a very limited anchoring role for two reasons. First of all, the Council and the Commission reflected a clear reluctance to establish an institutional/procedural framework where incentives and/or sanctions could be triggered by developments in Turkey's human rights record. This tendency was in contrast to that of the EP, which managed to use the JPC as a platform where progress in Turkey's policy reform could be compared with the list of required reforms. Between September 1988 and the Spring of 1991, the EP delegation to the JPC raised a number of substantive human rights issues and compared Turkey's performance with specified targets. This was done by obtaining written answers from the Turkish delegation to related questions and making sure that the replies were discussed thoroughly during the JPC meetings. The questions discussed included the abolition of Articles 141, 142, and 163 of the Turkish penal code that prohibited the organisation of communist or religious parties; the commutation of the death penalty into life sentences; the granting of an amnesty to all prisoners with long sentences; and the amendment of the procedural code for criminal offences, which was conducive to torture in police stations.[79]

The effectiveness of this strategy was increased by a temporary emphasis by the Council that human rights reforms was a condition for further development in EU-Turkey relations. Observing this convergence between the EP and the Council, the Turkish government did not object to the interventions of the EP in the JPC. In addition, both before and after the elections of 1991, Turkey carried out a number of further reforms. The first step in that direction was taken in September 1989, when the National Assembly voted in favour of reducing the application of the death penalty from 29 offences to 13 - just two months before the Commission' opinion on the membership application was made public. At about the same time, the Turkish government announced that it would extend its acceptance of the jurisdiction of the European Court of Human Rights beyond the three-year period announced in January 1987.[80] Partial reform continued after the negative verdict of the Commission in December 1989 on Turkey's

78 See, for example, Amnesty International (1990); and Amnesty International (1992).

79 For information on JPC meetings, various issues of the monthly bulletin *Info-Türk* can be consulted. See also, *The Financial Times*, 27.4.1989; EP Internal Documents *PE 139.059* of 6 February 1990; and *PE 141.174/Ann.* of 15 May 1990.

80 Dağı (1997), p. 3.

membership application. In 1991, Turkey introduced a number of improvements which included the permission to use the Kurdish language in publications from February 1991 onwards; the annulment of Articles 141, 142 and 163 of the penal code on 12 April 1991; the commutation of the death sentences to 20 years and life sentences to 15 years in the same month; and the early conditional release of a large number of political prisoners on 16 July 1991. In addition, the new government formed after the elections of October 1991 included in its programme a catalogue of targeted improvements in the area of human rights.

These developments, however, should be taken neither as indicators of Turkey's credible commitment to policy reform nor as a proof of the EU's anchoring function. The reform of the Turkish penal code was made part of the Anti-Terror Law (Law 3173), Article 8 of which punished any expression of separatism, violent or not, with long prison sentences and heavy fines. Therefore, the number of detentions and prosecutions under Article 8 increased dramatically from 1993 onwards, when the conflict with the PKK (The Kurdistan Workers' Party) intensified. In addition, human rights violations in Turkey became even more widespread from 1992-93 onwards, leading to an unprecedented number of 'disappearances' and extra-judicial executions.[81] The failure of the EU to emerge as an effective anchor in the face of these developments was dictated by the revealed preference for discreet diplomacy instead of supplementing the EP initiative by establishing a new platform for monitoring the pace and quality of Turkey's human rights reform. This preference was spelled out by the Spanish presidency in a number of the EP sessions in the first half of 1989. In the first statement, Mr. Ordonez told the EP that human rights issues had always been dealt with in both bilateral and joint EU contacts with Turkey.[82] Two months later, he informed the EP that specific EPC representations were made to the Turkish government on more than one occasions about Articles 141, 142 and 163 of the penal code. He assured the MEPs that the Turkish government was fully aware of the EPC's views on this matter.[83] The third statement was made 11 April 1989. In his reply to a parliamentary question, the president-in-Office once more drew attention to the EPC's contacts with Turkey and informed the EP that the Turkish government had undertaken to make sure that 'the application of the penal code is in accordance with the human rights standards' of the international conventions on human rights.[84]

---

81 Amnesty International (1996), pp. 13-19.
82 *Official Journal of the EC - Debates*, no. 2-373, January 1989, p. 90.
83 *Official Journal of the EC - Debates*, no. 2-376, March 1989, p. 48.
84 *Official Journal of the EC - Debates*, no. 2-377, April 1989, p. 91.

Finally, the Spanish foreign minister told the EP that 'as Turkey wishes to become a member of the EU, I must point out ... that it is this very Parliament who has the last word about the decision'.[85]

These statements, however, concealed more than they revealed. First of all, they disregarded the fact that the EU, from 1986 onwards, had been giving mixed signals about the seriousness of its criticism. It was an open secret that some member states [such as France, Belgium and the UK] were less opposed to Turkey's membership application than others [such as Germany, The Netherlands, and Greece]. Second, those statements also concealed the failure of the EU to devise a package of sanctions and incentives that signalled to Turkey in a transparent and credible manner the linkage between her human rights policy reform and the future of EU-Turkey relations. Third, the presidency's assurance that the EP would have the final say on the future of Turkey's relations with the EU ignored the fact that discreet diplomacy was in fact undermining the effectiveness of the EP's criticism. Finally, those statements concealed the fact that discrete diplomacy was essentially designed to enable the EU not only to accommodate the differences between the member states but also to be selective about when and to what extent human rights issues should be raised as an obstacle to Turkey's further integration into Europe. As a result, it was not surprising to observe that the EU failed once again to emerge as an effective anchor for policy reform in Turkey in early 1990s - when negotiations on the Matutes Package paved the way for Turkey's further integration, albeit at a level less than membership. This failure was confirmed in the EP's 1992 report, which suggested that there was less scope for effective EU interventions given that the EU and Turkey were inclined to settle on an intermediate solution to the membership question and Turkey turned its attention to the post-Soviet space, including the Black Sea Area, the Caucasus and Central Asia.[86]

The third occasion on which the EU failed to act as an effective anchor was the conclusion of the EU-Turkey customs union in 1995. During negotiations in 1994, it was evident that EU statements on the link between the customs union and improvements in Turkey's human rights record lacked any credibility. On the one hand, the press was being fed with briefs pointing to the gap between the EU standards and Turkey's human rights record. On the other hand, the Council and the member states signalled at various occasions that the customs union would be signed even though Turkey's human rights reform remained highly limited. The most graphic

---

85 *Official Journal of the EC - Debates*, no. 2-378, May 1989, p. 70.

86 Info-Türk, no. 187, May 1992, p. 4. See also, *Agence Europe*, 19.3.1992, p. 4.

expression of this preference was made by the British foreign secretary, Mr. Hurd, in January 1994. During his visit to Turkey, Mr. Hurd told the press that 'Turkey should continue to be fully involved in the evolving arrangements for European defence.' Echoing Dr. Kissinger's statements in the 1970s, he also added that EU's relationship with Turkey was 'not a luxury but a necessity'. This 'realist' view was based on the argument that Turkey was at the centre of commercial and political dynamics in the eastern Mediterranean and a potentially stabilising factor for the region, including the Turkic republics of the former Soviet Union.[87] The election success of the pro-Islamic Welfare Party in March 1994 gave an added impetus to EU efforts to push for a customs union and political dialogue despite continued deterioration in Turkey's human rights record.

The determination to subsume human rights issues under strategic and commercial interests was so strong that the sentencing of four Kurdish MPs to 15 years of imprisonment in December 1994 led only to a temporary delay in the Council's decision to approve the customs union. Although the German foreign minister, Mr. Kinkel, stated to the EP categorically that the EU would not sanction the agreement until Turkey improved her human rights record[88], the Council did just the opposite in March 1995 and exerted pressure on the EP to secure the latter's assent in December 1995. On the occasion of signing the customs union agreement on 6 March 1995, the French foreign minister stated that 'this conclusion marked the will to break with the tensions and resentments of the past'. The EU, he added, was sure that Turkey's constitutional reforms 'would come in weeks or months to come'.[89] This was yet another manifestation of the unrealistic assumption that gradual and partial openings towards Turkey would induce the latter to carry out policy reform. Obviously, this assumption was not a result of naiveté. On the contrary, it reflected the EU's tendency to minimise the risks involved in anchoring Turkey's policy reform. The risk-minimising strategy involved the trading-off of a convergence process determined by Turkey's discretion with limited concessions which could be either withdrawn or frozen by pointing to the lack of sufficient reform as and when the EU saw fit. The implication of this approach for the anchor/credibility dilemma in EU-Turkey relations is not difficult to anticipate. On the one hand, Turkey would be enabled to present cosmetic improvements as genuine policy reform given that her commitment is specified only in general terms. On the other hand, the EU's criticism of Turkey failures would become less credible

---

87 *The Financial Times*, 20.1.1994 and 21.1.1994. See also, The Guardian, 21.1.1994.

88 *The Guardian*, 15.12.1994.

89 *Agence Europe*, 6/7.3.1995, p. 6; and 8.3.1995, p. 4.

and effective as the latter tends to treat such criticism as a pretext designed to avoid Turkey's closer integration with the EU.

The result of the Turkish constitutional reform of July 1995 and the amendment of Article 8 of the Anti-Terror Law in October 1995 confirmed the first prediction, whilst developments after the EP's approval of the customs union lent support to the latter. The so-called constitutional reform package included 20 articles of the 1982 constitution, but only 13 of these were amended to some extent. The overall result of the July reform was to remove the statements in the preamble of the constitution praising the military coup of 12 September 1980; to allow students to become members of political parties; to grant public sector employees the right for collective bargaining (but without the right to strike); and to lower the voting age from 21 to 18.[90] Despite these limited improvements, the Commission stated that the result 'reaffirmed the credibility of the Turkish government's commitment to comply with obligations arising out of the European Convention of Human Rights'. Therefore, it urged the EP to give its assent in December and stated that the customs union would bring substantial advantages to the EU and consolidate Turkey's role in the region.[91] Similarly, the reform of the Anti-Terror Law in October 1995 was also limited. Despite the reduction in the maximum sentences from 5 to 3 years, 'separatist propaganda' remained a personable offence. In fact, Mehdi Zana, the former Mayor of the south-eastern province of Diyarbakir and a campaigner for Kurdish autonomy, was retried under the new Article 8 in November 1995 for a speech he had made earlier in the EP's plenary session. According to Amnesty International, public prosecutors in Turkey began to request charges under other articles of the penal code (for example Article 312 banning the 'incitment to hatred') to circumvent any constraint in sentencing imposed by the 'reform' Article 8.[92]

Despite these developments, the EP gave its consent to the customs union agreement in December 1995 under intense pressure from the Commission and the member states. Even the British Labour Party (which was still in opposition) exerted pressure on its group in the EP to vote in favour of the customs union with Turkey. The major factor that made the pressure work was the way in which the Commission, the Council and the member states blurred the transparency/divisibility of the human rights issues by linking them with a 'European interest' that the EP was expected to defend. Although the EP adopted a resolution calling for a permanent

90 *Agence Europe*, 24/5.07.1995, p. 4.
91 *Agence Europe*, 23.11.1995, p. 7.
92 Amnesty International (1996), pp. 17-19.

monitoring of Turkey's human rights record and periodical reporting by the Commission, this attempt remained essentially a face-saving exercise. That was because the conclusion of the customs union, despite declared announcements by both parties that it would improve the prospect for Turkey's integration, was not a comprehensive package that would anchor Turkey's policy reform. It constituted merely a new indicator of the EU's tendency to achieve high returns (i.e., convergence by Turkey) at lower risks. That even the EP was inclined to comply with this policy line was confirmed by a symbolic yet significant gesture: the presentation of the Sakharov Prize to Leyla Zana , one of the Kurdish MPs imprisoned in December 1994, was postponed so that the presentation did not coincide with the assent on the customs union.[93]

Developments after the entry into force of the customs union confirmed another implication of the EU's failure to act as an anchor for policy reform in Turkey. Developments in 1996 and 1997 demonstrated that the major factor that shaped the EU's relatively lenient approach towards Turkey's human rights record in 1994-95 was the EU's intention to trade off the upgrading of the EU-Turkey relations with an indefinite postponement of Turkey's membership. In other words, the EU was prepared to adopt a lenient stance against Turkey in order to induce the latter to settle on the customs union as an arrangement that, from the EU's point of view, would serve two purposes: keeping Turkey in Europe's orbit and avoiding Turkish membership for the foreseeable future. A signal to that effect was given in September 1996, when the Commissioner for external political relations, Mr. van den Broek, told the Turkish foreign minister that the EU 'did not wish to isolate Turkey', but it would find it very difficult to deepen the EU-Turkey relations in the face of Turkey's poor human rights record.[94] That this signal was not a reflection of the Commissioner's personal preferences was confirmed with the conclusions of the Luxembourg summit in December 1997. The Luxembourg summit confirmed Turkey's eligibility for accession, but it provided for a framework that, once again, left the pace and quality of the policy reform to be determined by Turkey. With the exception of the invitation to participate in European Conferences, the European Council made it explicit that the strengthening of EU-Turkey relations would depend, *inter alia*, on Turkey's political and economic reforms, alignment of her human rights standards with those of the EU, and protection of minorities.[95]

---

93 *Agence Europe*, 13.12.1995, p. 3.

94 *Agence Europe*, 28.9.1996, p. 3.

95 *Bulletin of the EU*, no. 12-1997, Inernet version, p. 5.

Given that these requirements had been evident for decades and the fact that the EU was prepared to devise a different strategy of locking the CEECs into a framework where policy reform went hand in hand with further integration, the question that arises here is obvious: why did the EU decide to treat Turkey as a special case? The answer suggested by the preceding analysis is that the EU was not prepared to undertake the risks associated with Turkey's accession given the history of the latter's non-credible commitment to policy reform. This factor constituted a major difference between the Turkish case and that of the CEECs. Although the reform history of the CEECs was short, it was characterised by a tendency to adopt the EU standards as a means of legitimating and consolidating the post-Soviet regimes. This reform history made the CEECs willing to trade off the short-term costs of convergence with the long-term benefits of integration. Because of the reduced risks that this tendency implied for the EU, the latter was induced to act as an anchor that would reduce the probability of policy reversals by locking the policy reform in the CEECs into a pre-accession framework of incentives and sanctions triggered off on the basis of transparent criteria. In contrast, the EU was unwilling to anchor Turkey's policy reform because the perceived risks were augmented not only by the extent of Turkey's divergence from EU standards but also by the non-credible nature of the Turkish governments' commitment to convergence.

This is a typical example of anchor failure. As indicated earlier, the EU can emerge as an anchor for policy reform only when the declared European orientation of the third countries is credible. But almost by definition, such countries' need for an anchor is minimal or non-existent. What is more challenging and meaningful is to act as an anchor for policy reform in a country such as Turkey where the probability of policy reversals is high. Instead of rising to this challenge, the EU, because of its tendency to secure policy convergence in associated countries at low risks, opted for a pseudo-solution to the anchor/credibility dilemma that characterised its relations with Turkey. On the one hand, it tended to leave it up to Turkey to determine the pace and the quality of her policy reform. On the other hand, it tended to raise Turkey's human rights record as an obstacle to the strengthening of the EU-Turkey relations when and as this was deemed necessary. Obviously, this strategy was costly for Turkey because it provided the EU with a high degree of discretion in determining the level at which Turkey would be integrated, but it was also an acceptable second-best as it provided Turkey with a scope to maintain her non-credible commitment to converge towards EU standards.

Under these conditions, Turkey's relations with the EU would continue to be characterised by the predictable consequences of the anchor/credibility dilemma. Given the EU's reluctance to internalise the risks associated with Turkish membership, Turkey's demands for accession will be rejected on the grounds that Turkey's convergence towards EU standards is unsatisfactory. Instead, Turkey will be offered intermediate solutions such as the customs union, political dialogue, or microeconomic cooperation in dynamic sectors in order to encourage market-based integration through joint ventures. Because of the second-best nature of these intermediate solutions, Turkey will continue to question their relevance until the EU can come up with new intermediate options that will re-affirm the EU's recognition of Turkey's European vocation. The implication of this strategic interaction for policy reform in Turkey and the latter's integration into the EU is not difficult to predict: the pace and quality of the policy reform may continue to be sub-optimal and Turkey may remain the only applicant failing to join the EU despite the fact that she now has the longest standing association agreement and is linked to the EU with a customs union.

Conclusions

One of the conclusions that can be derived from the analysis above is that the emergence and consolidation of the EU's human rights policy vis-à-vis third countries is neither an erratic process determined by inter-state interaction nor a uniformly cumulative process driven by supranational actors such as the Commission or the EP. The EU's human rights policy can be better described as a drive towards policy convergence determined by the need to legitimate the national and EU systems. The outcomes of the convergence process, i.e., the coherence and effectiveness of the EU's human rights policy as well as the contributions of the supranational actors - are positively related to the level of societal assertiveness defined as awareness of human rights issues but negatively related to the ability of the member states to blur the transparency/divisibility of those issues. Therefore, the development of the EU's human rights policy *vis-à-vis* third countries has been both cumulative and erratic - depending on the combination of the explanatory variables. The analysis in section 7.1 suggests that this explanation is more compatible with the existing evidence compared to state-centric explanations that treat the state as a closed entity and focus on external factors or interdependence as explanatory variables.

Another conclusion is that, at a given level of societal assertiveness, the ability of the member states to blur the transparency/divisibility of the human rights issues will depend not only on their preferences but also on the risk/incentive structure that the EU as a whole would be faced with as a result of a third country's European orientation. In other words, the degree of co-ordination in and effectiveness of the EU's human rights policy will depend on the risks implied by the intensity of the relations with third countries and the willingness of the latter to pay an 'entry fee' in terms of convergence towards EU standards. If the third country's European orientation is either non-credible or limited to economic relations that do not involve substantial EU commitments, the risks that the EU must tackle are either too high or too low to make a co-ordinated EU response to that country's human rights record feasible or necessary. If, however, the third country's European orientation is credible it is in the interest of the EU to ensure the maximum level of convergence before establishing closer links with and/or integrating that country. The feasibility of the policy co-ordination required for this purpose will be increased because the risks associated with a credible European orientation are higher than those associated with limited relations but more manageable than those associated with a non-credible European orientation. Therefore it was not surprising to observe that the EU proved capable of assuming an anchoring role towards the CEECs because of the lower risks implied by the latter's credible commitment to convergence, but incapable of playing a similar role towards Turkey because of her non-credible commitment to policy reform.

Finally, between 1980 and 1985, the EU demonstrated a clear tendency to adopt a low profile policy towards Turkey's human rights record because of the fact that the military coup and the length of the transition from a military to a civilian regime excluded the possibility of a membership bid from Turkey. Under this condition, the level of policy-coordination remained limited and the stance of the co-ordinated policy was lenient because there was no imminent need to manage the risks that would have been entailed by a Turkish bid for membership. Therefore, the Council, the Commission and the member states left Turkey to determine the return to democracy at her own pace and limited the EU's pressure on Turkey to the EP's initiatives which were functional mainly for keeping Turkey's human rights record under the spot lights. From 1986 onwards, however, the risk/incentive structure that the EU faced was affected by Turkey's attempts to upgrade her relations with the EU, including the possibility of membership. Under this condition, and given the history of Turkey's non-credible commitment to convergence, the EU increased its criticism of Turkey's human rights record without adopting an effective anchoring role in terms of setting incentives and sanctions designed to reduce the probability of reversals in Turkish policy reform. This 'anchoring failure' interacted with Turkey's non-credible commitment to convergence and ensured the continuity of the anchor/credibility dilemma that produced sub-optimal results for both sides.

8 General Conclusions

In the preceding chapters, we have argued that the continuity in the EU's reluctance to anchor Turkey's policy reform and the latter's repeated failure to converge towards EU standards can be analysed in the light of what we describe as an anchor/credibility dilemma. The anchor/credibility dilemma is an endogenous outcome of state-society interaction and its severity depends on the levels of societal assertiveness and issue transparency/divisibility. The second argument we have made is that international developments such as the end of the Cold War can bear upon the anchor/credibility dilemma only to the extent that they affect the nature of the state-society interaction in terms of issue of transparency/divisibility and societal assertiveness. In developing these arguments, we have drawn upon the theory of endogenous policy-making reviewed in chapter 1, but we have also tried to transcend the latter's shortcomings by proposing two amendments. First, future policy options available to the policy-makers must be considered as a function of not only the existing cost/incentive structure, but also of past and current decisions. Secondly, and as a corollary of the first proposition, policy-makers can improve on the outcomes of past policy decisions by incorporating all available information (including the information concerning past mistakes) into their current decisions. Taking into account these propositions and the evidence examined in the preceding chapters, we will demonstrate below that the anchor/credibility dilemma - even though it has been determined endogenously by state-society interaction - can be resolved positively or negatively if policy-makers in the EU and Turkey declare their true objectives and re-write the contact between them accordingly.

The concept of anchor depicts the extent to which the EU is able to undertake risks and/or impose sanctions with a view to reduce the probability of policy reversals in Turkey as an associated country. While the undertaking of risks in favour of an associated country reduces the cost of convergence towards EU standards, the ability to impose sanctions increases the cost of deviations from the policy reform required for convergence. In chapter 2, we have demonstrated that the EU's anchoring capacity would be limited to transparent/divisible policy areas because policy-makers cannot undertake risks in favour of third countries or penalise policy reversals therein unless the consequences of such actions are compatible with package deals based on either inter-country or inter-group traded-offs within the EU. In non-transparent/non-divisible policy areas such as foreign policy or immigration policy, the EU's anchoring capacity would be even lower because either the member states themselves or some societal groups could equate the policy issue with an overarching national interest that cannot be traded off as part of a package deal. This limitation will be more pronounced the higher is the perceived cost of Turkey's accession.

Because of its limited anchoring capacity, the EU has insisted on Turkey's prior convergence towards European standards to ensure that the risks associated with eventual membership are reduced to manageable levels. This risk-averse tendency could be seen not only in contractual documents such as the AA, the AP and the CU agreement, but also in individual policy decisions examined in chapters 4-7. Given the cost/incentive structure determined by state-society interaction in the EU and the probability of policy reversals in Turkey, the theory of endogenous policy-making would suggest that the EU's risk-averse policy is rational and inevitable. The EU's risk aversion is rational because it reflects all available information concerning the costs and benefits of anchoring Turkey's policy reform. It is also inevitable because it is the equilibrium outcome of the strategic interaction between the EU and Turkey, both of whom are concerned with reducing their risks and increasing their benefits. In our approach, however, the EU's risk aversion is a product of state-society interaction which determines the cost/incentive structure endogenously and the failure of EU policy-makers to incorporate all available information, including the information related to past mistakes. In other words, the EU's risk-averse strategy (i.e., its anchoring capacity) may be neither a rational nor an inevitable outcome unless EU policy-makers restrict the range of future policy options by: (i) taking decisions which blur the transparency/divisibility of the policy issues, and/or (ii) failing to base those decisions on all available information, including the information indicating that past policy decisions have actually failed to secure the declared objective of anchoring Turkey into Europe.

That the EU's anchoring capacity is an endogenous outcome of state-society interaction is evident from the evidence examined in the preceding chapters. For example, we have shown in chapter 2 that the EU's anchoring capacity is not uniform across policy issues and levels of societal assertiveness. Under high levels of issue transparency/divisibility and societal assertiveness, member states are induced and enabled to reduce the scope for shifts in constituent loyalties by approximating and integrating their policies. However, when issue transparency/divisibility or societal assertiveness is low, shifts in constituent loyalties can be reduced through control-reliant methods, which generate policy diversion rather than approximation. We have also shown that the EU's anchoring capacity would vary accordingly: it would be high when issue transparency/divisibility and societal assertiveness are high, but low when these variables are low. These analytical conclusions are supported by the evidence examined in chapters 4-7. The EU's anchoring capacity declines as we move from the area of trade policy where the level of societal assertiveness and issue transparency/divisibility is high towards immigration, foreign policy and human rights, where the level of either issue transparency/divisibility and/or societal assertiveness is low.

Underlying these tendencies is the extent to which the member-states are likely to present a particular policy issue as a matter of national interest that cannot be negotiated either because of their own preferences or due to societal veto. Because issue transparency/divisibility is not only a technical property, the policy-maker's past and current decisions about a particular policy issue become a crucial factor that determines future preferences as well as the ability of societal forces to act as veto groups. Chapters 4-7 provide significant evidence suggesting that the EU's anchoring capacity has been determined not only by an exogenously-given level of issue transparency/divisibility as the standard endogenous policy analysis would suggest, but also by the extent to which EU member states tended to blur that given level of transparency/divisibility. For example, the EU extended only partial and conditional agricultural concessions to Turkey not because the consequences of these concessions could not be shared among the member states, but because of the way in which the latter tied their hands by establishing the CAP in the first instance. A similar blurring of the issue transparency/divisibility was evident in the area of free movement. The EU failed to comply with the AP in this area not because the risks associated with the principle of free movement were unmanageable, but because of the way in which intra-EU free movement was based on the principle of excluding non-EU nationals. Finally, EU member states failed to co-ordinate their human rights policies *vis-à-vis* Turkey not because the externally-given transparency/divisibility of the issues in this area was low but because tended to link these issues with non-transparent/non-divisible foreign policy, security and economic objectives.

The failure of the EU policy-makers to take into account all available information is also evident from the analysis in chapters 4-7. The information ignored by EU policy-makers included not only the lessons that could be learned from the sub-optimal functioning of the EU-Turkey association for three decades, but also the fact that an associated country's convergence towards EU standards was nothing but a special case of international policy co-ordination. The incorporation of this information into policy decisions would have enabled the EU to improve on the sub-optimal outcomes of the existing contracts by devising new contracts regulating the distributional consequences of the policy co-ordination between itself and Turkey. The analysis in the preceding chapters clearly demonstrates that this has not been the case. While existing contracts, including the CU agreement, failed to address the distributional consequences of Turkey's convergence towards EU standards, the signals given by the EU during the association period reflected a clear tendency to undertake only partial commitments towards Turkey. In addition, these commitments were undertaken with a view to avoid the risks associated with membership which, in fact, could have been reduced had the EU been capable of acting as an effective anchor.

The credibility problem faced by Turkish policy-makers is also a function of state-society interaction, which unfolds in the context of a control-reliant mode of governance. As demonstrated in chapter 3, the Turkish state is a major economic actor who also defines the national interest. In that chapter, we have also shown that the discretion built into the policy-making process generates further discretion required by the need to internalise private risks, which arise out of the uncertainty caused by the role of the state in the economy and its competition with the private sector for limited resources. The implications of this state of affairs for Turkey's relations with the EU could be seen in chapters 4-7, where we have seen frequent departures from the declared objective of converging towards EU standards. Turkish governments of all shades have consistently failed to carry out the necessary economic and political reforms, and the divergence between Turkey's policy on Cyprus and that of the EU increased despite Turkey's membership application in 1987. Turkey's failure to carry out the necessary economic reforms resulted in the suspension of tariff dismantling during the transition period, granting of subsidies on investment and export, and introduction of *ad hoc* surcharges on imports. Her failure to carry out the political reforms produced similar but more damaging consequences. The Turkish state deviated from its commitment to convergence towards EU standards in terms of democracy and respect for human rights. In addition, it reduced the scope for future political reforms by suppressing and marginalising the societal forces demanding democratisation.

The anchor/credibility dilemma analysis suggests that the EU, even if it plays an effective anchoring role as defined in this book, may not be able to resolve the credibility problem underpinning the frequent policy reversals in Turkey. This possibility, however, cannot be invoked as a reason for avoiding such a role for a number of reasons. First, the EU's failure to assume an effective anchoring role is very likely to exacerbate the credibility problem with which Turkish policy-makers are faced. The evidence examined in chapters 4-7 clearly demonstrates that this has actually been the case. The EU's reluctance to act as an effective has both induced and enabled successive Turkish governments to renege on their commitments to converge towards the EU's economic and political standards as well as its principles concerning relations between European states. Given the EU's declared objective of anchoring Turkey into Europe as a stable country and a large market, these outcomes indicate that the EU's reluctance to anchor Turkish policy reform has been a self-defeating choice.

Second, the experience of the EU itself suggests that the effectiveness of an anchor depends not only on the existence of clearly-defined procedures that the anchoring country could adhere to, but also on policy co-ordination rules providing incentives and triggering sanctions which would increase the cost of defection. While the failure of the early attempts at monetary integration in the 1970s and the crises of the EMS in 1992-93 confirm the negative consequences of the lack of such rules, redistributive mechanisms such as the structural funds confirm that compensation payments can actually induce national governments to bear the cost of policy convergence and integration required by the Single Market project. The EU's own experience also suggests that sanctions must be an integral part of the policy co-ordination regime. Irrespective of whether or not the convergence criteria were actually necessary from an economic policy point view, they were necessary in the context of the policy convergence required by monetary union. The threat that member states failing to meet these criteria would remain outside the monetary union has contributed not only to economic policy convergence but also to the credibility of the future monetary policy stance. What we observe in the case of EU-Turkey relations is that the EU has consistently avoided the challenge of defining and insisting on transparent rules for incentives and/or sanctions which would increase the cost that Turkey would have to pay for policy reversals. This tendency was evident with respect to the most contentious issues in EU-Turkey relations, such as immigration, human rights and the Cyprus problem.

Third, the reluctance to assume an anchoring function meant that the EU, like Turkey, has also been interested in securing a significant scope for discretion. The EU used the discretion provided in the contractual documents extensively and, sometimes, in a manner that rewarded Turkey's policy reversals. For example, the analysis in chapter 4 shows that the EU extended agricultural concessions to Turkey despite the fact that Turkey had not taken any significant step towards agricultural policy reform. Also, the analysis in chapters 6 and 7 demonstrates that the EU normalised its relations with Turkey and concluded the CU agreement without securing contractual commitments concerning the settlement of the Cyprus problem and the quality of the democratisation process. To a large extent, these choices were made by exploiting the discretion provided in existing contractual documents and with a view to secure a delay in Turkey's membership. The anchor/credibility dilemma analysis suggests that the EU should have taken into account the fact that such discretion and the motives behind it would only induce Turkey to discount the significance of convergence towards EU standards and engage in further policy reversals.

In addition to these findings, the anchor/credibility dilemma analysis has enabled us to the existing knowledge about EU-Turkey relations by providing new insights into a number of substantive issues. We have demonstrated in chapter 4 that the Turkish argument concerning the level of EU protectionism against Turkish export of T&C products and the tendency of the existing literature to take this argument at face value must be questioned. The existing evidence suggests that restrictions imposed on Turkish T&C export were less significant than those imposed under the MFA on the export of other Mediterranean countries. The level of restriction was also less damaging than what a unilateral application of the safeguard clause under the AP would have implied. As a result, Turkey became the largest supplier of the EU market in a number of heavily protected products. Also, her market share increased significantly after informal restraint agreements were signed with Turkish exporters in 1982 and 1986. This finding suggests that Turkey's criticism of EU restrictions on Turkish T&C export was essentially motivated by the perceived opportunity to make further inroads into the EU market when other suppliers were largely excluded under MFA restrictions.

Another Turkish argument that must be questioned concerns the impact of Greek membership on EU-Turkey relations. As indicated in chapter 6, Greece tried to influence the EU's policy towards Turkey by invoking not only the Cyprus problem but also the issues in Greco-Turkish relations. Nevertheless, it would be a gross exaggeration to suggest that the general stance of the EU's policy towards Turkey was influenced by Greece. The EU normalised relations with Turkey in 1986, agreed on the Matutes Package of 1992, and signed the customs union agreement in 1995 despite the fact intra-EU decisions on some elements of these initiatives had to be agreed upon unanimously. Therefore, the existing evidence suggests that the EU, despite Greek attempts at blocking major developments in EU-Turkey relations, was able to upgrade its relations with Turkey. The irrelevance of the 'Greek factor' becomes more evident when one takes into account the fact that the EU's revealed preference for keeping the EU-Turkey association on track after the accession of Greece was a continuation of its policy towards Turkey before Greece became a member in 1981. The continuity was especially evident in the EU's tendency to strengthen its relations with Turkey both before and after 1981, albeit with a clear preference for delaying Turkey's membership as much as possible.

The anchor/credibility dilemma analysis enables us to interpret the 'Greek factor' within a broader perspective. One can speak of a 'Greek factor' in EU-Turkey relations in the sense that Greek objections to the strengthening of the EU-Turkey relations provided both Turkey and the EU with a pretext to detract attention from their respective failures to fulfil their convergence and anchoring obligations. Had the EU signalled its willingness to embrace Turkey's membership, successive Greek governments would have found it highly difficult, if not impossible, to be so much vociferous about the strengthening of the EU-Turkey relations. Also, had Turkey been committed credibly to converge towards EU standards, there would have been less reason for Greek governments to be concerned about the strengthening of the EU-Turkey relations because Turkey would have adopted a different approach to the settlement of the Cyprus problem and the issues in Greco-Turkish dispute. The 'Greek factor' must also be interpreted differently in the specific context of the Cyprus problem in EU-Turkey relations. The evidence examined in chapter 6 suggests that the accession of Greece reduced the feasibility of the *enosis* option and enhanced the viability of an independent Cypriot state, to which the only threat came from Turkey because of her continued military presence and her progressive integration of the Northern Cyprus. As the Greek-Cypriot leadership upgraded their European orientation in an attempt to benefit from the EU umbrella, the EU was induced to increase its involvement in the Cyprus problem in order to secure a settlement and reduce the risks associated with Cyprus' accession. Given these dynamics, Turkey's criticism of the EU for succumbing to Greek pressure is not only an erroneous but also a self-defeating strategy.

A third insight concerns the impact of the developments in Central and Eastern Europe on the EU's approach to Turkish membership and the alleged change in Turkey's foreign policy. It is an almost received wisdom to assert that the EU's interest in Turkey has declined and Turkey has begun to look beyond Europe after the collapse of the Soviet Bloc. The evidence examined in chapters 4-7, however, indicates clearly that continuity in the EU's approach to Turkey has been the rule rather than the exception. One aspect of the continuity in the EU's policy has been the tendency to subscribe to a narrow definition of anchor, which involves economic and political links that would keep Turkey within the Western zone of influence. Therefore, the EU-Turkey association survived the collapse of the Soviet Bloc and has been upgraded by the customs union. The other aspect of the continuity involves the strengthening of the economic and political links with Turkey without (and preferably as a substitute for) an effective anchoring function. In other words, the EU's policy towards Turkey has always been vague and non-committal so far as the latter's membership is concerned. Although the packaging of this reluctance has changed over time, such superficial changes cannot and should not be taken as evidence of change in the policy stance itself. Similarly, the evidence in chapters 4-7 also indicates that Turkey's commitment to a European orientation was non-credible not only after but also before of the developments in Eastern Europe. The lack of a credible commitment was evident not only from Turkey's failure to carry out the reforms required for closer ties with the EU, but also from her defiance of repeated EU calls for a settlement of the Cyprus problem and a peaceful resolution of the dispute with Greece.

The fourth insight provided by the anchor/credibility dilemma analysis enables us to reinterpret the intensification of the EU criticism towards Turkey after the latter's membership application in 1987. The evidence examined in chapters 6 and 7 demonstrates that the EU, after 1987, assumed a more critical stance against Turkey with respect to the Cyprus problem and Turkey's human rights abuses. The contrast between this critical stance and the lenient approach until the mid-1980s has prompted Turkish governments to argue that the EU was in fact using the Cyprus and human rights issues as an alibi to avoid Turkey's membership. This argument is only partially correct because it is based on the assumption that the EU's accommodating approach until the mid-1980s was essentially less damaging for Turkey's relations with the EU. However, what the evidence in chapters 6 and 7 suggests is that the EU's reluctance to impose sanctions against Turkey during the pre-1987 period was in fact more damaging for EU-Turkey relations for two reasons. On the one hand, the leniency of the EU's approach until 1987 made it less costly for Turkey to deviate from her declared objective of integrating with Europe. Therefore, what appeared to be a favourable policy stance was in fact nothing but an indicator of the EU's failure to act as an effective anchor. Because of this failure, the probability of Turkey divergence from EU standards was increased and her chance of securing a positive response to her membership application was reduced. On the other hand, the leniency of the EU's pre-1987 approach concerning the Cyprus problem and human rights issues was due to the lower risks implied by the lack of an imminent membership application. In other words, it was due to political convenience rather than the significance attached to Turkey's role in Europe. Therefore, there was no guarantee that the discretion used in developing the lenient approach would not be also deployed to develop a more critical position that would be functional for preventing Turkey's membership.

Finally, the anchor/credibility dilemma analysis also enables us to provide a new interpretation of the contrast between the EU's policy on intra-EU free movement and its policy on extra-EU immigration. The evidence examined in chapter 5 indicates that the former is inclusive and has supranational dimensions whereas the latter is exclusionist and has been developed through intergovernmental procedures. We have demonstrated that this contrast cannot be explained by referring to state sovereignty or xenophobic societal attitudes only. The state-centric account cannot explain why EU member states invoke the concept of sovereignty to exclude third-country nationals but not the nationals of other member states, whereas the society-centric account is inadequate for explaining why EU nationals in a particular member state would be prepared to share with other EU nationals the privileges they enjoy because of their territorially-defined nationality. The anchor/credibility analysis enables us to address these questions by referring to the domain of the state-society interaction which, in the specific case of intra-EU free movement, was redefined in such a way that it would correspond to a 'European' rather than 'national' realm. Therefore, it was possible to explain the contrast mentioned above by arguing that the redefinition of the domain over which nationality-based privileges are enjoyed has actually increased the transparency/divisibility of the policy issues concerning intra-EU migratory flows. Under this condition of increased transparency/divisibility, policy integration and inclusion became feasible as well as desirable options.

We have also shown that EU policies on intra-EU free movement and extra-EU immigration are in fact the two sides of the same coin despite the contrast between them in terms of policy-making procedures and policy stance. Once the domain over which nationality-based privileges can be enjoyed was redefined, the exclusion of third-country nationals became necessary to satisfy the demands of the EU nationals for 'club services'. In addition, the method of EU policy-making with respect to third-country immigration remained intergovernmental because the nationality principle excluded non-EU nationals and reduced the risk of spill-over effects that could arise from different national immigration policies. Therefore, the exclusion of non-EU nationals and intergovernmentalism, i.e., the indicators of a 'fortress Europe', have actually preceded the Single Market with which they are associated in the existing literature. As we have indicated in chapter 6, 'fortress Europe' was created in 1968, not 1986.

Thus far, we highlighted the general conclusions that can be derived from our analysis of the existing evidence on EU-Turkey relations. In what follows, we elaborate on whether the anchor/credibility dilemma in EU-Turkey relations can be resolved given the findings outlined above. As we have already indicated, the anchor/credibility dilemma specified in this book is a result of state-society interaction that can generate different levels of EU anchoring capacity and Turkish commitment to policy reform, depending on the extent of issue transparency/divisibility and societal assertiveness. In other words, it is neither dictated by a structural exigency nor does it reflect an inevitable outcome determined by a rational choice made on the basis of all available information. Therefore, the endogenous policy analysis suggests that there is scope for improvement should future policy decisions be based on all available information including the information relating to the sub-optimal consequences of past and current decisions. It also suggests that current policy decisions themselves influence the expectations held by societal forces and, thereby, can change the cost/incentive structure under which they have been taken. In other words, the range of policy options available to policy-makers depends not only the cost/incentive structure as determined by the parameters of the state-society interaction up to the current period, but also on the policy-maker's past and current decisions.

Given these results, we can argue that a solution to the anchor/credibility dilemma is possible if the *contractual principle* governing EU-Turkey relations is redefined to reflect the fact issues in EU-Turkey relations are essentially policy co-ordination problems. Before elaborating on whether a redefinition of the contractual principle will necessarily entail higher costs for either party, we shall explain what the principle should involve and why this simple proposal may be conducive to a solution of the anchor/credibility dilemma. The evidence analysed in this book suggests that the major defect of the existing contractual arrangements between the EU and Turkey is the degree of discretion they provide for. To a large extent, this discretion reflects the parties' preference for avoiding their obligations not only under extraordinary conditions or structural exigencies but also when it is politically convenient. Therefore, the new principle must minimise the possibility of avoiding contractual obligations for political convenience.

One point that must be made at the outset is that the proposed redefinition of the contractual principle does not require the conclusion of a new agreement between the EU and Turkey. On the contrary, it assumes that EU-Turkey relations would continue to be governed by the existing contracts, including the CU agreement. What is required, however, is the incorporation of this principle into detailed provisions of the existing contracts so that that all rights are linked to *transparent performance criteria* designed to serve two purposes: (i) monitoring Turkey's convergence towards EU standards and the EU's compliance with her obligations; and (ii) triggering automatic entitlement to rights once the performance criteria are met or imposition of sanctions when they are not. The new principle would also require that all derogations from the obligations under the contracts are linked to *derogation thresholds* applicable to both parties and specified in terms of the following indicators: unemployment rates; market penetration; levels of migratory flows; and international or regional developments which, although not caused by the actions of the parties, may affect their contractual performance. Unless the party deviating from its obligations provide evidence that its deviation is justified under any of these indicators, part or all of the contract would be frozen and penalties would be applicable. In other words, the opposite party would be allowed to avoid its share of the costs involved in the policy co-ordination process, which aims to secure Turkey's convergence towards EU standards and her eventual integration.

An agreement on this principle and the announcement of a credible commitment thereto by both parties would influence societal expectations accordingly. The revision of expectations would reduce the cost of implementing the revised contracts because, as societal forces recognise the fact that the scope for special treatment has declined, the transparency/divisibility of the policy issues in EU-Turkey relations would increase. Consequently, the scope for policy innovation would improve and both the EU and Turkey would be better placed to remain committed to their contractual obligations. Also, a new contractual arrangement should not necessarily increase the cost to be born by either party as long as convergence towards European standards and integration are their true objectives. Under this condition, it is possible to maintain all existing rights and obligations provided for in existing contractual documents, including the AA, the AP, the CU agreement, and the decisions of the Association Council. The only change that would occur will be limited to insertion of agreed thresholds or criteria that should allow for monitoring of both parties' performance under the contract. Up to this stage, and assuming that both parties are committed to ensure Turkey's integration into the EU when a specified convergence towards the standards set by the *acquis communautaire* is achieved, the only increase in the cost for both parties will be limited to the increase in the cost of negotiating the performance criteria and derogation thresholds, and establishing the institutions that would monitor implementation. Given the sub-optimal outcomes of EU-Turkey relations over the last three and a half decades, these negotiation and implementation costs are very likely to be negligible compared to the cost of past failures.

Obviously, the assumption that both parties are committed to convergence and integration is too restrictive. Therefore, if either party or both are actually not committed to Turkey's integration as specified above, then the rewriting of the contractual principle would entail higher costs for the party which lacks that commitment. The higher cost would result not because the new contractual principle would necessarily entail additional commitments beyond what already exists in current contracts, but because it would require the non-committed party to act in accordance with a contractual outcome that it does not subscribe to. The evidence examined in chapters 4-7 suggests that neither the EU nor Turkey have acted in line with the objective of convergence and integration, which is codified in existing contracts and repeated in policy announcements. In our view, this lack of commitment is not dictated by structural exigencies or the efficient use of all available information. It is rather caused by the failure of both parties to engage in adaptive learning and acknowledge the cost of the sub-optimal outcomes achieved over the last three and a half decades. Nevertheless, there is no guarantee that the EU and/or Turkey would rise up to this challenge. Therefore, there is a significant probability that they might reject a proposal such as ours on the grounds that it is unfeasible or unrealistic. Would such a rejection invalidate the proposal made above?

We would argue that a rejection would not make our proposition redundant for a number of reasons. First of all, the rejection would confirm our argument that the anchor/credibility dilemma in EU-Turkey relations is neither rational or inevitable. Given that the proposition could reduce the costs of convergence and integration as indicated above, a rejection would confirm our view that the lack of credible commitment is a result of the parties' preference for discretion and their failure to learn from past policy decisions, both of which generates sub-optimal outcomes. Second, the rejection would bring into the open the fact that both EU member states and Turkey have been misleading their constituents by declaring a commitment to convergence and integration on the one hand but rejecting to act accordingly on the other. The disclosure of this information is not insignificant for constituents who would prefer transparent information for expectation formation and risk assessment.

Third, the coexistence of a formal commitment to integration and convergence with a divergent practice generates two types of sub-optimal results. On the one hand, uncertainty would continue to impair EU-Turkey relations because of either party's deviations from contractual obligations, which can be neither justified nor penalised because of the discretion built into those contracts. To the extent that this is the case, both parties would be better off agreeing on a new contract which does not include integration and convergence as ultimate goals. On the other hand, bargaining over issues in the absence of transparent rules would protract the negotiation process and produce inefficient results. Such inefficiency would be caused by the lack of transparent information about the objectives of either party and exacerbated by the tendency to politicise the issues under negotiation. Under this condition, both parties would also be better off should they take this information into account and revise their future decisions accordingly. Therefore, and as a final word, we would state that the future of EU-Turkey relations would be determined by both parties' choices, as the sub-optimal outcomes of the last three and a half decades have also been.

Bibliography

1 Books, Book Chapters and Journal Articles

Abadan-Unat, N. et al. (1976), *Migration and Development: A Study of the Effects of International Labour Migration in Bogazliyan District*, Ajans Türk Press, Ankara.

Agathocleous, N. (1993), 'Cyprus and the European Community', in J. Charalambous and G. Georghallides (eds.), *Focus on Cyprus*, University of North London Press, London, pp. 155-64.

Aggarwal, V.K. (1983), 'The Unravelling of the Multi-Fibre Agreement, 1981: An Examination of International Regime Change', *International Organisation*, vol. 37, no. 4, pp. 617-45.

Ahmad, F. (1993), *The Making of Modern Turkey*, Routledge, London.

Aktan, O.H. and Baysan, T. (1985), 'Türkiye Ekonomisinin Dünya Ekonomisine Entegrasyonu: Liberasyon, Karşılaştırmalı Üstünlük ve Optimum Politikalar (The Integration of Turkish Economy into the World Economy: Liberalisation, Comparative Advantages, and Optimal Policies), *METU Studies in Development*, vol. 12, no. 1 and 2, pp. 49-106.

Amnesty International (1992), 'Turkey: Torture, Extrajudicial Executions, 'Disappearances', AI Index: Europe 44/39/92, London.

Amnesty International, (1993), 'The Challenges of Change: Preparation for the CSCE Human Dimension Implementation Meeting', Warsaw, 27 September - 15 October 1993', (Working Paper), London.

Anderson, J. (1991), 'Sceptical Reflections on a Europe of Regions: Britain, Germany and the ERDF', *Journal of Public Policy*, no. 1, pp. 417-47.

Andrews, B. (1984), 'The Domestic Content of International Behaviour', *International Organisation*, vol. 38, no. 2, pp. 321-27.

Apostolou, A. (1998), 'Turkey, the European Union and Cyprus', Paper presented in Seminars on Turkey, School of Oriental and African Studies, mimeograph, London.

Armaoğlu, F. (1963), *Kıbrıs Meselesi 1954-59: Türk Hükümetinin ve Kamuoyunun Davranışları (The Cyprus Issue 1954-59: The Attitudes of Turkish Government and Public Opinion)*, Faculty of Political Sciences, Ankara.

Ashley, R. (1984), 'The Poverty of Neorealism', *International Organisation*, vol. 38, no. 2.

Ataöv, T. (1970), *NATO and Turkey*, Sevinç Printing House, Ankara.

Averyt, W. (1975), 'Eurogroups, Clientela and the European Community', *International Organisation*, vol. 29, no. 4, pp. 949-72.

Avi, S. (1976), 'The Community and the Mediterranean Basin', in K.J. Twitchett, *Europe and the World: The External Relations of the Common Market*, Europa Publications, London, pp. 77-120.

Ayberk, U. (1978), *Le Méchanism de la Prise des Décisions Communautaires en Matière de Relations Internationales*, Emile Bruylant, Bruxelles.

Backus, D. and Driffil, J. (1985), 'Inflation and Reputation', *American Economic Review*, vol. 75, pp. 530-38.

Baldwin, D.A. (1985), *Economic Statecraft,* Princeton University Press, Princeton, N.J.

Balkır, C. (1993), 'Turkey and the European Community: Foreign Trade and Direct Foreign Investment in the 1980s', in C. Balkır and A.M. Williams, (eds.), *Turkey and Europe*, Pinter Publishers, London, pp. 123-25.

Barro, R. (1986), 'Recent Developments in the Theory of Rules versus Discretion', *Economic Journal*, vol. 96, pp. 23-37.

Beitz, C.R. (1979), *Political Theory and International Relations,* Princeton University Press, Princeton, N.J.

Bianchi, R. (1984), *Interest Groups and Political Development in Turkey*, Princeton University Press, Princeton, N.J.

Bicchieri, C. (1993), *Rationality and Coordination*, Cambridge University Press, Cambridge.

Birand, M.A. (1984), *30 Sıcak Gün (The 30 Hot Days),* Milliyet Publications, Ankara.

Birand, M.A. (1986), *Türkiye'nin Ortak Pazar Macerası* (*Turkey's Common Market Adventure)*, Milliyet Publications, Ankara.

Birand, M.A. (1991), 'Turkey and the Davos Process: Experiences and Prospects', in D. Constas (ed.), *The Greek-Turkish Conflict in the 1990s: Domestic and External Influences*, Macmillan, London, pp. 27-39.

Birsel, İ. (1983), *Avrupa Ekonomik Topluluğu ve Türkiye-AET İlişkileri (European Economic Community and Turkey-EEC Relations)*, Dışişleri Akademisi Yayınları, Ankara.

Blokker, N. (1989), *International Regulation of World Trade in Textiles,* Martinus Nijhoff, Dordrecht.

Bohning, W.R. (1987), 'The Scope of the EEC System of Free Movement of Workers', *Common Market Law Review*, vol. 10, no. 1, pp. 81-86.

Bölükbaşı, S. (1992), 'The Turco-Greek Dispute: Issues, Policies and Prospects', in C.H. Dodd (ed.), *Turkish Foreign Policy: New Prospects*, Eothen Press, Huntingdon, pp. 27-54.

Boratav, K. (182), *Türkiye'de Devletçilik (Etatism in Turkey)*, Savaş Yayınevi, Ankara.

Bourgeois, J.H.J. (1987), 'The Common Commercial Policy: Scope and Nature of Powers', in E.L.M. Völker, *Protectionism and the European Community* (2nd ed.), Kluwer Law and Taxation Publishers, Deventer, pp. 1-16.

Bourguignon, R. (1990), 'The History of the Association Agreement between Turkey and the European Community', in A. Evin and G. Denton (eds.), *Turkey and the European Community*, Leske and Budrich, Opladen, pp. 56-57.

Bozer, A. (1987), 'Turkey's Relations and Prospects with the European Community', *Turkish Review*, vol. 2, no. 3, pp. 9-14.

Buergenthal, T. (1992), 'CSCE Human Dimension: The Birth of a System', in A. Clapham and F. Emmert (eds.), *Collected Courses of the Academy of European Law: The Protection of Human Rights in Europe (vol. 1, book 2)*, Martinus Nijhoff, Dordrecht, pp. 163-209.

Bunyan, T. (1991), 'Towards an Authoritarian European State', *Race and Class Journal of Black and Third World Liberation*, vol. 32, no. 3, pp. 19-27.

Callovi, G. (1992), 'Regulation of Immigration in 1993: Pieces of the EC Jig-Saw Puzzle', *International Migration Review*, vol. 26, no. 2, pp. 353-72.

Cameron, D.R. (1992), 'The 1992 Initiative: Causes and Consequences', in M.S. Alberta (ed.), *Europolitics: Institutions and Policymaking, The 'New' European Community*, The Brookings Institution, Washington D.C., pp. 23-74.

Campanella, M.L. (1991), 'Proactive Policy-Making: The New Role of the State Actor', *Government and Opposition*, vol. 26, no. 4, pp. 480-99.

Carleton, D. (19985), 'The Foreign Policy of Human Rights: Rhetoric and Reality from Jimmy Carter to Ronald Reagan', *Human Rights Quarterly*, vol. 7, no. 2, pp. 205-229.

Cendrowicz, M. 'The European Community and Turkey: Looking Backwards, Looking Forwards', in C.H. Dodd (ed.), *Turkish Foreign Policy: New Prospects*, The Eothen Press, Wistow, pp. 9-26.

Charalambous, J. and Georghallides, G. (eds.) (DATE), *Focus on Cyprus*, University North London Press, London.

Clapham, A. and Emmert, F. (eds.) (1992), *Collected Courses of the Academy of European Law: The Protection of Human Rights in Europe (vol. 1, book 2)*, Martinus Nijhoff, Dordrecht.

Claude, R.P. and Burns, H.W. (eds.) (1992), *Human Rights in the World: Issues and Action*, University of Pennsylvania Press, Philadelphia.

Coates, K. (1992), *Human Rights in the World: A Report to the European Parliament* (Nottingham, Spokesman).

Cohan, A.S. (1991), 'Eurotexts and Eurothought: Changing Approaches to the Study of the European Community', *Review of International Studies*, vol. 17, no. 2, pp. 193-200.

Collins, S. (1988), 'Inflation and the European Monetary System', in F. Gaivazzi et al. (eds.), *The European Monetary System*, Cambridge University Press, Cambridge, pp. 112-33.

Constas, D. (ed.) (1991), *The Greek-Turkish Conflict in the 1990s: Domestic and External Influences*, Macmillan, London.

Coplin, W. (1965), 'International Law and Assumptions about the State System', *World Politics*, vol. 17, pp. 615-34.

Cox, R.W. (1981), 'Social Forces, States and World Orders: Beyond International Relations Theory', *Millennium: Journal of International Studies*, vol. 10, no. 2, pp. 126-55.

Cox, R.W. (1990), 'Production, the State and Change in World Order', in E-O. Czempiel and J.N. Rosenau (eds.), *Global Changes and Approaches to World Politics for the 1990s*, Lexington Books, Lexington, pp. 37-50.

van Dartel, R.J.P.M. (1987), 'The EEC's Commercial Policy Concerning Textiles', in E.L.M. Völker (ed.), *Protectionism and the European Community*, Kluwer Law and Taxation Publishers, Deventer, pp. 121-58.

Dodd, C.H. (ed.) (1992), *Turkish Foreign Policy: New Prospects*, The Eothen Press, Wistow.

Dolan, M.B. (1983), 'European Restructuring and Import Policies for a Textiles Industry in Crisis', *International Organization*, vol. 37, no. 4, pp. 538-615.

Donnelly, J. (1985), *The Concept of Human* Rights, St. Martin's Press, New York.

Dummett, A. and Andrew, N. (1990), *Subjects, Citizens, Aliens and Others: Nationality and Immigration Law*, Weidenfeld and Nicolson, London.

Dunleavy, P. and O'Leary, B. (1987), *Theories of the State: The Politics of Liberal Democracy*, Macmillan, London.

Duparc, C. (1992), *The European Community and Human Rights*, Office for Official Publications of the EC, Luxembourg.

Dyer, H.C. and Mangasarian, L. (eds.) (1989), *The Study of International Relations: the State of the Art*, Macmillan, London,.

Economist Intelligence Unit, (1990), *European Trends: Key Issues and Developments in the EC, EFTA and the Single Market*, no. 3.

Economist Intelligence Unit (1994), *EIU Country Report on Cyprus*, 4th Quarter, London.

Economist Intelligence Unit (1994-95), 'Country Profile: Cyprus, 1994-95', *The Economist Intelligence Unit*. London.

Edgeworth, F.Y. (1925), *Papers Relating to Political Economy* (vol. I), Macmillan, London.

Eeckhout, P. (1994), *The European Internal Market and International Trade: A Legal Analysis*, Oxford University Press, Oxford.

Eisenstadt, J.N. and Ahimeir, O. (eds.) (1985), *The Welfare State and Its Aftermath*, Barnes and Noble, London.

Eralp, A. (1993), 'Turkey and the European Community in the Changing Post-War International System', in C. Balkır and A.M. Williams (eds.), *Turkey and Europe*, Pinter Publishers, London, pp. 24-44.

Eralp, A. (1998), 'Turkey in the European Union in the Aftermath of the Cold War', in L. Rittenberg (ed.), *The Political Economy of Turkey in the Post-Soviet Era: Going West and Looking East?* Praeger, London, pp. 37-51.

Ersel, H. and Kumcu, E.M. (1995), 'İstikrar Programı ve Kamu Dengesi (Stability Programme and the Public Sector Balance)', TUSİAD (Turkish Industrialists and Businessmen's Association), *Türkiye için Yeni bir Orta Vadeli İstikrar Programına Doğru (Towards a Medium-Term Stability Programme for Turkey)*, TUSİAD Publication no. T/95, Istanbul, pp. 171-192.

Ertekün, N.M. (1981), *In Search of a Negotiated Cyprus Settlement*, Ulus Matbaacılık, Nicosia.

Esche, M. (1990), 'A History of Greek-Turkish Relations', in A. Evin and G. Denton (eds.), *Turkey and the European Community*, Laske and Budrich, Opladen, pp. 101-16.

Etzioni, A. (1967), 'Mixed-Scanning: A Third Approach to Decision-Making', *Public Administration Review*, vol. 27, no. 5, pp. 385-92.

Etzioni, A. (1968), *The Active Society: A Theory of Societal and Political processes*, The Free Press, New York.

Euroconsult Ltd. (1991), *Cyprus and the European Community*, Nicosia.

European Political Cooperation (1989), 'Intervention du Ministre des Affaires Etrangères de L'Espagne au Nom des Douze Etats Membres de la Communauté Européenne a L'occasion de l'inauguration de la première reunion the la Conference sur la Dimension Humaine', Paris, 30.5.1989.

European Political Cooperation (1990), 'Statement by the Minister of Foreign Affairs of Ireland on Behalf of the Twelve at the 46th Session of the UNCHR, Geneva, 2.2.1990.

Evans, P., Reuschmeyer, D. and Skocpol, T. (eds.) (1985), *Bringing the State Back In*, Cambridge University Press, Cambridge.

Evans, T. and Wilson, P. (1992), 'Regime Theory and the English School of International Relations: A Comparison', *Millennium: Journal of International Studies*, vol. 21, no. 3, pp. 329-51.

Evin, A. and Denton, G. (eds.) (1990), *Turkey and the European Community*, Leske and Budrich, Opladen.

Falk, R.A. (1971), *This Endangered Planet: Prospects and Proposals for Human Survival*, Random House, New York.

Falk, R.A. (1992), 'Theoretical Foundations of Human Rights', in R.P. Claude and B.H. Weston (eds.), *Human Rights in the World: Issues and Action*, University of Pennsylvania Press, Philadelphia, pp. 31-41.

Farer, T.J. (1992), 'The United Nations and Human Rights: More than a Whimper, Less than a Roar', in R.P. Claude and B.H. Weston (eds.), *Human Rights in the World Community: Issues and Action*, Philadelphia, University of Pennsylvania Press, pp. 227-43.

Farrands, C. (1979), 'Textile Diplomacy: The Making and Implementation of European textile Policy, 1974-78', *Journal of Common Market Studies*, vol. 8, pp. 22-39.

Ferguson, Y. H. and Mansbach, R.W. (1988), *The Elusive Quest: Theory and International Politics,* University of South Carolina Press, Columbia, South Carolina.

Flora, P. (1985), 'On the History and Current Problems of the Welfare State', in J.N. Eisenstadt and O. Ahimeir (eds.), *The Welfare State and Its Aftermath*, Barnes and Noble, London, pp. 11-30.

Foreign Affairs Committee (1987), *Report on Cyprus*, HMSO, London.

Forsythe, D.P. (1984), *American Foreign Policy in an Uncertain World*, University of Nebraska Press, Lincoln, Nebraska.

Fouwels, M. (1997), 'The European Union's Common Foreign and Security Policy and Human Rights', *Netherlands Quarterly Review of Human Rights*, vol. 15, no. 3, pp. 291-324.

Francois, J.F. (1997), 'External Bindings and the Credibility of Reform', in A. Galal and B. Hoekman (eds.), *Regional Partners in Global Markets: Limits and Possibilities of the Euro-Med Agreements*, Centre for Economic Policy Research/Egyptian Centre for Economic Studies, London and Cairo, pp. 35-48.

Friends of Cyprus (Session 1986-87), 'Memorandum Submitted to the House of Commons Foreign Affairs Committee', (Paper no. 23-iii), *Parliamentary Papers*, vol. 6, pp. 32-40.

Gandia, D. (1981), *The EEC's Generalised System of Preferences and other Agreements*, Allanheld Osmun Co., Montclair, N.J.

Garett, J.G. (1992), 'International Co-operation and Institutional Choice: the European Community's Internal Market', *International Organisation*, vol. 46, pp. 533-60.

Giavazzi, F. and Miller, M. (eds.) (1988), *The European Monetary System*, Cambridge University Press, Cambridge.

Giavazzi, F. and Pagano, M. (1988), 'The Advantage of Tying One's Hands: EMS Discipline and Central Bank Credibility', *Economic Review*, vol. 32, pp. 1055-82.

Giddens, A. (1979), *Central Problems in Social Theory*, Macmillan, London.

Ginsberg, R.H. (1988), 'The European Community and the Mediterranean', in J. Lodge (ed.), *Institutions and Policies of the European Community*, Frances Pinter, London, pp. 154-67.

Ginsberg, R.H. (1989), *Foreign Policy Actions of the European Community: The Politics of Scale*, Lynne Rienner Publishers, Boulder, 1989.

Goodwin-Gill, G.S. (1978), *International Law and the Movement of Persons Between States*, Clarendon Press, Oxford.

Graubard, S.B. (ed.) (1964), *A New Europe?* Oldbourne Press, London.

Grete, B. (1993), 'Control in Immigration policy: A Closed Europe in the Making', in R. King (ed.), *The New Geography of European Migrations*, Belhaven Press, London, pp. 100-15.

Grilli, E.R. (1993), *The European Community and the Developing Countries*, Cambridge University Press, Cambridge.

Groom, A.J.R. (1990), 'The Setting in World Society', in A.J.R. Groom and P. Taylor (eds.), *Frameworks for International Co-operation*, Pinter Publishers, London, pp. 3-11.

Groom, A. J. R. and Taylor, P. (eds.) (1990), *Frameworks for International Co-operation*, Printer Publishers, London.

Groux, J. (1983), 'Mixed Negotiations', in D.O. Keeffe and H.G. Schermes (eds.), *Mixed Agreements*, Kluwer Law and Taxation Publishers, Deventer, pp. 23-28.

de Gucht, K.L.G.E. (1988), *Report on Human Rights in the World and Community Policy on Human Rights for the Year 1987-88*, no. A 2-329/88, Office for Official Publications of the EC, Luxembourg, p. 32.

Guerrieri, P. and Padoan, P.C. (1989), 'Integration, Cooperation and Adjustment Policies', in P. Guerrieri and P.C. Padoan (eds.), *The Political Economy of European Integration: States, Markets and Institutions*, Harvester Wheatsheaf, New York, pp. 1-30.

Gürel, S. (1985), *Kıbrıs Tarihi (History of Cyprus)*, Kaynak Yayınları, Istanbul.

Haaland-Matlary, J. (1994), 'Integration Theory and International Relations Theory: What Does the Elephant Look Like Today and How Should It Be Studied?', Paper Submitted to the 2nd ECSA-World Conference on Federalism, Subsidiarity and Democracy in the European Union, Brussels.

Haas, E.B. (1964a), *Beyond the Nation State*, Stanford University Press, Stanford.

Haas, E.B. (1964b), 'Technocracy, Pluralism and the New Europe', in S.B. Gruda (ed.), *A New Europe?* Oldbourne Press, London, pp. 65-71.

Haas, E.B. (1968), *The Uniting of Europe* (2nd ed.), Stanford University Press, Stanford.

Haas, E.B. (1969), 'Letter to the Editor', *Journal of Common Market Studies*, vol. 8, no. 1, p. 70.

Haas, E.B. (1975), *The Obsolescence of Regional Integration Theory*, University of California, Institute of International Studies, Berkeley.

Hall, J.A. (ed.) (1986), *States in History*, Oxford University Press, Oxford.

Hall, P.A. (1986), *Governing the Economy: The Politics of State Intervention in Britain and France*, Oxford University Press, Oxford.

Halliday, F. (1989), 'State and Society in International Relations: A Second Agenda', in H.C. Dyer and L. Mangasarian (eds.), *The Study of International Relations: the State of the Art*, Macmillan, London, pp. 40-59.

Halliday, F. (1992), 'International Society as Homogeneity: Burke, Marx, Fukuyama', *Millennium: Journal of International Studies*, vol. 21, no. 3, pp. 453-461.

Hammar, T. (ed.) (1990), *Democracy and the Nation State: Aliens, Denizens and Citizens in a World of International Migration*, Avebury, Aldershot.

Hargreaves Heap, S. P. and Varoufakis, Y. (1997), *Game Theory: A Critical Introduction*, Routledge, London.

Harrison, G.W., Rutherford, T.F. and Tarr, D.G. (1996), *Economic Implications for Turkey of a Customs Union with the European Union*, World Bank, Washington, D.C.

Harrison, R.J. (1975), *Europe in Question: Theories of Regional International Integration* (2nd. ed.), George Allen and Unwin, London.

Heisler, M.O. (1992), 'Migration, International Relations and the New Europe: Theoretical Perspectives form Institutional Sociology', *International Migration Review*, vol. 26, no. 2 pp. 596-621.

Henkin, L. (1990), 'Law and Politics in International Relations: States and Human Values', *Journal of International Affairs*, vol. 44, pp. 183-208.

Heper, M. (1988), 'State and Society in Turkish Political Experience', in M. Heper and A. Evin (eds.), *State, Democracy and the Military: Turkey in the 1980s*, Walter de Gruyter, Berlin, pp. 1-10.

Heper, M. (1991), 'The State and Interest Groups with Special Reference to Turkey', in M. Heper (ed.), *Strong State and Economic Interest Groups: The Post-1980 Turkish Experience*, Walter de Gruyter, Berlin, pp. 1-23.

Heper, M. and Evin, A. (eds.) (1988), *State, Democracy and the Military: Turkey in the 1980s*, Walter de Gruyter, Berlin.

Hershlag, Z.Y. (1960), *Turkey: An Economy in Transition*, Martinus Nijhof, The Hague.

Hershlag, Z.Y. (1968), *Turkey: The Challenge of Growth*, E.J. Brill, Leiden.

Herz, J. (1989), 'The Territorial State Revisited - Reflections on the Future of the Nation-State', in M. Williams (ed.), *International Relations in Twentieth Century: A Reader*, Macmillan Education, Houndmills, pp. 80-98.

Heyd, U. (1950), *Foundations of Turkish Nationalism: The Life and Teachings of Ziya Gokalp*, Luzac and Co., London.

Hill, C. (1983), 'National Interests - The Insuperable Obstacles?', in C. Hill (ed.), *National Foreign Policies and the European Political Cooperation*, George Allen and Unwin for the Royal Institute of International Affairs, London, 185-202.

Hill, C. (1988), 'Research into the EPC: Tasks for the Future', in A. Pijpers et al. (eds.), *European Political Cooperation in the 1980s: A Common Foreign Policy for Western Europe?* Martinus Nijhoff, Dordrecht, pp. 211-22.

Hill, C. (1993), 'The Capability-Expectations Gap, or Conceptualising Europe's International Role', *Journal of Common Market Studies*, vol. 31, no. 3, pp. 305-29.

Hirschman, A.O. (1970), *Exit, Voice, Loyalty: Responses to Decline in Firms, Organisations and States*, Cambridge University Press, Cambridge, M.A.

Hirschman, A.O. (1981), 'Three Uses of Political Economy in Analysing European Integration', in A.O. Hirschman, *Essays in Trespassing: Economics to Politics and Beyond*, Cambridge University Press, Cambridge, pp. 266-84.

Hoekman, B. and Djankov, S. (1997), 'Towards a Free Trade Agreement with the European Union: Issues and Policy Options for Egypt', in A. Galal and B. Hoekman (eds.), *Regional Partners in Global Markets: Limits and Possibilities of the Euro-Med Agreements*, Centre for Economic Policy Research/Egyptian Centre for Economic Studies, London and Cairo, pp. 129-55.

Hoffmann, S. (1966), 'Obstinate or Obsolete? The Fate of the Nation State and the Case of Western Europe', *Daedalus*, vol. 95, no. 3, pp. 862-915.

Hoffmann, S. (1982), 'Reflections on the Nation-State in Western Europe Today', *Journal of Common Market Studies*, vol. 21, no. 1/2, pp. 21-37.

Holland, M. (ed.) (1991), *The Future of European Political Co-operation: Essays on Theory and Practice*, Macmillan, London.

Hollifield, J.F. (1992a), *Immigrants, Markets and States: The Political Economy of Post-War Europe*, Harvard University Press, Cambridge, Mass.

Hollifiled, J.F. (1992b), 'Migration and International Relations: Cooperation and Control in the European Community', *International Migration Review*, vol. 26, no. 2, pp. 568-95.

Hönnekop, E. and Hans, U. (1982), 'The Status of Immigrant Workers in the Federal Republic of Germany', in E-J. Thomas (ed.), *Immigrant Workers in Europe: Their Legal Status*, UNESCO, Paris.

Hotelling, H. (1990), 'Stability in Competition', in A.C. Darnell (ed.), *The Collected Economics Articles of Harold Hotelling*, Springler-Verlag, New York.

Huntington, S. (1993), 'The Clash of Civilisations', *Foreign Affairs*, vol. 72, no. 3, pp. 22-48.

Ifestos, P. (1987), *European Political Cooperation: Towards a Framework of Supranational Diplomacy?* Avebury, Aldershot.

Ikenberry, G.J. (1988), 'Conclusions: An Institutional Approach to American Foreign Economic Policy', *International Organisation*, vol. 42, no. 1, pp. 219-43.

İKV (1988), *Turkey's Position in the Face of the European Community According to the IKV's Studies*, IKV Publications no. 66, Istanbul.

Info-Türk (1986), *Black Book on the Militarist 'Democracy' in Turkey* Info-Türk, Brussels.

International Labour Organisation (1974), *Some Growing Employment Problems in Europe*, Second European Regional Conference, Report II, ILO, Geneva.

International Labour Organisation (1990), *Informal Consultation on Migrants from Non-EEC Countries in the Single European Market After 1992*, ILO, Geneva.

Jacobs, F.G. (ed.) (1976), *European Law and the Individual*, North-Holland Publishing, Amsterdam.

Jansen, J.M. (1985), 'The Political Economy of Group Membership', *American Political Science Review*, no. 1, pp. 79-96.

Kılınç, U. (1990), *Türkiye - Avrupa Topluluğu İlişkileri (Turkey - European Community Relations)*, TOBB Publications, Ankara.

Kahler, M. (1987), 'The Survival of the State in European International Relations', in S.C. Maier (ed.), *Changing Boundaries of the Political ???: Essays on the Evolving Balance Between the State and Society, Public and Private in Europe*, Cambridge University Press, Cambridge, pp. 287-319.

Karpat, K.H. (1959), *Turkey's Politics: The Transition to a Multi-Party System*, Princeton University Press, Princeton, N.J.

Kassim, H. (1994), 'Policy Networks and European Union Policy Making: A Sceptical View', *West European Politics*, no. 4, pp. 15-27.

Katzenstein, P. (1978), *Between Power and Plenty: Foreign Economic Policies of Advanced Capitalist States*, University of Visconsin Press, Madison.

Kazancigil, A. (ed.) (1986), *The State in Global Perspective*, Gower Publishers, Aldershot.

Kazgan, G. (1989), *Summary Report of the Manufacturing Survey with Special Reference to Turkey's Integration with the European Community*, Friedrich Ebert Foundation Research Results, Istanbul.

Keating, M. (1988), *State and Regional Nationalism: Territorial Politics and the European State*, Harvester and Wheatsheaf, New York.

Keeffe, O.D. and Schermes, H.G. (eds.) (1983), *Mixed Agreements*, Kluwer Law and Taxation Publishers, Deventer.

Keman, H. (1997), 'Approaches to the Analysis of Institutions', in B. Steunenberg and F. van Vught (eds.), *Political Institutions and Public Policy: Perspectives on European Decision Making*, Kluwer Academic Publishers, Dordrecht, pp. 1-27.

Keohane, R.O. (1984), *After Hegemony: Collaboration and Discord in the World Economy*, Princeton University Press, Princeton, N.J.

Keohane, R.O. (1986), 'Theory of World Politics: Structural Realism and Beyond', in R.O. Keohane (ed.), *Neorealism and Its Critics*, Columbia University Press, New York, pp. 158-203.

Keohane, R.O. (1989), *International Institutions and State Power: Essays in International Relations Theory*, Westview Press, London.

Keohane, R.O. and Hoffmann, S. (1990), 'Conclusions: Community Politics and Institutional Change', in W. Wallace (ed.), *The Dynamics of European Integration*, Pinter Publishers for the Royal Institute of International Affairs, London, pp. 276-300.

Keohane, R.O. and Hoffmann, S. (1991), 'Institutional Change in Europe in the 1980s', in R.O. Keohane and S. Hoffmann (eds.), *The New European Community: Decisionmaking and Institutional Change*, Westview Press, Boulder, pp. 1-39.

Keohane, R.O. and Nye, J. (1977), *Power and Interdependence: World Politics in Transition*, Little Brown, Boston.

Kerremans, B. (1996), 'Do Institutions Make a Difference? Non-institutionalism, Neo-institutionalism, and the Logic of Common Decision-Making in the European Union', *Governance*, vol. 9, no. 2, pp. 217-40.

Keyder, Ç., 'Les dilemmas de l'occidentalisation en Turquie', in S. Mappa (ed.) (1992), *L'Europe de Douze et les autres: integration ou auto-exclusion?* Editions Karthala, Paris, p. 241-56.

Kindleberger, C.P. (1967), *Europe's Post-War Growth: The Role of Labour Supply*, Harvard University Press, Cambridge: Mass.

King, R. (ed.) (1993), *The New Geography of European Migrations*, Belhaven Press, London.

Kirkpatrick, J. (1979), 'Dictatorships and Double Standards', *Commentary*, no. 68, pp. 34-35.

Kirman, A. and Widgren, M. (1995), 'Voting in the European Union: European Economic Decision-Making: progress or paralysis', *Economic Policy* 21, pp. 421-60.

Kiso, J.O. (1997), 'COREPER and the Political Committee: Damaging for CFSP?', *Cambridge Review of International Affairs*, col. 10, no. 2, pp. 141-53.

Kohlhase, N. (1981), 'The Greco-Turkish Conflict form a European Community Perspective', *The World Today*, vol. 37, no. 4, pp. 127-34.

Krasner, S.D. (1978), *Defending the National Interest: Raw Materials Investment and US Foreign Policy*, Princeton University Press, Princeton, N.J.

Krueger, A.O. (1974), *Turkey: Foreign Trade Regimes and Economic Development*, Columbia University Press, Princeton.

Krueger, A. (1978), 'The Role of Exchange Rate Policy in Opening Up the Economy', Paper Prepared for Economic and Social Studies Conference Board, Istanbul.

Kuper, L. (1992), 'The Sovereign Territorial State: The Right to Genocide', in R.P. Claude and B.H. Weston (eds.), *Human Rights in the World Community: Issues and Action*, University of Pennsylvania Press, Philadelphia, pp. 69-78.

Kydland, F. and E. Prescott (1977), 'Rules Rather than Discretion: The Inconsistency of Optimal Plans', *Journal of Political Economy*, vol. 85, pp. 473-92.

Kyle, K. (1997), *Cyprus: In Search of Peace*, Minority Rights Groups International, London.

Laipson, H. (1991), 'United States Policy Towards Greece and Cyprus since 1974', in D. Constas (ed.), *The Greek-Turkish Conflict in the 1990s:* Domestic and External Influences, Macmillan, London, pp. 160-74.

Land, J.W. (1970), *The Role of Government in the Economic Development of Turkey: 1923-63*, Rice University, Houston.

Lasok, D. and Soldatos, P. (eds.) (1981), *Les Coomunautés Européennes en Fonctionnement*, Bruylant, Bruxelles.

Layton-Henry, Z. (1992), *The Politics of Immigration, 'Race' and 'Race Relations' in Post-War Britain*, Blackwell, Oxford.
Leander, A. (1994), *'Robin Hood' Politics? Turkey Probing a New Model in the 1990s'*, European University Institute (Working Paper. 94/9), San Domenico.
Lehne, S. (1991), *The CSCE in the 1990s: Common European Home or Potemkin Village*, Wilhelm Braumüller, Vienna.
Lewis, A.W. (1954), 'Economic Development with Unlimited Supplies of Labour', *Manchester School of Economic and Social Studies*, no. 22, pp. 139-91.
Lewis, G. (1988), 'Turkey's Historical and Cultural Approach to Europe', in E. Manisalı (ed.), *Turkey's Place in Europe*, The Middle East Business and Banking Magazine Publications, Ankara, pp. 25-35.
Lindberg, L. (1966), 'Integration as a Source of Stress on the European Community System', *International Organisation*, vol. 20, pp. 233-65.
Lindberg, L. and Scheingold, S. (1970a), *Europe's Would-Be Polity*, Prentice-Hall, N.J.
Lindberg, L.N. and Scheingold, S.A. (1970b), *Europe's Would-be Polity: Patterns of Change in the European Community*, Prentice Hill, Englewood-Cliffs, N.J.
Linklater, A. (1993), 'Men and Citizens in International Relations', in H. Williams et al. (eds.), *A Reader in International Relations and Political Theory*, Open University Press, Buckingham, pp. 309-25.
Lucas, R.E. (1972), 'Expectations and Neutrality of Money', *Journal of Economic Theory*, vol. 4, pp. 103-24.
Ludlow, P. (1991), 'The European Commission', in R.O. Keohane and S. Hoffmann (eds.), *The New European Community: Decisionmaking and Institutional Change*, Westview Press, Boulder, pp. 85-132.
Ludlow, P. (1992), 'Europe's Institutions: Europe's Politics', in G.F. Treverton (ed.), *The Shape of the New Europe*, Council of Foreign Relations Press, New York, pp. 59-91.
Macleod, I., Hendry, I.D. and Stephen, H. (1998), *The External Relations of the European Communities*, Oxford University Press, Oxford.
Maghoori, R. and Ramberg, B. (eds.) (1982), *Globalism vs. Realism*, Westview Press, New York.
Maier, P. (1995), 'Political Parties, Popular Legitimacy and Public Privilege', *West European Politics*, no. 3, pp. 40-57.
Maier, S. (ed.) (1987), *Changing Boundaries of the Political: Essays on the Evolving Balance Between the State and Society, Public and Private in Europe*, Cambridge University Press, Cambridge.
Mancini, F. (1988), 'Opinion on the Cases of 281/85, 283-85/85 and 287/85: Germany and others vs. the Commission', *Common Market Law Reports*, vol. 51, part 636, pp. 11-47.

Mancini, G.F. (1991), 'The Making of a Constitution for Europe', in R.O. Keohane and S. Hoffmann (eds.), *The New European Community: Decision-Making and Institutional Change*, Westview Press, Boulder, pp. 177-94.
Mango, A. (1990), 'Turkish Foreign Policy', in A. Evin and G. Denton (eds.), *Turkey and The European Community*, Leske and Budrich, Opladen, pp. 95-99.
Mann, M. (1986), 'The Autonomous Power of the State: Its Origins, Mechanisms and Results', in J.A. Hall (ed.), *States in History*, Oxford University Press, Oxford, pp. 109-36.
Mappa, S. (ed.) (1992), *L'Europe de Douze et les autres: Integration ou Auto-exclusion?* Editions Karthala, Paris.
Marc, W. (ed.) (1989), *International Relations in Twentieth Century: A Reader*, Macmillan Education, Houndmills.
Mardin, S. (1983), 'Relations between Turkey and Western Europe', *D__ Politika*, vol. 10, no. 3-4, pp. 27-49.
Marks, G. (1992), 'Structural Policy in the European Community', in A.M. Sbragia (ed.), *Euro-politics: Institutions and Policymaking in the New European Community*, The Brookings Institution, Washington, D.C., pp. 191-224.
Martin, P.L. (1991), *The Unfinished Story: Turkish Labour Migration to Western Europe*, ILO, Geneva.
Matheson, J. and Henry E. (1991), 'The Immigration Issue in the Community: An ACP View', *The Courrier: ACP - EC*, no. 129 pp. 56-59.
McDonald, R. (1998), 'Cyprus' Prospect for EU Accession', Paper submitted to the Association of Cypriot, Greek and Turkish Affairs (ACGTA), mimeograph, London.
McGhee, G. (1990), *The US-Turkish-NATO Middle East Connection: How the Truman Doctrine and Turkey's NATO Entry Contained the Soviets*, Macmillan, London.
Meinardus, R. (1991), 'Third-Party Involvement in Greek-Turkish Disputes', in D. Constas (ed.), *The Greek-Turkish Conflict in the 1990s*, Macmillan, London, pp. 157-63.
Melitz, J. (1988), 'Monetary Discipline, Germany and the European Monetary System', in F. Giavazzi et al. (eds.), *The European Monetary System*, Cambridge University Press, Cambridge, pp. 51-79.
Melitz, J. (1985), 'The Welfare Case for the European Monetary System', *Journal of International Money and Finance*, no. 4, pp. 488-506.
Michelmann, H.J. (1981), 'The Community Decision-Making Process', in D. Lasok and P. Soldatos (eds.), *Les Coomunatiués Européennes en Fonctionnement*, Bruylant, Bruxelles, pp. 147-70.
Miliband, R. (1983), 'The Capitalist State: Two Exchanges with Nicos Poulantzas', in R. Miliband, *Class Power and State Power: Political Essays*, Verso, London, pp. 26-49.

Miliband, R. (1984), *The State in Capitalist Society: The Analysis of the Western System of Power*, Quartet Books, London.

Milward, A.S. (1992), *The European Rescue of the Nation-State*, Routledge, London.

Milward, A.S. (1993), 'Conclusions: The Value of History', in A.S. Milward et al., *The Frontier of National Sovereignty: History and Theory 1945-1992*, Routledge, London, pp. 182-201.

Milward, A.S. and V. Sorensen (1993), 'Interdependence or Integration? A National Choice', in A.S. Milward et al., *The Frontier of National Sovereignty: History and Theory 1945-1992*, Routledge, London, pp. 1-32.

Mitrany, D. (1966), *A Working Peace System*, Quadrangle Books, Chicago.

Mitrany, D. (1975), *The Functional Theory of Politics*, London School of Economics and Political Science, Martin Robertson, London.

Moe, T. (1990), 'The Politics of Structural Choice: Toward a Theory of Public Bureaucracy', in O. Williamson (ed.), *Organisation Theory from Chester Barbard to the Present and Beyond*, Oxford University Press, New York.

Moravcsik, A. (1991), 'Negotiating the Single European Act: National Interests and Conventional Statecraft in the European Community', *International Organisation*, vol. 45, no. 1, pp. 19-56.

Moravcsik, A. (1993), 'Preferences and Power in the European Community: A Liberal Intergovernmentalist Approach', *Journal of Common Market Studies*, vol. 31, no. 4, pp. 473-524.

Morgenthau, H.J. (1960), *Politics Among Nations: The Struggle for Power and Peace* (3rd ed.), Alfred A Knopf, New York.

Mortensen, J. (1990), *Federalism vs Co-ordination: Macroeconomic Policy in the European Community*, Centre for European Policy Studies, Brussels.

Mouzelis, N. (1987), *Post-Marxist Alternatives: The Construction of Social Orders*, Macmillan, London.

Mouzelis, N. (1988), 'Marxism or Post-Marxism?', *New Left Review*, no. 167, pp. 107-23.

Mower, A. Glenn Jr. (1980), 'The Implementation of Human Rights through European Community Institutions', *Universal Human Rights*, vol. 2, no. 2, , pp. 43-59.

Mower, A.G. Jr. (1987), *Human Rights and American Foreign Policy: The Carter and Reagan Experiences*, Greenwood Press, New York.

Moyser, G. and Wagstaffe, M. (eds.) (1987), *Research Methods for Elite Studies*, Allen and Unwin, London.

Mueller, D.C. (ed.) (1997), *Perspectives on Public Choice: A Handbook*, Cambridge University Press, Cambridge.

Nadel, S.F. (1956), 'The Concept of Social Elites', *International Social Science Bulletin*, vol. 8, no. 3, pp. 413-24.

Nas, T.F. (1992), 'The Impact of Turkey's Stabilisation and Structural Adjustment Program: An Introduction', in T.F. Nas and M. Odekon (eds.), *Economics and Politics of Turkish Liberalisation*, Lehigh University Press, Bethlehem, pp. 11-25.

Nettl, J.P. (1968), 'The State as a Conceptual Variable', *World Politics*, vol. 20, no. 4, pp. 559-92.

Neuwahl, N.A. (1991), 'Joint Participation in International Treaties and the Exercise of Power by the EEC and Its Member States: Mixed Agreements', *Common Market Law Review*, vol. 28, pp. 717-40.

Nolan, C.J. (1985), 'The Influence of Parliament on Human Rights in Canadian Foreign Policy: A Comparative and International Journal of the Social sciences, Humanities and Law', *Human Rights Quarterly*, vol. 7, no. 3 pp. 373-90.

Nolte, G. (1988), 'Case Law: The Court of Justice', *Common Market Law Review*, vol. 25, pp. 403-415.

Nordlinger, E.A. (1981), *On the Autonomy of the Democratic State*, Harvard University Press, Cambridge, Mass.

North, D. (1990), *Institutions, Institutional Change and Economic Performance*, Cambridge University Press, Cambridge.

Northedge, F.S. (1976), *The International Political System*, Faber and Faber, London.

Nugent, N. (1994), *The Government and Politics of the European Union*, Macmillan, London.

OECD (1987/1988 and 1995), *OECD Economic Survey: Turkey*, OECD, Paris.

OECD (1978), *Migration, Growth and Development*, OECD, Paris.

Offe, C. (1985), 'New Social Movements: Challenging the Boundaries of Institutional Politics', *Social Research*, vol. 52, pp. 817-68.

Olson, M. (1965), *The Logic of Collective Action*, Harvard University Press, Cambridge, Mass.

Öncü, A. (1984), 'Cumhuriyet Döneminde Odalar (Chambers in the Republican Era)', *Cumhuriyet Dönemi Türkiye Ansiklopedisi (The Encyclopedia of the Republican Turkey)*, pp. 1568-75.

Öniş, Z. and Riedel, J. (1996), *Economic Crisis and Long Term Growth in Turkey*, World Bank, Washington, D.C.

Oppenheim, L. (1905), *International Law: Volume I, Peace*, Longmans, Green and Co., London.

van Outrive, (1992), 'Legislation and Decision-Making in Europe: Police Cooperation and Human Rights', Paper Submitted to the Twentieth Conference of the European Group for the Study of Deviance and Social Control, Padova, mimeograph, Italy.

Özal, T. (1986), 'Speech Delivered at the Royal Institute of International Affairs', *Turkish Review*, vol. 1, no. 3, pp. 131-135.

Özal, T. (1991), *Turkey in Europe and Europe in Turkey*, Rüstem and Brothers, Nicosia.

Pastore, M. (1992), 'Towards the Building of a Fortress Europe?', *The Bulletin of the European group for the Study of Deviance and Social Control*, no. 4, pp. 26-35.

Pease, K.K. and Forsythe, D.P. (May 1993), 'Human Rights, Humanitarian Intervention and World Politics', *Human Rights Quarterly*, vol. 15, no. 2, pp. 290-314.

Pelkmans, J. (1993), *Opening Up the Euro-Market for Textiles*, Centre for European Policy Studies, Brussels.

Penninx, R. (1982), 'A Critical Review of Theory and Practice: The Case of Turkey', *International Migration Review*, vol. 16, pp. 781-818.

Persson, T. (1988), 'Credibility of Macroeconomic Policy: An Introduction and Broad Survey', *European Economic Review*, vol. 32, no. 2/3, pp. 519-32.

Petersen, J. (1992), 'The European Technology Community: Policy Networks in a Supranational Setting', in D. Marsh and R.A.W. Rhodes (eds.), *Policy Networks in British Government*, Oxford University Press, Oxford, pp. 226-48.

Petersen, J. (1995), 'Decision-Making in the European Union: Towards a Framework for Analysis', *Journal of European Public Policy*, vol. 2, no. 1, pp. 69-93.

Pierson, P. (1994), *Dismantling the Welfare State?* Cambridge University Press, New York.

Pierson, P. (1996), 'The Path to European Integration: A Historical Institutional Analysis', *Comparative Political Studies*, vol. 29, pp. 123-63.

Pieterse, J.N. (1991), 'Frictions in Europe', *Race and Class Journal of Black and Third World Liberation*, vol. 32, no. 3, pp. 3-10.

Pijpers, A. et al. (eds.) (1988), *European Political Cooperation in the 1980s: A Common Foreign Policy for Western Europe?* Martinus Nijhoff, Dordrecht.

Pijpers, A.E. (1991), 'European Political Co-operation and the Realist Paradigm', in M. Holland (ed.), *The Future of European Political Co-operation: Essays on Theory and Practice*, Macmillan, London, pp. 8-35.

Pizzorno, A. (1964), 'The Individualistic Mobilisation of Europe', in B.S. Graubard (ed.), *A New Europe?* Oldbourne Press, London, p. 269.

Plender, R. (1976), 'An Incipient Form of European Citizenship', in F.G. Jacobs (ed.), *European Law and the Individual*, North-Holland Publishing Company, Amsterdam.

Plender, R. (1988), *International Migration Law* (2nd ed.), Martinus Nijhoff, Dordrecht.

Pollack, M.A. (1996), 'The New Institutionalism and EC Governance: Promise and Limits of Institutional Analysis', *Governance*, vol. 9, no. 4, pp. 429-58.

Pomfret, R. (1986), *Mediterranean Policy of the EC: A Study of Discrimination in Trade*, St. Martin's Press, New York.

Poulantzas, N. (1975), *Political Power and Social Classes*, (Translation by T. O'Hagan), Verso, London.

Puchala, D.J. (1972), 'Of Blind Men, Elephants and International Integration', *Journal of Common Market Studies*, vol. 10, no. 3, pp. 267-84.

Putnam, R.D. (1988), 'Diplomacy and Domestic Politics: The Logic of Two-Level Games', *International Organisation*, vol. 42, no. 3, pp. 427-60.

Redmond, J. (1993), *The Next Mediterranean Enlargement of the European Community: Turkey, Cyprus and Malta?* Dartmouth, Aldershot.

Reiss, H. (ed.) (1970), *Kant's Political Writings*, translation by H.B. Nisbet, Cambridge University Press, Cambridge.

Republic of Cyprus (1984), Press and Information Office, *The Cyprus Problem*, Zavallis Press, Nicosia.

Republic of Cyprus (1991), Press and Information Office, *Resolutions Adopted by the UN on Cyprus Problem*, Nicosia.

Rhodes, R.A.W. (1990), 'Policy Networks: a British Perspective', *Journal of Theoretical Politics*, vol. 2, pp. 293-317.

Richardson, J. (1995), 'The Market for Political Activism: Interest Groups as a Challenge to Political Parties', *Western European Politics*, no. 1, pp. 116-39.

Richardson, J. (1996), 'Policy-Making in the EU', in J. Richardson (ed.), *European Union: Power and Policy-Making*, Routledge, London, pp. 3-23.

Rodrik, D. (1990), 'Some Policy Dilemmas in Turkish Macroeconomic Management', in T. Aricanli and D. Rodrik (eds.), *The Political Economy of Turkey: Debt Adjustment and Sustainability*, St. Martin's, New York.

Rogoff, K. (1987), 'Reputational Constraints on Monetary Policy', *Carnegie-Rochester Conference Series on Public Policy,* Cambridge University Press, Amsterdam, pp. 141-82.

Rosenau, J. (1969), *Linkage Politics: Essays on the Convergence of National and International Systems*, Free Press, New York.

Rosenau, J. (1969), 'Towards the Study of National-International Linkages', in J. Rosenau, *Linkage Politics: Essays on the Convergence of National and International Systems*, Free Press, New York, pp. 44-63.

Roth, A.H. (1949), *The Minimum Standard of International Law Applied to Aliens*, A.W. Sijthoff's Uitgeversmaatschappij N.V., Leiden.

Russo, M. and Tuilo, T. (1988), 'Monetary Policy Coordination within the European Monetary System: Is There a Rule?', in F. Giavazzi and M. Miller (eds.), *The European Monetary System*, Cambridge University Press, Cambridge, pp. 292-356.

Sachs, J. and Charles, W. (1986), 'The Economic Consequences of President Mitterand', *Economic Policy*, vol. 2, pp. 262-322.

Sandholtz, W. and Zysman, J. (1989), '1992: Recasting the European Bargain', *World Politics*, vol. 42, no. 1, pp. 95-128.

Saraçoğlu, R. (1995), 'İstikrar Programı Üzerinde Düşünceler (Thoughts on Turkey's Stability Programme)', TUSİAD, *Türkiye için Yeni bir Orta Vadeli İstikrar Programına Doğru (Towards a Medium-Term Stability Programme for Turkey)*, TUSİAD Publication no. T/95, Istanbul, pp. 195-204.

Sargent, T.J. and Wallace, N. (1976), 'Rational Expectations and the Theory of Economic Policy', *Journal of Monetary Economics*, vol. 2, pp. 169-84.

Sbragia, A.M. (ed.) (1992), *Europolitics: Institutions and Policymaking in the 'New' European Community* The Brookings Institution, Washington D.C.

Scharpf, F.W. (1988), 'The Joint Decision Trap: Lessons from German Federalism and European Integration', *Public Administration*, vol. 66, pp. 239-78.

Schermes, H.G. (1983), 'A Typology of Mixed Agreements', in D.O. Keeffe and H.G. Schermes (eds.), *Mixed Agreements*, Kluwer Law and Taxation Publishers, Deventer, pp. 23-28.

Schlegel, D. (1986), 'Turkish-European Pragmatism', *Aussenpolitik: German Foreign Affairs Review* vol. 37, no. 3, pp. 283-302.

Schmitter, P.C. (1969), 'Three Neofunctional Hypotheses About International Integration', *International Organisation*, vol. 23, no. 1 pp. 161-66.

Schmitter, P.C. (1970), 'Central American Integration: Spill-Over, Spill-Around and Encapsulation', *Journal of Common Market Studies*, vol. 9, no. 1, pp. 1-48.

Schmitter, P.C. (1981), 'Interest Intermediation and Regime Governability in Contemporary Western Europe and North America', in S.D. Berger (ed.), *Organising Interests in Western Europe*, Cambridge University Press, Cambridge.

Schneider, V. et al. (1994), 'Corporate Actor Networks in European Policy Making: Harmonising Telecommunications Policy', *Journal of Common Market Studies*, no. 4, pp. 473-98.

Schutte, J.E. (1991), 'Schengen: Its Meaning for the Free Movement of People in Europe', *Common Market Law Review*, vol. 28, pp. 549-70.

Schwarze, J. (1987), 'Towards a European Foreign Policy: Legal Aspects', in J.K. de Vree, P. Coffey, and R.H. Lauwaars (eds.), *Towards a European Foreign Policy: Legal, Economic and Political Dimensions*, Martinus Nijhoff, Dordrecht, pp. 69-76.

Schwed, J-J. (1989), 'La Turquie et la Communauté Européenne', in J. Thobie and S. Kançal (eds.), *Turquie, Moyen-Orient, Communauté Européenne*, L'Harmattan, Paris, pp. 359-70.

Sen, F. (1989), 'Problems and Integration Constraints of Turkish Migrants in the Federal republic of Germany', *World Employment Programme Working Paper*, ILO, Geneva.

Shaw, S. (1976), *Reform, Revolution and Republic: The Rise of Modern Turkey*, Cambridge University Press, New York.

Shlaim, A. and Yannopoulos, G. (eds.) (1976), *The EEC and the Mediterranean Countries*, Cambridge University Press, Cambridge.

Siedentopf, H. and Hauschild, C. (1988), 'The Implementation of Community Legislation by the Member States: A Comparative Analysis', in H. Siedentopf and J. Ziller (eds.), *Making European Policies Work: The Implementation of the Community Legislation in the Member States - Volume I, Comparative Synthesis*, Sage, London, pp. 1-83.

Siedentopf, H. and Ziller, J. (eds.) (1988), *Making European Policies Work: The Implementation of the Community Legislation in the Member States - Volume I, Comparative Synthesis*, Sage, London.

Simmonds, K.R. (1988), 'The Concenrtation of Community Migration Policy', *Common Market Law Review*, vol. 25, p. 200.

Slater, M. (1982), 'Political Elites, Popular Indifference and Community Building', *Journal of Common Market Studies*, vol. 21, no. 1/2, pp. 69-87.

Somers, F. (ed.) (1991), *European Economies: A Comparative Study*, Pitman, London.

Sönmezoğlu, F. (1991), *The Cyprus Problem: Attitudes and Positions of the Sides Involved*, Istanbul University Press, Istanbul.

Stephanou, C. and Tsardanides, C. (1991), 'The EC Factor in the Greece-Turkey-Cyprus Triangle', in D. Kostas (ed.), *The Greek-Turkish Conflict in the 1990s: Domestic and External Influences*, Macmillan, London, pp. 207-230.

Straubhaar, T. (1985), 'The Significance of Labour Migration for the Workers' Countries of Origin', *Intereconomics: Review of International Trade and Development*, vol. 20, no. 1, pp. 15-20.

Straubhaar, T. (1988), 'International Labour Migration within a Common Market: Some Aspects of EC Experience', *Journal of Common Market Studies*, vol. 27, no. 1.

Streeck, W. and Philippe C.S. (1991), 'From National Corporatism to Transnational Pluralism: Organised Interests in the Single European Market', *Politics and Society*, vol. 19, no. 2, pp. 133-64.

Sullivan, M.P. (1982), 'Transnationalism, Power Politics and the Realities of the Present System', in R. Maghoori and B. Ramberg (eds.), *Globalism vs. Realism*, Westview Press, New York, pp. 195-221.

Szabo, S.F. (1979a), 'Social Perspectives and Support for Human Rights in Germany', *Universal Human Rights*, vol. 1, no. 1, pp. 81-98.

Szabo, S.F. (1979b), 'Contemporary French Orientations Toward Economic and Political Dimension of Human Rights', *Universal Human Rights*, vol. 1, no. 3, pp. 61-76.

Szabo, M. (1993), 'Nationalism, Nation State and Prospects of Democratisation in Eastern Europe', in J. Iivonen (ed.), *The Future of the Nation State in Europe*, Edward Elgar, Aldershot, pp. 219-45.

Tabellini, G. (1986), 'Central Bank Reputation and the Monetisation of Deficits: The 1981 Italian Monetary Reform', *Economic Inquiry*, vol. 25, pp. 185-200.

Tacar, P. (1989), 'Demand d'Adhésion de la Turquie aux Communautés Européennes: Motifs Politiques Turcs et Réactions Communautaires', in J. Thobie and S. Kançal (eds.), *Turquie, Moyen-Orient, Communauté Européenne*, L'Harmattan, Paris, pp. 343-70.

Taylor, P. (1982), 'Intergovernmentalism in the EC in the 1970s: Patterns and Perspectives', *International Organisation*, vol. 36, no. 4, pp. 741-66.

Taylor, P. (1990), 'Consociationalism and Federation as Approaches to International Integration', in A.J.R. Groom and P. Taylor (eds.), *Frameworks for International Co-operation*, pp. 172-84;

Taylor, P. (1991), 'The European Community and the State: Assumptions, Theories and Propositions', *Review of International Studies*, vol. 17, no. 2, pp. 109-25.

Taylor, P. (1992), 'The Institutional and Constitutional Implications of the Maastricht Agreement'. Memorandum submitted to the House of Commons, Foreign Affairs Committee, HMSO, London.

Tekeli, İ. and İlkin, S. (1974), *Savaş Sonrası Ortamında 1947 Türkiye İktisadi Kalkınma Planı (Turkey's 1947 Development Plan in the Post-War Environment)*, The Middle East Technical University, Ankara.

Tekeli, İ. and S. İlkin (1993a), *Türkiye ve Avrupa Topluluğu: Ulus Devletini Aşma Çabasındaki Avrupa'ya Türkiye'nin Yaklaşımı* I *(Turkey and the EC: Turkey's Approach to Europe Attempting to Transcend the Nation State I)* (Ankara, Ümit Yayıncılık, 1993).

Tekeli, İ. and S. İlkin (1993b), *Türkiye ve Avrupa Topluluğu: Ulus Devletini Aşma Çabasındaki Avrupa'ya Türkiye'nin Yaklaşımı II (Turkey and the EC: Turkey's Approach to Europe Attempting to Transcend the Nation State II)* (Ankara, Ümit Yayıncılık, 1993).

Tezel, Y.S. (1986), *Cumhuriyet Döneminin İktisadi Tarihi (Economic History of the Republican Era)*, Yurt Yayınları, Ankara.

Therborn, G. (1986), 'Neo-Marxist, Pluralist, Corporatist, Statist Theories of the Welfare State', in A. Kazancigil (ed.), *The State in Global Perspective*, Gower Publishers, Aldershot, pp. 204-31.

Thobie, J. and Kançal, S. (eds.) (1989), *Turquie, Moyent-Orient, Communauté Européenne*, L'Harmattan, Paris.

Thomas E-J. (ed.) (1982), *Immigrant Workers in Europe: Their Legal Status*, UNESCO, Paris.

Thrandart D. (ed.) (1992), *Europe - A New Immigration Continent*, Litz Verlag, Münster.

Thrandart, D. (1992), 'Europe - A New Immigration Continent: Politics and Policies Since 1945 in Comparative Perspective', in D. Thrandart (ed.), *Europe - A New Immigration Continent*, Litz Verlag, Münster, pp. 13-74.

TOBB (1990), *Planlı Dönemde Rakamlarla Türkiye Ekonomisi (The Turkish Economy Under Planning)*, TOBB, Ankara.

Togan, S. and Yılmaz, A. (1995), 'Türkiye ve Avrupa Birliği (Turkey and the European Union), in TUSIAD, *Türkiye için Yeni bir Orta Vadeli İstikrar Programına Doğru (Towards a Medium-Term Stability Programme for Turkey)*, TUSİAD Publication no. T/95, Istanbul, pp. 121-167.

Tovias, A. (1977), *Tariff Preferences in Mediterranean Diplomacy*, St. Martin's Press, New York.

Treverton, G.F. (ed.) (1992), *The Shape of the New Europe*, Council of Foreign Relations Press, New York.

Tsakaloyannis, P. (1980), 'The European Community and the Greek-Turkish Dispute', *Journal of Common Market Studies*, vol. 19, no. 1 (1980), pp. 35-54.

Tsardanidis, C. (1983), *The Politics of EEC-Cyprus Association Agreement: 1972-82* (Unpublished Ph.D. Thesis, University of London, London School of Economics and Political Science), London.

Tsardanidis, C. (1984), 'The EC-Cyprus Association Agreement: Ten Years of a Troubled Relationship 1973-83', *Journal of Common Market Studies*, vol. 22, no. 4, pp. 351-76.

Tsebelis, G. (1990), *Nested Games: Rational Choice in Comparative Politics*, University of California Press, Berkeley.

Tsebelis, G. (1994), 'The Power of the European Parliament as a Conditional Agenda Setter, *American Political Science Review*, vol. 81, pp. 129-42.

Tsoukalis, L. (1992), *The New European Economy: The Politics and Economics of Integration*, Oxford University Press, Oxford.

Tulloch, P. (1975), *The Politics of Preferences: EEC Policy Making and the Generalised System of Preferences*, Croom Helm, London.

TUSİAD (1978), *AET İle İlişkileri Özel Kesim Nasıl Değerlendiriyor? (How Does the Private Sector View the Relations with the EEC?)*, TUSIAD Publication no. T/78.1.51, Istanbul.

TUSİAD (1995), *Türkiye için Yeni bir Orta Vadeli İstikrar Programına Doğru (Towards a Medium-Term Stability Programme for Turkey)*, TUSIAD Publication no. T/95, Istanbul.

TUSİAD (1997), *Perspectives on Democratisation in Turkey*, TUSIAD publications, Istanbul.

Twitchett, K.J. (1976), *Europe and the World: The External Relations of the Common Market*, Europa Publications, London.

Uçtum, M. (1992), 'The Effects of Liberalisation of Traded and Non-Traded Goods Sector: The Case of Turkey', in F.N. Tevfik and M. Odekon (eds.), *Economics and Politics of Turkish Liberalisation*, Lehigh University Press, Bethlehem, 143-54.

Ugur, M. (1988), *Continuity in the Economic Policy of Turkish Government: 1930-60* (Unpublished MSc. Thesis Submitted to the London School of Economics and Political Science), London.

Ugur, M. (1995), 'Freedom of Movement vs. Exclusion: A Re-interpretation of the 'Insider'-'Outsider' Divide in the European Union', *International Migration Review*, vol. 29, no. 4, pp. 964-999.

Ugur, M. (1996a), *The European Community's External Policy-Making Process: The Case of the EC-Turkey Association, 1973-93*, (Unpublished Ph.D. Thesis Submitted to the London School of Economics and Political Science. London.

Ugur, M. (1996b), 'Customs Union as a Substitute for Turkey's Membership?', An Interpretation of EU-Turkey Relations', *Cambridge Review of International Affairs*, vol. 10, no. 1, pp. 11-29.

Ugur, M. (1998), 'Explaining Protectionism and Liberalisation in European Union Trade Policy: The Case of Textiles and Clothing', *Journal of European Public Policy*, vol. 5, no. 4, pp. 655-73.

Urwin, Derek (1991), *The Community of Europe: A History of European Integration Since 1945*, Longman, London.

Vincent, R.J. (1986), *Human Rights and International Relations*, Cambridge University Press, Cambridge.

Völker, E.L.M. (1987), 'The Major Instruments of the Common Commercial Policy of the EEC', in E.L.M. Völker (ed.), *Protectionism and the European Community* (2nd ed.), Kluwer Law and Taxation Publishers, Deventer, pp. 17-56.

de Vree, J.K., Coffey, P. and Lauwaars, R.H. (eds.) (1987), *Towards a European Foreign Policy: Legal, Economic and Political Dimensions*, Martinus Nijhoff, Dordrecht. Pierre C.R. and Burns, H.W. (eds.) (1992), *Human Rights in the World: Issues and Action*, University of Pennsylvania Press, Philadelphia.

Wallace, H. (1987), 'Negotiations, Conflict and Compromise: The Elusive Pursuit of Common Policies', in H. Wallace, W. Wallace and C. Webb (eds.), *Policy-Making in the European Community*, John Wiley and Sons, Chichester, pp. 43-80.

Wallace, W. (1983), 'Introduction: Cooperation and Convergence in European Foreign Policy', in C. Hill (ed.), *National Foreign Policies and the European Political Cooperation* George Allen and Unwin for the Royal Institute of International Affairs, London, pp. 1-16.

Wallace, W. (1987), 'Less than a Federation, More than a Regime: The Community as a Political System', in H. Wallace, W. Wallace and C. Webb (eds.), *Policy-Making in the European Community* (2nd ed.), John Wiley and Sons, Chichester, pp. 403-34.

Wallace, W. (1990), 'Introduction: The Dynamics of European Integration', in W. Wallace (ed.), *The Dynamics of European Integration*, Pinter Publishers for the Royal Institute of International Affairs, London, pp. 1-24.

Wallace, W. and Allen, D. (1977), 'Political Cooperation: Procedure as a Substitute for Policy', in H. Wallace, W. Wallace, and C. Webb, *Policy Making in the European Communities*, John Wiley and Sons, London, pp. 227-246.

Wallerstein, M. (1989), 'Union Organisation in Advanced Industrial Democracies', *American Political Science Review*, no. 2, pp. 163-64.

Waltz, K.N. (1979), *The Theory of International Politics*, Addison Wesley, Reading, Mass.

Webb, C. (1987), 'Theoretical Perspectives and Problems', in H. Wallace, W. Wallace and C. Webb (eds.), *Policy-Making in the European Community*, John Wiley and Sons, Chichester, pp. 1-41.

Webber, F. (1991), 'From Ethnocentrism to Euro-Racism', *Race and Class Journal of Black and Third World Liberation*, vol. 32, no. 3 pp. 11-17.

Weber, M. (1968), *Economy and Society: An Outline of Interpretative Sociology*, (eds.) G. Rot and C. Wittich, Bedminster Press, New York.

Weiler, J. and Wessels, W. (1988), 'EPC and the Challenge of Theory', in A. Pijpers et al. (eds.), *European Political Cooperation in the 1980s: A Common Foreign Policy for Western Europe?* Martinus Nijhoff, Dordrecht, pp. 229-58.

Weiner, M. (1985), 'International Migration and International Relations', *Population and Development Review*, vol. 11, pp. 441-55.

Weintraub, E.R. (1992), *Towards a History of Game Theory: Annual Supplement to Volume 24, History of Political Economy*, Durham and London.

Wessels, W. (1995), 'Theories and Strategies for European Integration: The Fusion Thesis', Paper Submitted to UACES Annual Conference, Cambridge.

Weston, A., Cable, V. and Hewitt, A. (1980), *The EEC's Generalised System of Preferences*, Overseas Development Institute, London.

Weston, B.H., Lukes, R.A. and Hnatt, K.M. (1992), 'Regional Human Rights Regimes: A Comparison and Appraisal', in R.P. Claude and B.H. Weston (eds.), *Human Rights in the World Community: Issues and Action*, University of Pennsylvania Press, Philadelphia, pp. 244-55.

Williams, H. et al. (eds.) (1993), *A Reader in International Relations and Political Theory*, Open University Press, Buckingham.

Williams, S. (1991), 'Sovereignty and Accountability in the European Community', in R.O. Keohane ' S. Hoffmann (eds.), *The New European Community: Decisionmaking and Institutional Change*, Westview Press, Boulder, pp. 155-176.

Wooley, J.T. (1992), 'Policy Credibility and European Monetary Institutions', in A.M. Sbragia (ed.), *Euro-politics: Institutions and Policymaking in the 'New' European Community*, The Brookings Institution, Washington D.C., pp. 157-90.

Wornham, T. (1994), *The Immigration Lawyer's Guide to the Turkey-EC Association Agreement*, Immigration Law Practitioners' Association, London.

Yavuz, M.H. (1992), 'Cyprus and International Politics', *Cyprus Review*, vol. 4, no. 2, pp. 135-42.

Zürcher, E.J. (1993), *Turkey: A Modern History*, I.B. Tauris and Co., London.

2 Official Documents and Reports

Central Bank of the Republic of Turkey, *Annual Reports* (1982, 1985, 1987, 1989, and 1993)

Commission of the EC (1974), 'The Social Action Programme', *Bulletin of the EC*, no. 2/74, pp. 18-36.

Commission of the EC (1975), *Implementation of Point 10 of the Final Communiqué Issued at European Summit Held in Paris on 9-10 December 1974 Concerning a Passport Union*, COM(75)/322/final, Brussels.

Commission of the EC (1976), 'An Action Programme in Favour of Migrant Workers', *Bulletin of the EC*, Supplement 3/76, pp. 14-25.

Commission of the EC (1978), *Proposal for a Council Directive Concerning the Approximation of Legislation of the Member States in order to Combat Illegal Migration and Illegal Employment*, COM(78)86/final, Brussels.

Commission of the EC (1979a), 'Memorandum on the Accession of the European Communities to the ECHR', *Bulletin of the EC, Supplement 2/79*, pp. 6-21.

Commission of the EC (1979b), *Communication to the Council Concerning Consultation on Migration policies vis-à-vis Third Countries*, COM(79)115/final, Brussels.

Commission of the EC (1985a), *Communication to the Council on Guidelines for a Community Policy on Migration*, COM(85)48/final, Brussels.

Commission of the EC (1985b), 'Decision Setting Up a Prior Communication Procedure on Migration Policies in Relation to Non-Member Countries', *Official Journal of the EC*, no. L217, pp. 25-26.

Commission of the EC (1989a), *The Turkish Economy: Structure and Developments*, SEC(89)2290/final, Brussels.

Commission of the EC (1989b), *Opinion on Turkey's Request for Accession to the Community*, SEC(89)2290/final, Brussels.

Commission of the EC (1990a), *Communication to the Council on Relations with Turkey*, SEC(90)1017/final, Brussels.

Commission of the EC (1990b), *Communication on Community Accession to the European Convention and Some of Its Protocols*, SEC(90)2087/final, Brussels.

Commission of the EC (1991), *Communication to the Council and the Parliament on Human Rights, Democracy and Development Cooperation Policy*, SEC(91)61/final, Brussels.

Commission of the EC (1993), *Opinion on the Application by the Republic of Cyprus for Membership*, COM(93)313/final, Brussels.

Commission of the EC (1994), *Communication on Migration and Asylum Policies*, COM(94)23/final, Brussels.

Commission of the EC, Ankara Office (1977), *Turkey-EEC Relations*, 1963-1967, Head of Ankara Office, Ankara.

Council of the EC (1961), 'Regulation 15/61 on the Definition of Free Movement', *Journal Officiel des Communautes Européennes*, no. 57, p. 1075.

Council of the EC (1964a), 'Regulation 38/64 on Free Movement', *Journal Officiel des Communautés Européennes*, no. 62 p. 965.

Council of the EC (1964b), 'Agreement on the Adoption of Common Position prior to EC-Turkey Association Council Meetings', no. 64/737/EEC, *Official Journal of the EC*, no. 217, p. 3703.

Council of the EC (1964c), 'Agreement on the Financial Protocol to the EC-Turkey Association', no. 64/739/EEC *Official Journal of the EC*, no. 217, p. 3709.

Council of the EC (1968), 'Regulation 1612/68 Free Movement', *Official Journal of the EC*, no. L257, p.1.

Council of the EC (1971), 'Regulation 1842/71 on the introduction of safeguard measures against Turkey', *Official Journal of the EC*, no. L192, pp. 14-15.

Council of the EC (1974), *Treaties Establishing the European Communities*, Office for Official Publications of the EC, Luxembourg.

Council of the EC (1976), 'Resolution of 9 February 1976 on the Action Programme for Migrant Workers and Members of their Families', *Bulletin of the EC*, Supplement 3/76, pp. 7-8.

Council of the EC (1980), 'Resolution of 27 June 1980 on Guidelines for a Community Labour Market Policy', *Official Journal of the EC*, no. C168, p. 4.

Council of the EC (1982), 'Regulation 288/82 on Common Rules for Imports', *Official Journal of the EC*, no. L35, pp. 1-44.

Council of the EC (1983), 'Regulation 3420/83 on Trade with State-Trading Countries', *Official Journal of the EC*, no. L346, p. 6.

Council of the EC (1985), 'Resolution on Guidelines for a Community Policy on Migration', *Official Journal of the EC*, no. C186 p. 4.

Council of the EC (1992), *Treaty on European Union*, Office for Official Publications of the EC, Luxembourg.

Council of the EC, General Secretariat (1973-1988), *Annual Review of the Council's Work*, Office for Official Publications of thc EC, Luxembourg.

Council of Europe (1982), *Human Rights Information Sheet*, vol. 1, no. 11.

Council of Europe (1985), *Yearbook of the European Convention on Human Rights*, Martinus Nijhoff, Dordrecht.

EC-Turkey Association Council (1973a), 'Additional Protocol', *Official Journal of the EC*, no. C113, pp. 17-31.

EC-Turkey Association Council (1973b), 'Association Agreement', *Official Journal of the EC*, no. C 113/2, pp. 2-10.

EC-Turkey Association Council (1973c), 'Agreement Establishing an Association between the EEC and Turkey', *Official Journal of the EC*, no. C 113, pp. 2-7.

EC-Turkey Association Council (1976), 'Association Council Decision 2/76', Council of the EC, *Collected Acts: EEC-Turkey Association* (Luxembourg, Office for Official Publications). (Loose file).

EC-Turkey Association Council (1980), 'Association Council Decision 1/80', in Council of the EC, *Collected Acts: EEC-Turkey Association*, Luxembourg, Office for Official Publications, (Loose file).

European Parliament (1974), 'Resolution on a European Migrant Workers' Charter', *Official Journal of the EC*, no. C76 pp. 25-26.

European Parliament (1975), Committee on External Relations, *Opinion on Recommendations of 11 October 1974 Adopted by the EEC-Turkey Joint Parliamentary Committee, European Parliament Working Documents*, no. 448/74.

European Parliament (1976), 'Opinion of the Committee on Agriculture', *European Parliament Working Documents, 1976-77*, no. 548/76, pp. 37-43.

European Parliament (1977a), *Opinion of the Committee on Agriculture*, PE 47.089/final.

European Parliament (1977b), *Report of the Committee on External Relations on the Recommendation Adopted by the EEC-Turkey Joint Parliamentary Committee*, PE 47.089/final.

European Parliament (1979a), *Report of the Committee on External Relations on the Recommendation Adopted by the EEC-Turkey Joint Parliamentary Committee*, PE 57.075/final.

European Parliament (1979b), 'Report of the Committee on External Relations on the Recommendations Adopted by the EEC-Turkey Joint Parliamentary Committee', *European Parliament Working Documents* 1978-79, no. 644/78.

European Parliament (1985), 'Resolution on Consolidating the Internal Market', *Official Journal of the EC*, no. C175 p. 233.

European Parliament (1987a), 'Resolution on Human Rights and Community Policy on Human Rights', *Official Journal of the EC*, No. C99, p. 162.

European Parliament (1987b), 'Resolution on the Armenian Question', *Official Journal of the EC*, no. C190, pp. 119-121.

European Parliament (1988a), *Report on the Situation in Cyprus*, no. A 2-317/87.

European Parliament (1988b), *Report of the Political Affairs Committee on the Role of the EP in the Field of Foreign Policy in the Context of the Single European Act*, no. 2-86-88.

European Parliament (1989a), 'Resolution on the Pimenta Report', *Official Journal of the EC*, no. C96, p. 213.

European Parliament (1989b), 'Resolution on a Community Instrument with a Binding Character', *Official Journal of the EC*, no. C120, p. 51.

European Parliament, Council of the EC and Commission of the EC (1977), 'Joint Declaration on Fundamental Rights', *Official Journal of the EC*, C103, p. 1.

European Political Cooperation (1986a), 'Memorandum on the Action Taken in the Field of Human Rights by the EPC', *EPC Documentation Bulletin*, vol. 2, no. 1, p. 157.

European Political Cooperation (1986b), 'Statement on Human Rights', *EPC Documentation Bulletin*, vol. 2, no. 2, pp. 57-59.

European Political Cooperation (1989), 'Intervention du Ministre des Affaires Etrangères de L'Espagne au Nom des Douze Etats Members de la Communauté .

European Political Cooperation (1990), 'Statement by the Minister of Foreign Affairs of Ireland on Behalf of the Twelve at the 46th Session of the UNCHR'. Reproduced in *European Parliament Working Documents*, no. PE 141.372/Ann.

Foreign Affairs Committee (1987), House of Commons Foreign Affairs Committee, *Third Report on Cyprus*, HMSO, London.

Member States of the EC (1964), 'Internal Agreement on the Establishment of Common Positions', no. 64/737/EEC, in *Journal Officiel des Commautés Européennes*, no. 217, p. 3703.

Member States of the EC (1964), 'Internal Agreement on Financial Aid to Turkey', no. 64/739/EEC, *Official Journal of the EC*, no. 217, p. 3709.

OECD, *Continuous Reporting System on Migration (SOPEMI)* (OECD), various vols., Paris.

Presidency of the EPC (1986), 'Memorandum on the Activities of the Twelve in the Field of Human Rights', *European Political Cooperation Documentation Bulletin*, vol. 2, no. 1, European University Institute, Florence, p. 157-160.

Select Committee (1975), House of Commons Select Committee on Cyprus, 'Examination of Witnesses', Doc. no. 694, in *Parliamentary Papers*, vol. 14, HMSO, London.

Select Committee (1976), House of Commons Select Committee on Cyprus 'Examination of Witnesses', Doc. no. 331, *Parliamentary Papers*, vol. 17, HMSO, London.

State Institute of Statistics (1996), *Turkey and World Foreign Trade*, Ankara.

State Planning Organisation (1990), *Türkiye-Avrupa Topluluğu İlişkileri (Turkey - European Community Relations)*, State Planning Organisation Publication no. DPT2230 - AETB23, Ankara.

Under-Secretary for Treasury and Foreign Trade (1996), *Kamu İktisadi Teşebbusleri 1980-86 Yıllığı (State-owned Economic Enterprises 1980-86 Annual Report)*, DSİ Basım, Ankara.

United Nations (1975-83), Office for Public Information, *Yearbook of the United Nations*, vol. 29/37, United Nations, New York.

3 Periodicals

Agence Europe: Agence Internationale d'Information pour la Press (English Edition), Luxembourg and Brussels.
Annual Reports of the EEC-Turkey Association, Association Council, Brussels.
Annual Review of the Council's Work, Office for Official Publications of the EC, Luxembourg.
Bulletin of the European Communities, Office for Official Publications of the EC, Luxembourg.
Cumhuriyet, Turkish Daily, Istanbul.
Cyprus Bulletin, Republic of Cyprus, Press and Information Office, Nicosia.
Cyprus News, Cyprus High Commission, London.
Eurobarometer: Public Opinion in the European Community, Office for Official Publications of the EC, Luxembourg.
EPC (European Political Cooperation) Documentation Bulletin, European University Institute, Florence.
Hürriyet, Turkish Daily, Istanbul.
Info-Türk: Monthly Bulletin, Brussels.
Le Monde ,Paris.
Milliyet, Turkish Daily, Istanbul.
Official Journal of the EC: Documents (C Series), Office for Official Publications of the EC, Luxembourg.
Official Journal of the EC: Legislation (L Series) Office for Official Publications of the EC, Luxembourg.
Official Journal of the EC - Debates of the European Parliament, Office for Official Publications of the EC, Luxembourg.
Sabah, Turkish Daily, Istanbul.
The Daily Telegraph, London.
The Economist, London.
The Financial Times, London.
The Guardian, London.
The International Herald Tribune, New York, London, Paris.
The New York Times, New York.
The Times, London.
Türkiye - Avrupa Birliği Derneği Bülteni (Turkey - European Union Studies Association Bulletin), Ankara.

Index

For Product Safety Concerns and Information please contact our EU representative GPSR@taylorandfrancis.com Taylor & Francis Verlag GmbH, Kaufingerstraße 24, 80331 München, Germany

Batch number: 10725911

Printed by Printforce, the Netherlands